Violence in American Schools

A New Perspective

Edited by

Delbert S. Elliott
Beatrix A. Hamburg
Kirk R. Williams

D0556375

CAMBRIDGE
UNIVERSITY PRESS

PUBLISHED BY THE PRESS SYNDICATE OF THE UNIVERSITY OF CAMBRIDGE
The Pitt Building, Trumpington Street, Cambridge CB2 1RP, United Kingdom

CAMBRIDGE UNIVERSITY PRESS
The Edinburgh Building, Cambridge CB2 2RU, UK   http://www.cup.cam.ac.uk
40 West 20th Street, New York, NY 10011-4211, USA   http://www.cup.org
10 Stamford Road, Oakleigh, Melbourne 3166, Australia

© Cambridge University Press 1998

First published 1998

Printed in the United States of America

Typeset in Palatino 10/13 pt, in Quark XPress™ [AG]

*A catalog record for this book is available from
the British Library*

Library of Congress cataloging-in-publication data is available.

ISBN 0 521 59450 2 hardback

Violence in American Schools
A New Perspective

In this volume, experts from a range of disciplines use a variety of perspectives, notably those of public health, criminology, ecology, and developmental psychology, to review the latest research on the causes of youth violence in the nation's schools and communities and on school-based interventions that have prevented or reduced it. They describe and evaluate strategies for the prevention and treatment of violence that go beyond punishment and incarceration. The volume offers a new strategy for the problem of youth violence, arguing that the most effective interventions use a comprehensive, multidisciplinary approach and take into account differences in stages of individual development and involvement in overlapping social contexts, families, peer groups, schools, and neighborhoods. This book can be used profitably by school teachers and administrators, scholars, policy makers, and those who work with young people at risk, as well as by the general reader who is concerned with current social problems.

Delbert S. Elliott is Professor of Sociology, Director of the Program on Problem Behavior, and Director of the Center for the Study and Prevention of Violence at the Institute of Behavioral Science, University of Colorado. He has served on numerous national committees on youth and violent behavior, and he is a Fellow of the American Society of Criminology. In 1995 he received the ASC Edwin H. Sutherland Award for outstanding contributions to the field of criminology.

Beatrix A. Hamburg is President of the William T. Grant Foundation and Professor of Psychiatry and Pediatrics at the Mount Sinai School of Medicine. She has held appointments at the Stanford University School of Medicine and the Harvard Medical School. She is a member of the Advisory Committee of the National Center for Injury Prevention and Control at the Centers for Disease Control and Prevention.

Kirk R. Williams is Professor of Sociology and Associate Director of the Center for the Study and Prevention of Violence at the Institute of Behavioral Science, University of Colorado. His research, including work on conflict and violence, deviance and social control, juvenile delinquency, and human development, has been supported by the Colorado Department of Public Health and Environment, the U.S. Department of Justice, and the Centers for Disease Control and Prevention.

Contents

Acknowledgments

We are indebted to many persons who made significant contributions to this volume but whose names do not appear as authors or editors. Each chapter was reviewed anonymously by a person or persons with recognized expertise in the specific area covered by the chapter. This group included truly distinguished researchers and scholars who served as outside reviewers: Gilbert Botvin, John Burton, Aushalom Caspi, Denise Gottfredson, Peter Greenwood, Nancy Guerra, Robert Haggerty, Jane Quinn, Mercer Sullivan, Jackson Toby, and James Wright. In addition to these outside reviewers selected by the editors, authors of specific chapters also asked colleagues to review their chapters. These reviewers include: Larry Steinberg and Nancy Guerra (Chapter 3); John Coie, Debra Pepler, David Farrington, JoAnn Fraser, and Ailana Winters (Chapter 4); Jackson Toby (Chapter 5); Devon Brewer (Chapter 7); J. R. Newbrough, Mark Singer, and Anne Brodsky (Chapter 10); and Laura Greiner (Chapter 13). We are grateful for the high quality of these reviews and their contribution to the scholarly rigor of the individual chapters.

Several of the authors would also like to acknowledge financial and other types of support for their work on these chapters. Jeffrey Fagan and Deanna Wilkinson (Chapter 3) received partial support from the Harry Frank Guggenheim Foundation and the National Institute of Justice; Rolf Loeber and Magda Stouthamer-Loeber (Chapter 4) were partially supported by grants from the National Institute of Mental Health (MH48890) and the Office of Juvenile Justice and Delinquency Prevention (86-JN-CX-0009), and acknowledge the special computational assistance of Mary Lamatre; David Hawkins, David Farrington, and Richard Catalano (Chapter 7) acknowledge the support of Claire Hall and the Institute of Criminology, Cambridge University, and the Office of Juvenile Justice and Delinquency Prevention for grant support; and Ray Lorion (Chapter 10) received funding support from the National Institute of Mental Health (MH38725 and MH42968–06A). Points of view expressed in these chapters are those of the authors and do not necessarily represent the official positions of these agencies.

We would also like to thank two editors who worked tirelessly with us to prepare the manuscript for publication. Christie Lerch worked on the early submitted chapters and Jami McCormick edited the later chapters and made Cambridge formatting and style changes on all chapters in the final preparation of the manuscript. Linda Newman, assistant to Betty Hamburg at the W. T. Grant Foundation, also assisted with the editing and checking of references on several chapters.

Special thanks go to Kelley Coffin-Ingraham at the Center for the Study and Prevention of Violence for the overall coordination and management of the project. In the last few months Tiffany Shaw assumed this role at the center. This was a long and difficult task. Kelley became engaged, married, and then conceived, carried, and delivered a baby while managing this project. We appreciate both the quality of Kelley's and Tiffany's work and their patience and good humor while dealing with 22 authors, two technical editors, and three general editors.

Finally, our greatest debt is to Betty Hamburg, president of the W. T. Grant Foundation, who together with the senior editor conceived of this book at a breakfast meeting early one morning in San Diego, California; and to a subsequent grant from the W. T. Grant Foundation to the Center for the Study and Prevention of Violence that allowed us to commission authors to write these chapters and contract for the editorial assistance and management of the overall project. This volume reflects the commitment of the foundation to the support and promotion of a healthy and successful course of adolescent development for all of our children as the most effective strategy for the prevention of violence.

Contributors

Larry Aber, Ph.D.
National Center for Children of
    Poverty
Columbia University
New York, New York

Richard F. Catalano, Ph.D.
Social Development Research
    Group
University of Washington
Seattle, Washington

Marcia R. Chaiken, Ph.D.
LINC
Alexandria, Virginia

Delbert S. Elliott, Ph.D.
Center for the Study and
    Prevention of Violence
University of Colorado
Boulder, Colorado

Jeffrey Fagan, Ph.D.
Center for Violence Research and
    Prevention
Columbia University
New York, New York

David P. Farrington, Ph.D.
Institute of Criminology
Cambridge University
Cambridge, England

Beatrix Hamburg, M.D.
William T. Grant Foundation
New York, New York

Margaret A. Hamburg, M.D.
New York City Department of
    Health
New York, New York

J. David Hawkins, Ph.D.
Social Development Research
    Group
University of Washington
Seattle, Washington

John H. Laub, Ph.D.
College of Criminal Justice
Northeastern University
Boston, Massachusetts

Janet L. Lauritsen, Ph.D.
Department of Criminology and
   Criminal Justice
University of Missouri
St. Louis, Missouri

Rolf Loeber, Ph.D.
Western Psychiatric Institute and
   Clinic
University of Pittsburgh
Pittsburgh, Pennsylvania

Raymond P. Lorion, Ph.D.
University of Maryland
College Park, Maryland

Steven Marans, M.S.W., Ph.D.
Child Study Center
Yale University School of Medicine
New Haven, Connecticut

James A. Mercy, Ph.D.
National Center for Injury
   Prevention and Control
Centers for Disease Control and
   Prevention
Atlanta, Georgia

Mark L. Rosenberg, M.D., M.P.D.
National Center for Injury
   Prevention and Control
Centers for Disease Control and
   Prevention
Atlanta, Georgia

Faith Samples, Ph.D.
National Center for Children of
   Poverty
Columbia University
New York, New York

Mark Schaefer, Ph.D.
Child Study Center
Yale University School of
   Medicine
New Haven, Connecticut

Ronald D. Stephens, Ph.D.
National School Safety Center
Westlake Village, California

Magda Stouthamer-Loeber, Ph.D.
Western Psychiatric Institute and
   Clinic
University of Pittsburgh
Pittsburgh, Pennsylvania

Deanna L. Wilkinson, Ph.D.
Center for Violence Research and
   Prevention
Columbia University
New York, New York

Kirk R. Williams, Ph.D.
Center for the Study and
   Prevention of Violence
University of Colorado
Boulder, Colorado

I. Introduction

1. Violence in American Schools: An Overview

DELBERT S. ELLIOTT, BEATRIX HAMBURG,
& KIRK R. WILLIAMS

Introduction

Historically, our schools have been relatively safe havens from violence. However, over the past decade there has been an epidemic of youth crime. The violence on the streets and in some of our homes has spilled over into the schools. In recent years, the nation has been deeply shocked by several dramatic, incomprehensible multiple killings of students at school by their classmates. Fortunately such episodes are rare. However, on a daily basis many students, parents, and teachers are aware of threats or bullying and they experience pervasive anxiety about violence. Across the nation there is grave concern that our children are no longer as safe from intimidation, serious injury, or death as they once were while at school or on their way to or from school. This is the issue that we address in this book. Why has the level of youth violence escalated so steeply over the past decade? What are the impacts of this change on the priorities and functioning of the school; on teaching and on the learning and developmental outcomes for our children?

The societal response to this epidemic has been largely limited to increasingly harsh and lengthy sentencing with little evidence that this approach is deterring violence or rehabilitating young offenders. What is needed are new insights into the causes of this epidemic and new intervention strategies for making our schools safer places of learning. There are bodies of knowledge across diverse fields, not typically linked to criminology, that, taken together, have much to contribute to the understanding of these issues. They also point the way to implementing a range of integrated approaches for the prevention of the widespread youth crime and violence that have had such a disturbing ripple effect in our schools.

In this volume, new perspectives, methods, and data are presented from multiple scientific fields: social ecology, child and adolescent development, life course studies, criminology, and the field of public health. We believe these integrated approaches to the study of youth violence may be new to some readers. A brief description of each of these areas is given in the latter part of this chapter along with a guide to the location of chapters of the book in which each approach is more fully described and its contribution to the understanding of youth violence is explained.

The Violence Epidemic of the Nineties

Children and teens are often afraid to go to school. Once at school, many are afraid to go into the restrooms or out on the playground. Others live in fear that they will be shot or hurt by classmates who carry weapons to school. This fear is not totally unfounded:

- A 14-year-old honor student in Moses Lake, Washington, walked into a math class armed with a high-powered rifle and two handguns. He opened fire and killed the teacher and two students and critically wounded another student (Staff, 1996).
- In Portland, Connecticut, a junior high school student was suspended for refusing to remove his hat. He subsequently returned to school with an assault rifle, killed the janitor and seriously wounded the principal and a secretary (Office of Juvenile Justice and Delinquency Prevention, 1989).
- Two students, aged 13 and 11, set off the fire alarm at Westside Middle School in Jonesboro, Arkansas, and then ran to the trees near the school. As students and teachers filed out of the building, they opened fire killing a teacher and four students and wounding eleven others (Staff, 1998).
- A teenager in Lynville, Tennessee, angry about a traffic accident, carried a rifle into a crowded school hallway and opened fire. A teacher and a student were killed (Staff, 1996).

The 1978 release of the Safe School Study Report to Congress launched the first shocking statistics regarding violence in American schools. This report indicated that approximately 282,000 students and 5,200 teachers were physically assaulted in secondary schools every month (National Institute of Education, 1978). A 1996 national poll of American adolescents commissioned by Children's Institute International revealed that nearly half (47%) of all teens believe their schools are becoming more violent, and one of every ten reported a fear of being shot or hurt by classmates who carry weapons to school. More than 20% reported being afraid to go to the restrooms because these are unsupervised areas where students are frequently victimized (Children's Institute International, 1996; Harris & Associates, 1993; Walker et al., 1996). In 1993 the National Education Association formally called for a coordinated effort by national, state, and local governments to combat growing violence in the nation's schools.

The increased youth violence in the 1990s is not unique to schools. Between 1984 and 1994, the homicide rate for adolescents doubled and the number of nonfatal violent victimizations increased nearly 20%. On a typical day in 1992, seven juveniles were murdered. These dramatic increases in juvenile homicides took place at a time when the homicide rates for most other age groups were declining. The nonfirearm-related rate remained essentially unchanged during this period; the increase was driven almost totally by handgun homicides (Snyder & Sickmund, 1995). Chapter 6 of this volume (Mercy and Rosenberg) discusses this aspect of the violence problem in detail.

The surge in violence during the late '80s and early '90s included more than homicides. Between 1988 and 1991, the rate of juvenile arrests for nonlethal violent crimes (e.g., assaults, robberies, and rapes) increased by 38% (Snyder & Sickmund, 1995). The Monitoring the Future study, involving a national sample of high school seniors, also found an 18% increase in the proportion of students reporting a serious assault on another person between 1984 and 1994 (Maguire & Pastore, 1996). Although this increase was not dramatic in terms of increased episodes (Elliott, 1994a; Osgood et al., 1989), hostile confrontations became much more lethal as the number of youths carrying guns and other weapons increased substantially (Huizinga, 1997). Fights that in earlier years resulted in black eyes, bloody noses, or minor bruises now often involved a death or serious injury. It was primarily urban African American youth who were at increased risk of being murdered during this period. In the 1990s homicide became the second leading cause of death among adolescents and the leading cause of death among African American male adolescents (Fingerhut, 1993; Snyder & Sickmund, 1995).

In addition to the increased lethality of violent confrontations resulting from the use of firearms, there were more seemingly "random" violent events, innocent bystanders killed in drive-by shootings, and assaults on strangers with little provocation (Elliott et al., 1993; Fox, 1996). Plus, violence now erupted in places previously thought to be safe: the post office, McDonald's restaurants, shopping malls, commuter trains, and in the hallways and classrooms of schools. These three features of violence in the 1990s – increased lethality, more random violence, and fewer safe places – largely account for the high levels of fear experienced by both children and adults (Elliott, 1994a).

Violence in and Around Schools

Victimization, Serious Assaults, and Guns

The rate of victimization at school is quite high. In 1991, more than half (56%) of juvenile victimizations occurred at school or on school grounds.

Few of these youth (20%) reported their victimization to the police, and less than half reported the victimization to either the police or school officials. However, most of this victimization was in the form of theft, vandalism, or threats of violence without a weapon. The peak time for violent victimizations involving juveniles begins at 3:00 P.M., the typical end of the school day for most children and teenagers. For older adolescents, the risk of violent victimization remains relatively high from 3:00–11:00 P.M. and drops dramatically after midnight (Richters, 1993; Snyder & Sickmund, 1995).

The majority of *serious* violent events, like those newspaper accounts cited at the beginning of this chapter, occur either at or near the victim's home or out in the streets in the victim's neighborhood. Indeed, the increases in serious levels of violence in school buildings and on their surrounding grounds are relatively modest compared to those occurring in homes, neighborhoods, and communities. Compared to individual homes and neighborhoods, schools are still *relatively* safe contexts for children. In 1994, only 13% of violent crimes occurred on school grounds and most of these violent events involved minor assaults. Only 7% of serious assaults and 4% of robberies took place at school (Hanke, 1996; Harris et al., 1993; Maguire & Pastore, 1996; Snyder & Sickmund, 1995). In a national study of violent deaths associated with schools between 1992 and 1994, 105 violent deaths were identified, with most victims being students (72%) and males (96%). The overall incidence rate for violent deaths was .09 per 100,000 student years (Kachur et al., 1996). The proportions of deaths occurring during classes or other school activities and before or after official school activities were approximately the same. In fact, youth are three times *less likely* to encounter weapon-related crimes at school than on the streets in their neighborhood (Department of Justice, 1991).

There is clear evidence that weapons are more frequently being carried into schools (California Department of Education, 1990; Callahan & Rivara, 1992; Kingery et al., 1996; Maguire & Pastore, 1995). Between 1987 and 1994, gun carrying at school increased 138% in central Texas. In California the number of guns confiscated doubled between 1985 and 1988. In the Texas study, those who carried guns, compared to those who did not, were much more likely to have been victimized in the prior year, to enter dangerous situations repeatedly, to have used crack cocaine, to have less knowledge about means of avoiding fighting, and to feel a greater obligation to fight under a wider variety of situations (Kingery et al., 1996). In the American Teacher survey (Harris & Associates, 1993), students receiving poor grades were three times as likely to carry a gun to school as those earning good or fair grades.

The level of nonfatal violence involving injury at school is more substantial when self-reported data are used rather than official arrest data, as much of this violence goes unreported to authorities. A 1995 national self-reported study indicated 5% of high school seniors reported being injured by an armed offender while at school in the past year. The proportions of males and African Americans injured by an armed offender at school during the past year was higher, with the rate for African Americans (6.8%) being two times that of whites, and the proportion of males (7%) being two and a half times that for females. Weapon-related injury rates are higher for high school seniors than younger students, but the general assault rates (with or without weapons) on younger students are substantially higher than might be expected from official police and school disciplinary records (Maguire & Pastore, 1995). In a Centers for Disease Control and Prevention study involving a national sample of 9th through 12th graders in 1993, 9% of males and 5% of females reported being threatened or injured on school property in the last year (Maguire & Pastore, 1995); and in a national survey of 6th to 12th graders, nearly 18% reported being hurt by another student at school (PRIDE, 1996).

These rates of violent victimization and injury are substantially higher in large, inner city high schools. In a study of ten inner city public schools in California, Louisiana, New Jersey, and Illinois (Sheley, McGee, & Wright, 1995), 30% of males and 16% of females reported they had been assaulted at school or on the way to and from school; two-thirds reported they personally knew someone who had been shot or stabbed, or otherwise assaulted while in school. In summary, whether using official records or self-report information, rates of violent victimization and offending have been increasing in the nation's schools over the past decade. The fact that school is a relatively safer context than the home or streets in the neighborhood (Hanke, 1996; Maguire & Pastore, 1996) provides little comfort – the rates are still very high in and around schools. This level of violence is clearly unacceptable.

While the objective risk of becoming a victim of violence may be greater at home and in the neighborhood, the *perceptions* of safety at school do not reflect this difference. In a 1995 national Gallup poll, teenagers reported feeling safest at home, next safest in their neighborhood, and then at school. The places seen as least safe were public transportation, walking to and from a friend's house after dark, and in the area around their school. Nearly half of adolescents reported that their schools are becoming more violent, and only 24% reported that their neighborhoods are becoming more violent. Both the neighborhood and school are now seen as unsafe places, with approximately 40% reporting they sometimes feel unsafe in *both* settings (Maguire & Pastore, 1995). In a study of inner city schools, 15% reported they were afraid at school almost all of the time (Sheley, McGee, & Wright, 1992). In the American Teacher national survey (Harris & Associates, 1993), more than half of all students surveyed worried to some degree about being physically attacked in or around school. While a majority of teachers (77%) feel very safe in and around school, this perception varies greatly with the quality of the school; only 44% of teachers who think their school provides a fair or poor education feel safe at school. These teachers also are more likely to report that violence has increased in their school over the past year. Teachers from secondary as compared to elementary schools are also more likely to believe that the levels of school violence have increased (21% vs. 14%). Many (44%) law enforcement officials, especially those in urban areas (59%), also believe that violence has increased in their local public schools.

Violence and the Social Climate of the School

The real or perceived threat of violence at school has clearly influenced the way principals manage, teachers teach, and students learn. In a national survey of secondary school principals (Price & Everett, 1997), one-third reported they had already implemented some type of violence prevention or safe school program; another third indicated they were planning to implement such a program. Most of the remaining principals reported they were either unsure of the need for such a program or of which programs were effective.

In the American Teacher survey (Harris & Associates, 1993), one-third of teachers reported that because of the threat of violence, both teachers and students in their school were less eager to go to school. A much larger proportion (43%) of urban teachers held this opinion. One-third of all teachers and two-thirds of teachers from poor quality schools believed teachers were less likely to challenge or discipline students as a direct result of the threat of violence; half of all teachers reported that students were less likely to pay attention to learning in the classroom. One in four students believed violence has lessened the quality of their education. The effects of violence appear to be even greater for students who are struggling academically. More than one-third of these students reported that the threat of violence has made them want to change schools and makes them less inclined to pay attention in class.

Gang activity is increasingly being carried into the schools. Huff and

Trump (1996), in a study of youth gangs in Cleveland, Ohio, Denver, Colorado, and south Florida, report that half of their respondents acknowledged that members of their gangs had assaulted teachers; 70% admit their gangs assaulted students; more than 80% said gang members took guns and knives to school; and more than 60% claimed gang members sold drugs at school. Clearly, gangs no longer view the school as a "neutral zone" where gang activity ceases. Gang "turf" issues have infiltrated schools (Parks, 1997).

The real costs of violence go far beyond the individual injury and physical suffering resulting from the violent act, although these costs should not be minimized or trivialized. The fear and trauma in the nation's schools are having an impact on the entire school context and *all* students in these contexts: on teaching practices; children's readiness and capacity for learning; hiring and retention of teachers, administrators, and other school staff; the openness and accessibility of the campus; student rights to privacy; the physical building and grounds; and the quality of the learning environment more generally. This is the problem we address in this volume: How can our schools and their local neighborhoods stop the violence? How can we create safe schools for our children?

National, State, and Local Responses to School Violence: An Overview

There has been a dramatic shift in the public's perception of the seriousness of violence. In 1982 only 3% of adults in a national poll identified crime and violence as the most important problem facing this country; by August of 1994, more than half identified crime and violence as the nation's most important problem. Throughout the 1990s, violence has been viewed as a more serious problem than the high cost of living, unemployment, poverty and homelessness, and health care. Again in 1994, violence (together with a lack of discipline among students) was identified as the "biggest problem" facing the nation's public schools. Among America's high school seniors, violence is the problem these young people worry about most frequently – more than drug abuse, economic problems, poverty, race relations, or nuclear war (Maguire & Pastore, 1996).

The public's view of the causes of this crisis focuses primarily on deficiencies or dysfunctions in the family, public schools, and the criminal justice system. When respondents in a 1994 national survey were asked to identify which part of society is to blame for the increase in crime, the courts and prison system were most frequently identified, followed closely by the home and school (Maguire & Pastore, 1995). When asked about the causes of violence in schools, the number one cause identified was a lack of parental discipline and control; the second was the breakdown in family structure and dysfunctional lifestyles (Maguire & Pastore, 1995). Secondary school principals also identified lack of parental supervision most frequently as the cause of school violence. For principals, the second most frequent cause identified was a lack of parent involvement with the schools (Price & Everett, 1997). But the public is divided when asked about how society should deal with this problem. Nearly equal proportions endorse "three strike" legislation calling for life prison terms without parole and spending tax money on youth prevention and treatment programs (Maguire & Pastore, 1995). Overall, however, there is greater support for the more punitive legal responses involving longer prison sentences; hiring more police; waiving youthful offenders age 13 and older into adult courts and, if convicted, into adult prisons; enacting laws prohibiting the manufacture, sale, and possession of semiautomatic assault rifles; and laws prohibiting the purchase of a gun by youth under 18 or by those with a prior official record.

Government policies at all levels primarily reflect this punitive, legalistic approach to violence prevention and control. At the national and state levels, there have been four major policy and program initiatives introduced as violence prevention or control strategies in the 1990s: (1) the use of judicial waivers, transferring violent juvenile offenders as young as age ten into the adult justice system for trial, sentencing, and incarceration; (2) legislating new gun control policies, e.g., the Brady Act; (3) the development and operation of "boot camps" or "shock incarceration" programs for young offenders, oriented toward instilling discipline and respect for authority through a military-like regimen of physical conditioning, work, and the strict enforcement of rules; and (4) the use of community policing to create police-community partnerships aimed at more efficient community problem solving and reductions in violence, drug abuse, and other community crime problems.

Two of these initiatives are purely reactive: they involve ways in which society responds to violent acts after they occur. Two are more preventive in nature, attempting to prevent the initial occurrence of violent behavior. The justification of judicial waivers and boot camps for juveniles is primarily a "just deserts" philosophy, i.e., youthful offenders should be punished more severely for serious violence. But there is no research evidence to suggest either strategy will have any increased deterrent effect over processing these youth in the juvenile justice system or in traditional correctional settings (MacKenzie & Brame, 1995; MacKenzie, Shaw, & Souryal, 1992;

Peterson, 1996; Podkopacz & Feld, 1996; Shaw & MacKenzie, 1992). In fact, while the evidence is limited, it suggests that the use of waivers and incarceration in adult prisons as compared to juvenile institutions results in longer processing time and longer pretrial detention, disproportionate use of waivers for minority youth, much lower probability of any treatment while in custody, and an increased risk of subsequent offending when released (Bishop et al., 1996; Elliott, 1994a; Fagan, 1996; Frazier, Bishop, & Lanza-Kaduce, 1997). The research evidence on the effectiveness of community policing and gun control legislation is very limited and inconclusive.

There are some genuine prevention efforts sponsored by both federal and state governments, by private foundations, and by private businesses (National Research Council, 1993), although the investment in these efforts is small compared to the "get tough" approaches identified. At the federal level, the major initiative involves the Safe and Drug-Free Schools and Communities Act of 1994. This act provided $630 million in federal grants during 1995 to the states to implement violence (and drug) prevention programs in and around schools, in order to help the states meet the seventh National Education Goal of the America 2000 initiative. The intent of this legislation was to fund ". . . violence prevention, early intervention, rehabilitation referral, and education in elementary and secondary schools (including intermediate and junior high schools)." State Departments of Education and local school districts are currently developing guidelines and searching for violence prevention programs demonstrated to be effective. Most of the violence prevention programs currently being employed in the schools, e.g., conflict resolution curricula, peer mediation, individual counseling, metal detectors, and locker searches and sweeps, have either not been thoroughly evaluated or have been evaluated and found to be ineffective (Gottfredson, 1997; Lipsey, 1992; Tolan & Guerra, 1994; Webster, 1993). It remains to be seen if any significant reductions in violent offending will result from the Safe and Drug-Free Schools and Community initiative.

When examining the dollars allocated to national and state strategies for addressing the violence crisis, there is a clear priority – get tough on violent offenders and build more prisons to hold them. This suggests that the nation is investing far more resources in building and maintaining prisons than in primary prevention programs. Such investments imply an emphasis on reacting to violent offenders after the fact and removing them from the community, rather than preventing children from becoming violent offenders in the first place and retaining them in the nation's communities as responsible, productive citizens. Of course, if no effective prevention strategies or programs are available, there is no real choice between these strategies. This is the critical issue facing the country. Can the onset of serious violent behavior be prevented?

Summary

With strong public support, the national policy response to these deep concerns about youth violence has been one of increasingly harsh punishment of juveniles. The rates of incarceration have been rapidly rising and "shock incarceration" boot camps for juveniles have become very popular. Children as young as 10 years old can be tried as adults and, if convicted, jailed with adult criminals. These policies have proved to be both prohibitively expensive as well as unsuccessful in either deterring crime generally or decreasing recidivism on the part of convicted offenders. Instead, harsh imprisonment serves as a school for crime in which youth learn criminal skills and attitudes that virtually assure a life as a career criminal. For these reasons, such policies are beginning to be questioned within the law enforcement field.

The rising rates of preventable death and disability of children and youth directly attributable to youth violence underscore the significance of the public health issues and need for mobilizing public health approaches. At the same time, there is an emerging concern that the epidemic of youth violence is a signal of serious erosion of the underpinnings of healthy growth and development of children and youth. Many schools are failing to help children achieve the high or acceptable levels of academic proficiency within their reach. Far too many children and youth have no dependable adult support or guidance. Between a quarter and a third of American children and adolescents lack safe havens for after-school activities and have no opportunities for meaningful, prosocial community service. Youth unemployment is high for legal jobs but there are enticing inducements to participate in the illegal economy. Youth often express deep pessimism about future life chances or, at times, even doubt that they will survive the violence to become adults.

Purposes and Objectives of this Volume

We are at a critical crossroads in this country. Will we continue to build more and more prisons to house our children and teens, or will we redirect more of our limited resources to the prevention of violence and promotion of healthy, productive, and nonviolent transitions into adulthood? It is well known that there is a pattern of sharp increase in delinquency and crime beginning at ages 13–14 that peaks at about age 18 and steeply declines for serious forms of violence after age 21 (Elliott, 1994b). Thus any effective violence prevention effort will necessarily focus on children and adolescents. It is crucially important to have broad knowledge about the complex web of factors that either enhance or diminish the likelihood that particular youths will be victims or perpetrators of violence as they approach and pass through the developmental period of heightened risk. The critical question is: How can we mount an effective prevention effort? This is the central theme of this volume.

What do we know about the causes of violent behavior? What programs and intervention strategies demonstrate effectiveness in preventing the onset of violent behavior, or in terminating or controlling the violence of those who have already initiated violent behavior? Given the limited evaluations of current violence prevention programs, how can our research inform new intervention strategies and policies? How might we approach the violence problem in a more proactive way? What is the role of the school and community in violence prevention? These are the questions addressed in this book. Stated simply, we want to summarize what is known about the causes and developmental course of violent behavior; review what prevention strategies have proved effective in preventing school violence; and make recommendations for applying scientific knowledge to the design and implementation of new violence prevention programs, policies, and intervention strategies. To accomplish this goal we have divided the volume into five parts: Introduction, Understanding Child and Youth Violence, School-Based Interventions, Community-Based Interventions, and Conclusions.

Violence Prevention

Our focus is on violence prevention. The authors have agreed to a common definition of "violence" for this volume: "Violence refers to the threat or use of physical force with the intention of causing physical injury, damage, or intimidation of another person." We are concerned with interpersonal forms of violence. At the most serious level, this includes homicide, aggravated assault, armed robbery, and forcible rape, the offenses included in the FBI violent crime index. It also includes shoving, punching, hitting, and throwing objects when the intent is to harm or intimidate another human being. Verbal and psychological abuse are not included in our definition of violence. Forms of physical violence that generally involve no intended injury or intimidation, e.g., hitting, slapping, shoving, and pushing, which are common among siblings and friends, are also excluded. While these forms of physical violence most often involve good-natured play, they may also be antecedents to the more serious forms of violence considered here. We are not claiming that forms of psychological and verbal abuse and physical violence without apparent intent for injury are unimportant or have no significance for more serious forms of violence. However, it is important to make the distinction between a possible *cause* or risk factor for serious violence and the actual perpetration of serious violent acts.

The term "prevention" has been used to describe several different objectives: (1) avoiding the *onset* of violent behavior in a general population of persons who have not yet become involved in violent behavior (typically referred to as primary prevention); (2) *terminating* all involvement in violent behavior on the part of persons who previously have been involved in violent behavior (typically referred to as secondary prevention); and (3) reducing the frequency or *rate* of violent offending in some general population or among persons who have already initiated violent offending (which could be either a primary or secondary prevention). Our major concern is with primary prevention, although each of these types of prevention will be described at points throughout the volume. We have chosen not to focus on secondary prevention, particularly as it involves arrested, convicted, or incarcerated samples of youth. We are more concerned with that population of children and adolescents who have not yet come to the attention of the justice system for their involvement in violent crimes. We emphasize prevention efforts designed to intervene before it becomes necessary for a formal justice system intervention.

Unfortunately, there is a very limited body of evaluation research on programs specifically designed to prevent violent behavior. Most early prevention programs are designed to prevent a set of antisocial behaviors that emerge in childhood, such as aggressive behavior (e.g., fighting, bullying, pushing), lying, stealing, cruelty to animals, obstreperousness (i.e., resisting control in a noisy, boisterous, and unruly manner), and setting fires. During the adolescent years, prevention programs also focus on a broader set of "problem behaviors," which include delinquent acts (e.g., stealing, gang fights, minor and serious assaults, public disorder, fraud), substance abuse, and teenage pregnancy. Childhood aggression sometimes involves behavior that would meet our definition of violence. Delinquency prevention programs typically include violent behavior as one of several behaviors they target for prevention, but since it is relatively rare, few prevention programs have narrowly focused their programs on violent behavior and evaluated the program's effectiveness on the basis of lower onset or frequency of violent acts. These definitional issues must be sorted out in the research literature. The authors in this volume have endeavored to be as clear as possible about their use of the agreed upon definition.

There is a rationale for assuming that research findings on delinquent behavior in general can be applied to violence as well, and that the demonstrated effectiveness of delinquency prevention programs can be viewed as indicators for the effectiveness for violence prevention. First, evidence suggests that delinquent acts are embedded in a highly interrelated cluster of problem behaviors as a general lifestyle. Second, additional evidence suggests that a core set of causes is common to all of the behaviors in this cluster. Finally, there is a clear developmental progression from minor delinquent acts to more serious ones, with the serious interpersonal violent acts (e.g., aggravated assaults, robbery, rape, and homicide) being the final set of behaviors in this sequence (Elliott, 1986, 1993, 1994b). It is therefore possible to argue that an intervention effective in preventing the minor forms of delinquency earlier in the developmental sequence than violent delinquent acts should be effective in preventing violence. Nonetheless, the ultimate proof of effectiveness of a violence prevention program or policy will be direct evidence of reductions in the onset and frequency of violent acts. But lacking such definitive research findings, evidence that a program or policy is effective in preventing delinquent acts more generally will be accepted as evidence that this program/policy should be effective in preventing violence. This assumption reflects the current state of knowledge about violence and provides an informed basis for designing violence prevention strategies and interventions.

We also allowed our authors to consider childhood physical aggression (i.e., aggressive behaviors) as an early form of violence for children under the age of ten. It is one of the strongest predictors of serious violent offending during adolescence, and most researchers consider it a childhood form of violence (Loeber & Hay, 1997; Moffit, 1993). Early childhood prevention programs that target aggressive behaviors are thus considered violence prevention programs. For those in the second decade of life, violent behaviors are those identified in our general definition of violence. Some leeway is given when considering preventive interventions targeting adolescents; if violent acts are included as part of a broader set of delinquent acts in the evaluation of the program or policy, we consider these interventions to be violence prevention interventions.

Focus on Schools

Our focus is on violence in and around the schools and on creating a safe context in which children and adolescents can learn effectively and also master the developmental tasks that are the foundation for their effective participation in adult society. While the school is the primary social context of interest, we also examine the community in which it is located, since the nature of this surrounding social context has a significant influence on how the school carries out its educational mission and determines whether there will be a larger social climate that either supports or impedes the school's efforts.

There are several reasons for viewing the school as a critical social context for violence prevention efforts. First, the school and its immediate neighborhood are the settings in which much of the interpersonal conflict and violence occurs. It is at school that children and youth with divergent backgrounds and experiences come together to develop personal competence and skills and to compete for academic rewards, peer acceptance, and social status. Violence in this context disrupts the learning and skill acquisition process, seriously undermining the central mission of the school. As Hillary Rodham Clinton recently observed about children when calling for safer schools, "if we can't keep them safe, we can't expect them to learn."[1]

Schools also have a key role to play in the early identification of youth who are at risk of initiating violence and in marshaling the resources and expertise to eliminate, reduce, or buffer the conditions and factors that lead youth into violent behavior. The earlier that children who are truly at risk for adopting violent coping strategies can be identified, the better the chances for an effective intervention. Because the large majority of children attend public schools, it is often more cost effective to deliver an intervention in the school setting.

Most of the known risk factors for violence (e.g., poverty; abuse; neglect; ineffective parenting; dysfunctional families; disorganized neighborhoods; organized gangs; high levels of exposure to violence, drugs, and crime) reside in the family and larger community. Still, the prospects for developing interventions that are effective and can be sustained over time must involve the community *and* the school in a joint effort or partnership. Children bring their experiences in their families and neighborhoods with them to school and thus the effects of these experiences spill over into the school. Any effective resolution of these risk factors must involve the larger community as well as the school. In some instances, these problems actually emerge for the first time in the school, as children with very different socialization experiences must interact and compete with each other for grades and social status in this new setting. Methods for solving conflict in the home with one's parents and siblings may work reasonably well in that context but not in school. Moreover, ways of obtaining attention and rewards on the street in the neighborhood may not be effective at school.

Finally, the school is itself a little community, with its own norms and social structure, a complete social environment that affects children and youth in infinite subtle ways – much like the family and local neighborhood. A significant amount of children's lives is spent at school. In some instances the school, often unwittingly, creates a normative climate that supports violence or contributes to its use as a means for resolving conflict and redressing actual or perceived wrongs. This appears to happen in many inner city schools, even while they are offering courses in conflict resolution and nonviolence. Much of what is learned and reinforced about violence and nonviolence at school does not come directly from the formal curriculum. It is learned, instead, through the informal social messages that reflect the organization of the school and the values and behavior of teachers, principals, staff, and other students. Like any other learning in life, it occurs through observation and social experience. The social climate of the school can have a significant effect on the rates of violent behavior in the classroom, on the school grounds, and even in the neighborhoods surrounding the school. This issue is addressed in detail in Chapter 10 (Lorion). Our objective is to focus primarily on the school and secondarily on the community, as it influences the school's efforts to provide a safe, violence-free learning environment.

New Perspectives on School Violence

Historically, most of the research on interpersonal violence has been done by criminologists. We seek to broaden this perspective in several important ways to provide a fresh look at the violence problem and to learn from diverse disciplinary approaches. Integration of theoretical models, methods, and data from other fields that study the same or related issues can advance our scientific understanding of youth violence as well as increase the spectrum of options available for designing new, soundly based programs and policies. Four such perspectives are presented in this volume:

1. *Social-Ecological Perspective.* Research shows that social context plays an important role in generating and shaping attitudes, beliefs, and behavior (Bronfenbrenner, 1979, 1989). From a social-ecological perspective, violent behavior is an

adaptive response a youth makes to a particular social context. The behavior is the result of personal past history, personal traits, and dispositions of an individual interacting with characteristics of the social setting that could serve to trigger, facilitate, or inhibit the overt expression of violence for that specific person. Thus, it extends our understanding of violent behavior to include the patterns of person–environment interactions that explain the differing individual responses to superficially similar situations. The social-ecological perspective also stimulates study of the stability or flexibility of behaviors across diverse contexts. Loeber and Stouthamer-Loeber (Chapter 4) discuss the stability (or not) of physical aggressiveness of children at home and in the school.

In the field of criminology there is also a long tradition of work on delinquency prevention programs, which includes early educational enrichment (e.g., Head Start), cognitive development, moral development, social and academic skill development, and parent effectiveness training (see, e.g., Tolan & Guerra, 1994). Nearly all of these programs represent attempts to achieve change on an individual basis ignoring the social contexts in which persons learn attitudes, beliefs, and behavior as they interact with parents, siblings, relatives, neighbors, teachers, and other youth (parent effectiveness training is an important exception). Based on current evidence, an effective intervention is one that changes the nature of *interactions* by changing the person, the context, or both.

Violence prevention initiatives targeting social contexts involve attempts to change the characteristics of the family situations and neighborhoods in which children grow up, including the schools they attend. This focus will be more evident in some chapters than others, but it is a theme we attempted to include wherever possible.

2. *Life Course Perspective.* Recent longitudinal research has made it possible to study violence by following the same individuals from early childhood through adolescence and into adulthood with a single developmental conceptual paradigm guiding the study (Elder, 1985, 1994; Caspi, Elder, & Herbenner, 1990). This framework also includes studies of the sociohistorical cohort effects on individual behavior due to the impact of unique historical events such as the Great Depression or the Vietnam War. Much is learned from the study of specific time periods, but those findings must be judiciously assessed as to their applicability to other contexts.

As a result of rich databases from life course studies, there is no longer a dependence on the synthesis of cross-sectional data collected from different individuals, different historical cohorts, or different demographic groups as the primary knowledge base for understanding changes in behavior over the life span. We now know there are multiple causal paths into violent offending, which vary depending on the stage of life course development or involvement in transitions into new social contexts (e.g., school, peer groups, marriage, work). From life course studies we also know that violence is often intermittent and of short duration (Catalano & Hawkins, 1996; Elliott et al., 1989; Moffit, 1993; Sampson & Laub, 1993; Simons et al., 1994).

Traditionally, research on delinquency and criminal violence has been cross-sectional, with findings based on a particular point in time or phase of the life course. Further, each selected phase tends to be the intellectual domain of a different academic discipline, and each discipline has different assumptions, theories, methods, and data sources. Early childhood studies of conduct disordered and highly aggressive children (psychology) were seldom linked to studies of adolescents who were involved in serious violent crimes (sociology, criminology); and studies of delinquency among adolescents rarely used a life course approach and followed them into adulthood to determine which ones continued their violence, which ones did not, and what accounted for this difference (Elliott, 1994b; Rand, 1987; Sampson & Laub, 1990). As a result, conditions identified as leading to aggressiveness in childhood appear to be different from those identified during adolescence as leading to serious violence; and those associated with adult violence appear to be different from those associated with childhood aggression and adolescent violence. Very little integration of research findings across different stages of the life span was accomplished.

We have asked our authors to incorporate a life course perspective into their chapters to the extent this is possible, given the particular body of research they are reviewing.

3. *Developmental Perspective.* The effect of personal violent encounters and/or exposure to high levels of violence on developmental processes is a central theme. A key proposition for this volume is that violence is not only a destructive form of behavior for individual perpetrators and victims, but its occurrence contaminates the school and community environments, interfering with normal learning processes and arresting or delaying the successful completion of the developmental tasks of childhood and adolescence. This problem is discussed in Chapter 10 (Lorion). A corollary is that successful mastery of youth development tasks can act as a protective factor to prevent violence and promote the healthy adaptation to life across many social settings. This theme is highlighted in Chapter 7 (Hawkins, Farrington, and Catalano).

We also consider the developmental progression of violent behaviors themselves, from persistent forms of minor aggressiveness in childhood to physical fighting in early adolescence to aggravated assaults, robbery, rape, and homicide in the mid to late adolescent years. These issues are discussed in Chapter 4 (Loeber and Stouthamer-Loeber). A clear understanding of the interactions of individual characteristics and contextual conditions that facilitate escalation in violence levels over the life course will allow us to design targeted and more timely interventions for preventing, interrupting, and terminating these processes.

In designing prevention programs, it is also necessary to consider the developmental appropriateness of different intervention strategies. The question is: Does the intervention take into account the developmental stage of the child or youth targeted for the intervention by using risk and protective factors appropriate to the individual's developmental stage? For example, dyadic parent-child training programs may be effective with young children and early adolescents who are at risk for adopting violent coping strategies; but they are not appropriate, and may even have negative effects, if employed for older adolescents who are at that stage of life when they seek independence from parents and look to peers for approval and status. Likewise, attempting to teach elementary school children how to deal with peer pressure for engaging in sex, violence, or drugs before they have experienced the onset of puberty is not likely to be effective because they have no understanding of the intense need for peer approval, badges of adult status, and establishing one's sexual identity that emerge with this developmental change. All of the chapters have a developmental focus, addressing one or more of these specific issues.

4. *Public Health Model.* The public health model is the operational framework for this volume. This approach is described in detail in Chapter 2 (Hamburg). Prevention is the hallmark of the public health approach. The level of death and disability due to youth violence cannot be ignored as a serious public health issue. The public health approach brings a proven set of concepts, tools, and measures to the prevention and reduction of youth violence.

The impressive increases in lifespan, declining rates of many diseases, and improvements in health status over the past century are more attributable to the use of public health prevention measures than to direct medical treatment or bio-medical advances. The core elements of this approach provide a practical set of guidelines for designing and implementing prevention initiatives. They include: (1) community-based methods for identifying the sources of the problem; (2) the use of epidemiological data and analyses to identify the risk and protective factors associated with the problem; (3) ongoing surveillance and tracking of the problem and the identified risk/protective factors to establish trends in their prevalence and incidence; (4) designing community-based interventions to reduce or elimi-nate risk factors and enhance or introduce protective factors; (5) evaluation and monitoring of these interventions to establish and improve their effectiveness; and (6) public education to share information about strategies that are effective or not effective.

We have adopted the language of the public health model and refer to factors that influence violent offending and victimization as "risk" factors and "protec-tive" factors. Risk factors are those personal attributes and contextual conditions that increase the likelihood (or risk) that a person will become involved in violent behavior; protective factors refer to those personal attributes and contextual con-ditions that reduce this likelihood or risk, or that buffer (protect) against risk fac-tors.[2] We use these and other public health tools, concepts, and procedures in ref-erence to the violence problem in the nation's schools and communities and to make specific recommendations for intervention programs. Chapters 8 (Samples and Aber) and 9 (Stephens) focus specifically on proven programs, practices, and strategies for creating and maintaining a safe school environment. Chapters 11 (Marans and Schaefer) and 12 (Chaiken) review what is known about effective vi-olence prevention programs in the community generally and specifically for the af-ter-school hours when most violence occurs.

Charge to the Authors

Each of the authors in this volume is a nationally recognized expert on the violence issues they were asked to address in their respective chapters. We brought all of the authors together for two separate conferences, one in Boulder, Colorado, and one in New York City. At the initial meeting, we discussed the overall objectives and general themes of the volume as out-lined. We asked each author to prepare a coherent, integrated, state-of-the-art summary of the research on the topic or content area being ad-dressed and to make specific recommendations for the design and implementation of effective violence prevention interventions in the school or community, if such recommendations seemed justified by the available evidence. At the second conference, we reviewed and compared detailed outlines of each chapter, looking for gaps or overlaps in material that would be redundant, discussed and agreed on some common termi-nology for the volume, discussed some limitations in the available data, and again reviewed the general perspectives and themes we had asked each author to address.

Intended Audience

This book has many audiences. It is not a technical research monograph written for researchers. It *is* for: persons in the general public who seek deeper understanding of youth violence; school personnel, such as board members, teachers, and administrators; medical and public health practitioners; policy makers; corrections and law enforcement officials; social services specialists; members of parent-teacher associations; community organization members and staffs; program planners and developers; and for those interested in or directly involved in violence prevention activities or policy making.

While we have attempted to summarize and integrate the available research findings and to report on the intervention and policy implications of this body of knowledge with rigor and scholarly documentation, we have also asked our authors to present this information in clear and nontechnical language. We hope that we have achieved this goal.

Data Limitations

There was general agreement that the available research on youth violence has two important limitations. First, there is a gender bias in the earlier studies of youth violence. Prior to 1980 there were relatively few general population studies of violence perpetrated by females and even fewer evaluations of violence prevention programs targeting high-risk females. The recent national studies of violence, delinquency, and substance abuse in general population samples (e.g., the Monitoring the Future Study and the National Youth Survey) include both males and females in their samples. Gender bias is not a problem for studies of violent victimization and treatment of victims. These studies have routinely included both males and females in their samples. Still, in the general body of research, there is continuing gender bias.

Second, much of the research on adolescent violence focuses on children and youth in large urban schools and cities. While it is true that a disproportionate amount of the violence occurs in large, inner city schools, neither suburban nor rural schools have escaped the escalating levels of violence. Moreover, these different settings may involve different organizational and resource problems for mounting effective violence prevention initiatives. These two data limitations will become apparent in the reviews presented in many of the chapters, and from the outset we acknowledge that they affect the ability to generalize findings in certain areas.

Data Sources

There are two primary types of data available for etiological (i.e., explanatory) and epidemiological (i.e., descriptive) studies of violent offending or victimization. Evaluation studies also rely on these two types of data to assess post-treatment involvement in violent behavior. The first involves the official records of criminal justice agencies: the police, the courts, and correctional institutions. These official data contain information about apprehended violent offenders and crimes reported to the police. These agencies do not typically maintain records of victims of violence. Some other victimization records are kept. There are official records of homicide victims maintained by the FBI and official victimization records for child abuse victims maintained by child protective services agencies, but apart from these official data, there are little official data on victims. The second primary source of data is self-reports from victims or perpetrators of violence. Both victim and offender data are available from self-report studies.

These two data sources are both relevant to our interest in violent offending and victimization, but they are measures of different things, and this distinction is important (Elliott, 1995; Kitsuse & Cicourel, 1963). Self-reported data are direct measures of individual involvement in criminal behavior that may or may not come to official notice. Officially generated police and court records reflect the activity of these agencies, as they respond to those criminal acts that come to their attention. Self-reports are a broad measure of behavior; official records measure the justice system's response to that behavior, if and when it is known to them. Both are considered valid and reliable measures of their respective activities (Geerken, 1994; Hindelang et al., 1981; Huizinga & Elliott, 1986; Kitsuse & Cicourel, 1963).

Many violent acts are never reported to the police (Elliott, 1995; Hindelang et al., 1981). Many violent perpetrators and victims are related to each other, dating, or friends. They view violent acts as a family or personal matter and simply do not want the police involved. Many victims are afraid of retaliation by the perpetrator if they report the violence to the police, and many view violence as unimportant or are convinced that nothing will come of reporting it to the police (U.S. Department of Justice, 1994). What gets reported to the police is a relatively small subset of all violent offenses actually committed, and how they respond to this subset of offenses and offenders is a function of local police policies, characteristics of the offenders and the situations in which the violence occurred, the willingness of victims and witnesses to report and testify about what happened, and the quality of the physical evidence to support an arrest and formal charge. Police records reflect police activity as they respond to crimes and attempt to maintain the public order. District attorney and court records are also records of the activities of these agencies.

As might be expected, these two types of data provide very different estimates of the prevalence and frequency of violent acts and the characteristics of violent offenders (Elliott, 1994b, 1995; Hindelang et al., 1981; Huizinga & Elliott, 1986). There is clear evidence that most violent incidents, other than homicides, are unreported to the police and never appear in official records. Further, when compared to self-reported victimization or offender data, official record data indicate greater gender and race differences in violent offending. There are also differences in estimates of how long individuals are involved in violence (i.e., career length), the pattern of offenses, and the number of offenses committed by each offender.

Finally, there is no reason to believe that those persons with an arrest for a violent act are a representative sample of all persons committing violent acts, or that those acts found in arrest charges are representative of all violent acts committed. Official data should not be interpreted as if these data were measures of violent behavior; self-reported data are the more appropriate measures of behavior. (Homicide is an important exception.) Official records, on the other hand, are the most appropriate data for studying how the police and courts are responding to violent behavior: how the society is responding to this behavior through its official law enforcement agencies.

Objectivity

We asked our authors to be straightforward and forthright in their descriptions of the research findings and evidence of program and intervention effectiveness (or lack thereof). Many of the violence prevention programs and intervention strategies described in this volume have not been subjected to a rigorous, scientific evaluation. The fact is we do not know if these programs or interventions are effective or not. When their costs are high or there are alternatives that are *known* to be effective, the absence of any evidence of effectiveness is a sufficient basis for challenging the use of these programs or policies. If there are no alternatives known to be effective and the costs are modest, a case may be made for using untested prevention programs for a time, pending a careful evaluation.

There are also a number of programs that have been rigorously evaluated and the evidence indicates they do *not* work. In fact, some interventions have been demonstrated to have negative effects, i.e., they make matters worse, actually increasing the risk of violence for those participating in the intervention (Finckenauer, 1982; Lipsey, 1992). This conclusion may offend some – those who have invested much effort and put their very hearts into these programs – but in the interests of our children and the taxpayers who underwrite most of these programs and policies, we cannot waffle on this evidence.

Fortunately, we also have good evidence that some programs and policies are effective. It was the task of each author to sort out what can and cannot be said about the effectiveness of existing prevention efforts and to recommend new strategies that are grounded in the existing research findings, when that seems justified.

Conclusion

For many Americans, the epidemic of youth violence in this decade is a sentinel marker of a sharp decline in the fundamental well-being of the nation's children and youth. At the national level, we have responded to this escalation in violence with a relatively narrow, reactive set of criminal justice policies that focus on increased punitive sanctions and incarceration of child and teen offenders. Too little attention has been paid to violence prevention efforts or to redirecting troubled, at-risk youth toward nonviolent coping strategies, prosocial activities, and acquiring the skills and competencies needed for a successful transition into adult roles.

We believe there is a useful body of theory and research in the social and behavioral sciences that can be applied to the violence problem and its prevention. Our understanding of the interplay of personal attributes and dispositions and contextual conditions that enhance or diminish the chances that particular youth will become involved in serious forms of violent behavior during their adolescent years has improved greatly over the past decade. We attempt to summarize this body of knowledge and to explore how it can inform violence prevention programs and initiatives in schools and communities, and how it might direct future policy making at the local and national level.

Notes

1. This quote is from an address by Mrs. Clinton on September 11, 1996, at "In Harm's Way: A National Forum on Children and Violence," sponsored by the Children's Institute International in Beverly Hills, California.

2. There is a more technical meaning for "protective factor," but the definition given here has become the common meaning for this term (see Garmezy, 1985).

References

Bishop, D. M., Frazier, C. E., Lanza-Kaduce, L., & Winner, L. (1996). The transfer of juveniles to criminal court: Does it make a difference? *Crime and Delinquency, 42*, 171–191.

Bronfenbrenner, U. (1979). *The ecology of human development.* Cambridge, MA: Harvard University Press.

Bronfenbrenner, U. (1989). Ecological systems theory. In R. Vasta (Ed.), *Annals of child development – Six theories of child development: Revised formulations and content issues* (pp. 1–103). Greenwich, CT: JAI Press.

California Department of Education. (1990). *School crime in California for the 1988–1989 school year: Standard school crime reporting program.* Sacramento, CA: Author.

Callahan, C., & Rivara, F. (1992). Urban high school youth and handguns. *Journal of the American Medical Association, 267*, 3038–3041.

Caspi, A., Elder, G., Jr., & Herbenner, E. (1990). Childhood personality and the prediction of life course patterns. In L. Robbins & M. Rutter (Eds.), *Straight and deviant pathways from childhood to adulthood* (pp. 13–35). New York: Cambridge University Press.

Catalano, R. F., & Hawkins, J. D. (1996). The social development model: A theory of anti-social behavior. In J. D. Hawkins (Ed.), *Delinquency and crime: Current theories* (pp. 149–197). New York: Cambridge University Press.

Children's Institute International. (1996). *Armed and ready for school.* Los Angeles, CA: Pacific Visions Communication.

Department of Justice. (1991). *School crime: A national crime victimization survey report* [NCJ-131645]. Washington, DC: U.S. Government Printing Office.

Elder, G., Jr. (1985). Perspectives on the life course. In G. Elder, Jr. (Ed.), *Life course dynamics* (pp. 23–49). Ithaca, NY: Cornell University Press.

Elder, G., Jr. (1994). Time, human agency and social change: Perspectives on the life course. *Social Psychology Quarterly, 57*, 4–15.

Elliott, D. S. (1986). Self-reported violent offending: A descriptive analysis of juvenile violent offenders and their offending careers. *Journal of Interpersonal Violence, 1*(4), 472–514.

Elliott, D. S. (1993). Health-enhancing and health-compromising lifestyles. In S. G. Millstein, A. C. Petersen, & E. O. Nightingale (Eds.), *Promoting the health of adolescents: New directions for the twenty-first century* (pp. 119–145). New York: Oxford University Press.

Elliott, D. S. (1994a). Youth violence: An overview. *Congressional Program: Children and Violence, 9*(2), 15–20.

Elliott, D. S. (1994b). Serious violent offenders: Onset, developmental course and termination. *Criminology, 32*, 1–22.

Elliott, D. S. (1995, November). *Lies, damn lies and arrest statistics.* Paper presented at the American Society of Criminology Meetings, Chicago, IL.

Elliott, D. S., Huizinga, D., & Menard, S. (1989). *Multiple problem youth: Delinquency, drugs and mental health problems.* New York: Springer-Verlag.

Elliott, D. S., Williams, K. R., Mattson, B. A., Haack, D. M., & Cook, L. (1993). *Violence in Colorado, 1976–1991: A focus on homicide.* Denver, CO: Colorado Department of Health.

Fagan, J. (1996). The comparative advantage of the juvenile versus criminal court sanctions on recidivism among adolescent felony offenders. *Law and Policy, 18*, 77–112.

Finckenauer, J. (1982). *Scared straight! And the panacea phenomenon.* Englewood Cliffs, NJ: Prentice-Hall.

Fingerhut, L. A. (1993). Firearm mortality among children, youth and young adults 1–34 years of age, trends and current status: United States, 1985–1990. In *Advance data from vital and health statistics, 231.* Hyattsville, MD: National Center for Health Statistics.

Fox, J. A. (1996). *Trends in juvenile violence. A report to the U.S. Attorney General on current and future rates of juvenile offending.* Washington, DC: U.S. Department of Justice, Bureau of Justice Statistics.

Frazier, C. E., Bishop, D. M., & Lanza-Kaduce, L. (1997, May). *"Get tough" juvenile reforms: Does "adultification" make matters worse?* Paper presented at the symposium on the Future of the Juvenile Court. Philadelphia, PA: University of Pennsylvania, School of Social Work.

Garmezy, N. (1985). Stress-resistant children: The search for protective factors. In J. E. Stevenson (Ed.), *Recent research in developmental psychopathology* (pp. 213–233). Book supplement to *Journal of Child Psychology and Psychiatry, 4.*

Geerken, M. (1994). Rap sheets in criminological research. *Journal of Qualitative Criminology, 10*, 3–21.

Gottfredson, D. (1997). School-based crime prevention. In L. Sherman, D. Gottfredson, D. MacKenzie, J. Eck, P. Ruter, & S. Bushway (Eds.), *Preventing crime: What works, what doesn't, what's promising: A report to the United States Congress* (pp. 1–74). Washington, DC: U.S. Department of Justice, Office of Justice Programs.

Hanke, P. J. (1996). A profile of rural Texas youth who carry handguns to school. *Journal of Criminal Justice, 24*, 207–226.

Harris, L. and Associates. (1993). *Violence in America's public schools: A survey of the American teacher.* New York: Metropolitan Life Insurance Company.

Hindelang, M. J., Hirschi, T., & Weis, J. G. (1981). *Measuring delinquency.* Beverly Hills, CA: Sage.

Huff, R. C., & Trump, K. S. (1996). Youth violence and gangs: School safety initiatives in urban and suburban school districts. *Education and Urban Safety, 28*, 4492–4503.

Huizinga, D. (1997, February 27). *Over-time changes in delinquency and drug use in the 1970s and the 1990s.* Paper presented at the Western Society of Criminology, Honolulu, HI.

Huizinga, D., & Elliott, D. S. (1986). Re-assessing the reliability and validity of self-report delinquency measures. *Journal of Quantitative Criminology, 24*, 293–327.

Kachur, S. P., Stennies, G., Powell, K., Modzeleski, W., Stephens, R., Murphy, R., Kresnow, M., Sleet, D., & Lowry, R. (1996). School-associated violent deaths in the United States, 1992–1994. *Journal of the American Medical Association, 275*, 1729–1733.

Kingery, P. M., Pruitt, B. E., & Heuberger, G. (1996). A profile of rural Texas youth who carry handguns to school. *Journal of School Health, 66*, 18–22.

Kitsuse, J., & Cicourel, A. (1963). A note on the uses of official statistics. *Social Problems, 11*, 131–139.

Lipsey, M. W. (1992). Juvenile delinquency treatment: A meta-analytic inquiry into the variability of effects. In T. D. Cook, H. Cooper, D. S. Cordray, H. Hartman, L. V. Hedges, R. J. Light, T. A. Louis, & F. Mosteller (Eds.), *Meta-analysis for explanation: A casebook* (pp. 83–127). New York: Russell Sage Foundation.

Loeber, R., & Hay, D. (1997). The key issues in the development of aggression and violence from childhood to early adulthood. *Annual Review of Psychology, 48,* 371–410.

MacKenzie, D. L., & Brame, R. (1995). Shock incarceration and positive adjustment during community supervision. *Journal of Quantitative Criminology, 11,* 11–142.

MacKenzie, D. L., Shaw, J. W., & Souryal, C. (1992). Characteristics associated with successful adjustment to supervision: A comparison of parolees, probationers, shock participants, and shock dropouts. *Criminal Justice and Behavior, 19,* 437–454.

Maguire, K., & Pastore, A. L. (Eds.). (1995). *Sourcebook of criminal justice statistics – 1994. U.S. Department of Justice, Bureau of Justice Statistics.* Washington, DC: U.S. Government Printing Office.

Maguire, K., & Pastore, A. L. (Eds.). (1996). *Sourcebook of criminal justice statistics – 1995. U.S. Department of Justice, Bureau of Justice Statistics.* Washington, DC: U.S. Government Printing Office.

Moffit, T. (1993). Adolescent limited and life-course persistent anti-social behavior: A developmental typology. *Psychological Review, 100,* 674–701.

National Institute of Education. (1978). *Violent schools-safe schools: The Safe School Study report to Congress.* Washington, DC: U.S. Department of Education.

National Research Council. (1993). *Losing generations.* Washington, DC: National Academy Press.

Office of Juvenile Justice and Delinquency Prevention. (1989, October). Weapons in schools. *Juvenile Justice Bulletin,* p. 1. Washington, DC: U.S. Department of Justice.

Osgood, D. W., O'Malley, P. M., Bachman, J. G., & Johnston, L. D. (1989). Time trends and age trends in arrest and self-reported illegal behavior. *Criminology, 27,* 389–417.

Parks, C. P. (1997). Gang behavior in the schools: Myths or reality. *Educational Psychology Review, 7,* 41–68.

Peterson, E. (1996). *Juvenile boot camps: Lessons learned* [OJJDP Fact Sheet # 36]. Washington, DC: Office of Juvenile Justice and Delinquency Prevention.

Podkopacz, M. R., & Feld, B. C. (1996). The end of the line: An empirical study of judicial waiver. *The Journal of Criminal Law and Criminology, 86,* 449–492.

Price, J. H., & Everett, S. A. (1997). A national assessment of secondary school principals' perceptions of violence in the schools. *Health Education and Behavior, 24,* 218–229.

PRIDE. (1996). 1994–1995 national summary, United States Grades 6–12. In K. Maguire & A. L. Pastore (Eds.), *Sourcebook of criminal justice statistics – 1995* (p. 280, Table 3.59). Washington, DC: U.S. Government Printing Office.

Rand, A. (1987). Transitional life events and desistance from delinquency and crime. In M. Wolfgang, T. Thornberry, & R. Figlio (Eds.), *From boy to man: From delinquency to crime* (pp. 134–162). Chicago: University of Chicago Press.

Richters, J. (1993). The NIMH community violence project: I. Children as victims of and witnesses to violence. *Psychiatry, 56,* 7–21.

Sampson, R. J., & Laub, J. H. (1990). Crime and deviance over the life course: The salience of adult bonds. *American Sociological Review, 55,* 609–627.

Sampson, R. J., & Laub, J. H. (1993). *Crime in the making: Pathways and turning points through life.* Cambridge, MA: Harvard University Press.

Shaw, J. W., & MacKenzie, D. L. (1992). The one-year community supervision performance of drug offenders and Louisiana DOC-identified substance abusers graduating from shock incarceration. *Journal of Criminal Justice, 20,* 501–516.

Sheley, J. F., McGee, Z. T., & Wright, J. D. (1992). Gun-related violence in and around inner-city schools. *American Journal of Diseases of Children, 146,* 677–682.

28   Delbert S. Elliott, Beatrix Hamburg, & Kirk R. Williams

Sheley, J. F., McGee, Z. T., & Wright, J. D. (1995). *Weapon related victimization in se-lected inner-city high school samples* (NCJ-151526). Rockville, MD: National Criminal Justice Reference Service.

Simons, R. L., Wu, C., Conger, R. D., & Lorenz, F. O. (1994). Two routes to delin-quency: Differences between early and late starters in the impact of parenting and deviant peers. *Criminology, 32,* 247–276.

Snyder, H. N., & Sickmund, M. (1995). *Juvenile offenders and victims: A national re-port.* Washington, DC: Office of Juvenile Justice and Delinquency Prevention.

Staff. (1996, March 3). Shootings at schools prompt new concerns about violence. *The New York Times,* p. 8.

Staff. (1998, March 25). 5 are killed at school; boys, 11 and 13, are held. *The New York Times,* pp. A1, A20.

Tolan, P., & Guerra, N. (1994). *What works in reducing adolescent violence: An empiri-cal review of the field.* Boulder, CO: University of Colorado, Center for the Study and Prevention of Violence.

U.S. Department of Justice. (1994). *Criminal victimization in the United States, 1994* [Bureau of Justice Statistics, NCJ-162126]. Washington, DC: U.S. Government Printing Office.

Walker, H. M., Horner, G. S., Bullis, M., Spraque, J. R., Spraque, D. B., & Kaufman, M. J. (1996). Integrated approaches to preventing antisocial behavior patterns among school-aged children and youth. *Journal of Emotional and Behavioral Dis-orders, 4*(4), 194–209.

Webster, D. W. (1993). The unconvincing case for school-based conflict resolution. *Health Affairs, 12,* 126–141.

II. Understanding Child and Youth Violence

2. Youth Violence Is a Public Health Concern

MARGARET A. HAMBURG

Introduction

Youth violence has become one of the most serious public health problems in the United States. This chapter presents an overview of the public health approach to preventing violent behaviors and to reducing the death and injuries that result from violence. This chapter reviews the nature and scope of the problem, emphasizing why violence constitutes a public health problem and how the tools of public health can be effectively brought to bear on the design, implementation, and evaluation of meaningful school- and community-based interventions. Risk factors important in the incidence and severity of youth violence are considered, with special focus on those that emerge when the problems associated with youth violence are approached using the public health model. Finally, this chapter concludes with a discussion of the serious social, economic, and public policy challenges to the implementation of a public health approach to violence reduction, as well as a proposal for an agenda for the future of public health research in this important area.

Framing the Issue: What Is Violence?

In Chapter 1 of this volume, the editors offer a definition of violence as "the threat or use of physical force with the intention of causing physical injury, damage, or intimidation of another person." This definition will serve as the foundation for this chapter. Intentionality is at the heart of this definition, and distinguishes injuries inflicted with intent to harm from injuries that are truly unintentional and result from accidents such as motor vehicle mishaps, falls, poisonings, drownings, fires, and burns. The distinction is an important one. While all injuries combined are the leading cause of death among children and adolescents in the United States, intentional violence, alone, accounts for one-third of all injury deaths. It should be noted there is some overlap in the antecedents of intentional and nonintentional violence; impulsivity, for example, appears to be associated with both forms of violence, as are many aggressive and drug-related behaviors. The underlying configuration of causes of intentional violence, however, is quite different than that of unintentional violence. Thus intentional violence is reduced and prevented through different interventions. Intentional violence has two forms: it may be directed toward oneself as manifested by suicides or attempted suicides, or directed toward others as interpersonal violence. In keeping with the major themes and focus of this volume, this chapter focuses on interpersonal violence, including homicides, assault, sexual assault, child abuse, and child sexual abuse.

Demographics of Youth Violence

Violence is a term that refers to both a subset of behaviors (i.e., the acts that produce injuries) and the outcomes of those behaviors (i.e., the injuries themselves). While violence affects every socioeconomic level of American society, intentional interpersonal violence disproportionately involves young people as both perpetrators and victims. In 1989, for example, almost half of the estimated 4.2 million nonfatal crimes of violence in the United States were committed by youth between the ages of 12 and 24 (Mercy, 1993). In 1991, persons age 10 to 24 years accounted for 55% of all arrests for murder in the United States (Lowry et al., 1995). Self-report studies have suggested the age of highest risk for the initiation of serious violent behavior is 15–16 years, while youth age 16–17 years have the highest rates of participation in serious violence. After age 17 participation in violence drops dramatically; the vast majority – 80% – of young people who behaved violently during their adolescence cease violent behaviors by age 21 (Elliott, 1994).

In addition to perpetrating violence, young people are also at considerable risk of becoming victims of violence. In 1991, approximately 3.4 million assaults, robberies, and rapes were committed against young people age 12–24 years; nonfatal injuries occurred in about 1.1 million of these attacks (Centers for Disease Control and Prevention, 1995; Fingerhut et al., 1992; Lowry et al., 1995). Data from the National Crime Victimization Survey suggest young people are up to 4.5 times more likely than adults to be victims of violent crimes. Rates of violent victimization for youth age 12–15 years are 62.7 per 1,000 persons, and 91.1 per 1,000 for youth age 16–19 years, whereas the violent victimization rate for adults age 35–49 years is only 20 per 1,000. In 1991, adolescents age 10 to 24 years were the victims of one-third of all homicides committed in the United States (Hawkins, Crosby, & Hammett, 1994). Homicide is the second leading cause of death among persons 15–24 years of age in this country, and the third leading cause of death for youth 10 to 14 years old. Among children age 1 through 9 years, homicide is the fourth leading cause of death in the United States (Fingerhut et al., 1992; Lowry et al., 1995).

These are national statistics. However, rates vary greatly by location; in New York City, for example, homicide is the leading cause of death for young men and women age 15–24 years (New York City Department of Health, 1993; see, e.g., Centers for Disease Control and Prevention, 1995; Fingerhut et al., 1992). What is clear is that local and national figures have risen dramatically during the past few decades. Between 1963 and 1990, the homicide rate nationwide increased 104%, from 4.9 to 10 per 100,000. However, during that same period the homicide rate for youth age 10 to 24 years skyrocketed 286%, from 3.7 to 14.3 per 100,000 (Lowry et al., 1995).

Among minority youth, especially African Americans, violence has struck with particular force. Homicide has been the leading cause of death among African American males and females between the ages of 15–24 years for more than ten years. In 1988, homicide was the leading cause of death among African American males age 15–24 years, the second leading cause of death for African American boys age 1 through 4 years and 10 through 14 years, and the third leading cause of death for African American boys age 5 through 9 years. In 1991, homicide was the leading cause of death for male and female African Americans 15–34 years of age (Hawkins et al., 1994).

Of particular concern have been increases in firearm-related deaths. Between 1984 and 1993, gun-related deaths of young African American males tripled, with the most dramatic rise among those 13 to 18 years old (see Figure 2.1); the gun-related deaths of 19- to 24-year-olds also increased significantly during that time (see Figure 2.2) (Kellerman, 1994). In 1990, gunshot wounds killed 4.7 times the number of 15- to 19-year-old African American males as were killed by HIV/AIDS (human immunodeficiency virus/acquired immune deficiency syndrome), sickle cell disease, and all other natural causes of death combined (Centers for Disease Control and Prevention, 1992). Young African American girls and women scarcely fared better: homicide was the leading cause of death for ages 15 through 24 years, the second leading cause of death for ages 10 through 14, and the third leading cause of death for ages 1 through 9 (Centers for Disease Control and Prevention, 1992). In recent years, the homicide rate

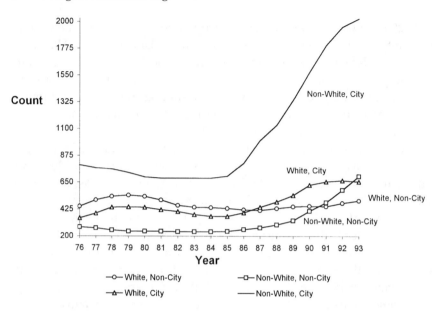

Figure 2.1. City and noncity homicide by age and race, United States, 1976–1993, Ages 13–18. *Data Sources:* New York City Department of Health, based on data from the Federal Bureau of Investigation, Uniform Crime Reports, and the U.S. Bureau of Census.

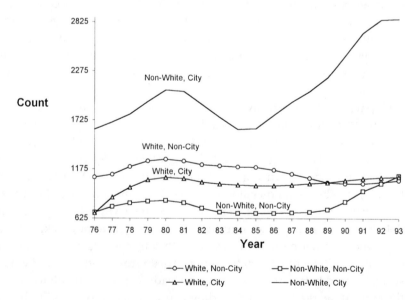

Figure 2.2. City and noncity homicide by age and race, United States, 1976–1993, Ages 19–24. *Data Sources:* New York City Department of Health, based on data from the Federal Bureau of Investigation, Uniform Crime Reports, and the U.S. Bureau of Census.

for African American females has risen faster than that of any other race/ gender grouping in the country; the most dramatic increase has been in the homicide rate of female infants less than one year of age (Tolan & Guerra, 1994).

School-Related Violence

As the levels of violence in the general society have risen sharply, it is a disturbing – though perhaps not surprising – corollary that the levels of violence in and around schools have also increased. The problem of violence in schools is known to reflect the violence occurring in the surrounding community. Evidence suggests that violence in schools derives mainly from factors external to schools, but may be precipitated or aggravated by the school environment. Student assaults on other students are the most frequent type of violence reported in schools. A recent study conducted by the Centers for Disease Control and Prevention (CDC) found that, nationally, half of boys and one-quarter of girls reported being physically attacked by someone at school (Centers for Disease Control and Prevention, 1992). Other researchers found 45% of urban school children reported witnessing someone being beaten or attacked in the preceding year (Tolan & Guerra, 1994). Nationwide, a 1993 CDC survey reported 16.2% of students had been in a physical fight on school property during the year preceding the study (Centers for Disease Control and Prevention, 1995). Approximately one-third of students had property stolen or deliberately damaged on school property during the preceding year, and more than 7% of students were threatened or injured with a weapon on school property during the preceding year, with male students significantly more likely than female students to have experienced threats or injuries (Centers for Disease Control and Prevention, 1995).

According to a recent national survey, more than one-third of all students in eighth and tenth grades reported they had been threatened with physical harm; 13% of students reported being attacked; and 14% of students had been robbed. A study in 1993 found that almost one-quarter of students in grades 3–12 nationwide reported being kicked, bitten, or hit by another student at school during the previous year; a similar percentage of students reported doing these things to someone else at school. Male students were more than twice as likely to engage in violence than female students, and students with poor grades were more likely to be both victims and perpetrators of violence (Lowry et al., 1995).

In recent years, weapon carrying by students in schools has become a growing source of violence and the threat of violence. Carrying a weapon significantly increases the possibility that a personal dispute will escalate to serious violence and result in death, disability, or other injury. A study by the National School Boards Association in 1993 reported 61% of all school districts nationwide cited weapons as a problem in schools, with the problem being particularly acute in urban schools (Lowry et al., 1995). The American School Health Association found in a 1988 national survey of eighth and tenth graders that 23% of male students and 5% of female students reported carrying a knife to school at least once during the previous year (Lowry et al., 1995). This corresponds closely with a study by the CDC that found nearly one-fourth of students nationwide had carried a weapon to school during the month preceding the survey (Centers for Disease Control and Prevention, 1995). A 1993 study, by the National Education Goals Panel, of eighth, tenth, and twelfth grade students found 9% of eighth grade students, 10% of tenth grade students, and 6% of twelfth grade students reported carrying a weapon such as a gun, knife, or club to school at least once during the previous month (Lowry et al., 1995). The highest rates of victimization were among eighth grade students: 19% reported having been threatened with a weapon, and 9% reported having been injured. At every grade level, African American and Hispanic students were more likely than white students to report being threatened or injured with a weapon at school (Lowry et al., 1995). (The special role of guns in violence is discussed in detail in Chapter 6 of this volume.)

Clearly, both violent incidents and threats of violence at school negatively affect students, school staff, and the educational process. In an atmosphere heavy with the threat of personal injury, students cannot learn and teachers cannot teach. A national study in 1993 found 22% of students in grades 3–12 were less eager to attend school because of the occurrence or threat of violence. Sixteen percent of students reported they were less willing to talk in class, and one-quarter of all student respondents believed the levels of violence they experienced or witnessed had a detrimental impact on the quality of their education (Lowry et al., 1995). A Centers for Disease Control and Prevention (CDC) survey reported that across the country in 1993, 4.4% of students had missed at least one day of school during the preceding month because they felt unsafe either at school or traveling to or from school. Hispanic and African American male and female students were significantly more likely than white male and female students to miss school because they felt unsafe (Centers for Disease Control and Prevention, 1995). The National Educational Goals Panel study in 1993 reported 7% of eighth grade students stayed home from school in the previous month because of fear (Lowry et al., 1995).

Health Consequences of Violence

From the rising trends of violence noted in the nation's communities and schools, it is possible to predict an increasing contribution of violence to the burden of illness and death borne by children and youth. In 1990 alone, homicide took the lives of 7,354 adolescents and young adults age 15–24 years. In the ten years between 1979 through 1989, the firearm homicide rate for persons 15 through 19 years of age in this country increased 61%, from 6.9 to 11.1 deaths per 100,000 population, a larger increase than for any other five-year age group (Fingerhut, Ingram, & Feldman, 1992). For each of these deaths, there are an estimated 100 nonfatal intentional injuries each year. Young people in the 15- to 24-year-old age group are at highest risk for the tens of thousands of head and spinal cord injuries caused by assaultive violence in the United States each year; these injuries result in the most significant long-term physical, neurological, and psychosocial disabilities. Of the estimated 1.6 million children who experience some form of abuse or neglect, rates of physical abuse tend to be highest among children and young adolescents 5 to 14 years of age (O'Carroll, Harel, & Waxweiler, 1993). Suicide rates for children and adolescents have doubled in the past 30 years, primarily as a result of increased use of firearms (Koop & Lundberg, 1992).

The personal health costs and economic costs to society of the devastation of violence are immense. In 1995 in New York City alone, interpersonal violence accounted for nearly 2,000 deaths, 11,000 hospitalizations, and hundreds of thousands of emergency room visits. In fact, violence is the leading cause of death for New Yorkers age 15–24 years (New York City Department of Health, 1993). Nationwide, the average cost of a violence injury, fatal and nonfatal, was $44,000 in 1992. The total medical cost of all violence that occurred in the United States was estimated at $13.5 billion in 1992, including $10.5 billion resulting from interpersonal violence such as murder, rape, assault, robbery, and arson (Elders, 1994). To these figures one must add the "costs" of years of potential life lost, and the psychological trauma resulting from intentional injuries. The latter costs are impossible to calculate, especially for children and adolescents who witness or experience violence at the most critical developmental stages in their lives. Although the health burden of violence strikes minority youth disproportionately, high rates of death and injury from violence in all racial and ethnic groups ensure that violence has without question become the most serious health problem facing all of our country's young people.

Youth Violence as a Public Health Issue

Traditionally youth violence has been addressed in the criminal justice or sociological domains and not as a concern for the public health system or health care providers. However, the continuing increases in rates of childhood and adolescent injury and death caused directly by violence have led to the recognition that the social institutions that have traditionally dealt with youth violence are losing ground. The criminal justice system, for example, though an important element in anti-violence efforts, cannot alone stem the rising tide of violence by and against youth. The criminal justice system generally responds after an act of violence has occurred, and thus cannot address either the complex causative factors that lead to youth violence or the various health consequences resulting from youth violence. Former Surgeon General C. Everett Koop and his colleague George D. Lundberg both assert that new approaches are required (Koop & Lundberg, 1992). In recent years, a proven, effective public health approach has become an increasingly important resource in the effort to prevent youth violence.

Violence would be a major public health concern based solely on the enormous toll it exacts on the health and well-being of the children and youth of America. There are, however, other even more compelling reasons for addressing violence as a public health problem. Public health efforts have had an immensely positive impact on the health status of Americans during the past century. The medical care system has benefited from a dazzling array of advances in biomedical technology, antibiotics, and treatment strategies during the past 100 years. Yet it is, in fact, public health measures that have had the greatest impact on reducing disease, increasing longevity, and improving the quality of life and health status of Americans. Since the turn of the century, the life expectancy of Americans has increased from 45 to 75 years. A recent report estimates only 5 of those 30 additional years gained can be attributed to the medical care system (U.S. Department of Health and Human Services, 1994). The most significant gains in health have come from public health programs, ranging from establishment of sanitary practices and protection of the food and water supply to control of communicable diseases through disease surveillance, contact tracing, immunization, diagnosis and treatment, and, when necessary, isolation (U.S. Department of Health and Human Services, 1994).

The success of the public health approach in addressing critical health concerns is in large measure based on its emphasis on primary prevention – that is, prevention taking place before the onset of disease or injury. Primary prevention identifies behavioral or environmental risk factors associated with disease conditions and takes steps to educate the community about, or protect it from, these risks. The major causes of premature death in America today are related to health-damaging behaviors involving violence, tobacco, alcohol, illegal substances, diet and activity patterns, motor vehicle driving practices, and risky sexuality. When health-related behaviors are the underlying causes of disease and death, public health measures for the modification of the health-damaging behaviors are essential for the reduction or prevention of the diseases. In these cases and others, public health principles and practices have demonstrated that appropriate preventive strategies can counteract or delay the onset of some diseases or disease progression.

It is clear, for example, that preventive interventions associated with the public health campaigns against smoking have led to the elimination of thousands of cases of lung cancer, other lung disease, and heart disease each year. As a result of the anti-smoking efforts in this country, the CDC estimates that approximately 1.6 million smoking-related premature deaths were prevented during the period 1964–1992, and an additional 4.1 million premature deaths will be prevented between 1993 and the year 2015 (U.S. Department of Health and Human Services, 1994). Similarly, public health interventions have played a pivotal role in achieving major health gains in infant mortality, low birth weight infants, childhood exposure to lead poisoning, vaccine-preventable childhood diseases, tuberculosis, heart disease and stroke, sexually transmitted diseases, and HIV/AIDS (U.S. Department of Health and Human Services, 1994).

The success of public health methods in significantly reducing motor vehicle injuries suggests the effectiveness of a broad public health approach to injury prevention. Over the past three decades this country has invested more than $250 million to discover ways to create safer cars, safer roads, and safer drivers. This effort has resulted in a marked decrease in the highway driving death rate, saving an estimated quarter-million lives over the past 30 years (U.S. Department of Health and Human Services, 1994; Wintemute, 1993).

Violence results from a confluence of multiple factors, including personal behaviors amenable to change, as well as family, neighborhood, and social systems that are themselves modifiable. Just as application of public health principles and comprehensive strategies reduced the number of deadly traffic accidents and the number of deaths attributable to tobacco use, the public health model can help to reduce the extent of injuries and deaths due to violence. In essence, the public health approach allows one to think about violence not as an inevitable fact of life but as a problem that can be prevented. As a consequence, the public health approach empowers individuals and entire communities to reduce the risk factors leading to violent behavior.

Public Health Model

The public health approach brings a systematic, time-tested, multidisciplinary set of practices and principles for reaching its prevention goals. It adds much needed new perspectives and dimensions to an understanding of the complexities of youth violence issues. The public health model includes a series of activities with real potential to mobilize the resources of medicine, mental health, social services, education, and substance abuse prevention to avert the epidemic of death, injuries, personal suffering, and wasted human potential resulting from youth violence. The essential features of the public health model are:

1. Community-based methods for problem identification and the development of solutions across entire population groups.
2. Health-event surveillance for gathering data to establish the nature of the health problem and to track the trends of its incidence and prevalence; also to track the relevant risk factors.
3. Epidemiologic analysis to identify risk factors and associated cofactors associated with the health problem.
4. Intervention design and evaluation.
5. Outreach/education/information dissemination.

Community-Based Approach

The heart of the public health model is a community-based approach. Such an approach incorporates a broad array of diverse strategies directed toward entire population groups rather than individual interventions such as those that take place with a patient in the doctor's office. Public health as the "physician to the population" thus has the responsibility to be the community organizer for prevention, forging collaborative relationships across community organizations, neighborhood associations, school systems, business coalitions, consumer groups, and others to identify problems, empower communities to organize and take action to prevent disease and injury, and protect themselves against risks to their health.

Health-Event Surveillance

Public health surveillance gathers information about health problems threatening communities, including data on who is most at risk, the geographic distribution of risks, and the capacity of available services to address the problems. Public health surveillance forms the basic tool for the health system as a whole. Surveillance of health events serves both as a sentinel alerting the community to new or reemergent threats, and as a research tool enabling the rapid implementation of interventions to stem the spread of disease.

The formidable data collection and surveillance instruments of the public health model allow the community to identify and respond to the full range of health problems, including violence, but also adolescent problem behaviors such as substance abuse and teen pregnancy, as well as infectious disease problems, including HIV/AIDS.

Data collection and surveillance have also helped society to better understand the relationship of certain risk factors to chronic disease conditions, such as the links between smoking and heart disease, or high fat diets and some forms of cancer.

Epidemiologic Analysis

Public health officials analyze surveillance data to assess the magnitude, characteristics, and impact of health problems on communities and population groups. Analysis of the epidemiologic data generated through surveillance helps public health officials to understand epidemics and emerging patterns of disease and injury, and the extent and prevalence of risks to health. Analysis and reporting of key dimensions of health status are vital to timely awareness of emerging problems, identification and containment of the source(s) of the problem, and the marshaling of appropriate interventions. Accurate analysis is also the foundation for effective allocation of resources to address priority health needs.

Intervention Design and Evaluation

Based on the findings of surveillance data and epidemiologic analysis, the public health model designs interventions to address specific health problems for the affected population group. Which strategies work best, for what groups of people, in what situations, and at what cost, both personal and economic, are the key considerations in the design of effective programs to promote healthy behaviors; prevent the expansion of health problems; and protect the environment, workplaces, housing, food, and the water supply. Evaluating the efficacy, effectiveness, and cost-effectiveness of interventions is a critical element of the public health approach.

Outreach/Education/Information Dissemination

The public health community serves as the health educator of the public (in contrast to the one-to-one educational and counseling intervention of the physician with a patient in the clinical setting). Outreach notifies and educates people about risks and protective measures, and helps to ensure the availability and accessibility of services.

Through health education and information dissemination efforts, public health has achieved marked success in changing behavioral patterns involving tobacco and alcohol use, diet, and exercise. The benefits of such changes may be difficult to calculate precisely, but they are clearly significant, whether measured in lives saved, decreased human suffering, or economic losses averted. For example, since 1970 there has been close to a 50% decline in the number of stroke-related deaths, largely attributable to public health measures rather than clinical care (U.S. Department of Health and Human Services, 1994).

Thus, the public health approach: (1) begins with a population-based perspective on problem identification and solution, in contrast to the individual intervention approach of the physician's office; (2) uncovers patterns and risk factors of health problems; (3) identifies who suffers from these problems and why; (4) designs and implements interventions based on a scientific analysis of the problem and what works to address the problem; (5) evaluates whether the programs work and to what extent; and (6) disseminates information about the intervention and the problem in general.

As noted previously, the techniques of public health have been effective in reducing the burden of many other preventable or controllable conditions, including communicable diseases such as smallpox and tuberculosis, chronic diseases such as coronary artery disease and lung cancer, and injuries such as motor vehicle injuries and head trauma. As this public health approach demonstrates, among the many advantages of framing violence as a public health problem is that this strategy shifts the debate from issues that may be polarizing (e.g., an individual's right to smoke) toward a discussion of improving a community's health and well-being. Thus public health can, for example, reframe the social debate about gun-related violence from incendiary issues such as gun control toward the more meaningful public health exchange about preventing firearm injuries, with the effect of bringing into the public discourse more voices representing diverse viewpoints – and added opportunities for effective intervention.

Applying the Public Health Model to the Problem of Youth Violence

It is important to note that the public health approach does not claim to have all the answers to the enormously complicated question of how to prevent violent behaviors and their consequences for America's children and youth. Rather, what the public health model offers is a practical, goal-oriented approach, the purpose of which is to discover not a single answer, but sets of answers that work for different groups in different contexts. Following are insights into the use of the public health approach in the prevention of youth violence, including consideration of some critical insights that have arisen from various studies.

Fashioning solutions to the complex social problem of violence depends on our abilities to understand the scope and nature of violence among children and youth in the United States. In order to reach this understanding, epidemiological surveillance and analysis are essential for: (1) tracking trends; and (2) identifying risk factors, vectors (i.e., the channels by which infection is transmitted), and influences. These activities develop the information base necessary for the subsequent design and evaluation of interventions. (The information contained in the "Demographics of Youth Violence" section of this chapter, for example, resulted from surveillance and analysis of youth in different settings.)

Tracking Trends

Research and surveillance monitor the magnitude of childhood and youth violence and violence-related injuries in order to help determine public health priorities at federal, state, and local levels for preventing violence-related injuries and deaths. Information generated through surveillance and analysis of epidemiological data guide the development of research and prevention programs, and monitor success in preventing injuries and deaths associated with violence, reducing the risk factors associated with violent behavior (e.g., weapon carrying in schools, physical fighting), and increasing the resiliency factors (e.g., improved conflict resolution skills, strong bonds with parents) that protect young people from violent behavior and its outcomes.

Identifying Risk Factors, Vectors, and Influences

Numerous studies have already been undertaken to probe the factors associated with youth violence. These studies serve the purpose of increasing knowledge about the causes of youth violence so society may identify targets (both populations and behaviors) amenable to preventive public health interventions.

Risk factors, cofactors, and influences important to the incidence and severity of youth violence have been identified. Evidence is mounting that youth violence is a learned behavior activated and influenced by the following individual and more general societal risk factors:

Family/Domestic Violence. Early learning experiences within the family provide the foundation for children's violent behavior. Initial causes of violence within the family have been traced to weak family bonding, including ineffective monitoring/supervision and parental indifference/rejection; exposure to violence in the home; and acquiring the expectations and values that support or tolerate the use of violence. In particular, childhood experiences with violence have clearly been associated with the development of violent behaviors throughout childhood and especially adolescence. Children as young as one year of age who were physically abused at home were found to be more than two times as likely as nonabused children to assault children and adults at school (Lowry et al., 1995; Tolan & Guerra, 1994; Widom, 1989a; Widom, 1989b).

Community Context. The neighborhoods in which children and adolescents grow and develop play very influential roles in young people's relationship with violence. Poverty, discrimination, and lack of opportunities for education and employment have all been identified as important risk factors for interpersonal violence. Because the nation's enclaves of poverty, and their related high population density, poor housing, and high unemployment – all associated with high rates of violence – are largely composed of racial minorities, particularly African Americans, these groups bear a disproportionate burden of the impact of violence. Yet it should be emphasized that research strongly indicates that poverty and residence in a low-income neighborhood more strongly predict violence than race or ethnicity (Lowry et al., 1995).

While the presence of gangs, drug distribution networks, violent role models, and rewards for violent activity characterize many low income communities, research suggests the critical factor influencing high rates of violence is the absence of effective social organization that helps to establish common values and norms, offers social support networks to residents, and reinforces effective social controls. In such neighborhoods, parents' efforts to teach their children alternatives to violence may be compromised by the lack of validation for violence-free lifestyles in the community. Discrimination, isolation from the wider society's labor market, and a dearth of social resources also help to shape children's attitudes toward violence by inhibiting the normal course of growth and development (Tolan & Guerra, 1994).

Schools/Peers. Youth living in areas characterized by a culture of violence in their homes and neighborhoods (particularly in areas of high levels of social disorganization, as described previously) often find it difficult to satisfy their needs for belonging, recognition, and acceptance through nonviolent outlets. School, which has the potential to offer positive outlets for satisfaction of those needs, may instead generate conflict and frustration, and, ultimately, violent responses from youth. Failure by young people to achieve academic success, peer approval, personal independence, self-efficacy, and satisfying interpersonal relationships within the school context may create stresses and conflicts that increase the likelihood of violence. Thus, while violence in schools may reflect the violence that pervades the surrounding community, the school environment itself presents the potential for giving rise to violence.

Research suggests that much school-related violence is linked to competition for status and status-related confrontations among peers. The peers with whom a child chooses to associate – his or her "crowd" – help to determine what behaviors he or she will model and adopt; the choice of friends is often influenced by early exposure to violence, problematic family and internal controls, and aggressive behavior patterns developed earlier in childhood. Additionally, some research suggests that grouping together students who are academically deficient and those who exhibit behavior problems may promote delinquent peer groups. Association with gangs, a type of peer group that provides the functions of a more formal identity and feelings of membership for youths in disorganized neighborhoods, may also contribute strongly to interpersonal violence as gang activity models, encourages, and rewards violent, peer-influenced antisocial behavior (Elliott, 1994).

The presence of gangs in schools also increases the likelihood of victimization for nongang members. Students who attend schools with gangs tend to be afraid of attack at school and on the way to and from school, and are more likely than students from schools without gangs to be victims of violent crime (Elliott, 1994).

An additional peer-related concern is that of sexual assault, particularly sexual assault within the context of dating (i.e., "date rape" or "acquaintance rape"). Research in this area reveals a number of disturbing trends; one study, for example, found more women had been victims of date rape than of rape by strangers (Buchwald et al., 1993; Lowry et al., 1995). Another study suggested that of female and male students who were forced to participate in a sexual act while on a date, less than one-quarter revealed the violence to anyone, in part because of their reluctance or inability to acknowledge their experience as violence (Lowry et al., 1995; Von et al., 1991). As with other forms of youth violence, victims of sexual assault tend to know their attackers, and alcohol and other drugs and/or weapons are often involved (Lowry et al., 1995).

Drugs/Alcohol. There is little question that a strong relationship exists between increasing levels of violence and the acquisition and use of drugs and alcohol. A 1989 study in New York City, for example, found more than half of all homicides were drug-related, with most involving the use or sale of crack cocaine (Lowry et al., 1995). Yet the connection between violence and substance abuse is complex, including different kinds and causes of violence. Some kinds of urban violence among young people, such as "turf" battles and drive-by shootings, appear related to drug distribution, often by youth gangs. Other kinds of violence, such as assaults, are often the means by which violent young people (and, of course, adults) acquire funds to buy drugs. Violence is also associated with the increased paranoia and irritability among the pharmacological effects of drugs such as cocaine, crack, "angel dust," and amphetamines. A good deal of indirect, often unintentional violence – including, motor vehicle accidents – is also often associated with drug use (Marwick, 1992).

Although given less attention, use of the drug alcohol can also be a powerful stimulus for youth violence. Research has suggested that at least half of all perpetrators of violence and their victims had been drinking, and the association between drinking and violence is especially strong in homicides and rapes involving people who know each other (Lowry et al., 1995; Rivara et al., 1997). The ease with which alcohol and drugs are available at schools appears to increase the likelihood that students will be attacked, or fear being attacked, in school or on their way to or from school (Lowry et al., 1995).

Media/Culture of Violence. The depiction and glorification of violence in television programs, movies, and other media expose children to a nearly unending cascade of modeled violence and aggression that fosters a general acceptance and even legitimization of violence within American culture at large (Comerci, 1996; Dukarm et al., 1995; Lowry et al., 1995; Tolan & Guerra, 1994). Some estimates suggest that by the time an American child has reached the age of 16, he or she has witnessed 200,000 acts of violence on television, including 33,000 murders (Lowry et al., 1995). Research has repeatedly claimed that violence observed in the media by children does increase aggressive and violent behavior in children and youth, creates unrealistic attitudes about the efficacy of aggressive behavior, predicts childhood violence and later crime, and desensitizes children to the horrors of real-life violence (Comerci, 1996; Dukarm et al., 1995; Lowry et al., 1995; Tolan & Guerra, 1994).

Guns. Evidence is mounting that the presence of a gun in a violent interaction significantly increases the likelihood of escalation of even relatively minor disputes into a lethal encounter in which one or more of the participants will be killed. In the past ten years the homicide rate for adolescents killed by firearms has increased more than 150%. Firearms are responsible for nearly three-quarters of all homicides of young African American men. And the presence of guns in schools continues to increase: an estimated 270,000 guns are brought to school each day in this country (Elliott, 1994). There is little doubt that violent events that involve guns are several times more likely to result in death than those involving knives or other weapons (Rosenberg et al., 1992).

As with alcohol and other drugs and violence in the media, the culture's ambivalence toward firearms – on the one hand decrying their destructive power, on the other connecting their use with highly valued qualities of American culture – creates a serious confusion in young people that muddies their abilities to make clear-cut, health-promoting life choices (Tolan & Guerra, 1994).

Biological Influences. Individual temperaments and acquired biological deficits may contribute to children's violent tendencies. For example, antisocial personality disorders, attention deficit disorders, impulsivity, lead and other neurotoxin exposures, and serious head injuries are among the factors that may impel a child toward violent behavior (Elliott, 1994).

While it is not possible to quantify all of the preceding risk factors at this point, certain of the most important cofactors, vectors, and influences to target public health interventions appear to be factors associated with family and domestic violence, factors related to schools and peers, factors related to alcohol and other drug use, and especially factors related to firearms. These factors appear to be not only the most strongly associated with violence but also those for which research has identified at least a hypothetical or tentative causal mechanism, and which appear to offer the most promising opportunities for modification through public health interventions. Moreover, these factors tend to appear in clusters rather than as isolated occurrences; the confluence of guns, peer conflicts, and drugs and alcohol, for example, can result in confrontations particularly prone to escalate into lethality. Such confluences of factors require multiple levels of interventions.

Designing Strategies for Intervention

A fundamental purpose of epidemiologic surveillance and analysis is to identify appropriate targets for violence prevention interventions. This includes consideration of which strategies work best, against which risk factors, for which target groups, in what circumstances, and at what costs. One of the critical findings of an analysis of the epidemiology of youth violence shows that while violence may be prevalent throughout society, risk for and types of violence differ among children and adolescents by socioeconomic status, age, gender, race, situation, and setting. For example, poor, urban, male African Americans are at greater risk of violence than adolescents who do not share those characteristics; African American males are most often killed by friends, while African American females are most often killed by their husbands or partners (Lowry et al., 1995). Similarly, adolescent males in general are at greatest risk of injury and death from physical fights, assaults, and robberies in the community, while young children and women are at greatest risk of nonfatal injuries in the home, due to sexual assault and violence including rape, child abuse, child sexual abuse, and assault by intimate partners (Lowry et al., 1995). Thus patterns of variations in risk for and circumstances of violence among risk groups revealed through analysis of surveillance data must guide the design of interventions to best serve and target specific populations, risks, and contexts.

Intervention categories for violence reduction address risks in the individual, the family, the school, and the community, as follows:

- Tolan and Guerra (1994) suggest three types of individual-level interventions: (1) those that address violence caused by problems in psychological processes (i.e., emotional, behavioral, and cognitive dysfunction); (2) psychoeducational interventions to prevent or reduce violence through programs that promote life skills, social competence, and conflict resolution capacity; and (3) psychoactive medication and behavioral interventions used for treating severe psychopathological forms of violent behavior.
- Family approaches include enhancing parenting skills to decrease the parent-

child interactions that promote aggression in children; improving parent management strategies to increase emotional engagement, appropriate monitoring, and family problem-solving skills; mobilizing resources; and helping the family learn to cope with stressful life circumstances.

- School-based interventions are those designed to alter school settings by: (1) changing teacher behavior management strategies to prevent violent behavior and encouraging student cooperation; (2) improving student motivation by enhancing reinforcement, improving communication between students, school staff, and families, and enhancing monitoring of students to identify youth at risk of developing violent behavior; and (3) changing school organizational structures and atmospheres in order to increase student and parent involvement and to establish programs to better meet students' special needs.
- Community- or neighborhood-level approaches attempt to integrate all of the primary institutions that serve youth within a community – families, health agencies, schools, employment, and juvenile justice – in a coordinated effort to develop effective neighborhood organization and a comprehensive range of services. Some recent studies illustrate the effectiveness of this approach. For example, the Harlem Hospital Injury Prevention Program has reported on two types of successful injury prevention programs using a public health approach to reduce injuries to children in northern Manhattan, including central Harlem (Laraque et al., 1995). The Adolescent Outreach Program and the Harlem Alternatives Program represent community-based approaches to violence reduction and gunshot injury prevention, respectively. In particular, the educational components of those projects were highly effective in reaching the intended community groups. Preliminary results also suggest these comprehensive programs were successful in reducing the risk for injuries specific to the age group 5–16-years of age (Laraque et al., 1995).

Similarly, a recent report from the CDC describes several studies across the country that evaluate the use of traditional tools of public health to address violence prevention (Satcher, 1995). This report is richly suggestive of the range of interventions accessible through use of the public health model. One study, for example, indicated that regular visits by health practitioners to the homes of unmarried, poor, teenage mothers reduced child abuse. Other studies showed the effectiveness of interventions ranging from laws against carrying firearms in public to training in communication, negotiation, and problem solving for middle school students (Satcher, 1995).

This abbreviated review of types of violence reduction interventions and case studies is not intended to be illustrative, comprehensive, or inclusive. Other chapters in this volume detail specific programs and strategies that illustrate these and other categories of interventions. The purpose is to provide an overview of the complexity and interrelatedness of the issues involved in violence reduction among children and adolescents. The important points are twofold. First, effective programs of intervention must be based on the disease patterns and risk factors identified through careful epidemiological surveillance and analysis. Second, the most effective violence reduction strategies must be both multidisciplinary and "multichanneled," incorporating combinations of strategies that address the diverse risk factors in a comprehensive intervention.

Evaluating/Measuring the Benefits of Intervention

A critical component of intervention strategies utilizing the public health model is the evaluation of the effectiveness of the violence reduction programs. The goal of program evaluation is to determine the efficacy of specific youth violence interventions in order to evaluate the benefits, costs, and consequences of implementation. Such evaluation should generate information allowing basic judgments to be made about which group(s) a program helps, what measurable violence-related behavioral outcomes result from the program's interventions, and specifications about how the intervention achieved its ends. Evaluation of an intervention's effectiveness can also be improved if its cost-effectiveness and any improvements it brings about in related problems can be addressed. Without these kinds of data, the impact of a program may not be reliably assessed, and its effectiveness and replicability not scientifically judged.

Disseminating Program Information

A final element of public health model interventions as applied to youth violence involves the identification, documentation, and sharing of information about successful models and approaches to violence reduction and prevention. The purpose of these activities is not only to increase public awareness about the extent and consequences of youth violence, but to share information on current research and documented successful prevention efforts so they may be implemented in other appropriate settings. Though last, this stage is a critically important one to help make as rapid progress as possible in reducing the burden of injuries and death resulting from violence.

Challenges to the Public Health Approach

Although the public health model's potential is gaining in prominence and credibility, the public health approach to the reduction and prevention of youth violence is not without its difficulties. Youth violence is a complex, multifaceted problem with multiple specific causes intimately intertwined with an array of America's most serious and intractable social and economic dilemmas: poverty; racism; the disintegration of families and entire communities; the increasing dearth of educational and employment opportunities for some of the nation's most disadvantaged and vulnerable citizens; overwhelming peer pressures; and a disruption of values and social norms. Each of these contributes in complicated ways to the problems associated with youth violence. While each deserves individual attention, it is an unfortunate fact that these problems are also irrevocably linked to other significant public health problems, such as the spread of HIV infection, high infant mortality rates, sexually transmitted diseases, tuberculosis, and overburdened hospital emergency rooms.

Complicating even further the ability to address these pressing health problems adequately is the deterioration of public health structures and functions across the country, due to a combination of short-sighted public policy making, fiscal neglect, and overconfidence. Despite the best intentions and wishes, there are no easy solutions for the complicated interplay of factors contributing to violent behavior by and against America's young people. Additionally, there is a need for collaborative efforts by every social institution affected by youth violence at local, state, and national levels. Educational institutions, public health systems, the medical establishment, mental health services, social services, the criminal justice system, the media, and substance abuse prevention and treatment facilities and organizations must all participate to the greatest extent possible.

Several essential reasons mandate this participation. The first is to ensure the comprehensiveness of the surveillance, intervention design, evaluation, and dissemination tasks characterizing a public health approach. For example, to be accurate and comprehensive, the collection, management, analysis, and exchange of data related to incidence and trends of youth violence for the purpose of information-based decision making must be gathered from many sources and must take place at local, state, and national levels. Collaboration thus promotes the continuous flow of information, ideas, and solutions between levels, agencies, and communities, and ensures that advances in research and programs are disseminated swiftly and meaningfully.

The second reason reflects the need to address community influences on behavioral risk factors for injuries and deaths resulting from violence. Public health itself is based on an understanding that interventions targeted at populations or communities affect the health and well-being of the individual. Changing behavior on a community-wide level thus requires innovations that far exceed the traditional model of medical health care services and incorporate social, political, and economic systems as stakeholders. This broadening of the focus from individual to a population perspective is consistent with the population-level approach of the public health paradigm; and collaboration is crucial to its success.

Future Research Needs in Prevention of Youth Violence

Addressing these challenges to the public health approach requires another kind of significant intervention: public health research. This must increase in importance as we struggle to understand the issues associated with youth violence. An ambitious program of public health research should focus on every component of the public health model noted in this chapter. For example, one needs to understand how best to forge and maintain effective broad-based community coalitions in different settings. Surveillance research will not only make epidemiologic trends more evident, but will help to evaluate how effective surveillance tools are in identifying trends.

Additionally, public health research should focus on identifying causative factors in the social environment contributing to youth violence. Research needs to identify and evaluate the effectiveness of measures for modifying behavioral and social practices that contribute to youth violence. Of particular interest is understanding the determinants of behavior change. More needs to be learned about what constitutes effective public health education, and how best to disseminate public health information. These questions affect a range of health and disease conditions beyond violence, yet there is surprisingly little data about what works, for whom, and why.

In short, a national public health research agenda must emphasize the entire spectrum of factors affecting youth violence, from basic research on the physiological aspects of violence to development of new surveillance technologies, to the design of a range of initiatives that can appropriately target specific populations and risk factors. Society's need for understanding this area of such compelling importance requires a strong commitment to continuing active public health research on youth violence prevention.

Conclusion

Youth violence has emerged as one of the nation's most urgent and disturbing public health problems. As with many behaviorally based public health problems, the enormous numbers of injuries and deaths resulting from youth violence are largely, if not entirely, preventable. The central theme of this chapter has been that preventing the injuries and deaths associated with youth violence requires a public health approach mobilizing a broad array of strategies and resources in a coordinated, multidisciplinary effort.

In addition, the public health approach to violence employs a time-tested, systematic set of practices and principles for reaching the goal of preventing the burdens of injury and death from increasingly threatening our nation's most vulnerable populations. Public health ensures that interventions are designed based on specific and extensive data concerning the full scope of the problem, its probable causes, and the design and evaluation of effective solutions.

At a time when the epidemic of interpersonal youth violence seems not only overwhelming but inescapable, the public health approach offers a source of hope for the future. It allows us to regard youth violence not as an inevitable state of affairs in a culture steeped in violence at the end of this violent century, but as a series of problems amenable to solutions. Ultimately the public health approach empowers both individuals to change their health-damaging behaviors and entire communities to act as positive agents of change to reduce the wholly unacceptable levels of violent behavior that plague this nation and imperil the futures of American youth.

References

Buchwald, E., Fletcher, P. R., & Roth, M. (1993). Are we really living in a rape culture? In E. Buchwald, P. R. Fletcher, & M. Roth (Eds.), *Transforming a rape culture* (pp. 7–9). Minneapolis, MN: Milkweed Editions.

Centers for Disease Control and Prevention. (1992). *Proceedings of the Third National Injury Control Conference*. Atlanta, GA: Author.

Centers for Disease Control and Prevention. (1995, March 24). Youth risk behavior surveillance: United States, 1993. *Morbidity and Mortality Weekly Report, 1995, 44*(SS-1), 5–34.

Comerci, G. D. (1996). Efforts by the American Academy of Pediatrics to prevent and reduce violence and its full effects on children and adolescents. *Bulletin of the New York Academy of Medicine, 73*(2), 398–410.

Dukarm, C. P., Holl, J. L., & McArarney, E. R. (1995, Summer). Violence among children and adolescents and the role of the pediatrician. *Bulletin of the New York Academy of Medicine, 72*(1), 5–15.

Elders, J. (1994, April). American violence is home grown. *Focus, 22*(4), 7.

Elliott, D. S. (1994). *Youth Violence: An overview*. Boulder, CO: University of Colorado, Center for the Study and Prevention of Violence.

Fingerhut, L. A., Ingram, D. D., & Feldman, J. J. (1992). Firearm and nonfirearm homicide among persons 15 through 19 years of age: Differences by level of urbanization, United States, 1979 through 1989. *Journal of the American Medical Association, 267*, 3048–3053.

Hawkins, D. F., Crosby, A. E., & Hammett, M. (1994). Homicide, suicide, and assaultive violence: The impact of intentional injury on the health of African Americans. In I. L. Livingston (Ed.), *Handbook of black American health: The mosaic of conditions, issues, policies, and prospects* (pp. 169–189). Westport, CT: Greenwood Press.

Kellerman, A. L. (1994). Firearm-related violence: What we don't know is killing us [annotation]. *American Journal of Public Health, 84,* 541–542.

Koop, C. E., & Lundberg, G. D. (1992). Violence in America: A public health emergency. *Journal of the American Medical Association, 267,* 3075–3076.

Laraque, D., Barlow, B., Durkin, M., & Heagarty, M. (1995). Injury prevention in an urban setting: Challenges and successes. *Bulletin of the New York Academy of Medicine: A Journal of Public Health, 72,* 16–30.

Lowry, R., Sleet, D., Duncan, C., Powell, K., & Kolbe, L. (1995). Adolescents at risk for violence. *Educational Psychology Review, 7,* 7–39.

Marwick, C. (1992). Guns, drugs threaten to raise public health problem of violence to epidemic. *Journal of the American Medical Association, 267,* 2993.

Mercy, J. A. (1993, Summer). Youth violence as a public health problem. *Spectrum, 66*(3), 26–30.

New York City Department of Health. (1993). *Injury mortality in New York City.* New York: New York City Department of Health, Office of Vital Statistics and Epidemiology.

O'Carroll, P. W., Harel, Y., & Waxweiler, R. J. (1993). Measuring adolescent behaviors related to intentional injuries. *Public Health Reports, 108,* 15–19.

Rivara, F. P., Mueller, B. A., Somes, G., Mendoza, C. T., Rushforth, N. B., & Kellerman, A. L. (1997). Alcohol and illicit drug abuse and the risk of violent death in the home. *Journal of the American Medical Association, 278*(7), 569–575.

Rosenberg, M. L., O'Carroll, P. W., & Powell, K. E. (1992). Let's be clear: Violence is a public health problem. *Journal of the American Medical Association, 267*(22), 3071–3072.

Satcher, D. (1995). Violence as a public health issue. *Bulletin of the New York Academy of Medicine: A Journal of Public Health, 72,* 46–56.

Tolan, P. H., & Guerra, N. G. (1994). *What works in reducing adolescent violence: An empirical review of the field.* Boulder, CO: University of Colorado, Center for the Study and Prevention of Violence.

U.S. Department of Health and Human Services. (1994). *For a healthy nation: Returns on investments in public health.* Washington, DC: Author.

Von, J. M., Kilpatrick, D. G., Burgess, A. W., & Hartman, C. R. (1991). Rape and sexual assault. In M. L. Rosenberg & M. A. Fenley (Eds.), *Violence in America: A public health approach* (pp. 95–122). New York: Oxford University Press.

Widom, C. S. (1989a). Child abuse, neglect, and violent criminal behavior. *Criminology, 27,* 251–271.

Widom, C. S. (1989b). The cycle of violence. *Science, 244,* 160–166.

Wintemute, G. (1993). Motor vehicles or firearms: Which takes a heavier toll? *Journal of the American Medical Association, 269*(17), 2213.

3. Social Contexts and Functions of Adolescent Violence

JEFFREY FAGAN & DEANNA L. WILKINSON

Introduction

In the past, violence research has been concerned with predicting why certain individuals are more disposed to violence than others. One consequence of this approach has been the development of theory and policy that view violence as a homogeneous behavior, and that overlooks potentially important variations in the motivations, behaviors, and characteristics of adolescents involved in violent acts. This variation exists not only *between* individuals, but *within* individuals over time.

Violence theory and research have paid little attention to these meaningful differences in the forms of violent acts among teenagers. Violence research often has failed to acknowledge its heterogeneity and the likelihood that different forms of violence have different motivations and are a response to different conditions and circumstances.[1] Empirical research shows teenagers are involved in a wide range of violent acts. Meaningful distinctions go beyond the simple "expressive violence" and "instrumental violence" and seek to locate violence within a framework where motivation interacts with social context to produce a violent act.

Violence research has rarely addressed the specific conditions and interpersonal dynamics that channel such dispositions into violent events (Luckenbill & Doyle, 1989). Few studies have examined the contexts, antecedents, or interpersonal dynamics of violent events among adolescents or young males in the inner city, especially the mechanisms that escalate personal disputes into assaults or homicide, nor have there been studies that have located these events within specific neighborhood, school, or other social contexts. Such an approach seems necessary to explain the increase in violence and fatalities among young males in general and the concentration of lethal violence in urban areas (Fingerhut, 1993; Sampson & Lauritsen, 1994). The social and cultural landscape of inner city neighborhoods described by

Anderson (1990, 1994), Sullivan (1989), Canada (1995), Decker and van Winkle (1996), and others provides further support for research focused on "situated transactions" (i.e., the interactions between people within specific places).

Violence research has increasingly adopted an event-based approach to explain violent interactions among people (Cornish 1993, 1994; Felson, 1993; Felson & Steadman, 1983; Katz, 1988; Luckenbill, 1977; Luckenbill & Doyle, 1989; Oliver, 1994; Polk, 1994; Sommers & Baskin, 1993). This approach views violent events as complex interactions among people, personal motivations, weapons, the social control attributes of the immediate setting, and the ascribed meaning and status attached to the violent act. This view addresses both the motivations that bring individuals to situations where violence occurs and the specific features that comprise the event.

This approach, therefore, does not deny the importance of the individual character traits that bring people to violent situations, such as "disputatiousness" (Luckenbill & Doyle, 1989), but does recognize the limitations of deterministic models that assume a simple relationship between personality and violent behavior. It recognizes that motivated individuals are placed in circumstances where disputes occur, and a variety of internal and interpersonal processes shape the outcome of such events. Accordingly, we view events as situated transactions, with specific rules that develop within specific social settings. These rules reflect the norms of groups in which violence is an accepted and rewarded behavior. There are "scripts" that govern how disputes are settled and when and where violence is used or avoided; such scripts convey the significance and status of violence within the broader adolescent culture.

This theoretical framework was originally developed to explain the dynamics of interpersonal disputes between *adults*. In this view, violence is a goal-oriented behavior (Kennedy & Forde, 1996; Tedeschi & Felson, 1994). Adolescent violence, however, involves a wide range of behaviors including not only disputes but other acts designed to achieve goals closely linked to the unique developmental needs of adolescence. The application of this framework to adolescent violence therefore must be extended to account for the unique developmental context of adolescence, as well as the types of social and situational factors that frame the everyday activities of youths.

In this chapter, we develop a conceptual framework for explaining adolescent violence in inner cities as a functional, goal-oriented behavior. Violence for adolescents serves specific purposes that reflect the stages of adolescent development. The goals are also specific to the social contexts in which adolescent violence occurs. This perspective makes possible explanations that sort out the effect of immediate factors such as the presence of bystanders, intoxicants, or firearms from the more distant influences of social psychological factors that predispose individuals toward violent responses. Event-based approaches are "theories of action" (Cornish, 1993, 1994) that describe the dynamic of a human interaction, taking into account both motivation and decision making within events.

The next section begins by examining several types of adolescent violence in specific contexts and analyzes the goals of these behaviors. Then we discuss the functions of adolescent violence. Following, we consider mediating factors that either inhibit or enhance the seriousness of violence. In the final section, we explore the internal dynamics of violent events.

Types and Contexts of Adolescent Violence

Adolescence is a time of stressful development, marked by changes in both physical appearance and social status. It is a developmental period characterized by physical stress, impoverished coping skills, and high vulnerability (Hamburg, 1974). It is a prolonged period, beginning with hormonal changes and ending with the transition to adult social roles, typically work. Adolescence is marked by a series of social transitions, including entry into middle/junior high school and differentiated school tasks, increasing use of peers as a critical reference group for exploration of social roles, exploration of opposite-sex relationships, and changing relations with parents and other adults. Adult expectations of teenagers are changing at the same time the adolescents' perceptions of themselves are undergoing basic changes. Adolescence also is a time of pursuit of some universal goals of adolescence: social affiliation, mastery, social identity, and autonomy.

The daily routines of child and adolescent development occur primarily within the specific contexts of neighborhood, family, school, and peer group. Apart from family, social interactions occur among groups of similarly situated children within schools or neighborhood peer groups. These contexts circumscribe social networks and daily interactions within these networks give rise to potential disputes and violence in three ways.

First, there are recurring interactions among individual youths. Adolescents see each other daily in school, on the journey to and from school, in their neighborhoods, and in a range of social activities such as parties or athletic events. Individuals rank each other in these contexts through a variety of social comparisons. These processes naturally give rise to competition and disputes.

Second, bystanders are present in contexts of adolescents' lives and they witness and participate in disputes and in the confirmation or withholding of status. Bystanders are a critical component of the escalation of disputes into violence. (See, e.g., Decker, 1996; Tedeschi & Felson, 1994.) Witnesses to disputes are the arbiters of their outcomes, and often the main arbiters of status. Accordingly, they play a crucial role in the initiation and settlement of disputes, at times encouraging violence for their own vicarious pleasure, or raising the stakes of a conflict so high that violence becomes a necessity to the participants in the dispute. From children on playgrounds to adolescents in street-corner groups, witnesses are a part of the landscape of social interactions and influence decisions about how to conduct social relations or settle disputes.

Third, the social position of the inner city affords limited avenues for children and adolescents to obtain the types of social status and roles available to children in other ecological contexts. Inner city residents tend to withdraw from organized communal life (Anderson, 1990). Social roles are dominated by street-oriented peer groups, with limited opportunity for broader participation in community life such as after-school groups, volunteer organizations, or unsupervised athletics (Short, 1996). Accordingly, adolescents often are unable to demonstrate the types of refined skills that bring status in later years: vocational or technical skills, analytic intelligence, or artistic talent. Alternatives to conventional status attainment, then, may be limited in the inner city to manifestations of physical power or domination, athletic performance, verbal agility, or displays of material wealth. Social status inordinately depends on one's position within social hierarchies, and for males those hierarchies often are established through manifestations of physical power or fighting (Guerra, Nucci, & Huesmann, 1994; Guerra & Slaby, 1990). The continual demand for personal "respect," coupled with limited avenues by which to attain it, sets up conflicts often resolved through fighting, an available pathway to high status.

As examples of the event-based theory, we shall illustrate the intentionality, purposefulness, and goal orientation of four types of violence common during childhood and adolescence in the inner city: childhood aggression, gang violence, robbery, and dating violence.[2] We then locate the goals and functions of these acts, and offer explanations for diversity of outcomes.

Childhood Aggression: Rough and Tumble Play

Violence has functional interpretations age-graded for developmental as well as social contexts. Aggression among children, some of which involves

physical fighting, is an important part of the development and maintenance of dominance hierarchies. "Rough and tumble" play-fighting and
chasing typically occur among children and often serve to differentiate
children and establish social hierarchies (Humphreys & Smith, 1987). In
observational studies, it may occupy as much as 10% of their unstructured
time. Moreover, partners in these exchanges appear to strengthen affinities
(i.e., friendships) through this form of play.

Rough and tumble play has been characterized as a "good-natured"
form of aggression, quite different from serious fighting. Observational
studies show that although the motor activities of rough and tumble play
are similar to fighting, fighting involves different facial expressions and
different social outcomes. The roles of dominance and submission are exchanged in rough and tumble play, by mutual consent, but these become
the outcomes of serious fighting (Smith & Hogan, 1980). As male children
age, rough and tumble play becomes an important forum for development
of fighting skills. And when rough and tumble play persists in a pattern of
physical aggression in pursuit of domination, it becomes *bullying*. Bullying
is a precursor of stable antisocial and aggressive behavior that may endure
into later adolescence and adulthood (Olweus, 1993, 1994).[3]

One of the constants across developmental stages is the ordering of dominance hierarchies among males based on fighting skills and toughness
(Humphreys & Smith, 1987; Pikert & Wall, 1981). The functional value of
rough and tumble play for younger children is threefold: affiliations and
friend selection, development of fighting skills, and initial establishment
of one's position in a dominance hierarchy. However, as children age into
adolescence, the forms and instrumental value of rough and tumble play
seem to change. For 12- and 13-year-old boys, rough and tumble play involves both intense and playful fighting (Neill, 1976). But the intense fighting often involves hostility, with the potential for injury and other distress
for the victim. What was playful behavior in a younger developmental
stage becomes with age more intense, purposeful, and consequential behavior that lies at the heart of dominance struggles.

While these struggles ensue on other social fronts as well, rough and
tumble play remains at the center of social hierarchies among male children as they grow into early adolescence, where physical dominance and
"toughness" are valued (Humphreys & Smith, 1987). When alternative
means of establishing social position (e.g., success in school or other prosocial activities) are attenuated, rough and tumble play is likely to continue
beyond childhood. However, its meaning, seriousness, and social value
change as adolescents enter a developmental context with increased social

diversity and competition for status. This transitional period is the stage at which rough play turns serious, and when the goals of childhood rough play transform into the more consequential violent behaviors of older adolescence.

Gang Violence

The assignment of status to young males based on toughness and fighting skills is an enduring theme of gang life. (See, e.g., Cohen, 1955; Miller, 1975; Short & Strodtbeck, 1965; Spergel, 1995; Vigil, 1988.) Gangs present an opportunity for involvement in peer groups during adolescent development. Gangs are social groups that value styles of exaggerated display of masculinity, risk taking, and autonomy. Violence often is part of the collective identity of the gang and its members (see, e.g., Keiser, 1969; Padilla, 1992). But gang violence is a heterogeneous phenomenon, with meanings and functions that vary according to the specific situation. Gangs provide a social context in which the potential for violence results from any number of concerns, including struggles for power within the gang, territorial battles with other gangs, initiation and detachment rituals, attaining high status, material gain, the expression of grievances, retribution, self-defense, defense of the gang, and reinforcement of collective identity. Each of these components of gang violence involves a functional or purposeful dimension.

As a social context, the gang is "ripe" for violence because there are frequent and repeated interactions among individuals; bystanders are readily present; status is valued and restricted; there is very low external (i.e., legal) social control (i.e., police) on activity; and violence can help individuals address the specific concerns previously noted. In addition, violent expression of grievances within and between gangs are normative, and cultural values about masculinity are typically strong in the gang context (Oliver, 1994; Tedeschi & Felson, 1994).

The establishment of social identity and the expression of masculinity are important components of negotiating and maintaining social position in the gang, and gang members adopt styles to express their "manhood" in several forms, including violence (Anderson, 1994; Vigil, 1988). Verbal aggression, or violent discourse, among street-corner groups can strengthen group cohesion (Miller, Geertz, & Cutter, 1961). Homophily of friendship patterns (Kandel, 1985) suggests gang members will have extensive and exclusive contact with like-minded and similarly situated adolescents, such as risk takers or impulsive individuals, reinforcing the central functional role of violence and increasing the opportunities for violence.

Finally, in the social world of gangs and the socially isolated neighborhoods in which they exist, the amplification of personal disputes into violence is normal. Many events of gang violence involve a grievance, such as the violation of physical space or social status. These may lead to violence within and between gangs. For example, conflict between two rival gangs often involves violation of territory or perceived insults to the gang. Conflicts within gangs may occur when members jockey for status or when a dispute arises over relations involving girlfriends or money. Blame accumulates over time in a gang conflict, and a grievance may recycle for long periods as the parties involved claim counter-grievances and then counter-counter grievances, and so on. The ready availability of guns increases the stakes in gang conflicts, and raises the potential seriousness of gang violence (Campbell, 1984; Vigil, 1988).

Robbery: Acquisitive Violence

Robbery is one of the most salient forms of violence in the American consciousness. Its unpredictability and the threat of serious harm make it one of the most feared crimes. Robbery offending is concentrated in late adolescence, with increasing rates starting at age 14 and peaking at age 19. Rates for 17- to 19-year-olds exceed rates for any other age category (Snyder & Sickmund, 1995).

For inner city youths, robbery provides a way of "campaigning for status . . . by taking the possessions of others" (Anderson, 1994). Goods obtained in robberies, whether valuable or seemingly trivial, are imbued with symbolic value for adolescents that far exceeds their material value. Not only do the goods have face worth, but they also symbolize the robber's ability to dominate another person, to control a victim, and to gain deference from others. According to Anderson (in press), while the material returns from robbery contribute socially and extrinsically to the accrual of status, the intrinsic rewards of status and dominance provide comfort, self-respect, and confidence. And it is only through violence, or the threat of it, that these robberies can be successful.

Especially among adolescents, robberies often are unplanned or hastily planned events, the result of a chance coming together of motivation and opportunity (Cook, 1976, 1980, 1991). The goals are acquisitive, but serious injuries also result from many robberies gone wrong. The presence of a firearm allows the opportunity for a robbery to become a homicide (Cook, 1980). In an examination of patterns of force in robbery, Luckenbill (1980) found that choice of "coercive lethal resources" (i.e., weapon or no weapon) determined the offender's "opening move" and the subsequent patterns of behavior in the robbery event. Luckenbill (1980) concluded:

> . . . based on the observations of the interviewed offenders, that offenders with lethal resources open the transformation process with a threat of force, whereas offenders with nonlethal resources open with incapacitating force. (p. 367)

Similarly, Skogan (1978) suggested the presence of a lethal weapon affects the type, timing, and sequence of events in a robbery. The availability of a firearm may encourage a robber to threaten "risky or harder" targets, anticipate little or no resistance from the victim, and rely on a threat of force which may or may not need to be followed through.[4] There are predictable stages for the robbery event, and when the victim's responses fail to meet the robber's expectations, threatened violence may become actual to gain compliance or to place the event back on its planned course (Feeney, 1986; Skogan, 1978). The use of force, including firing guns, often is not gratuitous in robberies, unless a robbery becomes a stage for acting out toughness or meanness. Although firearms are often present during robberies, their use in the course of a robbery may reflect other contingencies, or what Zimring and Zuehl (1986) called "recreational violence"[5] (see also Katz, 1988).

Adolescence is a developmental stage when abstract reasoning about the consequences of using guns and the cognitive capacity to read social cues are incomplete (Kagan, 1989; Steinberg & Cauffman, 1996). The choices in these situations may be seen as "black and white" or "all or nothing" for the adolescent robber. During the course of a robbery, the (presumably inexperienced) teenager armed with a weapon becomes an unstable performer in a scenario with outcomes dependent on a predictable set of interactions between the robber and victim. It is when the initial definition of the situation strays from robbery to a threat, personal slight, or conflict (in the wake of resistance) that seemingly irrational violence occurs. And if guns are present, the violence often results in death.

Dating Violence

Recent evidence shows domestic violence by men toward their female partners is a remarkably stable behavior over the developmental life course, beginning with dating violence during middle adolescence (Magdol, Moffitt, Caspi, et al., 1997). However, events in which teenage males assault their dates have rarely been examined to explain motivations or event dynamics. Date *rape* involves coercion to obtain sexual relations or alternative goals such as power, status, or self-esteem (Lloyd, Koval, &

Cate, 1989). Physical dating *violence* has other motives: control (Dobash & Dobash, 1992), coercion and maintenance of power (Yllo, 1988), or displays of domination or mastery (Makepeace, 1989).

An understanding of dating violence by adolescents involves recognition of the high-stakes sexual "game" that governs sexual codes and intimacy among youth (Anderson, 1990; Hagedorn, in press). There is little evidence that dating violence is especially prevalent in any specific demographic group. However, its meaning (i.e., functionality) may vary among different groups, reflecting the normative values regarding dating among different social networks, values that in turn reflect structural contexts that value or devalue women and male–female intimacy. Dating often is practice for adult roles, a process of experimentation and development of scripted behaviors governing intimacy. Part of the practice involves the management of gender roles, and identity formation for adolescents at a critical developmental stage requires success in such roles. Having a boyfriend or girlfriend is important for status and identity. The importance of this form of success is exaggerated by the attenuation of other means of success. The influence of social context lies in the meaning conveyed to gender roles and the functional value of intimacy. When normative patterns of relations devalue intimacy, the meaning of dating as a means to status is conflated with other forms of status, identity, and success. Thus, objectification supplants emotional attachment.

In this context, notions of masculinity combine with a material view of relationships to place dating in the context of the struggle for high status (Wilkinson, 1997). Males are assumed to be dominant and women subordinate. A violation of these expected gender roles can be interpreted as an insult or threat to respect. When conducted in front of an audience (i.e., in public), the stakes become high if the female behaves without respect for the male. Male violence is perceived as a necessary response to control one's girlfriend, a necessary step in maintaining not just control over "your woman," but in being a "man." Controlling and owning one's intimate partner are mandates of masculinity generally, and these motivations are heightened in a social milieu where taking someone's lover is tantamount to taking his possession. It is an assault on respect, and in many cases mandates a violent response.

In summary, these four types of violence have features in common. In all of them, violence has specific functions in meeting adolescents' needs. Violence occurs within a shared cognitive framework of purposefulness or "human guidedness" (Pernanen, 1991). All acts of violence can be interpreted as coercive actions that serve specific goals of adolescents.

Functions of Violence

According to Tedeschi and Felson (1994), goal-oriented behavior is motivated by the desire to achieve some outcome (i.e., terminal values) or means of acting (i.e., procedural values). It is the valued outcome (or goal) that motivates the use of violence, not some involuntary response to aversive stimuli. Tedeschi and Felson explain that the means of achieving the goal are also valued and play a part in fulfilling the objectives of the individual.

Violence researchers have studied the factors that both produce and inhibit conflict. Often, these factors involve exchanges between two individuals, or between an individual and other individuals in the surrounding situation.[6] Both Katz (1988) and Felson (1993) identified three primary goals of violent actions: (1) to compel and deter others, (2) to achieve a favorable social identity, and (3) to obtain justice. Also, there are three factors that explain how violence occurs, given these goals: (1) through the escalation of disputes over goods or status; (2) through competition for status and social identities, and (3) the role of third parties. Felson (1993) describes the dynamics of violent incidents, much like Luckenbill and Doyle (1989), calling the sequence of events a "social control process" (see also Black, 1983, 1993).[7]

Felson and Tedeschi (1995) describe the individual's decision-making process. They argue that doing harm and the threat of harm are often motivated by the desire to achieve personal goals, but situational factors – including interpersonal relationships between participants, the social interchange between participants, and third parties – affect the outcome, and the perceptions, judgments, expectations, and values of the perpetrator all play a part. That is, a violent event involves a sequence of decisions by the perpetrator, and the individual evaluates alternatives before carrying out a violent action. Felson and Tedeschi (1995) stress four elements of the decision: (1) the expected value of the outcome; (2) the expectations of success in reaching goals; (3) the anticipated costs of the act (e.g., arrest, injury); and (4) the likelihood of the costs. Expected high costs and third parties can be inhibitors of violence. The individual makes a choice to engage in violent behavior because it seems to be the best alternative available in the situation. Felson and Tedeschi (1995) explain that a decision maker is typically operating under some type of decision rule. They describe two rules: the "minimax" principle ("maximize benefits and minimize costs") and the "satisficing" principle ("good enough"). A decision-making framework thus examines what goes on in the perpetrator's mind during a violent event in terms of weighing the rewards and costs of an action while in pursuit of a goal. If an individual determines that the benefits outweigh the costs of the violent action, then he or she chooses to engage in the action.

Following we illustrate five goals important to adolescents that may result in violent acts. In some situations more than one goal may be sought, and, of course, a given individual may be involved in a variety of types of goal-oriented violent acts during one period of his or her life.

Impression Management: Achieving and Maintaining High Status

The establishment and perpetuation of the *sense of self* and of one's personal *image* in the minds of others are the goals of much violence. There can be a very low threshold for the use of violence for these ends. By the norms of some subcultures, excessive violence, including weapon use, is valued for males, gains social rewards, and gives great personal pleasure. Toughness has always been central to masculine identity in many settings of adolescent life (Hagedorn, 1997; Messerschmidt, 1993; Polk, 1994; Sante, 1991). Especially for males, the need to present a self that is powerful and impenetrable has become an important but dangerous method of commanding respect, honor, or economic advantage in the inner city (Anderson, 1994; Oliver, 1994; Polk, 1994). These needs are strengthened in inner cities when access to other sources of status is attenuated, and perceptions of power and masculinity are untempered by other norms.

Toughness requires young males to move beyond symbolic representation to physical violence. Physical prowess and the willingness to resort to violence to resolve interpersonal conflicts are hallmarks of adolescent masculinity (Anderson, 1994; Canada, 1995; Messerschmidt, 1993). Although these terms have been invoked recently to explain high rates of interpersonal violence among non-whites in central cities, toughness has always been highly regarded and a source of considerable status among male adolescents in a wide range of adolescent subcultures, from street-corner groups to gangs (Canada, 1995; Chambliss, 1973; Goffman, 1959, 1963, 1967; Whyte, 1943; Wolfgang & Ferracuti, 1982).

Displays of toughness always have an aesthetic or symbolic aspect: facial expression, symbols and clothing, physical posture and gestures, car styles, graffiti, and unique speech, all are part of "street style" used to convey an image of masculine toughness that may or may not be complemented by physical aggression. Though changing over time with tastes, these efforts at "impression management" to convey a "deviant aesthetic" and "alien sensibility" have been evident across ethnicities and cultures

(Katz, 1988). In disputes or conflicts, adolescents may employ "scripts" as part of a strategy of impression management to gain status and dominance in potentially violent transactions (Cornish, 1994; Tedeschi & Felson, 1994). For example, in street code, displays of toughness are directly related to reputation building, offering a deterrent value necessary to avoid continual attacks from other males seeking to build their own reputations. These are scripts of survival on the street (Anderson, 1994; Canada, 1995; Wilkinson & Fagan, 1996).

Materialism, Status, and Social Identity

The acquisition of material goods is another source of high status for adolescents. Exaggerated displays of material wealth have become part of street life for many (Anderson, 1990, 1994; Taylor, 1990). Adolescents use material possessions to express their own superiority and to attract attention (see, e.g., Connor, 1995; Eder et al., 1995; Majors & Billson, 1992). The necessary "props," including clothing, valuable jewelry, hairstyles, expensive sneakers, beepers, cellular phones, and flashy cars, have become part of the sorting process that occurs during this stage of social development. During adolescence, "fashion wars" are highly competitive and expensive to win. This social process is most distressing for members of lower socioeconomic classes, in which there is a strong disparity between the material goods desired and the legitimate opportunities to obtain them. The young male with many material possessions is admired, and many adolescents seek to demonstrate their right to high status by taking what they want from others. Billy, a 24-year-old, explained:

> Cool is no different between black and white. People killing people for a jacket, because they think it's cool. For a pair of shoes. There's more pressure in the black community to be cool, the negative type of cool. All the commercialism going around. Get what you want. (Majors & Billson, 1992, p. 11)

Such claims to high status can have violent consequences, both in terms of being a victim or a perpetrator of violence. Dress and action together convey certain meanings that frequently attract challenges to the "right" to own such desirable possessions. Majors and Billson (1992) argue that for street drug hustlers putting a "wardrobe" together is important in establishing prestige and making money. They explain that, like a Madison Avenue executive, "in order to make money, he must look like he already has money" (p. 81). The pursuit of material goods may assume a violent component that combines two goals: (1) the desire to possess and display material wealth, and (2) the domination involved in taking possessions from others.

Wealth is the most visible manifestation of individual power and achievement for adolescents in a social context that offers few sources of legitimate social status (Anderson, 1990; Taylor, 1990). Some recent gang studies suggest "materialism" has been elevated to a set of beliefs, and the goal of accumulating wealth has replaced the traditional gang goals of ethnic solidarity and neighborhood defense (Fagan, 1992; Padilla, 1992; cf. Moore, 1993). The use of the language of work (e.g., "getting paid," "going to work") to describe acquisitive violence signals an ideological shift in the social definition of work and the confounding of illegal and legal means of making money. The teenagers using this language pursued commodities that offered instrumental value as signs of wealth and success (Padilla, 1992; Sullivan, 1989).[8]

Power

Acquisition of wealth has elements of power as well, particularly when an audience confirms the twin functions of gaining wealth and domination of another to obtain wealth. Anderson (1994) points out that taking another person's possessions is a way of dominating that person, or showing one's ultimate control over another individual. But some acquisitive violence transcends this function to become a basis for domination. "Bad asses," robbers, and other fighters seem to gain much pleasure from violence, including the use of guns and other weapons (see Katz, 1988, chapters 3 and 6). Much of this pleasure may come from the feeling of power violence provides and from the pleasures of dominance and unrestrained "ultimate" aggression. The use of violence may reflect a total identity geared to dominate, if not humiliate, adversaries. Although this form of violence has a long history, its recent manifestation as what appears to be "senseless" violence may in fact simply reflect the changes brought about by the availability of weapons. Bullying also is a form of domination through physical aggression. This is evident, for example, in some gang contexts in which locura (i.e., extremely crazy) acts of violence establish one's status in the gang. Such violence is "senseless" only in the fact that the violence is an end in and of itself. Weapons, especially guns, can elevate the level of domination. Guns can be used tactically to disable an opponent, or to humiliate an opponent by evoking fear (thus causing humiliating behavior such as begging, tears, and soiling the pants).

Rough Justice, Social Control, and Self-Help

The ritualization of violence as social control is a sign of the replacement or supplement of formal law and social rules with street codes and values (Anderson, 1994; Black, 1983, 1993). Street codes emphasize toughness and quick, violent retribution for transgression of one's sense of self or insults to one's reputation. Such transgressions become grievances, and a response is mandatory. A failure to respond is a sign of weakness, and the ensuing loss of status is unacceptable. In contexts where formal social control is seen as either oppressive (i.e., serving an external dominant class) or illegitimate, street codes become normative and adopt the moral dimension formerly reserved for the law or other social institutions.

When it responds to the conduct of someone else, violence can be a form of self-help. For example, in the context of perceived wrongs or grievances, violence may be conceived of by the perpetrator as a moral behavior in pursuit of a form of justice. Some violence is an effort to achieve retribution, restitution, or compensation for perceived wrongs (Black, 1983; Luckenbill & Doyle, 1989; Tedeschi & Felson, 1994). Whether the violence is done with cool precision or in an impulsive outburst, the arousal of anger can be initiated by the desire to respond to a perceived assault against one's person or honor. In fact, among African Americans in the inner city there appears to be a code of honor, or "respect," whose violation calls for an active and often violent retaliation (Anderson, 1994; Horowitz & Schwartz, 1974; Katz, 1988; Kennedy & Forde, 1996; Luckenbill, 1977; Oliver, 1994; Polk, 1994).

Much gang violence assumes this retributive form, when one gang commits an assault against the person or honor of a member of another gang. In this case, collective liability is assigned to all gang members for the actions of one. Gang codes call for a swift response, and the retribution is often "an eye for an eye." Similar acts of retribution occur when perceived slights are directed at family members or boyfriends/girlfriends of gang members. In the course of a dispute, maintaining dominant status or "face" requires a response to an assault against one's honor or status (Felson & Steadman, 1983). Certain homicides have long been regarded as a form of self-help. From Wolfgang and Ferracuti's (1982) victim-initiated homicides to battered women's self-defensive homicide, self-help has motivated the use of lethal violence against the actions of another.

Violence also is used as a form of self-help in the settlement of monetary disputes in illegal business. Violence has been characterized as a necessary tool of the drug trade to protect money, protect dealers from assault and robbery, to settle disputes about money or drugs, to settle grievances regarding poor-quality or low weight drugs, or to guard against invasion of one's selling territory (Fagan & Chin, 1990; Goldstein et al., 1989; Sommers & Baskin, 1993). In drug dealing, violence is used by both adolescent and adult dealers to settle territorial conflicts and business disputes involving cash or drugs.[9]

Violence also is used to maintain organizational discipline and control in illegal enterprises. In gangs, drug dealing organizations, and other crime organizations, violence is used to punish violations of business principles or organizational norms and ultimately serves to reinforce the collective authority of the group or the individual authority of its leader. (See, e.g., Chin, 1995; Padilla, 1992; Taylor, 1990.)

Preemptive violence that incapacitates an antagonist is another form of self-help. Domestic homicides by women often involve a lethal assault on a batterer whom the victim believes may kill her or her children if not stopped preemptively (Browne, 1987). Other attacks are anticipatory acts intended to prevent a future victimization. Earlier, for example, we noted the importance of locura acts of violence by gang members as a sign to others of a capacity for unrestrained and seemingly unprovoked violence (see Vigil, 1988). Such acts also have deterrent value, as well. Katz (1988) describes how acts of "meaningless" violence in fact can benefit their committer by reinforcing common knowledge of his or her capacity for lethal and gratuitous violence. This violence not only provides intrinsic pleasure from domination, but also symbolizes and communicates one's status as someone not to be crossed.

Defiance of Authority

Defiance of authority is a common behavior in adolescence. Specific manifestations of youthful defiance, or rebellion, vary with the social position of the family and the community. Among disadvantaged populations, the expression of adolescent rebellion is more likely to involve violence (Hamburg, 1974; Messerschmidt, 1993). Indeed, what has been described as an "oppositional culture" may come to dominate and control the public space in economically and politically marginalized communities (Anderson, 1994; Bourgois, 1995). Opposition to social controls perceived as unfair or illegitimate is normative within this social context, especially among young males. Social controls experienced by youths can either be formal legal reactions by police or informal responses by peers, neighbors, or social institutions such as schools or the workplace. In such communities, intrinsic emotional rewards from behaviors defying the controls or behavioral norms of the larger society outweigh whatever material or social rewards may be forthcoming from compliance and conformity.[10]

Oppositional cultures, in part, arise initially from the violation of a sense of fairness by external forms of social control, especially the laws and the police (Tyler, 1990). Respect for punishers and belief in the fairness of the process of punishment contribute to the legitimacy of formal legal sanctions. The opportunity for the punished to provide a full interpretation of the events, to obtain a fair hearing, and to receive consideration and respect for their viewpoints all contribute to acceptance of the moral basis of the punishment.[11] Research over three decades shows in the group with the highest imprisonment rates – African American males – acceptance of the legitimacy of the actions of police and the courts is the lowest (Sherman, 1993). Sanctions perceived as unfair can provoke a defiant reaction, a feeling that violence against authorities gives them their "just desserts," or can simply provoke anger. They may also delegitimize the moral authority of the law and the punishers.

Defiance of conventional middle-class ideas of success or behavioral norms is part of oppositional culture (Sherman, 1993). In socially isolated, marginalized communities, negative views of conventional success create attitudes condemning achievement in school or the legitimate workplace. Such achievements are identified with an oppressive dominant economic and cultural order. Young people who pursue such success are themselves isolated and denied social standing in street networks in areas of social isolation and concentrated poverty. Defiance turns conventional success into an act of betrayal of others in the impoverished community.

Such communities experience high tension and struggle in everyday social discourse concerning any hint of social disapproval from the larger society or unfair expression of any power – whether state power or in interpersonal relations – that may be expressed through pent-up anger (Black, 1993). The exaggerated demand for respect in the inner city may reflect its absence in the everyday interactions between people in socially isolated communities and those in positions of authority (Anderson, 1994; Bourgois, 1995). Adding to the problem is the reliance on vigilante, illegal, or "populist" forms of social control, the rough justice that encourages immediate retaliation for perceived wrongdoing (Black, 1983; Felson, 1993). Thus, the rise of violence as a form of self-help – for redressing grievances, as self-defense – may be seen as a consequence of the decline of local authority.

Risk Taking and Impulsivity

There also are functions that address not only developmental status, but also provide intrinsic returns. Risk taking is one such function. Risk taking is part of the image of toughness for young males, and is typical of adolescent boys in all social contexts. Risk taking can be a part of the process of establishing a social identity that carries a high status.

Typically, explanations of violence include some type of dichotomy between instrumental and expressive forms of violence. Instrumental violence has been viewed as extrinsically motivated (i.e., a means to an end), while expressive (e.g., angry, hostile, or impulsive) violence has been portrayed as intrinsically motivated (i.e., an end in and of itself) (see Megargee, 1983). Typically these distinctions are used to separate the "rational" and "irrational" forms toward a better understanding of each type. When viewed as a functional behavior, this dichotomy causes unnecessary confusion. Interactionists basically argue that if one carefully examines the sequence of activities that occur in events previously classified as irrational, impulsive, or nongoal-directed from the participants' point of view one will find the behavior is more instrumental than not.

Pallone and Hennessy's (1993) neurogenic theory of violence suggests there are irrational acts of violence – acts that seemingly do not achieve a discernible goal – explained by a different set of factors. They emphasize neurologic and neuropsychological dysfunction that underlies impulsivity. The "tinderbox of violence" scenario suggests there are individual-environmental feedback loops that escalate the potential for violence within high-risk individuals. In other words, individuals with a "taste for risk" self-select risky environments in an effort to create opportunities for violent behavior. Restlessness limits the decision-making process to consider only the present rather than the future.

However, there are elements of choice and goal orientation in events that appear to be irrational or impulsive. For example, the selection of the environment where violence is perceived as normative is considered to be a rational choice. Since these individuals will be seeking a social environment supportive of risky activity, individuals with similar characteristics will hang out together. Pallone and Hennessy (1993) explain that such environments, with their high tolerance for risky behavior, present unprecedented opportunity to behave without deterrence, and with the full expectation of impunity; they systematically reinforce the misconstruing of costs, risks, and benefits associated with behavior. This type of imperfect decision making that seems on the surface irrational is simply what Cornish and Clarke (1987) refer to as "bounded rationality."

Pallone and Hennessy (1993) further describe habitual risk takers as "unreasonable adventurers." They do not perceive the danger in dangerous situations, and need increasingly more dangerous situations to experience a sustained "high" from risk taking. Clearly, this conceptualization could be useful, especially with regard to individuals' self-selecting of risky environments. Research is needed to sort out situational variation, neurological dysfunctions, and other social factors beyond learning.

Functions of Violence for Adolescent Girls

Despite greater research attention to violence among adult women in recent years (e.g., Sommers & Baskin, 1993), we know little about the functions of violence for adolescent females.[12] Recent research on female gangs in the inner city provides some insights into violence among young women, although much of it is filtered through the gendered lens of male gang researchers. Although girl gangs often report fighting, they fight less often and fight differently: they seldom use guns, and generally less often use weapons (Hagedorn, in press). But Campbell's (1984) groundbreaking study of female gangs in New York City depicted a world where violence was common, and where young women carried guns and other weapons (but rarely used them). Campbell (1990) suggested many female gangs had moved beyond the stereotypes of auxiliary to male gangs, and female gang members had also rejected the limited roles of carrying weapons, money, or drugs for male gang members. Nevertheless, rates of injury and homicide victimization for adolescents remain lower for females than males (Blumstein, 1995).

The pathways to violence for girls often differ from male pathways: young women who use violence more often experience aggression and violence in the home, and more often come from troubled or violent families (Campbell, 1993).[13] The functions of violence for girls often reflect gender relations between adolescent males and females, and gender roles exert constraints on violence among adolescent women. For example, childbearing and traditional gender roles serve to attenuate the involvement of young women in violence, both by placing competing demands on their time and by reinforcing the unbalanced allocation of power between males and females within adolescent social networks (Hagedorn, in press).

Campbell (1993) claims girl gangs often possess many "feminine" qualities while also pursuing instrumental goals through aggression, like males.

Girls worked heavily on their reputations for toughness, in the same way boys did, while also firmly embracing female gender roles: mother, lover, and companion to intimate partners; and sister to neighborhood girls. But, like males, girls also sought a social identity and status through toughness and reputation, including outrageous acts to demonstrate "heart," or courage. Many fights among girls reflect disputes involving males: boyfriends are thought of as emotional possessions, and disputes arise over ownership and control.[14] Moreover, like males, their pursuit of a tough identity is often designed to ward off attacks from other girls. Taylor (1993) expands on this and places female violence in the context of gender relations. He gives voice to young women whose violence serves to establish their toughness, which in turn can ward off physical attacks by males. Campbell (1993) agrees, citing the high prevalence of girls' victimization experiences from violence at the hands of fathers, beatings of their mothers they witnessed, and sexual and other physical assaults at the hands of neighborhood boys or men: "In the context of the routine violence that surrounds them, the attraction of the gang for . . . girls is not hard to see" (p. 136).

Accordingly, rather than embracing the functions of violence for boys, which emanate from conceptions of manhood and masculinity, female pursuit of toughness and other dimensions of violent identities seems to reflect a rejection of the violence of men toward women and the need for protection of self from men but also from other violent girls (Campbell, 1993). Obviously, much more research is needed on the questions of social identity (i.e., toughness, status), gender roles, and violence among adolescent women.

Mediators of Violence

We turn now to other key aspects of violent incidents: mediating influences (beyond the perpetrator) in the social situation; the internal dynamics of violent events; and social norms. Violent events are affected by factors present in the social setting where these events unfold. These contextual factors can provide additional information beyond the individual's own thoughts or serve as social controls that alter the decision-making processes of the participants. Mediators can influence the individual's evaluation of the rewards or costs of engaging in violence, affect his or her cognition or motivation (i.e., arousal), or shape his or her strategic thinking. We discuss three examples of mediating factors: bystanders, alcohol, and guns.

Bystanders

The role of bystanders and third parties in the unfolding of interpersonal disputes contributes significantly to the outcome. Tedeschi and Felson (1994) describe a variety of roles third parties play including instigators, peacekeepers, cheerleaders, and bouncers. In a public dispute, third parties constitute the audience, and their reaction has a strong effect on youthful participants. In dispute situations, the identities and associations of observers of potential conflict can deeply influence the thoughts, feelings, and behavior of the participants. For example, Felson (1982) found that when a dispute occurred between parties of the same sex, the presence of third parties increased the likelihood that a verbal disagreement would turn into a physical fight.

In Oliver's (1994) study of violent behavior by African American men in bars and bar settings, subjects described three primary roles for third parties: "mediators [peacekeepers], instigators, and instigating audiences." What Oliver defines as mediators we refer to as peacekeepers, meaning "third parties who actively attempted to intervene in an encounter between a respondent and an antagonist to deescalate conflict toward a nonviolent termination" (p. 98). Instigators were third parties who assumed a proactive stance in violent incidents by provoking one participant to argue or fight with another participant. An instigating audience consists of bystanders who encourage one or both participants in a dispute to resort to violence.

Black (1993) has also developed a useful system for analyzing third party involvement in violence. He identifies two roles – supportive and settlement – and two dimensions – degree of partisan intervention and degree of authoritative intervention. The supportive include the informer, adviser, advocate, ally, and surrogate, and the settlement roles include the friendly peacemaker, mediator, arbitrator, judge, and repressive peacemaker. The role of the third parties often depends on personal allegiance (or lack of it) to the main participants. Audience members allied with either the protagonist or the antagonist may each contribute to the escalation or deescalation of a dispute through verbal statements, body language, cheering, nonverbal social pressure, or physical acts of violence.

Alcohol

The views of Pallone and Hennessy (1993), discussed previously with regard to risk taking, are consistent with a long and rich literature that seeks to connect violence with the arousal effects of alcohol. Fagan (1990) identifies a range of arousal effects that provide several mechanisms for motivating violence. Cognitive effects, for example, include: inhibition of cues that normally control behavior (e.g., reduction in fear of retaliation and breaking rules), increased arousability, inability to judge the degree of threat in social situations, interference with communication and interpersonal interactions, altered self-presentation, and intensification of emotions. In addition, alcohol expectations are postulated to account for the relationship between alcohol use and aggression. Thus, it is possible that individuals behave aggressively when they are intoxicated because of these expectations.

Like other event-based approaches, these studies suggest an alcohol-related violent event results from an interaction among the individual, the substance, and the situation. Alcohol use can shape the nature and course of a violent episode, independent of the characteristics of the individuals involved. For example, injuries are more severe when alcohol is present (Pernanen, 1991). Alcohol is more often present in violent events that occur in public places when there is physical violence between strangers, and in violent incidents involving more than two people (Pernanen, 1991; Roman, 1981; Tedeschi & Felson, 1994).

Guns

Similarly, the presence and availability of guns among adolescent males can affect violent events through adolescents' attitudes and perceptions of danger, the nature of social interaction on the streets, decision making in potential or actual violent situations, the level of arousal, and social identity formation and maintenance. Guns have symbolic as well as strategic meaning for adolescent males. Gibbs and Merighi (1994) suggest guns are symbols both of masculinity and high status. The presence of guns in potentially violent situations raises the stakes in terms of both status and strategy (Fagan & Wilkinson, 1977, in press; Wilkinson & Fagan, 1996). Guns can perpetuate and refine the aesthetic of toughness, create an imminent threat of harm, help their users to claim the identity of being among the toughest, and are an ultimate source of power in resolving a dispute (Fagan & Wilkinson, in press-b; Sheley & Wright, 1995).

In our research in inner city neighborhoods in New York City, young males described a strong sense of the danger of their surroundings and a pervasive feeling of a lack of personal safety (Fagan & Wilkinson, 1997, in press; Wilkinson & Fagan, 1996). For the adolescent and young adult respondents, violence is expected and can erupt in a variety of situations. Public behavior on the streets is regulated by a general knowledge that life can be taken away at any moment (by guns, primarily). Possessing a gun for defense therefore plays a big part in providing a feeling of personal safety for these young people. The prevalence of guns, coupled with media emphasis on episodes of gun violence, help shape these perceptions of danger. Respondents reported "most" young males (i.e., 14 to 30 years old) can and did have guns in these inner city neighborhoods. Guns are available on the street to just about anyone who has the means to purchase, share, borrow, or steal them. Even boys of relatively low status can obtain access to firearms through associates, family members, or local drug dealers.

Where guns are readily available, individuals develop expectations and plans for handling their disputes which may or may not result in gun use, depending on a variety of situational factors. Certain actions or words warrant a violent response; if guns are available, guns are used in reply to a transgression or serious threat of harm. Having a powerful gun is valued both for intrinsic and extrinsic reasons. Guns may fulfill a variety of personal needs for adolescent males, including providing power, status, protection, and recreation. The presence of guns also has shaped the rules of fighting among teenagers. Pulling a gun automatically increases the intensity of the conflict and limits the number of choices available to all parties. Showing a gun (i.e., threatening someone) is a sign of disrespect and considered a violation of the other person's social and physical space. Someone who threatens with a gun must be willing to back up that threat by using the gun. Once an individual establishes that a gun will be necessary to handle a dispute or grievance, violence is likely to be initiated. Our research suggests "the potential for an attack to involve guns is nearly certain for the young men in our sample" (Fagan & Wilkinson, in press). Again, guns raise the stakes in a variety of ways and in many instances firearms trump all other logic.

The thought of dying does occur to the participants of these gun-related events. However, this cost competes with anticipated returns from gun violence: the thought of achieving or maintaining high status may hold more value than life itself. It appears that the young male may give more thought to what others may think of him and more attention to an attempt to match his behavior to his self-image as a powerful person than to the possibility of his own death or serious injury. As already noted, losing respect can be damaging to his personal safety, economic livelihood, and associations with peers (and sometimes family members). In summary, guns play an important role in this quest for respect on the street, and guns enhance a young man's potential for being tough. Their presence leads to their strategic use, often to maximize the attainment of the functional goals of violence.

Internal Dynamics of Violent Events

Violence researchers have come to understand that the personal disputes that can result in violence, like many other forms of human interaction, contain their own processes or dynamics that affect the outcome.[15] Numerous researchers have applied this approach to studies of violence among adults (e.g., Campbell, 1986; Felson, 1982; Felson & Steadman, 1983; Luckenbill, 1977; Luckenbill & Doyle, 1989; Oliver, 1994; Polk, 1994). The processual nature of violent interpersonal transactions is both rule-oriented and normative (Cornish, 1993).[16]

Each of these studies identifies three critical issues for understanding the interactions that occur within violent events: (1) the fact that disputes can escalate to violence, (2) the key role of status issues, and (3) the important role of third parties (i.e., bystanders). Felson (1993) describes the dynamics of violent incidents, similarly to Luckenbill and Doyle, calling the sequence of events a "social control process." Accordingly, violence may also reflect events that occur during the incident and may not always be predetermined by the initial goals of the participants (Felson & Steadman, 1983). It is the interaction of situational contexts (i.e., the structure of events) and human agency (i.e., functional goals and strategic decisions) that shapes the outcomes of disputes and violent events.

Violence as Scripted Behavior

The script framework is an event schema used to organize information about how people learn to understand and enact commonplace behavioral patterns. The theory borrows heavily from cognitive psychology and was first articulated by Abelson (1976, 1981). A script is a cognitive structure or framework that organizes a person's understanding of typical situations, allowing the person to have expectations and to make conclusions about the potential result of a set of events.

Cornish introduced the concept of "procedural scripts" to explain violent offenders' decision-making processes (see Cornish, 1993, 1994). Cornish uses the example of the "restaurant script" to explain the theory.[17] The specific situation largely determines the props, casts, scenes, paths, actions, roles, and locations. The script framework provides a useful way of understanding the decision-making process, including the participant's calculation of risks and strategic decisions. Cornish (1994) states: "The unfolding of a crime involves a variety of sequential dependencies within and between elements of the action: crimes are pushed along or impeded by situational contingencies – situated motives; opportunities in terms of settings; victims and targets; the presence of co-offenders; facilitators, such as guns and cars" (p. 8).

Research on child and adolescent violence suggests several ways in which the script theory can be used to understand violent events: (1) scripts are ways of organizing knowledge and behavioral choices (Abelson, 1976); (2) individuals learn behavioral repertoires for different situations (Abelson, 1981; Huesmann, 1988; Schank & Abelson, 1977; Tedeschi & Felson, 1994); (3) these repertoires are stored in memory as scripts and are elicited when cues are sensed in the environment (Abelson, 1981; Dodge & Crick, 1990; Huesmann, 1988; Tedeschi & Felson, 1994); (4) choice of scripts varies among individuals, and some individuals will have limited choices (see Dodge & Crick, 1990); (5) individuals are more likely to repeat scripted behaviors when the previous experience was considered successful (Schank & Abelson, 1977); and (6) scripted behavior may become automatic without much thought or weighing of consequences (Abelson, 1981; Tedeschi & Felson, 1994).

Equally important in the study of disputes is the question of how violence is avoided and how scripts are used for defusing disputes. Previous studies have looked exclusively at completed violent interactions that resulted in some sort of criminal justice system involvement. The events described by Luckenbill (1977, 1980) and by Felson and Steadman (1983), for example, were completed violent transactions. Such research has been one-sided and may have distorted understanding of disputes. Little is known about disputes that do not end in physical fights or firing a weapon.[18] Further research is needed to obtain a better understanding of the realm of possible scripts for defusing disputes in the world of young males and females.

Influence of Social Context on Violent Scripts

Finally, scripts are learned and reinforced within specific social contexts. Scripted behaviors by young adults reflect processes of socialization during the developmental stages preceding adolescence, just as adolescent violence does generally. Context, in this framework, is a social setting that serves several purposes: providing a stage where events play out for public consumption; creating expectations of specific behaviors given specific situations; providing a regulatory structure for behaviors (i.e., setting social costs and returns); and providing opportunities for specific forms of interaction that may lend themselves to violent or peaceful behavior. The latter might either refer to physical spaces or social spaces, such as drinking or drug use scenes, social scenes such as parties, and group processes such as gang cliques or street-corner groups.

Contexts and Street Codes. The development of scripts, the processes of decision making, and the social definitions of conflict and other functions served by violence, form in specific social contexts. These contexts shape normative definitions, imperatives or expected behaviors, and the costs and rewards of violence. Yet only a few studies have examined in depth the current social world of young inner city males (see Anderson, 1990, 1994; Canada, 1995; Fagan & Wilkinson, in press; Sullivan, 1989). Anderson's study of inner city Philadelphia is perhaps the most detailed description of violence and inner city life (Anderson, 1994, in press). According to Anderson (1994), the causes of inner city violence are determined by both social structure and social situation: "The inclination to violence springs from the circumstances of life among the ghetto poor – the lack of jobs that pay a living wage, the stigma of race, the fallout from rampant drug use and drug trafficking, and the resulting alienation and lack of hope for the future" (p. 81).

Anderson proposes there are two types of normative systems operating within the inner city context: the "decent" (i.e., locked into middle-class values) families, and the "street" (i.e., opposed to mainstream-society) families. He argues that although the majority of inner city residents are of the decent orientation, the street orientation has come to govern the normative system regarding human behavior in public spaces, especially among the young. Thus community norms on the street are regulated and enforced by the smaller minority who possess the street orientation. One adapts to the dangers of public spaces by developing a range of social identities to manage the threats and demands of a context that creates codes maintained by violence (Fagan & Wilkinson, 1997, in press; Wilkinson, 1997).

Social and material resources in conditions of social isolation are limited. Avenues to social status, respect, and material goods in other circumstances are provided by opportunities for social roles as worker–wage earner and vested neighborhood resident. In the inner city, opportunities for interaction with people in conventional roles are limited by the absence of services and conventional economic activities (Wilson, 1987, 1996). Where everyone is poor, status and respect often are earned by physical aggression and violence. Acquiring fighting skills is considered important as a means of survival in the inner city (see Sullivan, 1989, p. 113). Young children in the neighborhood are exposed to all types of interpersonal conflict, displays of physical domination, social approval for violent behavior, and limited definitions of respect. The street code is a determining factor in proving one's manhood and knowing how to behave accordingly when confronted with a variety of challenging situations.

Street codes, born in contexts of social isolation, largely determine the procedural scripts children acquire for handling interpersonal conflicts and identity formation. Children who are of street orientation will invariably learn scripts that accord with the street code, whereas "decent" youths may learn alternative scripts in addition to those in line with the code of the street. The process of self-preservation through displays of toughness, nerve, or violent behavior is considered a necessary part of day-to-day life for inner city adolescents, especially males (see Canada, 1995).

The norms that prevail in this context serve three functions: (1) conferring positive social value and status on specific behavior; (2) creating a set of behavioral expectations, with violence central to them, for responses to many forms of social interactions; and (3) providing a regulatory or deviant social control system that enforces behavioral codes supportive of violence. The status and reputations earned through these means provide street-oriented youth with positive feelings of self-worth and high status. Social isolation creates an alternative system of gaining positive identities and building self-esteem that is reflected in prevailing street codes.

Influence of Popular Culture. Popular culture has served as a transmitter, amplifier, and interpreter of inner city violence (LH Research, Inc., 1993; Staff, 1993). The symbols and trappings of guns, for example, are widespread in music and film, and often irony or mockery of violence by music and film artists is confused by the listeners and viewers with endorsement. Nevertheless, many media messages do cultivate perceptions among adolescents of an ecology of violence, danger, and fear. Norms supporting and justifying violence also are communicated through popular culture. Conceptions of manhood are presented that place a high value on "heart" – withstanding or engaging in acts of extreme violence – or even on the willingness to "take a bullet" (Gibbs & Merighi, 1994, p. 73).[19]

Many people view popular culture as a direct contributor to violence. Whether these cultural symbols of violence are internalized among violent teenagers is unclear. Although several studies report that repeated childhood exposure to media violence results in later violence (Huesmann & Miller, 1994), others have taken a more cautious view. Felson (1996), for example, reviews the literature on mass media effects and concludes that because the media compete with other sources of messages supporting violence, its direct effects are difficult to determine. In fact, what may appear to be the effects of the message itself may be conflated with "sponsor" effects, or the tacit approval and permissive atmosphere that accompany the showing of violent material (Wood, Wong, & Chachere, 1991).

Accordingly, although media violence may not directly reinforce violent behavior, it may contribute to the affective styles designed to convey threat and hardness. Thus, the milieu of fear and danger is reinforced and perhaps amplified by the popular media, as well as the poses and styles that express ways to manage threat and to convey toughness and control (Connor, 1995). These styles appeal to both white and minority youths in safer areas, whose lives unfold without the daily threat of violence, and for whom toughness has more limited value. Thus, popular culture has a diffusing effect on perceptions of threat and danger, on ways to communicate a tough or violent identity, and on the proliferation of cues that increase the likelihood of a violent reaction.

Interactions Between Individual and Contextual Influences
in Adolescent Violence

Throughout this discussion, we have emphasized an ecological-developmental framework in which violence reflects the hierarchical interaction of individual developmental needs and goals (e.g., identity, affinity, mastery, and defiance) within highly skewed social and structural contexts of neighborhoods and communities (Bronfenbrenner, 1979). These interactions have been observed both in qualitative research and in long-term studies of adolescents. For example, Jessor, Donovan, and Costa (1991) show that the joint influences of different psychosocial systems – the environmental system and the personality system – better explain the development of functional problem behaviors (like violence), compared to the explanatory power of either psychosocial system alone.[20]

A social interactionist view also anticipates influences from both personality and situational structures. There are personal motivational structures, predispositions, anticipation of what is likely to happen in a situation (i.e., perceived properties of the situation itself), and selective attention to those features of the context. There also are choice-structuring properties of situations, independent of the motivations and perceptions of individuals within those contexts, that shape decisions about whom to affiliate with and what to do when with them. These interactions of situational and individual factors shape the natural course of violent events, including whether violence is avoided even when its likelihood otherwise remains high. These interactions of perception and individual factors develop over time through the repeated interactions of individuals and settings that have properties perhaps independent of the individuals. That is, while there are contextual cues that trigger normative reactions, individuals may bring these expectations with them based on what Goffman (1983) terms "cumulative baggage."

The question is whether there are norms in those scenes and contexts, independent of the contributions of participants in these scenes, that shape the outcome of events leading to violence. Regardless of whether these norms exist in the minds of the individuals in those settings, we believe there are norms that emanate from scenes apart from the people in them, as evidenced in our research and other studies on contexts and settings (see, e.g., Brooks-Gunn et al., 1993; Crane, 1991; Kennedy & Forde, 1996; Majors & Billson, 1992; Tedeschi & Felson, 1994; Zinberg, 1984).

When nonviolent events escalate into violent ones, this nearly always involves the active instigation of people in the immediate setting, coupled with the expectancy of what is mandated as a behavioral response by the norms attached to these scenes and peer networks within the neighborhood. Some of this is internalized, and is anticipated in terms of the social response when word spreads in the neighborhood about how each participant behaved during the event. Accordingly, what looks situational may only be partially so, but it also cannot be explained entirely by the personalities of the individuals involved.

The debate between these two perspectives revolves around the question of social and self-selection. For example, "niche-picking" (Scarr and McCartney, 1983) refers to the fact that individuals are not randomly assigned to contexts (i.e., niches), but rather select them on the basis of their own individual characteristics. The process explains the difficulty of apportioning the effects of genes and environment, or individuals and contexts. Consider examples of social selection based on genotypes: intelligent children and adolescents select intelligent peers to spend time with, and spend more time on activities likely to provide intellectual stimulation. These activities, in turn, lead to intellectual development, which heightens niche-picking, or social and self-selection. Many studies suggest violent adolescents choose antisocial peers to hang out with, and engage in activities more likely to provide the sort of stimulation presumed to increase violent behavior (see, e.g., Cairns et al., 1988; Dishion et al., 1991; Schwendinger & Schwendinger, 1985). In each illustration, niche-picking is likely to reflect characteristics of the individual and strengthen the very characteristics that led the individual to pick the niche in the first place.

These processes have been observed among probability samples in longitudinal studies conducted in generally heterogeneous social areas where there is extensive variation in the orientation of the social networks of children and adolescents who live there. But the conditions within areas marked by high violence rates are hardly comparable to nonurban locales. In neighborhoods where adolescent violence rates are highest, choices of social networks and social situations are constrained by patterns of residential segregation, concentrated poverty, and social isolation. The results for adolescents in these circumstances include attenuated interactions with persons from outside the area and a general cut-off of normative influences and informal social controls from the dominant, mainstream community (Elliott et al., 1996; Sampson & Wilson, 1995; Wilson, 1991). Accordingly, the social structure of the neighborhood directs the adolescents to only one kind of status-producing niche, and in turn a narrowing of sources of social identity.

In summary, the interaction of individual and contextual factors in violent events reflects the internalized norms of neighborhoods into individual-level decision making within events, and their influence on scripts and social identity. Perceptions and decisions seem to be filtered through individual and personality variables – such as disputatiousness – to influence the development of behavioral scripts, but the scripts themselves reflect the accumulation of hundreds of social interactions in which violence underlies the exchange of status and identity. Thus, violent scripts and violent social identities become the foundation of developmental capital for children and teenagers growing up in these contexts of violence.

Conclusion

The analysis of violence in an event framework explicitly recognizes the dynamic interactions of individuals with one another, with other persons in their social networks or situational contexts, and with neighborhood contexts that bear on the course of violent events. This type of dynamic contextualism (Sampson, 1993) calls for research methods that address the person-in-context influences on violence. In addition to the study of communities and groups, this approach also requires an analysis of events themselves. Discerning the functions of violence requires an analysis of violent events, but events are the products of ongoing dynamics within communities: the influence of contexts combines with individual characteristics to shape events that accumulate toward developmental outcomes. These dynamics in turn are situated in a set of normative influences – codes, for example – that reflect the sum of these interactions. Accordingly, researchers face not only sampling challenges but also the challenges of measurement of processual dynamics and feedback processes. Understanding the developmental functions of violence requires the assessment over time of multiply determined, complex ecological dynamics. Addressing these challenges portends a paradigm shift many will welcome.

For many adolescents in urban areas, violence has had a pervasive influence on their social and cognitive development (Richters & Martinez, 1993). Coupled with high adolescent mortality and firearm injury rates, the prevalence of violence in their immediate social contexts objectifies and symbolizes their perceptions of risk and danger in the most common activities of everyday life. The absence or weakness of ordinary social controls means there are no buffers between their internalized sense of danger and the situations they deal with daily. Even when violence and danger are not immediately present, the constant emphasis on them in popular culture and urban legend enhances the perception of personal risk. Rituals of mourning and burial, whether real or mythologized, have become cultural touchstones reinforced and internalized in normative beliefs and attitudes about the inevitability of violence.

Violence has become an important part of the discourse of social interactions, with both functional (i.e., status and identity), material, and symbolic meaning (i.e., power and control), as well as strategic importance in everyday social dangers. The development of violence scripts and violent identities reflects processes of anticipatory socialization based on the perceived likelihood of victimization from violence and the perceived necessity to deter violent attacks by projecting an aura of toughness and danger. The result is a developmental ecology of violence, where beliefs about violence and the dangers of everyday life are internalized in early childhood and shape the cognitive framework for interpreting events and actions during adolescence. In turn, this context of danger creates, shapes, and highly values scripts skewed toward violence and underscores the central, instrumental role of violence in achieving the goals of aggressive actions or defensive violence in specific social contexts.

Notes

1. One important exception has been the theoretical and empirical literatures on drugs, alcohol, and violence. See, e.g., Fagan 1990, 1993a, 1993b; Goldstein, 1985, 1989; Pernanen, 1991.
2. The four illustrations do not imply a developmental progression or hierarchy. We selected four unique domains to illustrate the paradigm of situated transactions. Other domains of violence also can be analyzed from this perspective, including street-corner conflicts (Anderson, 1978; Whyte, 1943); ethnic conflicts (Thrasher, 1927); fraternity hazing or sporting event violence (Bufford, 1991; Goldstein, 1983); or sexual assaults (Tedeschi & Felson, 1994). Future work will include detailed analyses of these contexts of adolescent violence.
3. "Bullying involves patterned aggression toward peers, coupled with impulsivity and strong needs to dominate others" (Olweus, 1994, p.100).
4. In Skogan's (1978) hypothetical analysis of "life without lethal weapons," he suggests that without them robbers would face more resistance from victims (including fighting back or running away), have to use an increased amount of physical force to gain compliance, and need to select more vulnerable or easy targets for robberies. However, Cook (1980) found that in robberies victims were more likely to be injured by unarmed offenders (i.e., those not carrying guns) than by offenders with a gun. He concluded victims were sufficiently intimidated by a weapon to more readily comply with the offenders' demands.
5. A robbery is considered to be "recreational violence" when the primary purpose is for the entertainment and thrill of the perpetrators above any monetary rewards of the crime.
6. Violence is a function of events that occur during the incident and therefore is not predetermined by the initial goals of the participants (Felson & Steadman, 1983).
7. Black (1983) proposed that certain violent acts could be explained as attempts by the perpetrator to exert social control over another person when other mechanics of social control, such as the criminal justice agencies or informal rules of fairness, have failed. Accordingly, self-help occurs most frequently within the context of low formal social control or where laws are not enforced. Black (1993) argues the socioeconomic distribution of violent crime reflects these attempts at self-help within the context of societal neglect.
8. These trends should be viewed in the broader context of cultural changes in the 1980s that began not within inner cities, but more broadly across American society. The cultural emphasis on materialism and personal wealth provided an organizing framework for the development of norms and beliefs. Consumption was celebrated culturally in the media, and political leaders who symbolized these values came to power. Entrepreneurs were hailed as modern heroes whose individual economic triumphs were examples of the "cream" of society.
9. While an increase in homicides may have at one time reflected the expansion of the drug market, homicides now (nearly a decade after the emergence of crack cocaine markets) may reflect the residual effects of those markets. That is, guns that entered street networks during the expansion of drug markets remained part of the street ecology even as the drug economy subsided (Hamid, 1994).

10. Clearly, structural factors as well as human agency are at play in creating and perpetuating this alternative culture of the street. The material or social rewards of compliance and conformity are unequally distributed in American society. Urban racial minority communities are largely unrepresented in all major positions of power, whether political or economic (Wilson, 1996). Defiance of authority can also be viewed as a form of adaptation to structural constraints (see Bourgois, 1995).

11. Some argue inner city populations simply lack the "human and cultural capital" to be able to have positive experiences with the criminal justice system or other institutions (Bourgois, 1995).

12. Several studies have documented changes in the prevalence of female gangs and violence among women. Sommers and Baskin (1993) showed sharp increases in arrests of women for violence in New York City over a ten-year period from 1980–1990. Estimates of female participation in gangs range from 5% of all gang members (Curry, Ball, & Decker, 1996) to 10% (Miller, 1975). Nevertheless, adolescent female homicide victimization rates remain only a small fraction of adolescent male rates, and that fraction has not changed significantly since the early 1980s.

13. This is not to suggest boys are not victimized in the home; however, survey studies show these experiences affect girls' violence more powerfully than that of boys.

14. Campbell (1993) describes the violent logic that follows from these disputes: Discovering that a boyfriend has been unfaithful, female adolescents perceive this as the other girl's doing as boys are incapable of turning down an offer of sex, and even if they wanted to, their image and reputation as a man would suffer if word got out. "Coming on" to another girl's boyfriend entails both an emotional injury and an assault on her tough reputation (as someone whose possessions and self are not to be "messed with"). The issues seem to be framed in masculine terms, involving intimate partners as possessions, but they are also defined through the lens of their experiences as women and their understanding of gender roles from their families: transgressions of an intimate relation may launch a process of victimization and emotional betrayal. Thus these transgressions are to be stopped and require retribution, often through violence.

15. Felson (1993) distinguishes "predatory" violence from dispute-related violence, suggesting there are processual factors in dispute-related violence not evident in predatory assaults. Predatory violence is defined as physical aggression committed without provocation, while dispute-related violence involves a reaction to some alleged wrong. However, Katz (1988) suggests that even the most seemingly irrational violent acts have a logical and predictable sequence. There may be disputes between the aggressor and the victim, but there may appear to be no interaction between the two parties preceding the violent act. In these cases, the victim may be a proxy, surrogate, or symbolic target for the other disputant. Pallone and Hennessy (1993) also suggest that impulsive or tinderbox violence may be explained by angry arousal from disputes or grievances that preceded the violent act. The source of arousal, such as a disputant, may have long gone from the immediate vicinity of the violent act.

16. See Wilkinson and Fagan (1996), Wilkinson (1997), and Fagan and Wilkinson (in press) for a detailed analysis of these studies.
17. Cornish (1993) argues that in a restaurant we all know how to "enter; wait to be seated; get the menu; order; eat; get the check; pay; and exit" (p. 8). He maintains there are different levels of abstraction; for example, within the general script are related "tracks" that organize knowledge about the various kinds of restaurants, which require different procedures in specific contexts.
18. One process of mitigating the potential for violence in a dispute is the use of "accounts" by one or both participants (Scott & Lyman, 1968). Accounts are explanations that deny or mitigate responsibility for an offensive action. If the offended party accepts the excuse then the conflict may deescalate because blame will not be attributed to the antagonist and the grievance will be weakened or withdrawn. Giving an account acknowledges responsibility but claims there was some valid justification under the circumstances. Accounts can lessen the severity of harm if a physical fight occurs. (See Canada, 1995; Oliver, 1994, for illustrations.)
19. Gibbs and Merighi (1994), in their review of marginality and masculinity as dimensions of adolescent criminality generally, also suggest these influences conflate sexual identity and racial identity with masculinity. Toughness and violence are central to this identity formation, leading perhaps to the formation of violent identities.
20. Jessor et al. (1991) compared the variance explained in problem behaviors when predicted by the personality system versus the environmental system versus a developmental system that compares these perspectives. The environmental system developmentally situates adolescents in a network of peer influence including friends' approval for problem behaviors and friends' modeling of problem behaviors, plus parent-friend compatibility. The personality system has both motivational-instigation components, personal belief structures, and personal controls. Each dimension entails a range of personality and developmental markers, including such factors as value of academic achievement, self-esteem, and religiosity.

References

Abelson, R. (1976). Script processing in attitude formation and decision-making. In J. S. Carroll & J. W. Payne (Eds.), *Cognition and social behavior.* Hillsdale, NJ: Lawrence Erlbaum.

Abelson, R. P. (1981). Psychological status of the script content. *American Psychologist, 36*(7), 715–729.

Anderson, E. (1978). *A place on the corner.* Chicago: University of Chicago Press.

Anderson, E. (1990). *Streetwise: Race, class and change in an urban community.* Chicago: University of Chicago Press.

Anderson, E. (1994, May). Code of the streets. *The Atlantic Monthly,* pp. 81–94.

Anderson, E. (in press). *Violence and the inner city code of the streets.* Chicago: University of Chicago Press.

Black, D. (1983). Crime as social control. *American Sociological Review, 48,* 34–45.

Black, D. (1993). *The social structure of right and wrong.* Orlando, FL: Academic Press.

Blumstein, A. (1995). Youth violence, guns, and the illicit-drug industry. *Journal of Criminal Law and Criminology, 86*(1), 10–36.

Bourgois, P. (1995). *In search of respect: Selling crack in El Barrio.* New York: Cambridge University Press.

Bronfenbrenner, U. (1979). *The ecology of human development: Experiments by nature and design.* Cambridge, MA: Harvard University Press.

Brooks-Gunn, J., Duncan, G. J., Klebanov, P. K., & Sealand, N. (1993). Do neighborhoods influence child and adolescent development? *American Journal of Sociology, 99,* 353–395.

Browne, A. (1987). *When battered women kill.* New York: Free Press.

Bufford, B. (1991). *Among the thugs.* New York: Vintage Books.

Cairns, R., Cairns, B., Neckerman, H., Gest, S., & Gariepy, J. L. (1988) Social networks and aggressive behavior: Peer support or peer rejection? *Developmental Psychology, 24,* 815–823.

Campbell, A. (1984). *The girls in the gang.* New York: Basil Blackwell.

Campbell, A. (1986). The streets and violence. In A. Campbell & J. Gibbs (Eds.), *Violent transactions: The limits of personality* (pp.115–132). New York: Basil Blackwell.

Campbell, A. (1990). Female participation in gangs. In R. Huff (Ed.), *Gangs in America* (pp. 163–182). Newbury Park, CA: Sage.

Campbell, A. (1993). *Men, women and aggression.* New York: Basic Books.

Canada, G. (1995). *Fist, knife, stick, gun.* Boston: Beacon Press.

Chambliss, W. J. (1973). The saints and the roughnecks. *Society, 11,* 24–31.

Chin, K. L. (1995). *Chinatown gangs.* New York: Oxford University Press.

Cohen, A. (1955). *Delinquent boys: The culture of the gang.* Glencoe, IL: Free Press.

Connor, M. K. (1995). *What is cool? Understanding black manhood in America.* New York: Crown.

Cook, P. J. (1976). A strategic choice analysis of robbery. In W. Skogan (Ed.), *Sample surveys of the victims of crime* (pp. 173–187). Cambridge, MA: Ballinger.

Cook, P. J. (1980). Reducing injury and death rates in robbery. *Policy Analysis, 6*(1), 21–45.

Cook, P. J. (1991). The technology of personal violence. In M. Tonry & N. Morris (Eds.), *Crime and justice: An annual review of research,* Volume 14 (pp. 1–72). Chicago: University of Chicago Press.

Cornish, D. (1993, May, 26–28). Crimes as scripts. Paper presented at the Second Annual Seminar on Environmental Criminology and Crime Analysis. University of Miami, Coral Gables, FL.

Cornish, D. (1994). The procedural analysis of offending. In R. V. Clarke (Ed.), *Crime Prevention Studies.* Monsey, NY: Criminal Justice Press.

Cornish, D., & Clarke, R. (1987). Understanding crime displacement: An application of rational choice theory. *Criminology, 25,* 933–947.

Crane, J. (1991). The epidemic theory of ghettos and neighborhood effects on dropping out and teenage childbearing. *American Journal of Sociology, 96,* 1226–1259.

Curry, G. D., Ball, R., & Decker, S. (1996). Estimating the national scope of gang crime from law enforcement data. In C. R. Huff (Ed.), *Gangs in America* (pp. 21–38). Thousand Oaks, CA: Sage.

Decker, S. H. (1996). Reconstructing homicide events: The role of witnesses in fatal encounters. *Journal of Criminal Justice, 23*(5), 439–450.

Decker, S., & van Winkle, B. (1996). *Life in the gang.* New York: Cambridge University Press.

Dishion, T., Patterson, G., Stoolmiller, M., & Skinner, M. (1991). Family, school, and behavioral antecedents to early adolescents involvement with antisocial peers. *Developmental Psychology, 27,* 172–180.

Dobash, R. E., & Dobash, R. P. (1992). *Women, violence and social change.* New York: Routledge.

Dodge, K. A., & Crick, N. R. (1990). Social information processing bases of aggressive behavior in children. *Personality and Social Psychology Bulletin, 16,* 8–22.

Eder, D., with Evans, C., & Parker, S. (1995). *School talk: Gender and adolescent culture.* New Brunswick, NJ: Rutgers University Press.

Elliott, D. S., Wilson, W. J., Huizinga, D., Sampson, R. J., Elliott, A., & Rankin, B. (1996). The effects of neighborhood disadvantage on adolescent development. *Journal of Research in Crime and Delinquency, 33*(4), 389–426.

Fagan, J. (1990). Intoxication and aggression. In M. Tonry & J. Q. Wilson (Eds.), *Drugs and crime* (Vol. 13): *Crime and justice.* Chicago: University of Chicago Press.

Fagan, J. (1992). The dynamics of crime and neighborhood change. In J. Fagan (Ed.), *The ecology of crime and drug use in inner cities* [mimeo]. New York: Social Science Research Council.

Fagan, J. (1993a). Set and setting revisited: Influences of alcohol and illicit drugs on the social context of violent events. In S. E. Martin (Ed.), *Alcohol and interpersonal violence: Fostering multidisciplinary perspectives* [NIAAA Research Monograph No. 24]. Rockville, MD: National Institute of Alcohol Abuse and Alcoholism.

Fagan, J. (1993b). Interactions among drugs, alcohol, and violence. *Health Affairs, 12*(4), 65–77.

Fagan, J., & Chin, K. (1990). Violence as regulation and social control in the distribution of crack. In M. de la Rosa, B. Gropper, & E. Lambert (Eds.), *Drugs and violence* [NIDA Research Monograph No. 103, DHHS Pub. No. (ADM) 90–1721]. Rockville, MD: U.S. Public Health Administration, National Institute of Drug Abuse.

Fagan, J., & Wilkinson, D. L. (1997). Firearms and youth violence. In D. Stoff, J. Brieling, & J. D. Maser (Eds.), *Handbook of antisocial behavior.* New York: Wiley and Sons.

Fagan, J., & Wilkinson, D. L. (in press). Guns, youth violence, and social identity. In *Youth violence – Crime and justice: A review of research.* Chicago: University of Chicago Press.

Feeney, F. (1986). Decision making in robberies. In R. V. Clarke & D. Cornish (Eds.), *The reasoning criminal* (pp. 53–71). New York: Springer-Verlag.

Felson, R. B. (1982). Impression management and the escalation of aggression and violence. *Social Psychology Quarterly, 45,* 245–254.

Felson, R. B. (1993). Predatory and dispute-related violence: A social interactionist approach. In R. V. Clarke & M. Felson (Eds.), *Routine activity and rational choice: Advances in criminological theory,* Volume 5 (pp. 103–126). New Brunswick, NJ: Transaction Press.

Felson, R. B. (1996). Mass media effects on violent behavior. *Annual Review of Sociology, 22,* 103–128.

Felson, R., & Steadman, H. J. (1983). Situational factors in disputes leading to criminal violence. *Criminology, 21,* 59–74.

Felson, R., & Tedeschi, J. T. (1995). A social interactionist approach to violence: Cross-cultural applications. In R. B. Ruback & N. A. Weiner (Eds.), *Interpersonal violent behavior: Social and cultural aspects.* New York: Springer.

Fingerhut, L. A. (1993). Firearm mortality among children, youth and young adults 1–34 years of age, trends and current status: United States, 1985–1990. In *Advance data from vital and health statistics, No. 231.* Hyattsville, MD: National Center for Health Statistics.

Gibbs, J. T., & Merighi, J. R. (1994). Young black males: Marginality, masculinity and criminality. In T. Newburn & E. A. Stanko (Eds.), *Men, masculinities and crime: Just boys doing business?* (pp. 64–80). London: Routledge.

Goffman, E. (1959). *The presentation of self in everyday life.* Garden City, NY: Doubleday.

Goffman, E. (1963). *Stigma.* Englewood Cliffs, NJ: Prentice-Hall.

Goffman, E. (1967). The nature of deference and demeanor. In E. Goffman (Ed.), *Interaction ritual: Essays on face-to-face behavior* (pp. 47–95). Garden City, NY: Anchor Books.

Goffman, E. (1983). The interaction order. *American Sociological Review, 48,* 1–17.

Goldstein, J. (Ed.). (1983). *Sports violence.* New York: Springer-Verlag.

Goldstein, P. J. (1985). The drugs-violence nexus: A tripartite conceptual framework. *Journal of Drug Issues, 15*(4), 493–506.

Goldstein, P. J. (1989). Drugs and violent crime. In N. A. Weiner & M. E. Wolfgang (Eds.), *Pathways to criminal violence* (pp.16–49). Newbury Park, CA: Sage.

Goldstein, P. J., Brownstein, H., Ryan, P., & Belluci, P. A. (1989). Crack and homicide in New York City, 1989: A conceptually-based event analysis. *Contemporary Drug Problems, 16*(4), 651–687.

Guerra, N. G., Nucci, L., & Huessmann, L. R. (1994). Moral cognition and childhood aggression. In L. R. Huessmann (Ed.), *Aggressive behaviors: Current perspectives* (pp. 13–32). New York: Plenum.

Guerra, N. G., & Slaby, R. G. (1990). Cognitive mediators of aggression in adolescent offenders: II. Interventions. *Developmental Psychology, 26,* 269–277.

Hagedorn, J. (1997). Frat boys, bossmen, studs, and gentlemen: A typology of gang masculinities. In L. Bowker (Ed.), *Masculinities and violence.* Thousand Oaks, CA: Sage.

Hagedorn, J. (in press). Gang violence in the post-industrial era. In M. Tonry & M. Moore (Eds.), *Youth violence,* Volume 24 of *Crime and justice: A review of research.* Chicago: University of Chicago Press.

Hamburg, B. A. (1974). Early adolescence: A specific and stressful stage of the life cycle. In G. V. Coelho, D. A. Hamburg, & J. E. Adams (Eds.), *Coping and adaptation.* New York: Basic Books.

Hamid, A. (1994). *Beaming up.* New York: Guilford.

Horowitz, R., & Schwartz, G. (1974). Honor, normative ambiguity and gang violence. *American Sociological Review, 39,* 238–251.

Huesmann, L. R. (1988). An information processing model for the development of aggression. *Aggressive Behavior, 14*(1), 13–24.

Huesmann, L. R., & Miller, L. (1994). Long-term effects of repeated media exposure to violence in childhood. In L. R. Huessmann (Ed.), *Aggressive behaviors: Current perspectives* (pp. 153–186). New York: Plenum.

Humphreys, A. P., & Smith, P. K. (1987). Rough and tumble, friendship, and dominance in schoolchildren: Evidence for continuity and change with age. *Child Development, 38,* 201–212.

Jessor, R., Donovan, J., & Costa, F. M. (1991). *Beyond adolescence: Problem behavior and young adult development.* New York: Cambridge University Press.

Kagan, J. (1989). *Unstable ideas: Temperament, cognition, and self.* Cambridge, MA: Harvard University Press.

Kandel, D. B. (1985). On processes of peer influences in adolescent drug use: A developmental perspective. In R. K. Silbereisen, K. Eyferth, & G. Rudinger (Eds.), *Development as action in context: Problem behavior and normal youth development* (pp. 203–227). Berlin: Springer-Verlag.

Katz, J. (1988). *Seductions of crime: Moral and sensual attractions in doing evil.* New York: Basic Books.

Keiser, R. L. (1969). *The Vice Lords: Warriors of the streets.* New York: Holt, Rinehart and Winston.

Kennedy, L. W., & Forde, D. A. (1996). Pathways to aggression: A factorial survey of routine conflict. *Journal of Quantitative Criminology, 12,* 417–438.

LH Research, Inc. (1993). *A survey of experiences, perceptions, and apprehensions about guns among young people in America.* Cambridge, MA: Harvard University, School of Public Health.

Lloyd, S., Koval., J. E., & Cate, R. A. (1989). Conflict and violence in dating relationships. In M. Pirog-Good & J. E. Stets (Eds.), *Violence in dating relationships: Emerging social issues* (pp. 126–142). New York: Praeger.

Luckenbill, D. F. (1977). Homicide as a situated transaction. *Social Problems, 25,* 176–186.

Luckenbill, D. F. (1980). Patterns of force in robbery. *Deviant Behavior, 1,* 361–378.

Luckenbill, D. F., & Doyle, D. P. (1989). Structural position and violence: Developing a cultural explanation. *Criminology, 27,* 419–436.

Magdol, L., Moffitt, T. E., Caspi, A., Newman, D. M., Fagan, J., & Silva, P. (1997). Gender differences in partner violence in a birth cohort of 21-year-olds: Bridging the gap between clinical and epidemiological research. *Journal of Consulting and Clinical Psychology, 65*(1), 68–78.

Majors, R., & Billson, J. M. (1992). *Cool pose: The dilemmas of black manhood in America.* New York: Simon & Schuster.

Makepeace, J. (1989). Dating, living together, and courtship violence. In M. Pirog-Good & J. E. Stets (Eds.), *Violence in dating relationships: Emerging social issues* (pp. 94–107). New York: Praeger.

Megargee, E. I. (1983). Psychological determinants and correlates of criminal violence. In E. Wolfgang & N. A. Weiner (Eds.), *Criminal violence* (pp. 81–170). Beverly Hills, CA: Sage.

Messerschmidt, J. (1993). *Masculinities and crime: Critique and reconceptualization of theory.* Totowa, NJ: Rowman and Littlefield.

Miller, W. B. (1975). *Violence by youth gangs and youth groups as a crime problem in major American cities.* Report to the National Institute for Juvenile Justice and Delinquency Prevention. Cambridge, MA: Harvard Law School, Center for Crime and Justice.

Miller, W. B., Geertz, H., & Cutter, H. S. G. (1961). Aggression in a boys' streetcorner group. *Psychiatry, 24,* 283–398.

Moore, J. (1993). Gangs, drugs, and violence. In S. Cummings & D. Monti (Eds.), *Gangs* (pp. 27–48). Albany, NY: State University of New York Press.

Neill, S. R. (1976). Aggressive and non-aggressive fighting in 12 to 13 year old preadolescent boys. *Journal of Child Psychology and Psychiatry, 17,* 213–220.

Oliver, W. (1994). *The violent social world of black men.* New York: Lexington.

Olweus, D. (1993). *Bullying at school: What we know and what we can do.* Oxford, England: Blackwell.

Olweus, D. (1994). Bullying at school: Long-term outcomes for the victims and an effective school-based intervention program. In L. R. Huessmann (Ed.), *Aggressive behavior: Current perspectives.* New York: Plenum.

Padilla, F. (1992). *The gang as American enterprise.* New Brunswick, NJ: Rutgers University Press.

Pallone, N. J., & Hennessy, J. J. (1993). Tinderbox criminal violence: Neurogenic impulsivity, risk-taking, and the phenomenology of rational choice. In R. V.

Clarke & M. Felson (Eds.), *Routine activity and rational choice, Advances in criminological theory*, Volume 5 (pp. 127–156). New Brunswick, NJ: Transaction Press.

Pernanen, K. (1991). *Alcohol in human violence*. New York: Guilford.

Pikert, S. M., & Wall, S. M. (1981). An investigation of children's perceptions of dominance relations. *Perceptual and Motor Skills, 52*, 75–81.

Polk, K. (1994). *When men kill: Scenarios of masculine violence*. New York: Cambridge University Press.

Richters, J. E., & Martinez, P. (1993). The NIMH Community Violence Project: I. Children as victims of and witnesses to violence. *Psychiatry: Interpersonal and Biological Processes, 53*(1), 7–21.

Roman, P. A. (1981). Situational factors in the relationship between alcohol and crime. In J. J. Collins (Ed.), *Drinking and crime: Perspectives on the relationship between alcohol consumption and criminal behavior*. New York: Guilford.

Sampson, R. J. (1993). Linking time and place: Dynamic contextualism and the future of criminological inquiry. *Journal of Research in Crime and Delinquency, 30*(4), 426–444.

Sampson, R. J., & Lauritsen, J. L. (1994). Violent victimization and offending: Individual-, situational- and community-level risk factors. In A. J. Reiss, Jr. & J. A. Roth (Eds.), *Understanding and preventing violence*, Volume III (pp.1–115).

Sampson, R. J., & Wilson, W. J. (1995). Race, crime and urban inequality. In J. Hogan & R. Peterson (Eds.), *Crime and inequality* (pp. 37–54). Stanford, CA: Stanford University Press.

Sante, L. (1991). *Low life: Lures and snares of old New York*. New York: Farrar, Straus and Giroux.

Scarr, S., & McCartney, K. (1983). How people make environments: A theory of genotype environment effects. *Child Development, 54*, 424–435.

Schank, R., & Abelson, R. (1977). *Scripts, plans, goals and understanding*. Hillsdale, NJ: Lawrence Erlbaum.

Schwendinger, H., & Schwendinger, J. (1985). *Adolescent subcultures and delinquency*. New York: Praeger.

Scott, M. B., & Lyman, S. M. (1968). Accounts. *American Sociological Review, 33*, 46–62.

Sheley, J. & Wright, J. 1995. *In the Line of Fire: Youth, Guns, and Violence in Urban America*. New York: Aldine de Gruyter.

Sherman, L. W. (1993). Defiance, deterrence and irrelevance: A theory of the criminal sanction. *Journal of Research in Crime and Delinquency, 30*, 445–473.

Short, J. F., Jr. (1996). *Poverty, ethnicity and violent crime*. Boulder, CO: Westview.

Short, J. F., Jr., & Strodtbeck, F. L. (1965). *Group process and gang delinquency*. Chicago: University of Chicago Press.

Skogan, W. (1978). Weapon use in robbery. In J. Inciardi & A. Pottieger (Eds.), *Violent crime: Historical and contemporary issues*. Beverly Hills, CA: Sage.

Smith, P. K., & Hogan, T. (1980). Effects of deprivation of exercise play in nursery school children. *Animal Behavior, 28*, 922–928.

Snyder, H. N., & Sickmund, M. (1995). Juvenile offenders and victims: A national report [Monograph]. Washington, DC: U.S. Department of Justice, Office of Juvenile Justice and Delinquency Prevention.

Sommers, I., & Baskin, D. (1993). The situational context of violent female offending. *Journal of Research in Crime and Delinquency, 30*, 136–162.

Spergel, I. A. (1995). *Youth gangs: Problem and response*. Chicago: University of Chicago Press.

Staff. (1993, August 15). Hard-core rap lyrics stir black backlash. *The New York Times*.

Steinberg, L., & Cauffman, E. (1996). Maturity of judgment in adolescence: Psychosocial factors in adolescent decision making. *Law and Human Behavior, 20,* 249–272.

Sullivan, M. (1989). *Getting paid: Youth crime and unemployment in three urban neighborhoods.* New York: Cornell University Press.

Taylor, C. S. (1990). *Dangerous society.* East Lansing, MI: Michigan State University Press.

Taylor, C. S. (1993). *Women, girls, gangs, and crime.* East Lansing, MI: Michigan State University Press.

Tedeschi, J., & Felson, R. B. (1994). *Violence, aggression and coercive actions.* Washington, DC: APA Press.

Thrasher, F. M. (1927). *The gang: A study of 1,313 gangs in Chicago.* Chicago: University of Chicago Press.

Tyler, T. R. (1990). *Why people obey the law.* New Haven, CT: Yale University Press.

Vigil, J. D. (1988). *Barrio gangs.* Austin, TX: University of Texas Press.

Whyte, W. F. (1943). *Street corner society.* Chicago: University of Chicago Press.

Wilkinson, D. L. (1997, August 10). *Male adolescent social identity in the inner-city "war zone."* Paper presented at the American Sociological Association annual meeting, Toronto, Canada.

Wilkinson, D. L., & Fagan, J. (1996). Understanding the role of firearms in violence "scripts": The dynamics of gun events among adolescent males. *Law and Contemporary Problems, 59*(1), 55–90.

Wilson, W. J. (1987). *The truly disadvantaged: The inner city, the underclass, and public policy.* Chicago: University of Chicago Press.

Wilson, W. J. (1991). Studying inner-city social dislocations: The challenge of public agenda research. *American Sociological Review, 56,* 1–14.

Wilson, W. J. (1996). *When work disappears: The world of the new urban poor.* New York: Alfred A. Knopf.

Wolfgang, M., & Ferracuti, F. (1982). *The subculture of violence: Toward an integrated theory in criminology* (2nd ed.). Beverly Hills, CA: Sage.

Wood, W., Wong, F. Y., & Chachere, J. G. (1991). Effects of media violence on viewers' aggression in uncontrolled social interaction. *Psychological Bulletin, 109,* 371–383.

Yllo, K. (1988). *Feminist perspectives on wife abuse.* Newbury Park, CA: Sage.

Zimring, F. E., & Zuehl, J. (1986). Victim injury and death in urban robbery: A Chicago study. *Journal of Legal Studies, 15,* 1–40.

Zinberg, N. (1984). *Drug, set and setting.* New Haven, CT: Yale University Press.

4. Juvenile Aggression at Home and at School

ROLF LOEBER & MAGDA STOUTHAMER-LOEBER

Introduction

The development of aggression during childhood and adolescence can involve broad changes in child behavior across multiple settings. The most significant settings are the home and school. Children's aggression in the home is often, but not always, related to their aggression at school. This chapter focuses on the development of aggression in relation to parents and siblings in the home, and to teachers and peers in the schools.

Another key issue is to establish the relative importance of age-related developmental factors and environmental influences in determining the expression of different forms of disruptive behaviors including mild aggression, serious fighting, and criminal violence. In this chapter, we focus on the stability of such aggressive or violent behaviors. Stability refers to the maintenance of similar behavior across different settings and across time. We examine which early behaviors predict which later ones and, particularly, the risk factors for the most dysfunctional developmental pathways. An important goal is to identify specific adverse developmental pathways so interventions can be designed to change behavior before a negative path becomes too firmly set.

The term aggression as used in this chapter encompasses acts of varying degrees of severity from the upper end of normative aggressive acts to physical fighting to delinquency and also crimes, including rape, aggravated assault, and robbery. Hamburg (1995) discussed the distinctions between these different but related constructs:

> The historical roots of studies of youth violence in the criminology field have led to a focus on [violence and] crime as the basic construct[s]. Crime is a legal construct that varies across time, jurisdictions, and political climate. Therefore, [delinquency and] crime [have] severe limitations as [constructs] around which to build sound

scientific theories and rigorous research on basic patterns of individual behavior. As a result, attempts to rely on the use of the crime construct have led to a semantic confusion that has greatly complicated the effective use of the psychological and biosocial literatures in trying to marshal relevant data, to sort out significant issues, and to determine their relationship to the available crime statistics. Aggression, which is highly related to, but [clearly] not the same as, violence, has been the construct that has been studied most widely in the psychological and biosocial fields. In those fields, the concept of intentional harm, which is central to definitions of violence, is captured by devising a range of subcategories of aggressive behavior. There are categories that denote associated hostile intent or antisocial behavior of the individual. The most sophisticated research also investigates the varying expressions of aggression as influenced by the context in which the individual is behaving. (p. 13)

Aggression in the Schools

Primary consideration is given to aggression as a problem in schools because children spend a lot of time in schools. Since more is known about the development of antisocial behavior in general than about aggression in particular, we first examine aggression in the context of other antisocial acts. Antisocial behavior is an inclusive term that includes interpersonal aggression, but also encompasses a broad range of other behaviors such as cruelty to animals, theft, and destruction of property.

Prevalence of Aggression in Schools

There are several key aggressive behaviors apparent in school settings, each of which varies in seriousness. Among the moderately serious behaviors are hostile teasing, pushing, and bullying that are generally associated with boys' behavior (Farrington, 1993; Olweus, 1991). In addition, female students are known to display indirect forms of aggression, including behavior such as ostracism (Cairns, Cairns, Neckerman, Gariépy, & Ferguson, 1989; Hämäläinen & Pulkkinen, 1995; Lagerspetz, Björkqvist, & Peltonen, 1988). Among the most serious behaviors displayed, particularly by boys, are physical fighting, the use of weapons, robbery, and homicide. In addition, sexually aggressive acts, which vary from aggressive provocations to rape, should be noted.

Research indicates aggression in school is most often directed at peers, but teachers have also become the target of students' attacks (Callahan & Rivara, 1992; Johnston, O'Malley, & Bachman, 1993). Most of the aggression in schools, though, is displayed by male students and is directed at male students (Olweus, 1991). However, research increasingly shows female students also display overt aggressive acts, including physical fighting and carrying weapons. Overall, female incidents of aggression appear at lower but not negligible rates. For example, Cotten et al. (1994) found 26% of African American girls fought at middle school, and 16% carried a weapon to school, compared to 47% and 22% of the males, respectively.

Research shows weapon carrying varies by setting. For example, the number of students carrying a weapon is much higher in some schools than in other schools (Webster, Gainer, & Champion, 1993). Webster et al. found the worst school in terms of boys' carrying of guns (40%) was also the worst school for girls' carrying of knives (67%), and boys in the worst school carried knives and guns, whereas girls carried knives only. A survey of 11th graders in Seattle, Washington, showed 11.4% of the males owned a handgun, compared to 1.5% of the females. Weapon ownership was highly linked to use: 33% of the owners of a handgun had fired at someone (Callahan & Rivara, 1992), and it was highly linked to past victimization (Kingery, Pruitt, & Heuberger, 1996; Van Kammen & Loeber, 1995). Furthermore, weapon ownership is particularly high among known delinquents. Sommers and Baskin (1994) found 34% of a sample of female delinquents reported they had frequently carried weapons at school.

Surveys of the reasons for aggressive conflicts in schools show typical fights are about retaliation for teasing and for accidental or purposeful hurt or injury. In addition, conflicts tend to arise over rules of games, disputes over possession of toys or equipment, or territorial disputes (Boulton, 1993; Garofalo, Siegel, & Laub, 1987).

Children's physical aggression in schools is important not only because of the harm it inflicts but also because it has long-term consequences for settings beyond the school. Consistent physical aggression and bullying by boys in school predicts later antisocial acts, delinquency, and violent offending in the community (Farrington, 1989, 1991; Haapasalo & Tremblay, 1994; Loeber et al., 1991; Loeber, Tremblay, Gagnon, & Charlebois, 1989; Olweus, 1991; Pulkkinen & Tremblay, 1992; Stattin & Magnusson, 1989). The sequelae of physical aggression by girls have been less studied, but Hämäläinen and Pulkkinen (1995) found indirect defensive aggression, and offensive aggression at ages 8 and 14, respectively, as rated by teachers, predicted later delinquency in girls.

Relation of Aggression to Other Problem Behaviors

Juvenile disruptive behavior is related to other problem behaviors. Loeber and Schmaling (1985) examined 28 studies reporting parent and teacher ratings of disruptive child behavior. Their analysis showed a single dimension of disruptive behavior, with overt problem behavior (e.g., temper tantrums and attacks on people) clustering on one pole and covert problem behaviors (e.g., theft and setting fires) on the other pole. Disobedience was situated in the middle of the overt-covert continuum. More recently, Frick et al. (1993) repeated the analysis on an expanded number of studies involving more than 28,000 children. Their results basically replicated those reported by Loeber and Schmaling (1985; see also Fergusson, Horwood, & Lynskey, 1994). The findings suggest that aggressive and nonaggressive behavior problems, although somewhat related, are distinct entities.

Both overt and covert antisocial acts reflect a failure by children to successfully resolve distinct normative developmental tasks. Overt antisocial acts represent children's failure to learn to control their emotions and use nonconfrontational forms of interpersonal problem solving. In contrast, covert antisocial acts represent children's failure to accept personal responsibility and to be honest about their own actions and motivations. Covert acts also reflect children's misplaced ambition to obtain goods without payment or money without earning it. The conceptualization of antisocial behavior as a failure to master developmental tasks recognizes that just because persons meet one developmental task such as honesty, does not mean they will necessarily also meet another developmental task such as nonaggressive interpersonal problem solving. Children and youth can span the range of mastery from full mastery of tasks at all developmental stages to partial mastery, or to failure to master any of the age-appropriate tasks.

As mentioned, disobedience was somewhat in the middle of the overt-covert distribution. Disobedience, defiance, as well as truancy and running away from home, differ from most other disruptive behaviors in that they may not inflict the same degree of immediate distress on others as do overt and covert acts. Patterson (1980, 1982) considered disobedience a key to the development of overt and covert disruptive behaviors (see also Patterson, Reid, & Dishion, 1992). Although we focus here on overt aggressive acts, it should be realized that overt aggressive behaviors are correlated with both disobedience and covert nonaggressive delinquent behaviors. Also, the most aggressive boys are also at risk to develop covert behavior problems (Loeber & Schmaling, 1985).

Onset and Prevalence

Useful distinctions have been made between different severity levels of aggression, such as minor aggression without drawing blood, physical fighting, and violence in which there is physical injury. At what ages do juveniles first show these behaviors? Are there developmental orderings or sequences between behaviors in that less serious aggression tends to occur prior to serious aggression? And do juveniles who become violent first show less serious forms of aggression earlier in life?

Onset refers to the first occurrence of a particular behavior. Unfortunately, accurate onset data on juveniles' aggression in schools are quite rare. The apparent reasons are twofold: school-based studies do not tend to be cumulative and generally do not record whether or not an episode is the first occurrence of aggression or violence. Second, the collection of onset information is hampered by the fact that after grade school, middle school/junior high and senior high school students attend rotating classes supervised by different teachers. For these reasons, it is difficult to determine the ages of onset of physical aggression and other problem behaviors in middle/junior high and high schools.

In the absence of good onset data for children's aggression in school, one can review prevalence data on different forms of aggression at different grade levels. This method indirectly informs one about the onset or not of aggressive acts at each grade level studied. Prevalence refers to the rate of occurrence of behaviors at one specific time period. Of particular interest are differences in the prevalence of fighting and bullying in the early school years and prevalence figures over subsequent years. Such information is crucial for selecting target groups and optimizing the timing of interventions.

A Canadian study sheds some light on these issues of age at onset and prevalence. Haapasalo and Tremblay (1994) reported on a large community sample in Quebec and identified boys who, according to teachers, fought habitually at kindergarten (age 6) and subsequently at ages 10, 11, and 12. Taking together all the fighters at these four assessments, 8.3% fought at kindergarten *and* in at least two of the three ensuing years. Another 9.15% of all the fighters started fighting after kindergarten and were rated as high fighters in at least two of the three school years. Thus, an additional proportion of the fighters emerged during elementary school and became persisting fighters. It is not clear, however, whether the two groups of fighters were drawn from boys who were already highly aggressive at home.

Data from clinic-referred samples of children are important, too, because they shed some light on the onset of the most seriously affected groups. These studies reveal interesting gender differences in onset and prevalence. Teacher ratings of the prevalence of aggression show different patterns for clinic-referred girls and boys (Achenbach & Edelbrock, 1986). Fighting by referred girls initially has a lower prevalence than that by boys. For referred males most of the increase in the prevalence of fighting takes place by ages 8 to 9. Unexpected, perhaps, was the fact that teacher ratings of the prevalence of fighting in referred girls increased after ages 8 to 9 years and peaked at ages 14–15 years, when the prevalence became about the same as that of boys. These results show most referred boys who fight in school do so already by ages 8 to 9. For girls a much smaller early onset group is also apparent by that age, but in addition there is a clear late onset group of fighters that emerges during adolescence.

An examination of changes in prevalence of aggression is no substitute for data on the onset of aggression. Two caveats are in order. First, there is still a need for prospective studies to show the actual ages of onset. Second, because of the structure of middle/junior high and high schools, with students being seen by a given teacher for only a few hours per week and rarely by the same teacher supervising playgrounds and common areas, teachers' reports in such schools are less valid indicators of the aggression of their students.

Bullying can be a major form of aggression at school. Norwegian data (Olweus, 1991) showed the prevalence of students who were victims of bullying was consistently higher for boys than for girls in elementary schools, but for each gender the prevalence decreased considerably during the elementary school years, and continued to decrease in junior high school. In contrast, however, the percentage of boys (but not girls) who reported having bullied other students increased for boys between grades five and nine. Olweus (1991) noted the prevalence of bullying is partly a function of the age of bullies and the presence of older boys. He stated that "a considerable part of the bullying was carried out by older students" (p. 417). He pointed out that, generally, the younger students are, the higher the proportion of older, potential bullies they are exposed to (see also Warr, 1996). As students grow older, the age discrepancy decreases, which may explain the decrease in bullying with age noted earlier.

In summary, a proportion of boy fighters have already emerged during kindergarten. When the fighting persists during the first few grades of elementary school, these boys are highly likely to continue to fight at later grades. Other fighters emerge during the elementary school years, and possibly during middle/junior high and high school. Of clinic-referred children, most of the boys who fight appear already aggressive by ages 8 to 9. In contrast, there is a smaller early-onset group of referred girls, with most girls showing an onset of fighting subsequently during adolescence. Data on changes in bullying patterns also vary by gender and appear to peak between grades five to nine for boys. Early identification of the aggressive child is important because an early onset of antisocial and delinquent behavior is one of the most important markers for a career of chronic delinquency (Loeber, 1988; Moffitt, 1993).

Stability of Aggression

The next step is to ask how stable juveniles' aggression is over time? Olweus's (1979) survey of studies measuring the stability of aggression showed that on average the correlation between early and later aggression was .63 (.79 when corrected for measurement error), which is as high as the stability of intelligence over time. This finding appears to indicate that most of those scoring high on aggression early in life also score high on aggression later in life.

The high correlation between early and later aggression should be accepted with some reservations, though. First, as Loeber (1982) has shown, the most stable individuals are those who are at the extremes. Initially, they are either the least aggressive or the most aggressive. However, a large proportion of juveniles display fluctuating levels of aggression over time as a function of maturity, situation, or other influences (Le Blanc, Côté, & Loeber, 1991). Second, stability varies with age, with lower coefficients at an earlier age and higher coefficients at a later age. Specifically, Loeber (1982) reported the average stability correlation of aggression increased with age. The percentage of variance accounted for increased from 18.5% for 8-year-old cohorts to 44.9% in 13-year-old cohorts. As is generally true in development, instability in aggression is more apparent early in life; as children enter adolescence and young adulthood, their aggressive tendencies become more stable. Olweus's (1979) review of longitudinal studies based on teachers' ratings shows stability coefficients for aggression are moderately high, showing an average correlation of .56 (range .48–.70). Findings reported by Verhulst and Van der Ende (1991) show average stability coefficients of .34 and .52 for teacher-rated aggressive syndromes in boys and girls, respectively.

Since in most studies follow-up ratings often involved teachers different from those who completed the initial ratings, the agreement across raters lends support for the stability of aggression in students and weakens support for the notion that the stability estimates are contaminated by teachers' bias regarding certain students. However, the possibility cannot be discounted that aggressive students' negative reputations may be well known to many teachers.

A series of papers on physical fighting reported by teachers in schools in Quebec (Haapasalo & Tremblay, 1994; Loeber, Tremblay, et al., 1989; Tremblay, Loeber, et al., 1991) documented the high temporal stability of physical fighting by boys. The stability of fighting from kindergarten to first grade was not statistically significant. However, the stability of later fighting was enhanced when based on the presence of fighting in more than one year. For example, the likelihood that boys who fought both in kindergarten and in first grade also fought in the next year was 1.0. In contrast, in the absence of fighting at kindergarten and first grade, the probability of fighting in the subsequent year dropped to .29 (Loeber, Tremblay, et al., 1989; Tremblay, Loeber, et al., 1991).

Finally, stability of aggression in schools is increased when boys are highly aggressive in two settings, such as the home *and* the school. These boys are likely to remain stably aggressive in *both* settings. One unpublished study (Kirkpatrick, 1978, cited in Loeber, 1982) showed children with overt deviant behavior in both home and school were at higher risk to incur a contact with the police for delinquent behavior than children with overt deviant behavior in only one of the settings.

In summary, juvenile aggression tends to be stable over time, although it is not necessarily stable for all juveniles and under all measurement conditions. One of the research challenges is to identify youth *before* their aggression becomes stable. Some of the tools for early identification will be specific knowledge about ages of onset of aggression and the documentation of developmental pathways showing the trajectories for youth who escalate from minor forms of aggression to violence. This knowledge is important for the early identification of youth most at risk for violence, for the implementation of timely interventions, and for increasing scientific knowledge about patterns of aggression and the roots of violence.

Developmental Pathways

Research on the development of delinquency has been undertaken by Huizinga (1995) and Elliott (1994) utilizing analyses of longitudinal data from the National Youth Survey, and by Le Blanc, Côté, and Loeber (1991) in the analysis of Quebec longitudinal data. A finding common to all of the studies investigating the development of aggression and delinquency was

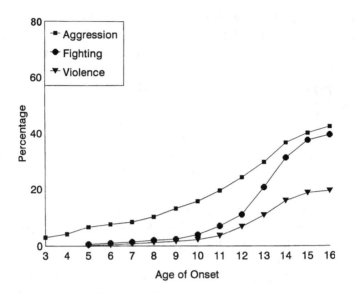

Figure 4.1. Development of minor aggression, physical fighting, and violence.

that less serious forms of delinquency precede the onset of more serious delinquent acts over time.

In order to investigate developmental pathways in aggression and violence in the Pittsburgh Youth Study, the authors created age of onset graphs using information about the boys' aggression from the boys and their parents and derived three categories (Loeber, Wung, et al., 1993). Onset graphs were very similar for annoying others and bullying (using parent information only) and, for that reason, were merged into the "minor aggression" category. For the same reason, physical fighting and gang fighting were merged in a single onset curve called "physical fighting." Finally, the onset curves for strong-arming, attacking someone to seriously hurt or kill, and forced sex were very similar and thus were merged into the category "violence." Figure 4.1 shows the three onset curves for minor aggression, physical fighting, and violence in the youngest sample (N=503) (Loeber, DeLamatre, Keenan, & Zhang, in press).

The graphs show the seriousness of aggression increases with age, a finding that is not surprising, but which does have important implications for interventions. Minor aggression emerged first, followed by physical fighting, which in turn was followed by the onset of violence. The results shown in Figure 4.1 constitute a replication of previous results from the middle and the oldest samples in the Pittsburgh Youth Study (Loeber, Wung, et al., 1993). In addition, retrospective information collected from a

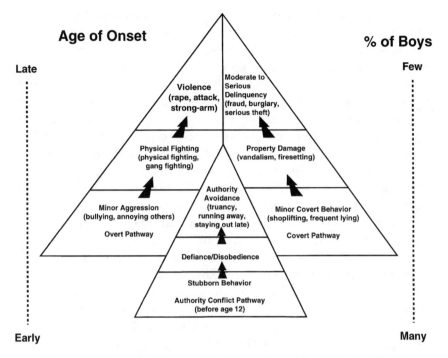

Figure 4.2. Three developmental pathways in problem behavior. *Data Source:* Loeber & Hay, 1994.

sample of clinic-referred girls and their parents showed similar developmental ordering of minor aggression, physical fighting, and violence (Loeber, Green, Keenan, & Navratil, 1995).

One of the vexing problems in violence is that it is difficult to predict because of its relative rarity. However, prediction can be enhanced by delineating development steps and then making predictions from one step to the next (Loeber, Wung, et al., 1993). There are several ways the development of aggression can be conceptualized in order to divide it into steps. Development in which individuals progress through a stepwise sequence of increasingly serious aggressive acts can be discussed as a developmental pathway.

Based on the previously mentioned meta-analyses showing overt and covert behavior problems (and disobedience as a third marker), the authors formulated and tested three developmental pathways of disruptive behavior (Loeber, DeLamatre, Keenan, & Zhang, in press; Loeber et al., 1993; Loeber, Keenan, & Zhang, 1997; see Figure 4.2). The overt pathway, which involves interpersonal aggression or violence, has three stages:

Stage 1, minor aggression (e.g., annoying others, bullying); Stage 2, physical fighting (e.g., fighting, gang fighting); and Stage 3, violence (e.g., attacking someone, strong-arming, forced sex). The covert pathway, which does not contain interpersonal aggression or violence, also has three stages: Stage 1, minor covert behavior (e.g., lying, shoplifting); Stage 2, property damage (e.g., setting fires, damaging property); and Stage 3, moderate to very serious forms of delinquency (e.g., "joyriding," pickpocketing, stealing from cars, fencing, illegal checks or credit cards, stealing cars, selling drugs, breaking and entering). The authority-conflict pathway does not contain interpersonal aggression or violence. This pathway fits best for boys engaging in these behaviors before 12 years of age, and has three stages: Stage 1, stubborn behavior; Stage 2, disobedience and defiance (e.g., doing things own way, refusing to do things); and Stage 3, authority avoidance (e.g., staying out late, truancy, running away).

Analysis of the Pittsburgh Youth Study data shows that although a large proportion of children show problems characteristic for the first step in the overt pathway, relatively few children progress through the full pathway to the most serious violent acts. Nonetheless, most boys who become violent have progressed through the full overt pathway, in that they displayed minor aggression first, followed by physical fighting, before they escalated to violence (Loeber, DeLamatre, et al., in press; Loeber, Keenan, & Zhang, 1997; Loeber, Wung, et al., 1993). The fit for the model is best when a distinction is made between "experimenters" (i.e., those who show a problem behavior temporarily) and "persisters" (i.e., those who continue in their problem behavior over time). More of the persisters than experimenters follow the overt pathway. The results agree with those reported by Elliott (1994) from the National Youth Survey showing that boys who advance to violence have practiced minor forms of aggression first.

A small proportion of boys follow more than one pathway (Loeber, Wung, et al., 1993). Boys who began to follow the overt pathway early were more likely to follow the covert pathway than boys on the covert pathway were to follow the overt pathway. Further, boys who followed multiple pathways were found to be more frequently delinquent both by self-reports and officially recorded juvenile offenses. The rate of offending was highest for boys following all three pathways (i.e., overt, covert, and authority-conflict). However, among the boys on two pathways, the rate was higher for boys on the overt/covert and the authority-conflict/covert pathways than for boys on the authority-conflict/overt pathways. Thus, early aggression is of particular importance because it is a predictor for entry into multiple pathways.

A literature search finds no studies focusing on within-individual changes in aggression specifically in school settings. However, the pathway model postulated previously (Loeber, DeLamatre, et al., in press; Loeber, Keenan, & Zhang, 1997; Loeber, Wung, et al., 1993) is based on information from parents and children, and it is unlikely these informants would have limited their reports of aggression to acts occurring in the home or in the community only. Future research must show whether or not the overt pathway also applies to school settings.

In summary, the prediction of serious outcomes such as violence can best be conceptualized according to a model in which steps toward violence are specified. That is, few individuals begin a full-blown violent career. Instead, they "ease" into it through minor offenses, and the earlier these begin, the more likely the individual will eventually show more serious examples of violent behavior. Thus, early onset of problem behaviors and children's position on the developmental pathway model's stage of problem behavior constitute important markers to identify those youth at highest risk for violence and who may need preventive interventions. It is unclear, however, to what extent these developmental pathways also apply to behavior in school, and whether pathways found for boys are also applicable to girls.

Development of Aggression in the Home and in School

Some children may show aggression in the home only, others in the school only, and a third group may show aggression in both settings. One cannot necessarily expect the association between children's aggression or problem behaviors in the home and in the school will be strong. A meta-analysis by Achenbach, McConaughy, and Howell (1987) reported a weak correlation of .32 for "undercontrolled" (i.e., aggressive, impulsive) child behavior across home and school, indicating a low correspondence for that behavior across the two settings.

Problem behaviors such as aggression and violence in multiple settings, like early age of onset, are a predictor of a more seriously deviant developmental pathway or outcome (Loeber, 1982). One way to address the consistency of behavior across settings is to ask about informant agreement. One might expect parent and teacher ratings of the problem behaviors of nonreferred children would have a higher agreement than for deviant children. Kolko and Kazdin (1993) found a correlation of .29 between externalizing problems as reported by parents and teachers, compared to a correlation of .48 for a nonpatient sample. Perhaps the most sophisticated measurement study on problem behaviors at home and school was carried out by Ramsey, Patterson, and Walker (1990) on a subsample of their longitudinal study. Constructs of antisocial behavior were based on different informants and measurement modes (i.e., rating reports and direct observations). There was weak statistical evidence for correlation between antisocial behavior in the home and the school. Antisocial behavior in the home accounted for 52% of the school antisocial construct (which in addition to antisocial behavior also included attendance and academic achievement). Whether the results also apply to aggression is not clear.

Thus, several studies support the idea that children's disruptive problems and aggression in the home are correlated with similar behavior at school. However, the statistical correlations vary from low to moderately high depending on sample type and measurement, and should be accepted with some caution. It is likely that parent ratings of children's aggression may be influenced by teachers' reports of the children's behavior at school, and similarly, teachers may be familiar with reports of children's behavior in the home. To avoid this possible rater bias in future studies it would be better to base results on independent observations of children's behavior both in the home and at school.

Few studies have addressed the percentage of aggressive youth who are aggressive in the home, the school, or in both settings. Loeber and Dishion (1984), in a cross-sectional study, found of all the fighters in a community sample of fourth, seventh, and tenth grade boys, 49% were fighters in the home only, 30% were fighters in the school only, and the remaining 21% fought both at home and in school. From these data it can be inferred that the highest percentage of fighters had a background of fighting at home (70%) compared to school only (51%). Fighters both at home and school were also the most deviant in terms of police contacts, self-reported delinquent lifestyle, disobedience to parents, and association with deviant peers. Those fighters also showed a trend toward a higher rate of coercive behaviors in the home (according to home observations) compared to fighters in the other groups.

In summary, the results indicate that boys who are known to fight often at home *and* in school probably are qualitatively more antisocial than boys who fight in the home or in school only. Either way, explanations are needed to explain differences in patterns of children's fighting in the home, the school, or both settings.

Models of Transmission Across Settings. Consistency of aggression across settings has been viewed by some as an expression of an antisocial trait, by others as due to environmental influences, and by still others as resulting from person–environment interactions (Lewis, 1990). We will briefly discuss different models conceptualizing the transmission of aggression across the settings of home and school.

Antisocial Trait Model. There has been considerable debate among scholars about whether antisocial behavior in juveniles is a stable personality trait that manifests itself across different settings (Loeber & Hay, 1994; Mischel, 1984; Patterson, 1982; Pepler & Slaby, 1994). When multiple sources of information are used, an antisocial trait stable across the settings of the home and the school can be documented, but the evidence is modest (Ramsey, Patterson, & Walker, 1990). Also, Charlebois and colleagues have demonstrated that behavioral consistency across situations is considerably enhanced by the researcher's judicious choice in the similarity of interaction partners (Charlebois, Tremblay, Gagnon, Larivée, & Laurent, 1989). For example, one can expect a higher consistency of children's problem behaviors when confronted with the same type of interaction partner in different settings. Thus, consistency can be higher in the presence of an interaction partner of similar age and gender (e.g., siblings vs. peers, parents vs. teachers, female vs. male peers, and female vs. male adults).

Formulations of the antisocial trait model have not been very explicit about what the mechanism is that produces consistency of behavior in different settings. Several explanations are plausible. Many hypothesize there is persisting perceptual bias that leads some aggressive juveniles to misinterpret neutral social acts as provocations directed at them and that triggers behaviors that then serve as a stimulus for aggression in the other person (Dodge, Bates, & Pettit, 1990; Dodge, Pettit, McGlaskey, & Brown, 1986). Since attributional biases (e.g., expectations, stereotypes) are within an individual, the internalized bias may be equally and readily expressed across different settings. That is, the attributional bias may manifest itself independent of social stimuli and, as a consequence, may be expressed in a similar manner in the home, in the school, and in other locations. As a sole explanation, the antisocial trait theory has few adherents. Environmental factors, including social interactions, have received more support.

Environmental Model. According to an environmental control, social learning, or transactional model (Patterson, 1982; Sameroff, 1975), juveniles' aggression is seen mostly as the product of external environmental factors and circumstances. This model has some components of the antisocial trait model in that it concerns both perpetrators and victims, each of whom are engaged in repeated aggressive interchanges, initially mostly in the home (Patterson, 1992). Extensive experience with aggression in the home with parents and siblings may severely limit a child's ability to resolve social conflict other than by aggression. Such an impaired child may have little alternative but to resort to the aggressive methods learned at home when confronted by social conflicts with peers in school. These aggressive interchanges initially may be of a less serious nature, but perpetrators and victims may learn over time that escalation to more serious forms of aggression can determine who will "win" and who will have to submit. Thus, repeated learning experiences sooner or later lead to an escalation of more serious forms of aggression.

Juveniles may respond to provocation or threat in two ways. First, they may respond to aggression in kind. Second, by witnessing aggressive acts between others or by becoming victimized, they may attempt to prevent their own victimization by arming themselves so that when confronted, they can quickly escalate their aggressive power in an effort to intimidate their aggressor into desisting. Several studies have shown a relationship between victimization and the carrying of weapons in or outside schools, but the strength of the association varies by gender and grade (Gottfredson & Gottfredson, 1985; Van Kammen & Loeber, 1995). Physically weaker juveniles may perceive the strategy of arming themselves as a preferable alternative to being victimized.

Consistency of aggression across different settings would only take place if contingencies (i.e., reinforcement and punishment) in one setting are duplicated in the other setting. In contrast, aggressive behavior patterns occurring only in one setting are thought to be caused by the presence of contingencies in that setting but not in the other setting. This formulation comes close to Herrnstein's (1961) matching law, which states that relative contingencies in multiple settings, rather than the absolute contingencies, should influence differential rates of behavior in each setting. Specifically, Conger and Simons (in press) stated "a child or adolescent will engage in a relatively high proportion of antisocial behavior compared to conventional behaviors within a specific context (family, peer group, school, or community) when: (1) reinforcement for antisocial behavior is relatively high, (2) punishment for antisocial behavior is relatively low, (3) reinforcement for conventional behavior is relatively low, and (4) punishment for conventional behavior is relatively high" (p. 25). Conger and Simons stressed that differences in the time that individuals choose to spend in different environments can be explained by the matching law. For example, aggressive youth usually choose to spend time in certain less supervisable areas of playgrounds of schools compared to more visible areas or in proximity to teachers.

However, evidence supporting the environmental model consists of the finding that once aggressive juveniles leave such aggression-prone settings (e.g., after leaving school), their own level of aggression will decrease. There is a great scarcity of environmental control studies showing how aggressive behavior of the same youths is modulated in different settings (Lewis, 1990).

Person–Environment Interaction Models. Most theorists and researchers of antisocial behavior have abandoned the pursuit of a pure antisocial trait or a pure environmental control model and, instead, integrate both in a person–environment interaction model (see, e.g., Elliott, Huizinga, & Ageton, 1985; Gottfredson & Hirschi, 1994; Patterson, 1992; Patterson et al., 1992). Several of the person–environment interaction models highlight the relationship between children's family functioning and their relationships with peers outside the home (see, e.g., Bierman & Smoot, 1991; Dishion, Patterson, Stoolmiller, & Skinner, 1991). Although valuable, more relevant for this chapter are models and studies combining social interactional perspectives with attention to settings. For example, Dumas (in press), expanding on the work by Blechman, Prinz, and Dumas (1995), postulated a coping-competence model of the development of aggressive behavior based on children's communication skills, attention processes in dysfunctional family interactions, and automaticity in cognition and social interactions with others. Basically, this model combines aspects of social skill deficits with social learning parameters to explain the development of aggression over time.

Definitive studies of how person–environment interaction models perform across settings are scarce (Lewis, 1990). In the best circumstances, such a model would have to be based on observations of the contingencies in two settings such as the home and the school in order to account for differences in the rate and severity of aggression in each setting. Moreover, as pointed out by Dumas (in press) and Patterson, Reid, and Dishion (1992), each setting can have distinct risk factors for increasing aggression. For example, deficiencies in parenting can be associated with the emergence of boys' aggression in the home. When children enter school, their behavior may be aggravated by negative classroom experiences and disturbed peer relations. Particularly aggressive children, poor academic performance, and rejection by their peers may constitute new risk factors for the escalation of aggression in school. Although models with changing risk factors are highly plausible, rigorous studies showing the mechanisms for the shift from aggression in the home to aggression in school are rare.

Differences and Direction of Transmission of Aggression Between Home and School

It is important to point out that aggression in school is not necessarily the same as aggression at home. First, the history of conflict and aggressive interchanges between children and their siblings and between children and their parents are usually more long-standing than between children and their peers in school and between children and their teachers. This longer history of conflict may mean that aggressive interchanges in the home will have more "automated" scripts (Dumas, in press) than those in school.

Second, what is probably unique to schools and less common in the home is aggression displayed within groups of children, particularly of the type in which several children target their aggression on a single child. Such ganging or mobbing (Olweus, 1984) can have several purposes. Groups of children may tease and scapegoat a particular victim, they may use the same techniques to punish the victim for an alleged transgression, or they may collectively rob the victim of some of his or her possessions, such as a coat, sneakers, or a weapon. It is plausible that such a group phenomenon of aggression is a developmental precursor of robbery committed by small groups of youths on the street, and of delinquent gang activity in the community.

Third, the availability of large numbers of younger peers in schools offers a plethora of choices of victims upon which to practice aggression. In addition, the presence of girls in school constitutes a pool for aggressive youths to practice gender-specific forms of aggression.

Two major unanswered questions are whether juveniles' stable aggression in school is an extension of their stable aggression in the home, or whether juveniles' stable aggression in the home results from their stable aggression in the school setting. A literature search has not found longitudinal studies addressing these questions.

The first option (i.e., transmission from home to school) assumes that factors influencing early forms of aggression are situated in the child and/or the home environment. In one variant, the impact of these factors continues at school age and extends into the school setting. In a second variant, generalization of aggression from the home to the school setting may result from similar risk factors in each setting (e.g., aggressive siblings in the home and aggressive peers in school), or through unique risk factors in either setting (e.g., familial psychopathology, victimization at school). Also, the emergence of new risk factors in the school setting, particularly through coercive peer interactions, may facilitate the generalization of aggression apparent in the home to the school setting. In a third and more probable version, risk factors in the home during the child's life at school continue to exercise their impact on aggression in the home, but the impact is enhanced by the presence of risk factors in the school.

The second option, that aggression for some children develops at school and then generalizes to the home, may seem less likely but is certainly possible. The pattern of risk factors in this case is only partly the same as that of the first option. The generalization of aggression from the school to the home setting may have similar risk factors in the school as in the home. However, protective factors in the home may have been responsible for the fact that aggression did not originate in the home. Probably only when new risk factors emerge in the home is it likely that aggression originating in the school may extend to the home setting as well.

In summary, of the three models of influences we postulated, the person–environment model appears the most plausible, given available, although limited, data. This implies that interventions probably are most effective if they can address both the individual characteristics of children (e.g., impulsiveness or hyperactivity) and the social contingencies that affect their aggressive responding. Based on current evidence, interventions in the home may be more beneficial than school programs, because there is evidence that juveniles' aggression in the home influences the level of their aggression in the school setting. At any rate, school interventions would also benefit from those in the home.

Family Risk Factors for the Development of Aggression at School

We will now review selected risk factors in the home that are associated with children's aggression at school: child abuse, parents' inadequate child rearing practices, disruptions in family functioning, antisocial parents, and aggressive interactions between siblings.

Child Abuse

Batsche and Knoff (1994) postulated that "a bully at school is a victim at home" (p. 166), which implies victimization at home is a precursor to the display of aggression at school. This is confirmed by survey studies. For example, Hotaling, Straus, and Lincoln (1989) reported that "children who are assaulted in the family are more likely to assault and commit property crimes outside of the family" (p. 364). In a large national survey the authors found "children who are *both* the victims of parental assaults and who witness spouse assault have a rate of assault against nonfamily children that is *six times higher* [emphasis added] than children from nonassaultive families (12.1% vs. 2.1%)" (p. 345; see also Widom, 1989).

It is likely physical abuse of children in the home setting alters their relationships with other adults outside the home. For example, Boney-McCoy and Finkelhor (1995) found that in a national sample of children ages 10 to 16, girls victimized by parental violence showed increased trouble with a teacher. Also, Smith and Thornberry (1995) found child physical or sexual maltreatment by a parent was associated with later violent offending and with the frequency of such offending. In one of the few prospective studies, Dodge et al. (1990) found physical abuse was a risk factor for later aggression in a sample of boys and girls. Other research has linked physical abuse to lower social effectiveness with peers and higher levels of aggression in the school setting (Rogosch, Cicchetti, & Aber, 1995).

That the relationship between abuse and child problems extends to aggressive acts is not surprising ("aggression begets aggression"). Some research suggests the relationship between child physical abuse and aggression in school is complex. Strassberg and colleagues (Strassberg, Dodge, Pettit, & Bates, 1994) reported higher levels of severity in parental punishment practices (i.e., spanking) predicted higher levels of teacher-rated boys' aggression toward peers in schools. Widom (1994) reports physically abused girls are more at risk for arrest for violent crimes during adolescence. Childhood neglect also predisposes children toward aggression and violence. And it was found that neglected males, compared to neglected females, were more at risk for violent crimes during adolescence (Widom, 1994).

Inadequate Child-Rearing Practices

Adequacy of child rearing, apart from abuse, is another risk factor. Several parental child-rearing practices in the home appear relevant for boys' aggressive behavior in school. Results from the Cambridge Study in Delinquency Development (Farrington, 1978, 1989) report harsh parental attitudes and discipline when a child is 8 years old correlated with teacher-rated aggression of boys at school ages 8 to 10 (but not aggression in school at ages 12–14). In a Norwegian study, Olweus (1980) found mothers' negativism, mothers' and fathers' power assertive methods, and mothers' permissiveness for aggression predicted boys' peer-rated aggression at school in sixth grade. Thus, several parental child-rearing practices in the home are known to be associated with boys' aggressive behavior in school.

Although such consistent results are impressive, they do not reveal: (1) to what extent poor parental child rearing may have been a reaction to the boys' aggression at home, (2) what proportion of the parents' negative child-rearing practices in the home were in response to the youths' aggressive behaviors at school, (3) whether poor parental child-rearing practices predicted the *onset* of aggression at school, and (4) whether the prediction held when aggression at home was partialled out.

Pettit, Bates, and Dodge (1993), using home observations in a longitudinal study, showed that mothers' coerciveness (but not fathers' coerciveness) predicted teacher ratings of first grade child externalizing behavior. Mothers' coercive behavior also predicted consistency of children's externalizing behavior both in the home and at school. The authors found lower rates of mothers' coercive behavior for children who scored high in a single setting only than for those who scored high in both. Loeber and Dishion (1984) focused on boys' fighting at home and at school and found mothers of boys who fought at school only were significantly more coercive as judged by home observations than mothers of boys who did not fight in either setting or fought at home only. One interpretation is that mothers of boys who fight in school only are successful in suppressing boys' aggression in the home by being strongly coercive to the boys at home as compared to mothers whose boys do not fight in either setting, but this requires confirmation through future research.

The question should be raised about whether the generalization of aggression from the home to school equally applies to boys and girls. The answer must be evaluated in light of the fact that the prevalence of mild to moderate aggression in girls is initially much lower than that of boys, and that the gender differences decrease with age (Maccoby & Jacklin, 1974; Rutter & Giller, 1983). However, gender differences in serious violence tend to increase with age, with a much larger percentage of males committing violent acts compared to females (Elliott, 1994).

Studies show, on average, the acquisition of aggression is gender-linked in that boys at home or in the school direct their physical aggression more often at other boys than at girls (Farrington, 1993; Warr, 1996). Likewise, most aggressive girls direct their aggression at girls rather than at boys. However, there can be a great difference in the availability of the same gender in each setting, with some families having mostly boys or girls as children but with schools having available an abundance of potential opponents and victims of the same gender. Since boys tend to be more aggressive than girls, it can be hypothesized that the higher the proportion of male siblings in a family the more likely such a family will produce aggressive juveniles. Additionally, as will be discussed later, highly aggressive boys raised in families with several female siblings may be at risk for committing sexual violence later in life.

Disruptions in Family Functioning

Disruptions of the family affect child rearing and hence children's aggressive tendencies. Farrington (1978) found marital disharmony in families with boys at age 8 was associated with aggression in school (as rated by teachers) at ages 8 to 10 years. Similarly, separation of a child from a parent before age 10 was associated with aggression during that same interval and was predictive of aggression at school at ages 12–14 (Farrington, 1989).

Parental Criminality

Studies have demonstrated that antisocial parents tend to have antisocial children (Loeber & Stouthamer-Loeber, 1986). In that context, it is likely parental antisocial behavior is one of the factors directly affecting boys' aggression in school. For example, Farrington (1978, 1989) found a convicted parent (before the child's age of 10) correlated with teacher ratings of aggression at ages 8 to 10 and predicted teacher ratings of boys' aggression at school by ages 12–14. It is unclear, however, to what extent the link between antisocial behavior in the parent and a child's aggression at school can be explained by heredity, social learning, poor child rearing practices, or a combination of all of these factors.

Aggressive Interactions Between Siblings

Most aggressive interchanges in the home take place between siblings (Patterson, 1982). For example, a study on children at high risk for disruptive behavior showed a highly conflictual sibling relationship increased the likelihood of aggression at school (Storashak, Bellanti, & Bierman, 1996). Presumably, there are many common elements in such aggressive dyads in each setting, such as the nature of coercive interchanges, including provocation, reaction, escalation, and deescalation. For instance, "horsing around" may develop into aggressive acts. Also, it may be safely assumed that there are common elements across settings in which aggressive episodes (or chains of behaviors) are triggered repeatedly and are linked over time. There is clearly a need, however, to compare observations of aggressive interchanges in the home with those in schools.

It can be argued that the parenting deficiencies previously discussed are not limited to the conflictual relationship between parents and their aggressive children, but also reflect deviant interactions between the aggressive children and their siblings. Thus, part of poor child rearing practices reflects parents' unwillingness or inability to stop chronic aggressive conflicts between siblings. Pepler, Corter, and Abramovitch (1982) wrote, for example, "interactions with brothers and sisters usually precede interactions outside of the family and thus may serve as a bridge between the family and peer systems" (p. 220). Thus, models of the development of aggression need to measure at least the following components in the home and at school: the nature and quality of sibling interactions; parents' child rearing practices in general, but particularly those practices affecting sibling relations; and the nature and quality of children's peer interactions, preferably in the context of teachers' disciplinary practices and teaching practices.

A study by Patterson, Dishion, and Bank (1984) uses poor parental disciplining and coercive child behavior with siblings to explain physical aggression in elementary school. Poor parental discipline was correlated with observed coercive acts between the target children and their siblings in the home. These interactions were strongly correlated with boys' physical aggression as rated by teachers, parents, and self-reports. Thus, the study showed the relevance of coercive interchanges between siblings and parental child rearing practices to children's physical aggression at school.

In summary, research shows that several factors situated in the family constitute risk factors associated with children's aggression in the school setting. It is less clear how family risk factors are associated with the onset of aggression at school, especially independent of risk factors in that setting. Moreover, since most studies have concerned only boys, it remains to be seen to what extent family risk factors are equally associated with aggression by girls in schools. It also remains to be established to what extent systematic changes in the risk factors in the home should be accompanied by changes in risk factors in the school in order to permanently lower children's risk of becoming aggressive or violent.

Important Issues about Aggression in Schools

Aggressive Peers

Aggressive youths often operate in groups, but do aggressive youths actually select aggressive peers over nonaggressive peers? Cairns and colleagues (Cairns, Cairns, Neckerman, Gest, & Gariépy, 1988) identified the most aggressive boys and girls in their longitudinal study and studied their social networks by comparing them to the networks of nonaggressive children. The authors found that very often aggressive children sought out and allied themselves with other aggressive children, although this varied somewhat with age and gender.

Major progress toward understanding aggression in peer groups has been made by observational studies of newly formed peer groups in laboratory play rooms. For example, Dodge, Price, Coie, and Christopoulos (1990) observed 5,263 aggressive behaviors in a total of 387 pairs of children in 29 peer play groups, each consisting of 6 first to third grade African American boys. Half of the aggressive interchanges took place in just 20% of the pairs. The observations revealed that boys who had been rejected in the classroom were more prone than nonrejected boys to develop mutually aggressive relations when paired together.

The importance of this type of observational work is that it can highlight processes leading to escalation of aggression, and the way highly aggressive children draw others into aggressive interchanges. It is important to learn more about the extent of aggressive interactions in the laboratory and whether they also represent the processes happening on school playgrounds (Pepler & Craig, 1995). Moreover, it is important to learn more about how networks of aggressive peers in school relate to the formation and operation of gangs outside of school.

Victims Becoming Aggressors

Some research findings indicate a proportion of children who are repeatedly aggressively victimized eventually become perpetrators of aggression themselves (Olweus, 1978), "but the process linking victimization to aggression is not well understood" (Hotaling, Straus, & Lincoln, 1989, p. 352). One of the moderators of the victim-to-aggressor process is likely to be the carrying of weapons. For example, the carrying of knives as reported by seventh and eighth graders was highly associated with their having been threatened or attacked by someone with a knife or gun. This effect was strongest for females (Webster et al., 1993). This concurs with longitudinal findings from the Pittsburgh Youth Study showing victimization was much more likely to predict adolescents' gun carrying than the reverse (Van Kammen & Loeber, 1995). A critical question remains about what proportion of highly aggressive children originate from repeated victimization in schools, and whether reactive forms of aggression decrease once children are moved to environments in which aggressive provocations by other students are uncommon.

Boys' Aggression toward Girls

The developmental origins of sexual assaults and rape has been little studied (Fagot, Loeber, & Reid, 1988). How often do boys direct aggression toward girls? And how does boys' aggression toward girls escalate? As to the first question, Olweus (1991), in his Norwegian study, found "boys carried out a large part of the bullying to which girls were subjected" (p. 420). As to the second question, it is probable most boys who advance to rape have already practiced lesser forms of aggression (such as extreme teasing and rough handling of girls). However, developmental pathways from less serious forms of sexual aggression to more serious forms have not yet been documented.

We hypothesize that sexual aggression flourishes when aggressive boys: (1) grow up in households with more sisters than brothers, and (2) when aggressive boys practice bullying and aggression on female students in school. School playgrounds offer many opportunities for boys to practice aggression toward females, particularly because the setting allows them to tease (Boulton, 1993), push, and hit females. Loeber, Weissman, and Reid (1983) found male adolescents arrested for assaultive crimes tended to have more sisters than brothers (see also Farrington & West, 1971), but this study did not demonstrate that sex-specific aggression in the home was related to sex-specific aggression at school. It is likely the practice of sex-specific aggression in school is associated with later aggression directed at women in the community, including rape, but there is a clear need for research on these issues.

Finally, results from the National Youth Survey indicate boys who have raped practiced minor aggression first, followed by more serious forms of violence (e.g., aggravated assault and robbery) prior to their committing rape (Elliott, 1994). Thus, sex-specific violence may conform to the same developmental course that applies to other forms of violence; nonetheless, uninhibited sexual desire is one unique component of sexual violence.

Boys' Assaults on Teachers

Assaults on teachers are not uncommon. Johnston et al. (1993), in a national survey, found during the 1991 school year 28% of public school teachers in high schools were verbally abused, 15% threatened with injury, and 3% were physically attacked by a student (cited in Batsche & Knoff, 1994). Little is known about the developmental background of students who physically assault teachers. However, it is likely such students feel little or no restraint in expressing their aggression to other adults such as parents or adult strangers in the street. Also, assault on an adult is more likely when youth already engage in other serious acts. For example, Callahan and Rivara (1992) found adolescents who owned a handgun were more likely to assault teachers.

What proportion of the students who assault a teacher also have assaulted their parents earlier in life? Loeber, Weissman, and Reid (1983) have shown adolescents arrested for an assault showed high rates of coercive behavior in the home that tended to outrank the rates of coercive behavior displayed by their siblings *or* parents. This is in contrast to "normal" families, in which parents issue higher rates of coercive behavior than their children. Thus, assault, and possibly assault directed at adults such as teachers, may have a basis in inverse dominance hierarchies in the family home. We postulate that domination of adults in the home may be one of the factors contributing to the development of predatory forms of violence outside the home, including strong-arming and robbery.

Aggression Following School Transitions

Youth who are aggressive at home, upon entry into elementary school, can spread the aggression to other students in that setting. In that respect, the aggressive child can be seen as the "bad" carrier who can transform previously peaceful school settings into ones characterized by high rates of aggression and victimization in which several children are drawn to become aggressors. Thus, contagion is thought to be instigated by one or more perpetrators, who by their provocative aggression draw others into similar disruptive behaviors (see Chapter 10 of this volume for a detailed discussion of this issue).

The extent to which children's aggression in one school is transmitted to the next school is still a question. It is not uncommon for very aggressive juveniles to be expelled from a school in which they have caused trouble. It is probable that after the acceptance of such students in another school, the behavior pattern will persist and might also cause contagion. However, precise data in this area are not available.

There is a scarcity of studies showing how much normal school transitions (e.g., from kindergarten to elementary school, from elementary to middle/junior high school, or from middle/junior high to high school) are followed by changes in the level of aggression. School transitions can have several effects. First, after each transition, children in the presence of new peers may need to reestablish a dominance structure (Perry, Perry, & Boldizar, 1990). As a result, one can expect a transition period in which aggression becomes a strategy by which a dominance hierarchy becomes established.

Another possibility is that school transitions break the link between bullies and their former, often junior, victims. Specifically, elementary school bullies who graduate to a middle/junior high school suddenly not only find themselves among the youngest generation in that school, but also face a shortage of younger victims in that setting. Olweus (1991), using Norwegian data, pointed out the percentage of boys who bullied other students dropped at grade 7 from about 12% to 8%. (Grade 7 was the first year of junior high school.) However, longitudinal analyses in the Pittsburgh Youth Study failed to show that physical aggression varied with school transitions, either from elementary to middle school, or middle to high school (Loeber & Smalley, 1995).

Aggression and School Dropout

A key question is whether leaving school is associated with a change in the level of children's aggression compared to their level of aggression while attending school. On the one hand, we would expect a decrease in aggressive acts because individuals are separated from peer groups in the school conducive to aggressive interchanges. Furthermore, risk factors specific to schools, such as forced proximity to peers in close quarters and frustrations associated with students' negative feelings of being pressed in aversive academic demands, disappear when students leave school. Thus, the contingencies affecting aggressive acts are likely to change considerably when individuals shift from the school setting to the community. On the other hand, leaving school means an increase in unsupervised time, which can be conducive to an increase in delinquent activities.

Nonetheless, leaving school is unlikely to generate a big change in behavior. Very often students who drop out early from school have already often been truant (Farrington, in press; Robins & Ratcliff, 1980). Moreover, even when attending school, children and youth engage in delinquency outside of school. For example, an inner city survey of juveniles (ages 13–19) showed just under one-quarter (22%) of their most recent fights took place at school, while about half (48%) of the fights occurred in the street (Hausman, Spivak, & Prothrow-Stith, 1994). Delinquent activities in other settings than the school may already have been ongoing for a long time, and as a consequence, leaving school may not affect individuals' level of delinquency outside school. Finally, aggression, unlike property crimes, may be more closely linked to a personality trait and thus may be less likely to vary as a consequence of students' leaving school.

Dropping out of school before reaching the maximum grade level is associated in some studies with a decrease in delinquency for individuals compared to their level of delinquency when attending school (see, e.g., Aseltine & Gore, 1993; Elliott & Voss, 1974; Le Blanc, Biron, & Pronovost, 1979). In other studies, though, dropout has been associated with an increase in delinquency (Krohn, Thornberry, Collins-Hall, & Lizotte, 1995; Thornberry, Moore, & Christenson, 1985).

Thus, there is conflicting evidence about the impact of leaving school, either at a normal age or at a precocious age, on subsequent delinquency. The literature is even less clear about to what extent the decrease or increase in delinquency also pertains to aggressive acts.

Conclusion

There are large differences among children in their stability of aggression, with some becoming highly stable in their aggression over time, and others showing fluctuating levels of aggression or even aggression that decreases over time. Yet children's aggressive behavior in school is moderately stable. The research on developmental pathways shows there are incremental stages of involvement in aggressive behavior, with markers that predict the likelihood of progression from mild aggression to serious involvement and, at times, eventual criminal violence. Knowledge of the onset and developmental pathways of aggression is useful for the planning of interventions.

Aggression in the home does relate to aggression in the school setting, and certain risk factors in the home predict aggression at school. Each out-of-home setting has specific risk factors. For those youth whose aggression is pervasive across settings, interventions must include strategies to decrease aggression in *each* setting. Although we have not considered community levels of violence, it is recognized that children's aggression in the home and at school also reflects the larger community context of norms for aggressive behavior and the overall levels of daily aggression and violence. Interventions, therefore, may suitably be targeted to community contexts as well as to home and school. These community issues are discussed in detail in Chapter 10 of this volume.

New directions in research are needed for several high-priority areas. First, more frequent and systematic surveys are needed to monitor the prevalence of different types of aggression across the full range of grade levels in schools. These surveys should include data on age of onset and nature of disruptive episodes, teacher information, and measures of school climate, in addition to describing characteristics of offenders and victims. This knowledge is needed in order to identify schools at highest risk and to monitor progress in risk reduction when interventions are introduced. Second, systematic research is needed to understand the complex linkages and interactions between aggression in the home, the school, and the community. Third, rigorous evaluations of experimental interventions are needed to examine how best to design programs to reach high-risk children and youth, in terms of selecting appropriate target groups, appropriate settings, and appropriate timings for optimal outcomes.

References

Achenbach, T. M., & Edelbrock, C. (1986). *Manual for the Teachers Report Form and teacher version of the Child Behavior Profile*. Burlington, VT: University of Vermont, Department of Psychiatry.

Achenbach, T. M., McConaughy, S. H., & Howell, C. T. (1987). Child/adolescent behavioral and emotional problems: Implication of cross-informant correlations for situational specificity. *Psychological Bulletin, 101*, 213–232.

Aseltine, R. H., & Gore, S. (1993). Mental health and social adaptation following the transition from high school. *Journal of Research on Adolescence, 3*, 247–270.

Batsche, G. M., & Knoff, H. M. (1994). Bullies and their victims: Understanding a pervasive problem in the schools. *School Psychology Review, 23*, 165–174.

Bierman, K. L., & Smoot, D. L. (1991). Linking family characteristics with poor peer relations: The mediating role of conduct problems. *Journal of Abnormal Child Psychology, 19*, 341–356.

Blechman, E. A., Prinz, R. J., & Dumas, J. E. (1995). Coping, competence, and aggression prevention. Part 1. Developmental models. *Applied and Preventive Psychology, 4*, 211–232.

Boney-McCoy, S., & Finkelhor, D. (1995). Psychosocial sequelae of violent victimization in a national youth sample. *Journal of Consulting and Clinical Psychology, 63*, 726–736.

Boulton, M. J. (1993). Proximate causes of aggressive fighting in middle school children. *British Journal of Educational Psychology, 63*, 231–244.

Cairns, R. B., Cairns, B. D., Neckerman, H. J., Gariépy, J. L., & Ferguson, L. L. (1989). Growth and aggression: I. Childhood to early adolescence. *Developmental Psychology, 25*, 320–330.

Cairns, R. B., Cairns, B. D., Neckerman, H. J., Gest, S. C., & Gariépy, J. L. (1988). Social networks and aggressive behavior: Peer support or peer rejection? *Developmental Psychology, 24,* 815–823.

Callahan, C. M., & Rivara, F. P. (1992). Urban high school youth and handguns. *Journal of the American Medical Association, 267,* 3038–3042.

Charlebois, P., Tremblay, R. E., Gagnon, C., Larivée, S., & Laurent, D. (1989). Situational consistency in behavioral patterns of aggressive boys: Methodological considerations on observational measures. *Journal of Psychopathology and Behavioral Assessment, 11,* 15–27.

Conger, R. D., & Simons, R. L. (in press). Life-course contingencies in the development of adolescent antisocial behavior: A matching law approach. In T. P. Thornberry (Ed.), *Developmental theories of crime and delinquency.* New Brunswick, NJ: Transaction Books.

Cotten, N. U., Resnick, J., Browne, D. C., Martin, S. L., McCarraher, D. R., & Woods, J. (1994). Aggression and fighting behavior among African-American adolescents: Individual and family factors. *American Journal of Public Health, 84,* 618–622.

Dishion, T. J., Patterson, G. R., Stoolmiller, M., & Skinner, M. L. (1991). Family, school, and behavioral antecedents to early adolescent involvement with antisocial peers. *Developmental Psychology, 27,* 172–180.

Dodge, K. A., Bates, J. E., & Pettit, G. S. (1990). Mechanisms in the cycle of violence. *Science, 250,* 1678–1683.

Dodge, K. A., Pettit, G. S., McGlaskey, C. L., & Brown, M. M. (1986). Social competence in children. *Monographs of the Society for Research in Child Development* [Serial No. 213], *51*(2), 1–85.

Dodge, K. A., Price, J. M., Coie, J. D., Christopoulos, C. (1990). On the development of aggressive dyadic relationships in boys' peer groups. *Human Development, 33,* 260–270.

Dumas, J. (in press). Home and school correlates of early at-risk status: A transactional perspective. In R. F. Kronick (Ed.), *At-risk youth: Theory, practice, and reform.* New York: Garland.

Elliott, D. S. (1994). Serious violent offenders: Onset, developmental course, and termination: The American Society of Criminology 1993 presidential address. *Criminology, 32,* 1–21.

Elliott, D. S., Huizinga, D., & Ageton, S. S. (1985). *Explaining delinquency and drug use.* Beverly Hills, CA: Sage.

Elliott, D. S., & Voss, H. L. (1974). *Delinquency and dropout.* Lexington, MA: Lexington Books.

Fagot, B., Loeber, R., & Reid, J. B. (1988). Developmental conditions which facilitate men's learning of violence toward women. In G. W. Russell (Ed.), *Violence in intimate adult relationships.* New York: Spectrum.

Farrington, D. P. (1978). The family background of aggressive youths. In L. A. Hersov, M. Berger, & D. Schaffer (Eds.), *Aggression and antisocial behavior in childhood and adolescence* (pp. 73–93). Oxford: Pergamon.

Farrington, D. P. (1989). Early predictors of adolescent aggression and adult violence. *Violence and Victims, 4,* 79–100.

Farrington, D. P. (1991). Childhood aggression and adult violence: Early precursors and life outcomes. In D. J. Pepler & K. H. Rubin (Eds.), *The development and treatment of childhood aggression* (pp. 5–29). Hillsdale, NJ: Lawrence Erlbaum.

Farrington, D. P. (1993). Understanding and preventing bullying. In M. Tonry (Ed.), *Crime and justice: Vol. 17* (pp. 381–458). Chicago: University of Chicago Press.

Farrington, D. P. (in press). Later life outcomes of truants in the Cambridge Study. In I. Berg & J. Nursten (Eds.), *Unwillingly to school* (4th ed.). London: Gaskell.

Farrington, D. P., & West, D. J. (1971). A comparison between early delinquents and young aggressives. *British Journal of Criminology, 11,* 341–358.

Fergusson, D. M., Horwood, J., & Lynskey, M. T. (1994). The comorbidities of adolescent problem behaviors: A latent class model. *Journal of Abnormal Child Psychology, 22,* 339–354.

Frick, P. J., Lahey, B. B., Loeber, R., Tannenbaum, L., Van Horn, Y., Christ, M. A. G., Hart, E. A., & Hanson, K. (1993). Oppositional defiant disorder and conduct disorder: A meta-analytic review of factor analyses and cross-validation in a clinic sample. *Clinical Psychology Review, 13,* 319–340.

Garofalo, J., Siegel, L., & Laub, J. H. (1987). School-related victimization among adolescents: An analysis of National Crime Survey narratives. *Journal of Quantitative Criminology, 3,* 321–338.

Gottfredson, G. D., & Gottfredson, D. C. (1985). *Victimization in schools.* New York: Plenum.

Gottfredson, M. R., & Hirschi, T. (1994). A general theory of adolescent problem behavior: Problems and prospects. In R. D. Ketterlinus & M. E. Lamb (Eds.), *Adolescent problem behaviors: Issues and research.* Hillsdale, NJ: Lawrence Erlbaum.

Haapasalo, J., & Tremblay, R. E. (1994). Physically aggressive boys from age 6 to 12: Family background, parenting behavior, and prediction of delinquency. *Development and Psychopathology, 8,* 443–455.

Hämäläinen, M., & Pulkkinen, L. (1995). Aggressive and non-prosocial behaviour as precursors to criminality. *Studies on Crime and Crime Prevention, 4,* 6–21.

Hamburg, B. A. (1995). President's report. In *William T. Grant Foundation annual report* (pp. 1–29). New York: William T. Grant Foundation.

Hausman, A. J., Spivak, H., & Prothrow-Stith, D. (1994). Adolescents' knowledge and attitudes about and experience with violence. *Journal of Adolescent Health, 15,* 400–406.

Herrnstein, R. J. (1961). Relative and absolute strength of response as a function of frequency of reinforcement. *Journal of the Experimental Analysis of Behavior, 4,* 267–272.

Hotaling, G. T., Straus, M. A., & Lincoln, A. J. (1989). Intrafamily violence and crime and violence outside the family. In L. Ohlin & M. Tonry (Eds.), *Family violence* (pp. 315–375). Chicago: University of Chicago Press.

Huizinga, D. (1995). Developmental sequences in delinquency: Dynamic typologies. In L. J. Crokett & A. C. Crouter (Eds.), *Pathways through adolescence* (pp. 15–34). Mahwah, NJ: Lawrence Erlbaum.

Johnston, L. D., O'Malley, P. M., & Bachman, J. G. (1993). *Monitoring the future study for goal 6 of the national education goals: A special report for the National Education Goals Panel.* Ann Arbor, MI: University of Michigan, Institute for Social Research.

Kingery, P. M., Pruitt, B. E., & Heuberger, G. (1996). A profile of rural Texas and adolescents who carry handguns to school. *Journal of School Health, 66,* 18–22.

Kirkpatrick, K. (1978). "Deviant behavior of children in multiple settings." Unpublished master's thesis, University of Oregon, Eugene, OR.

Kolko, D. J., & Kazdin, A. E. (1993). Emotional/behavioral problems in clinic and nonclinic children: Correspondence among child, parent and teacher reports. *Journal of Child Psychology and Psychiatry, 34,* 991–1006.

Krohn, M. D., Thornberry, T. P., Collins-Hall, L., & Lizotte, A. J. (1995). School dropout, delinquent behavior, and drug use: An examination of the causes and

124   Rolf Loeber & Magda Stouthamer-Loeber

consequences of dropping out of school. In H. B. Kaplan (Ed.), *Drugs, crime and other deviant adaptations: Longitudinal studies* (pp. 163–183). New York: Plenum.

Lagerspetz, K. M. J., Björkqvist, K., & Peltonen, T. (1988). Is indirect aggression typical of females? Gender differences in aggressiveness in 11 to 12 year old children. *Aggressive Behavior, 14,* 403–414.

Le Blanc, M., Biron, L., & Pronovost, L. (1979). Psycho-social development and delinquency evolution. *Adolescence, 15,* 126–159.

Le Blanc, M., Côté, G., & Loeber, R. (1991). Temporal paths in delinquency: Stability, regression and progression analyzed with panel data from an adolescent and a delinquent sample. *Canadian Journal of Criminology, 33,* 23–44.

Lewis, M. (1990). Models of developmental psychopathology. In M. Lewis & S. M. Miller (Eds.), *Handbook of developmental psychopathology* (pp. 15–27). New York: Plenum.

Loeber, R. (1982). The stability of antisocial and delinquent child behavior. *Child Development, 53,* 1431–1446.

Loeber, R. (1988). Natural histories of conduct problems, delinquency, and associated substance use: Evidence for developmental progressions. In B. B. Lahey & A. E. Kazdin (Eds.), *Advances in clinical child psychology: Vol. 11* (pp. 73–124). New York: Plenum.

Loeber, R., DeLamatre, M., Keenan, K., & Zhang, Q. (in press). A prospective replication of developmental pathways in disruptive and delinquent behavior. In R. Cairns (Ed.), *The individual as a focus in developmental research.* Thousand Oaks, CA: Sage.

Loeber, R., & Dishion, T. J. (1984). Boys who fight at home and in school: Family conditions influencing cross-setting consistency and discontinuity. *Journal of Consulting and Clinical Psychology, 52,* 759–768.

Loeber, R., Green, S. M., Keenan, K., & Navratil, J. (1995). "The development of antisocial behavior in clinic-referred girls." Unpublished manuscript, Western Psychiatric Institute and Clinic, University of Pittsburgh, Pittsburgh, PA.

Loeber, R., & Hay, D. H. (1994). Developmental approaches to aggression and conduct problems. In M. Rutter & D. H. Hay (Eds.), *Development through life: A handbook for clinicians* (pp. 488–515). Oxford: Blackwell.

Loeber, R., Keenan, K., & Zhang, Q. (1997). Boys' experimentation and persistence in developmental pathways toward serious delinquency. *Journal of Child and Family Studies, 6,* 321–357.

Loeber, R., & Schmaling, K. (1985). Empirical evidence for overt and covert patterns of antisocial conduct problems. *Journal of Abnormal Child Psychology, 13,* 337–352.

Loeber, R., & Smalley, M. (1995). *Unpublished data analyses on the longitudinal relation between boys' aggression and school transition.* Western Psychiatric Institute and Clinic, University of Pittsburgh, Pittsburgh, PA.

Loeber, R., & Stouthamer-Loeber, M. (1986). Family factors as correlates and predictors of juvenile conduct problems and delinquency. In N. Morris & M. Tonry (Eds.), *Crime and justice: An annual review of research* (Vol. 7). Chicago: University of Chicago Press.

Loeber, R., Stouthamer-Loeber, M., & Green, S. M. (1991). Age at onset of problem behavior in boys, and later disruptive and delinquent behavior. *Criminal Behavior & Mental Health, 1,* 229–246.

Loeber, R., Tremblay, R. E., Gagnon, C., & Charlebois, P. (1989). Continuity and desistance in disruptive boys' early fighting in school. *Development and Psychopathology, 1*(9), 39–50.

Loeber, R., Weissman, W., & Reid, J. B. (1983). Family interactions of assaultive adolescents, stealers, and nondelinquents. *Journal of Abnormal Child Psychology, 11,* 1–14.

Loeber, R., Wung, P., Keenan, K., Giroux, B., Stouthamer-Loeber, M., & Van Kammen, W. B. (1993). Developmental pathways in disruptive child behavior. *Development and Psychopathology, 5,* 101–132.

Maccoby, E. E., & Jacklin, C. H. (1974). *The psychology of sex differences.* Stanford, CA: Stanford University Press.

Mischel, W. (1984). Delay of gratification as process and as person variable in development. In D. Magnusson & P. Allen (Eds.), *Human development: An interactional perspective* (pp. 149–166). New York: Academic.

Moffitt, T. E. (1993). Adolescence-limited and life-cycle-persistent antisocial behavior: A developmental taxonomy. *Psychology Review, 100,* 674–701.

Olweus, D. (1978). *Aggression in the schools.* New York: Wiley.

Olweus, D. (1979). Stability of aggressive reaction patterns in males. *Psychological Bulletin, 86,* 852–857.

Olweus, D. (1980). Familial and temperamental determinants of aggressive behavior in adolescent boys: A causal analysis. *Developmental Psychology, 1,* 644–660.

Olweus, D. (1984). Aggressors and their victims: Bullying at school. In N. Frude & H. Gault (Eds.), *Disruptive behaviour in schools* (pp. 57–76). Chichester, England: John Wiley & Sons.

Olweus, D. (1991). Bully/victim problems among school children: Basic facts and effects of a school-based intervention program. In D. J. Pepler & K. H. Rubin (Eds.), *The development and treatment of childhood aggression* (pp. 411–455). Hillsdale, NJ: Lawrence Erlbaum.

Patterson, G. R. (1980). Children who steal. In T. Hirschi & M. Gottfredson (Eds.), *Understanding crime: Current theory and research. Vol. 18* (pp. 73–90). London: Sage.

Patterson, G. R. (1982). *A social learning approach, Vol. 3: Coercive family process.* Eugene, OR: Castalia.

Patterson, G. R. (1992). Developmental changes in antisocial behavior. In R. DeV. Peters, R. J. McMahon, & V. L. Quinsey (Eds.), *Aggression and violence throughout the life span* (pp. 52–82). London: Sage.

Patterson, G. R., Dishion, T. J., & Bank, L. (1984). Family interaction: A process model of deviancy training. *Aggressive Behavior, 10,* 253–268.

Patterson, G. R., Reid, J. B., & Dishion, T. J. (1992). *Antisocial boys: A social interaction approach, Vol. 4.* Eugene, OR: Castalia.

Pepler, D. J., Corter, C., & Abramovitch, R. (1982). Social relations among children: Comparison of sibling and peer interaction. In K. H. Rubin & H. S. Ross (Eds.), *Peer relationships and social skills in childhood* (pp. 209–227). New York: Springer-Verlag.

Pepler, D. J., & Craig, W. M. (1995). A peek behind the fence: Naturalistic observations of aggressive children with remote audiovisual recording. *Developmental Psychology, 31,* 548–553.

Pepler, D. J., & Slaby, R. G. (1994). Theoretical and developmental perspectives on youth and violence. In L. D. Eron, J. H. Gentry, & P. Schlegel (Eds.), *Reason to hope: A psychological perspective on violence and youth.* Washington, DC: American Psychological Association.

Perry, D. G., Perry, L. C., & Boldizar, J. P. (1990). Learning of aggression. In M. Lewis & S. Miller (Eds.), *Handbook of developmental psychopathology* (pp. 135–146). New York: Plenum.

Pettit, G. S., Bates, J. E., & Dodge, K. A. (1993). Family interaction patterns and children's conduct problems at home and school: A longitudinal perspective. *School Psychology Review, 22,* 403–420.

Pulkkinen, L., & Tremblay, R. E. (1992). Patterns of boys' social adjustment in two cultures and at different ages: A longitudinal perspective. *International Journal of Behavioral Development, 15,* 527–553.

Ramsey, E., Patterson, G. R., & Walker, H. M. (1990). Generalization of the antisocial trait from home to school settings. *Journal of Applied Developmental Psychology, 11,* 209–223.

Robins, L. N., & Ratcliff, K. S. (1980). The long-term outcome of truancy. In L. Hersov & I. Berg (Eds.), *Out of school* (pp. 65–83). New York: John Wiley & Sons.

Rogosch, F. A., Cicchetti, D., & Aber, J. L. (1995). The role of child maltreatment in early deviations in cognitive and affective processing abilities and later peer relationship problems. *Development and Psychopathology, 7,* 591–609.

Rutter, M., & Giller, H. (1983). *Juvenile delinquency: Trends and perspectives.* Middlesex, England: Penguin.

Sameroff, A. (1975). Transactional models in early social relations. *Human Development, 18,* 65–79.

Smith, C., & Thornberry, T. P. (1995). The relationship between childhood maltreatment and adolescent involvement in delinquency. *Criminology, 33,* 451–477.

Sommers, I., & Baskin, D. R. (1994). Factors related to female adolescent initiation into violent street crime. *Youth and Society, 25,* 468–489.

Stattin, H., & Magnusson, D. (1989). The role of early aggressive behavior in the frequency, seriousness, and types of later crime. *Journal of Consulting and Clinical Psychology, 57,* 710–718.

Storashak, E. A., Bellanti, C. J., & Bierman, K. L. (1996). The quality of sibling relationships and the development of social competence and behavior control in aggressive children. *Developmental Psychology, 32,* 79–89.

Strassberg, Z., Dodge, K. A., Pettit, G. S., & Bates, J. E. (1994). Spanking in the home and children's subsequent aggression toward kindergarten peers. *Development and Psychopathology, 6,* 445–461.

Thornberry, T. P., Moore, M., & Christenson, R. L. (1985). The effect of dropping out of high school on subsequent criminal behavior. *Criminology, 23,* 3–18.

Tremblay, R. E., Loeber, R., Gagnon, C., Charlebois, P., Larivée, S., & Le Blanc, M. (1991). Disruptive boys with stable and unstable high fighting behavior patterns during junior elementary school. *Journal of Abnormal Child Psychology, 19,* 285–300.

Van Kammen, W. B., & Loeber, R. (1995). *Adolescents and their guns: Relationship to delinquency and victimization.* Presentation at the meeting of the American Society of Criminology, November 1995, Boston, MA.

Verhulst, F. C., & Van der Ende, J. (1991). Four-year follow-up of teacher-reported problem behaviours. *Psychological Medicine, 21,* 965–977.

Warr, M. (1996). Organization and instigation in delinquent groups. *Criminology, 32,* 11–37.

Webster, D. W., Gainer, P. S., & Champion, H. R. (1993). Weapon carrying among inner-city junior high school students: Defensive behavior versus aggressive delinquency. *American Journal of Public Health, 83,* 1604–1608.

Widom, C. S. (1989). Does violence beget violence? *Psychological Bulletin, 106,* 3–28.

Widom, C. S. (1994). Childhood victimized and risk for adolescent problem behaviors. In M. E. Lamb & R. Ketterlinus (Eds.), *Adolescent problem behaviors.* Hillsdale, NJ: Lawrence Erlbaum.

5. The Interdependence of School Violence with Neighborhood and Family Conditions

JOHN H. LAUB & JANET L. LAURITSEN

Introduction

Despite the long-standing problem of school violence, relatively few comprehensive studies of violence in and around schools have been conducted. In sharp contrast, the links between neighborhood and family characteristics and violence have been the topic of extensive investigation in criminological research. In this chapter we summarize what is known about these relationships and integrate these findings with the literature on the study of school violence. Thus, our first objective is to show how and why an analysis of family and neighborhood conditions is essential to an understanding of school violence.

A second and equally important goal is to discuss the limitations of the common understanding of school violence. The conventional wisdom holds that school violence is a reflection of violence in the broader social context, that is, violence is imported into a school by the students, and by intruders from the neighborhood surrounding the school (see, e.g., Reiss & Roth, 1993). Although the evidence we will review finds this to be generally true, we will also find that the relationship between neighborhood crime and school violence is a complex one, and other factors (e.g., school context) must also be taken into account. Our conclusions warrant a sense of optimism concerning the development of school-based programs to reduce violence in and around schools. However, the level of optimism very much depends on the extent to which the complexity of the relationship is understood.

What follows is an integration of the literature on neighborhood and family conditions with the literature on school violence. Drawing on Bronfenbrenner's (1979) "ecological" perspective on human development, our view is that schools and students attending school are embedded in a broader social developmental context. Our focus, then, is on "persons in context," and it is our assumption that individual behavior is the product of the interaction between individual development and social contexts (e.g., the family, school, and neighborhood). For the purposes of this chapter, "violence" is defined as "the threat of or use of physical force with the intention of causing physical injury, damage, or intimidation." (For a more detailed discussion of definitions of violence, see Chapter 1 of this volume.) We will consider both violence students experience in school as well as violence they experience going to and from school, although little research has included the latter topic.[1]

Before we begin our review of the literature, an important analytical issue merits brief discussion. Criminologists pay close attention to the "level" of analysis used in studies of violence. Much existing research is conducted either at the individual (i.e., "micro") level or at the aggregate (i.e., "macro") level of analysis. (See Sampson & Lauritsen, 1994, for an extensive review.) Research focusing on the individual level of analysis asks what individual characteristics make that person more likely to commit violent acts or be victimized by violence. Both perpetration and victimization have been studied in this respect, and each has its own extensive literature.

When, however, the objective of the research is to describe the characteristics that distinguish neighborhoods with high rates of violence from those with low rates, then macrolevel analysis is used. The macrolevel analysis treats aggregate units such as neighborhoods, cities, or schools as the topic of inquiry and focuses on what it is about their respective social structures and cultures that produces different rates of violence. Factors that prove to be strongly related to neighborhood differences in violence are not necessarily strongly related to individual differences in violence, and vice versa, as we shall see. Therefore, inferences should not be made across levels of analysis.[2]

More advanced studies of violence employ multilevel analyses, in order to separate the unique influences of individual characteristics from those of neighborhoods or other social contexts. This analytical issue is familiar to educational researchers who investigate how a given classroom or school may influence students' academic achievement, independent of individual ability. Our review of the literature on violence is designed to provide insight into a similar question: What are the independent effects of specific neighborhoods, families, and schools on individuals' experiences with violence? Since not enough multilevel studies have yet been performed to clearly answer this question, we have instead assembled the best available evidence from a variety of studies (and levels of analysis) in order to discuss the interdependence of school violence with neighborhood and family conditions.

Neighborhoods and Violence

An extensive and longstanding literature exists, in the field of criminology, on the relationship between neighborhood characteristics and violent crime. Recent reviews of this research have summarized in detail the importance of community influences such as poverty and socioeconomic inequality; racial and ethnic composition; family composition; housing density and population turnover; and neighborhood disorder and neighborhood change (e.g., Sampson & Lauritsen, 1994). In this section, we focus on what is known about neighborhood differences in violence and discuss how these factors influence individuals' risk for performing or suffering violent acts.

Studies of neighborhood differences in rates of violent crimes (e.g., homicide, robbery, assault) traditionally rely on official data such as those in police reports and arrest rates. For an event to be recorded as a violent crime, it must be known to the police and regarded as a criminal event. Because there are often variations in victim reporting of crime and police practices of arrest and crime recording among different neighborhoods, these data may be incomplete. Fortunately, an alternative source of crime data is available for violent crimes such as robbery, aggravated assault, and rape. The National Crime Victimization Survey, or NCVS (U.S. Census Bureau) is an ongoing study designed to measure the extent of personal and household victimization in the United States. Interviews are conducted at six-month intervals with all household members 12 years of age and older in the sample. Using data, it is possible to estimate the number of violent victimizations not counted in official police data. Therefore, throughout our review we will note when conclusions based on official data differ from those based on self-report surveys.

Social Disorganization Theory

Research on the relationship between communities and crime begins by asking why certain neighborhoods have higher crime rates than others. One of the most influential explanations of neighborhood differences in crime, social disorganization theory, argues that three factors are crucial to understanding this variation. Low socioeconomic status, high population turnover, and racial and ethnic heterogeneity in an urban community are closely associated with high neighborhood crime rates because, it is argued, these factors have an impact on the ability of the community members to organize to achieve common goals. Neighborhoods with greater levels of the factors just mentioned are described as more "socially disorganized," meaning they contain relatively fewer social resources and social ties. This, in turn, affects the ability of residents to exert informal social control over delinquency, crime, and violence (Shaw & McKay, 1942/1969).

Research derived from this perspective has shown that certain urban neighborhoods have significantly higher crime rates and other social problems (including health problems), and, more important, these neighborhoods tend to have the highest levels of problems in the city, regardless of population composition. Such neighborhoods are often located near old industrial areas and are characterized by physical deterioration; a large number of rental properties and a low level of home ownership; residents of low socioeconomic status; high residential turnover; and a high percentage of immigrants and ethnic minorities (see Shaw & McKay, 1942/1969).

The influence of poverty on violence has preoccupied the majority of neighborhood studies since Shaw and McKay (1942/1969) demonstrated that economic conditions were highly correlated with juvenile delinquency rates in Chicago during the first part of the twentieth century. Chicago neighborhoods with greater proportions of families on relief, lower percentages of families owning homes, and with lower median rental values were found to have significantly higher rates of juvenile offending. Since then, researchers have studied a number of relevant factors across a variety of urban settings in order to discover the reasons for this relationship. The primary issue is whether poverty and economic deprivation in and of themselves have independent and direct effects on neighborhood violence, or whether these factors are associated with violence because they are related to other conditions typically found in disadvantaged neighborhoods.

Recent literature confirms Shaw and McKay's findings that disadvantaged neighborhoods experience higher rates of crime and violence. For example, Block (1979) found the same factors that predicted juvenile delinquency in the first part of the twentieth century were also significant predictors of homicide, robbery, and aggravated assault in the 1970s. Similar patterns are found when researchers are interested in predicting gang homicide rates. Curry and Spergel (1988) found the percentage of neighborhood residents living below the poverty level, the unemployment rate, and the level of mortgage investments in a neighborhood predicted the rate of gang homicides, and poverty continued to remain a significant factor even when factors such as the racial and ethnic composition of the neighborhood were taken into account. Such results suggest that economic conditions may have a direct effect on certain types of violence.

However, analyses of other communities, and studies using alternative data sources, have not always had the same results. Messner and Tardiff (1986) studied Manhattan neighborhoods and found that although poverty was certainly correlated with homicide rates, the correlation was no longer statistically significant once the percentage of African Americans in the population, as well as the divorce rate, were considered. They concluded that poverty and inequality alone are insufficient to account for neighborhood differences in violence, but that poverty in combination with a high level of family instability appears to be important. Similarly, Sampson's (1985, 1986) analyses of self-reported NCVS data (which includes data from more than one city) also suggest poverty alone has weak effects on violence. Instead, a neighborhood's family structure (as reflected, for example, in the percentage of households headed by females and the percentage divorced), as well as housing density and population turnover, appeared to be more closely related to violent victimization.

Shaw and McKay (1942/1969) themselves argued that poverty per se does not have a simple, direct effect on crime rates. Although they clearly showed that poorer communities have higher levels of crime, they also noted that crime rates did not rise in Chicago during the Great Depression, as one might have expected if economic deprivation was directly related to crime. Instead, they argued that neighborhoods with residents of low socioeconomic status tend to experience more difficulty in establishing the formal and informal social ties within the community necessary to controlling crime and violence. Recent evidence confirms this interpretation (see Bursik & Grasmick, 1993; Sampson & Groves, 1989). Socioeconomic conditions are strong predictors of neighborhood violence, particularly when they appear in conjunction with high rates of neighborhood and family instability.

Neighborhood instability in the form of high residential turnover is also an important predictor of high rates of violent crime. In disadvantaged communities, the majority of residents tend not to be committed to the community, but rather want to move away as soon as possible (see Bursik & Grasmick, 1993; Kornhauser, 1978; Shaw & McKay, 1942/1969; Skogan, 1986; Taub, Taylor, & Dunham, 1984). High population turnover in a neighborhood leads to reduced participation in local institutions, which in turn produces institutional disruption. Communities lacking strong local institutions such as well-functioning schools, strong churches, and successful businesses have a reduced capacity to exert informal social control over residents' behavior. High population turnover combined with population loss is especially problematic for neighborhood institutions (see Korn-hauser, 1978).

Several studies have documented that neighborhoods with high rates of population change experience greater levels of violence. For instance, Sampson (1985, 1986) found self-reported rates of violent victimization were greater in neighborhoods with higher rates of residential turnover, even af-ter taking into account other predictors of violence. Smith and Jarjoura (1988), analyzing data from neighborhoods in three cities, found residential mobility predicted rates of community violence, but only in lower income areas. In a longitudinal study explicitly designed to capture the types of changes facing urban communities, Taylor and Covington (1988) studied 277 Baltimore neighborhoods from 1970 through 1980. They reported low-income neighborhoods that were either "worsening" (with respect to in-creasing poverty concentration) or gentrifying (with increasing proportions of affluent residents, as measured by owner-occupied housing and higher family income) also experienced higher rates of violent crime. Thus, com-munity change appears to be an important component for understanding changes in violence rates, but the underlying mechanisms are different for different neighborhoods. In increasingly poor neighborhoods, violence ap-pears to be related to increased relative deprivation (i.e., relative status changes); in gentrifying neighborhoods, violence appears to be related to in-creased social disorganization (i.e., changes in relative stability).

Shaw and McKay (1942/1969) also argued that racial and ethnic hetero-geneity are strongly correlated with crime. However, several of their find-ings led them to conclude that this association was not due to any charac-teristic of a specific ethnic or racial group. Instead, they argued that racial and ethnic composition were predictors of crime rates because they, in turn, were highly correlated with patterns of urban growth and change, and hence with social disorganization.

Three findings led them to this interpretation. First, neighborhoods near decaying industrial areas maintained the highest rates of juvenile delin-quency despite nearly complete ethnic turnover during the early twenti-eth century. For example, certain neighborhoods in Chicago maintained the highest crime rates in the city, regardless of whether the neighborhood population was predominantly Italian, German, Polish, or African Ameri-can. Second, as immigrant groups migrated to other areas of the city, crime rates did not increase in those areas. Third, the crime rate for each racial or ethnic group varied across different types of neighborhoods in the city.

Since these findings appeared, criminologists investigating the effect of neighborhood racial and ethnic composition have continued to debate the causal significance of the relationship. Contemporary research continues to find that the percentage of African Americans in disadvantaged urban neighborhoods correlates with neighborhood violence rates. However, findings are mixed regarding whether or not this racial composition is directly and independently correlated with crime rates. If it is, this suggests there may be something unique to disadvantaged African American urban communities that contributes to higher violence rates.

This issue clearly has not been resolved. Several studies have found a strong relationship between racial and ethnic composition of a community and rates of violence (e.g., Roncek, 1981), whereas others (e.g., Curry & Spergel, 1988; Messner & Tardiff, 1986; Sampson, 1985) suggest other conditions in the neighborhood – especially family composition – account for this effect. Because of the methodological limitations of most existing community-level studies, the causal relationship between racial and ethnic composition and neighborhood violence is not yet completely understood (Sampson & Lauritsen, 1994).[3]

Several additional neighborhood conditions have also been found to affect violence rates. For instance, Sampson (1983) found that neighborhoods with higher proportions of multi-unit dwellings (e.g., apartment houses) had higher rates of assault and robbery than communities similar in other respects but with fewer multi-unit dwellings. Roncek's (1981) analyses of city blocks in San Diego and Cleveland also found that population density and the percentage of households headed by single adults (with or without children) were associated with greater violence, regardless of the age and racial composition of the neighborhood. Other studies (e.g., Smith & Jarjoura, 1988) support the notion that heterogenous population and housing density contribute to increased crime because in such communities residents are less likely to know their neighbors or to engage in what are referred to as "guardianship" behaviors (e.g., keeping an eye on each other's property) (Roncek, 1981; Taylor & Gottfredson, 1986).

In sum, factors such as low socioeconomic status, high population turnover, racial and ethnic heterogeneity, and high housing density are strong predictors of an area's violence rate because these conditions lower the neighborhood's capacity for social organization and, hence, for exerting informal social control. As we have noted, there is nothing inherent in low socioeconomic status or racial and ethnic composition in and of themselves that results in higher crime rates. However, when low socioeconomic status is combined with high residential turnover or population loss, the consequence is typically fewer formal and informal social networks within the neighborhood, as well as a lack of relationships with other neighborhoods in the city or with city government (Bursik, 1988; Kornhauser, 1978; Sampson, 1988).[4]

A neighborhood deficient in social networks has greater difficulty supervising or controlling adolescent peer groups, such as gangs and street-corner groups, who are likely to become involved in aggressive confrontations (Sampson & Groves, 1989). A relative lack of informal social ties also means residents are less likely to recognize strangers in the neighborhood, to intervene in violent situations on behalf of their neighbors or their neighbors' property, or to engage in guardianship activities (Skogan, 1986; Taylor, Gottfredson, & Brower, 1984). A community's ability to use informal social controls appears to be the key to understanding local levels of violence and disorder.

Participation in more formal networks such as neighborhood associations, school or church organizations, or local political organizations tends also to be lower in these communities. This lack of formal involvement is symbolic of the lack of community organization. This also contributes to reduced numbers of informal friendships within the neighborhood, which, as we have noted, results in reduced capacity for social control (Hunter, 1974; Kornhauser, 1978). Such neighborhoods develop a reputation as communities where no one "cares" enough to become involved with others, either formally with their community or informally with their neighbors. Wilson and Kelling (1982) have argued that this type of atmosphere can contribute to violence in general and to gang and drug activity in particular, because the community, by failing to sanction local offenders, attracts more offenders from elsewhere.

Without strong formal and informal social ties among adults within a neighborhood, it is unlikely strong ties to organizations and resources outside the neighborhood will develop. A lack of external ties in turn leaves the community relatively powerless to influence public policy decisions that will vitally affect neighborhood conditions. Policy decisions by the city government concerning such things as municipal code enforcement, maintenance of city property, closures of public schools, and withdrawal of other public services (e.g., health care) can further destabilize weakened communities. Such actions, in turn, negatively influence the business climate, discouraging businesses from locating there and "drying up" mortgage funds, which further escalates the neighborhood's deterioration. (See also Sampson & Lauritsen, 1994, for a more detailed review.)

Thus, a lack of informal and formal ties within a neighborhood and the lack of external ties influence the ability of community members to realize common goals, including the control of residents' criminal or violent behaviors. Moreover, this dynamic might also operate in the opposite direction: weak or ineffective external ties might result in city policy decisions that make it even more difficult for internal ties to form, thus exacerbating the problems of crime and violence.

Similarly, violence in a community can change the population composition of a neighborhood, increasing social disorganization (Bursik, 1986). For example, as crime increases, fear of crime in the neighborhood may also increase. Skogan (1986) describes how a higher level of fear of crime can lead to a spiral of decay as individuals withdraw from community life. This withdrawal further weakens social ties and hence informal social control, and may also produce deteriorating business conditions as customers become less willing to enter the neighborhood. Under these circumstances, people who are able to move away do so, and the result can be the increased social isolation of the disadvantaged community (see Wilson, 1987).

Neighborhood Composition

The effect of neighborhood composition on individual community members has been much discussed in the literature on violence and other developmental outcomes such as crime, drug use, and mental health problems. Do the neighborhood characteristics we have been examining affect behavior, or are they instead simply the result of economic sorting and other types of selection processes? Although it is not extensive, there is an emerging literature that examines this issue.[5] For instance, in their multilevel analysis of more than 3,000 individuals living in 321 different city blocks, Gottfredson, McNeil, and Gottfredson (1991) found that neighborhood population composition had a very small effect on individual delinquent behavior, once the effects of individual characteristics were taken into account.

Alternatively, in a study of the effects of neighborhood composition on child and adolescent development using data from the Infant Health and Development Program and the Panel Study of Income Dynamics, Brooks-Gunn and her colleagues (1993) found "reasonably powerful neighborhood effects . . . on childhood IQ, teenage births, and school-leaving, even after the differences in the socioeconomic characteristics of individual families are adjusted for" (p. 353). In addition, they found the absence of affluent neighbors had a much stronger effect on child development than the presence of low-income neighbors (see also Jencks & Mayer, 1990). Interestingly,

they also found white teenagers benefited more from the presence of affluent neighbors than did African American teenagers.[6]

Recently, Elliott and his colleagues (1996) examined the idea that the effects of poverty on adolescent development (e.g., prosocial competence,
conventional friendships, and problem behavior) are strongly influenced
by the organizational structure and culture of the neighborhood. Using
path analyses and multilevel causal modeling, these authors found the effects of neighborhood disadvantage in Denver, Colorado, and Chicago,
Illinois, varied with the kind of social organization and culture that
emerged in these neighborhoods as the residents interacted with one another. Although atypical, a few disadvantaged neighborhoods had relatively high levels of social control, strong informal support networks, and
high consensus on community norms and values. Under these organizational conditions, the level of poverty no longer had a negative influence
on adolescent development. Still, when individual characteristics were
taken into account, the effects of neighborhood composition and neighborhood organization on adolescent development were relatively modest.
More multilevel studies are needed to confirm these findings.

In the meantime, we do know neighborhoods have substantial influence
on schools as well as the students attending them. (See the section of this
chapter entitled "Neighborhoods, Families, and School Violence.") Some
research has contended that "the vast majority of students attend neighborhood schools and because school funding is related directly to family
and neighborhood wealth, public schools tend to be stratified by class,
race, and ethnicity . . . Therefore, student bodies reflect the composition of
the neighborhood" (National Research Council, 1993, p. 68). (Some objections to this view are also noted in a later section of this chapter.) Thus,
"white flight," zoning changes, and other housing policies can affect the
composition of a neighborhood, which in turn influences the schools (e.g.,
level of resources, quality of teachers, etc.) and rates of violent behavior
within the schools.

Families and Violence

The relationship between family characteristics and violence has also been
studied at various levels of analysis. From the perspective of the individual, researchers ask what characteristics of family structure and family
functioning contribute to an individual's disposition to be violent or to be
victimized by violence. A broad literature exists on this question, including extensive research on violence between spouses and among siblings,

the intergenerational transmission of violence, and the consequences of child abuse and child neglect. (See, e.g., Fagan & Browne, 1994; Loeber & Stouthamer-Loeber, 1986; Widom, 1989.) The relevant aspects of this literature for understanding school violence are reviewed elsewhere in this volume (see Chapter 4).

Here we focus our attention on how family composition and conditions within the neighborhood influence rates of violence within the community. As noted previously, family composition is a strong predictor of neighborhood violence rates. Neighborhoods where many heads of households are women or single adults, and neighborhoods with high divorce rates, have significantly greater levels of violence, including child abuse (Block, 1979; Garbarino & Crouter, 1978; Messner & Tardiff, 1986; Sampson, 1985; Smith & Jarjoura, 1988). In fact, several analyses suggest family composition has a stronger direct effect on violence than factors such as poverty or racial composition (Sampson, 1985).

How does the distribution of types of family composition in a neighborhood contribute to increased rates of violence in the community? Recall that such studies focus on the neighborhood rather than the individual. Therefore these findings do not necessarily indicate that individual children from single-parent homes experience more violence than those from two-parent homes. Regardless of their own family circumstances, youths living in a neighborhood with more single-parent homes are more likely to be victims and perpetrators of violence than youths living in predominantly two-parent neighborhoods. This finding can be interpreted in terms of the social disorganization theory, since neighborhoods in which most households are headed by single adults are also neighborhoods with fewer informal social ties.

Delinquency and aggression among children are known to be related to their parents' ability to care about, monitor, supervise, and punish the children's antisocial behavior appropriately (Patterson, 1980). However, as children age, they are increasingly less likely to be under their parents' direct supervision. Effective monitoring of adolescents' behavior when they are away from home requires sets of acquaintance and family networks. Much adolescent crime occurs in a peer-group context, when adolescents are not under the watchful eyes of their parents. Thus, in neighborhoods with relatively fewer available adults, the level of supervision is inevitably decreased. Relatedly, in neighborhoods where residents do not generally trust one another or know each other and their children, controlling adolescents' behavior becomes especially difficult. Unlike either single- or two-parent families in more organized neighborhoods, parents in these communities tend to be socially isolated from each other and are forced to rely on personal resources in raising their children. Thus, even if parents possess good parenting skills, the tasks of child rearing and of controlling adolescents' behavior in socially disorganized communities is much more difficult than in better-organized communities (Sampson, 1992). In Furstenberg's (1990) view, parenting skills interact with the community context of family structure. Furthermore, Coie and Jacobs (1993) argue "that in the most disadvantaged segments of urban communities, there is no critical mass of stable, achievement-oriented families to provide neighborhood cohesion, sanctions against maladaptive behavior, and support for basic community institutions" (p. 270).

Evidence supporting the idea that neighborhood characteristics can influence family functioning is found in Garbarino and Sherman's (1980) study of varying rates of child abuse in two neighborhoods matched on socioeconomic level and demographic composition. Taking into account differences in population composition, they found families in high-risk neighborhoods were exposed to "social impoverishment" – social isolation, sparse social networks, and weak systems of social support. Mothers in these high-risk neighborhoods were more apt to abuse their children than mothers in low-risk neighborhoods. (See also Garbarino & Kostelny, 1992.)

Extensive social ties with a community and firm embedment in those networks serve as a resource for both parents and their children. This involvement in community networks constitutes one's "social capital" (see Coleman, 1990; Sampson & Laub, 1993.) While "physical capital" generally refers to material resources, and "human capital" represents an individual's own skills and knowledge, social capital is a unique resource; it can be defined as the extent to which one has others to rely on for assistance and support. In terms of family management, increased social capital means residents share information about children and others in the neighborhood, thereby establishing community norms regarding acceptable and unacceptable behavior (Sampson, 1992). As Coleman (1991) notes, adequate social capital in the community is important for a child's success in school. Coleman writes: "The social capital of the community can to a considerable extent offset its absence in particular families in the community. For example, children from single-parent families are more like their two-parent counterparts in both achievement and in continuation in school when the schools are in communities with extensive social capital" (p. 10).

By recognizing the importance of social capital in children's lives and the fact that social networks and resources are not equally developed in all communities, the contextual effects of neighborhood conditions on individual behavior can be better understood.[7]

A cautionary note is necessary. Most research on family context has been restricted to the macrolevel. Consequently, it is possible some part of the relationship between family structure and neighborhood violence is due to a selection effect, since persons who live in single-adult households may possess individual characteristics that make them more likely to be involved in violence. This is not likely the case, however, as individual-level analyses do not report a very strong relationship between family structure and aggression (Loeber & Stouthamer-Loeber, 1986).

Research that focuses attention on how neighborhood conditions interact with family functioning is relatively rare, but most useful. In an intriguing study, Peeples and Loeber (1994) found a significant effect of neighborhood context on juvenile delinquency, despite taking into account both individual and family factors (e.g., degree of parental supervision). Similarly, Stern and Smith (1995) identified five factors that may have an impact on the family/delinquency nexus: economic hardship (i.e., poverty, low social class, job instability, and social dependence); a disadvantaged neighborhood; life distress; social isolation; and lack of partner support. Using data from the Rochester Youth Development Study, they found the addition of neighborhood characteristics doubled the amount of variance explained by family characteristics alone. More important, their analyses showed that the "disadvantaged neighborhood" factor had a direct effect on delinquency, as well as an indirect effect on family life (specifically, parent/child involvement).

Other studies have not confirmed these results. Robins (1966) found neighborhood factors did not predict juvenile antisocial behavior, once antisocial behavior by parents was taken into account. Clearly, more studies are needed of the relative effects of family functioning and individual characteristics within different neighborhood contexts before definitive conclusions can be drawn.[8]

In sum, the association between neighborhood family context and area levels of crime and violence, while not a primary focus of early macrotheories, has been well documented. Neighborhoods characterized predominantly by single-parent households tend to have fewer social resources to draw upon for supervising youths and monitoring their behavior. When neighborhoods lack sufficient social networks, adolescents growing up there have fewer opportunities to develop the necessary social capital to succeed in life. The consequence of these conditions for such neighborhoods is relative social isolation and a weak capacity to restrain many types of antisocial behavior (Sampson & Laub, 1993).

Although that is the case, it is important to point out that neighborhoods can promote positive development in children and adolescents. Just as a stable family can provide a protective or buffering influence on an impulsive child, a stable neighborhood can have a protective influence on dysfunctional families and individuals by providing resources and social support for healthy development. For example, network facilitation, life and social skills building, and support groups can improve parenting skills. Parent/child involvement is encouraged in a positive neighborhood environment, when parents have a supportive network (Stern & Smith, 1995). In addition, social norms and opportunity structures within the neighborhood specify that prosocial behaviors will be encouraged and rewarded and antisocial behaviors will be discouraged and sanctioned. (See Jessor, 1993, for an overview of this perspective.)

Neighborhoods, Families, and School Violence

It is apparent from the literature that a neighborhood's socioeconomic status, racial and ethnic composition, population turnover and loss, housing and population density, and family structure can affect parents' ability to raise their children to live safe and productive lives. It is not surprising that schools in such neighborhoods inherit the difficulties of the community as well as the problems of the children who live there. We have argued that social resources, informal networks, and social capital are key elements in understanding neighborhood differences in crime, disorder, and violence.

Despite pleas from many researchers who study school violence not to ignore the community context, relatively few empirical studies have systematically examined the relationship between macrolevel community characteristics and crime and violence in schools. To date, several studies have examined the association between school crime rates and neighborhood crime rates, and between delinquency in schools and in the community (Gold & Moles, 1978; McDermott, 1983; Menacker, Weldon, & Hurwitz, 1990; National Institute of Education, 1978). The general conclusion from these studies is crime in schools is a reflection of crime in the community.

Gottfredson and Gottfredson's (1985) important analysis of data from the Safe School Study confirmed the fact that neighborhood social disorganization is correlated with the level of disorder and violence in American schools.[9] In a study of more than 23,000 teachers and 31,000 students in 642 junior and senior high schools, they investigated the extent to which community characteristics such as social class, urbanicity, and unemployment are associated with teacher and student victimization rates across schools. They also examined whether community crime rates were related to school crime and disorder rates independent of those three factors, and how school characteristics (e.g., student body composition, staffing and resources, organizational climate, and security measures) predicted school crime rates, taking into account community characteristics.

Gottfredson and Gottfredson found that neighborhood and school characteristics correlated strongly with teacher self-reports of victimization, but did not correlate strongly with all student self-reports of victimization. For example, community characteristics and student body racial and ethnic composition were strongly related to teacher victimization rates, whereas these same measures were only weakly related to student victimization. A possible reason could be that student reports of incidents are generally less valid than those of adults. The fact that the weakest relationships were obtained in the analyses of the youngest respondents – young junior high school students – conforms to findings from other research indicating young adolescents are likely to include relatively minor incidents in their reports of violence victimization (Garofalo, Siegel, & Laub, 1987). Another reason could be that the community factors that influence teacher victimization are not the same as those that affect student victimization (Toby, 1986).

When teacher victimization rates were examined in both junior and senior high schools, school factors (e.g., resources, teachers' reports of governance, educational climate, and disciplinary standards) were found to be significant predictors of teacher victimization rates. Also related were students' reports of the social climate of their schools. For instance, teacher victimization rates were higher in schools in which students reported being less attached to the school, and less likely to believe in conventional social rules. However, the effects of these various reports of school conditions were dwarfed by the influences of community and student body composition.

When these same school factors were examined for their effects on student victimization rates, the authors found very similar associations. As for "disciplinary climate," schools whose students reported that the disciplinary rules were clear and fair tended to have lower rates of student-reported victimization. Yet, even though school disciplinary climate was found to be statistically significant, Gottfredson and Gottfredson (1985) concluded the effect was small: In fact, they found that "in contrast to the analyses for teacher victimizations, *all* predictors combined are weakly associated with student victimizations" (p. 130). Furthermore, they argued, one cannot assume the disciplinary climate is responsible for the lower rates: it may be that school disorder and failure to enforce the rules are responsible for students' views of the disciplinary climate, or that both conditions are a function of the composition of the student body.

When factors like neighborhood composition and social disorganization were considered in additional analyses, other school factors were also found to predict school crime rates. Sound school administration was found to be associated with reduced teacher and student victimization. Also, schools with academic orientations tended to have lower rates of teacher victimizations (though somewhat higher rates of student-reported theft). Gottfredson and Gottfredson concluded that although community characteristics and student body composition are the major determinants of school crime, school administration can have an independent effect.

Even though data from the Safe School Study indicate neighborhood social disorganization is a primary predictor of school crime, the methodological design of the study does not permit a more detailed assessment of what specific processes account for this relationship. This research does illustrate that community poverty and unemployment, urban location, percentage of student families on welfare, student and teacher racial or ethnic composition, peer and nonacademic ties, and students' academic abilities are all related to school crime rates, but the causal direction and mechanisms responsible for each of these influences are not completely understood.

For instance, as Toby (1986) points out, the data were not collected or analyzed in such a way as to permit a distinction to be made between violent acts by intruders and violent acts by students. If violence against teachers is disproportionately committed by intruders, then this may partly explain the differences found in the significance of various neighborhood factors. Crimes perpetrated by intruders (or by alienated and unmotivated students) require different types of policy responses than crimes committed by students who are committed to receiving an education (Toby, 1995).

These limitations of the Safe School Study are a result of its cross-sectional survey design, and also of the failure of the survey to collect more detailed data on the students' own offending behaviors. To clearly understand how factors such as disciplinary practices or security procedures can independently influence violence in schools, some form of longitudinal, randomized experiment is required. Unfortunately, no such demonstration projects have yet been undertaken.

Several other studies exist on the relationship between schools, neighborhoods, and crime. For example, Hellman and Beaton (1986), in their study of Boston public schools, found that suspension rates were higher in school districts that contained higher percentages of poor quality housing, higher population density, and greater population turnover. Interestingly, suspension rates were not significantly related to neighborhood income level, unemployment, or racial and ethnic composition. Even more intriguing, Hellman and Beaton's analysis revealed community influences (measured within the school districts) on school suspension rates varied by type of school. More specifically, the "community characteristic" factor had no effect on the middle school (grades 6–8) suspension rate, but it had a strong effect on the high school (grades 9–12) suspension rate. This study suggests the influence of the community on a school may be affected by the school's level. However, the use of student suspensions as a measure of school violence has some serious drawbacks. School suspensions cover a wide variety of misbehaviors, and the data reported are likely to be incomplete, owing to differences in official processing in various schools. Therefore these findings should be used cautiously.

More recently, Sheley, McGee, and Wright (1992) assessed gun-related violence in and around ten inner city high schools in five cities. Using self-report data, they found that gun-related violence that occurs in and around inner city schools is mainly imported from outside the school. That is, "a dangerous environment *outside* the school, as opposed to a dangerous environment *inside* the school, was a better predictor of weapon-related victimization at or during travel to and from school" (Sheley, McGee, & Wright, 1995, pp. 10–11; see also Sheley, McGee, & Wright, 1992). These authors concluded "it appears that schools do not generate weapon-related violence as much as they represent the location (exactly or approximately) where violence spawned outside the institution is enacted" (p. 11). Unfortunately, this study does not directly measure community-level factors, nor does it address concerns about selection effects. In addition, although this is one of the first studies to gather data on violence experienced on the way to and from school, the authors do not differentiate this form of violence from violence occurring in school in their published analyses.[10]

Another issue of concern is the relationship between gangs in the community and gangs in school. Surprisingly, there has been relatively little empirical research done on this topic (see Ralph et al., 1995). Of particular importance here is a study mentioned by Spergel (1990, p. 238) that suggests "student opportunity transfers and busing programs" can spread gang violence into a school or from the school back to the students' neighborhood.

It does appear that the problem of gangs in school is different from the problem of gangs on the street, as gangs at school are younger and involved in relatively less serious offenses. It should be noted that a large number of the gang members were not in school (e.g., they dropped out, were suspended, or were expelled). However, although a small percentage of school discipline code violations were gang-related, these incidents were disproportionately serious, comprising 12% of the weapon violations, 26% of the robberies, and 20% of the aggravated batteries (Spergel, 1990).

In a study using national-level data from the National Crime Victimization Survey and the National Household Education Survey, Ralph and his colleagues (1995) found students attending schools with gangs reported higher rates of victimization and higher levels of fear, and were more likely to carry weapons to school than students at schools without gangs. At this time, it is not known whether gangs in schools are merely imported from the surrounding neighborhood or the result of more complex processes of selection, density of peer networks, family influences, and individual propensities toward violence.

Finally, the question of *how* school context might influence an individual student's involvement in interpersonal violence was investigated in a sophisticated multilevel analysis by Felson and his colleagues (1994). Using data from more than 2,200 male students in 87 different high schools, the researchers uncovered several important findings about violence by adolescent males. First, by summarizing the information provided by students within each school, they found peer group cultures concerning academic achievement and approval for the use of violence differed from school to school. Schools in which students felt academic success was very important tended to be schools in which students were opposed to the use of violence. Second, these dimensions of a school's culture affected each student's risk for violence, over and above the risk associated with the student's own values regarding violence.

Felson and his colleagues (1994) thus demonstrated that violent responses to provocations meet with greater peer approval in some schools than others, and that peer group support for violence has a unique influence on involvement in violence. As they argue, "When group-level values predict behavior, independent of individual-level values, it suggests the operation of a social control process. Delinquency involves public compliance and impression management, rather than private acceptance or internalization of one's schoolmates' values" (p. 168). They contend these peer group processes occur within small groups in which youths are involved in routine social interactions with one another. "If boys are expected to retaliate when provoked, it appears that they are more likely to engage in violence and other delinquent behavior, no matter what their personal values may be" (p. 170; see also Chapter 3 of this volume).

Taken as a whole, the best available evidence from the literature on neighborhoods, families, school context, and violence allows us to draw two broad conclusions. First, neighborhood conditions such as high population turnover and loss, heterogeneity, poverty, and family structure are strong predictors of a neighborhood's violent crime rate and general crime rate. The best explanations for how these factors operate are the social capital and social disorganization models. The evidence suggests disadvantaged communities are more likely to lack the social resources and informal networks necessary for developing and maintaining local institutions and for helping parents acquire the social capital essential to deter their children from violence and delinquency.

Second, the strongest predictors of school violence rates are local neighborhood crime rates, or direct measures of community disorganization. Students attending school bring with them the problems of their families and residential community. In this sense, school violence is a reflection of neighborhood context and student body composition.[11] However, the most sophisticated research to date suggests these are not the only factors, and school violence may be influenced by school policies regarding discipline, security, and dropping out, and by small group interactions that develop within the school that encourage youths to respond violently to routine provocations. The most effective school responses to violence and delinquency will, therefore, be those that develop the social resources of their students.

Distinguishing Neighborhood, Family, and School Effects

School violence, we have found, is largely dependent on neighborhood and family conditions, although it is clear to us there are many aspects of these relationships not presently known. The problem of distinguishing the influence of neighborhood from the influence of school is a difficult one. In a recent review, Farrington (1993) concluded no longitudinal study has successfully separated individual, family, peer network, school, and community influences on adolescent antisocial behavior.

With respect to the community's influence on school violence, the problem is both conceptual and methodological. Often the geographical boundaries of the neighborhood do not coincide with those of the school district, which creates enormous problems in data collection and comparison. In any case, Reiss (1995) argues, "schools are rarely a microcosm of the communities in which they are located" (p. 307; cf. Mayer, 1991). Students in a given school may not even come from the community in which the school is located; for example, the *New York Times* reported students in Terlingua, Texas, are bused 89.7 miles to and from their high school in Alpine, Texas (Verhovek, 1994). Moreover, it has been common practice in large cities like Boston to bus students from one community to another for the purpose of racial integration; 65% of the students in the Boston public schools are bused to their schools.[12] Policies that allow parents to choose which school their child attends also make the neighborhood/school linkage more tenuous and complex. In sum, we cannot automatically assume the community is a "structural property of schools," and we must treat the community as an independent source of variation in order to avoid confounding community and school effects (Reiss, 1995).

Efforts to measure school effects are further confounded by the presumed influence of adolescent peer networks (Reiss, 1995). Although peer networks operate in both the community and the school, the density of peers is greater in the school, so peer group influence might well be greater there. Students represent pools of both potential offenders and potential victims who come into frequent contact with each other, often in the absence of capable guardians (Garofalo, Siegel, & Laub, 1987). Moreover, given recent changes in the demographic character of inner cities, large urban schools increasingly bring together children and adolescents at high risk for both offending and victimization (Toby, 1995).

Directions for Further Research

In our view, future research on the relationship between neighborhoods, families, schools, and violence should address the following issues:

1. *Selection Effects.* We have strong evidence that individual development and family characteristics are crucial in understanding the violence occurring in schools. However, taking into account selective migration to and from particular schools and neighborhoods is essential in order to distinguish selection effects on school violence from school and community influences. Toby (1995) discusses in detail these selection effects with regard to both students and teachers. In our view, the problem of selection effects is as much a conceptual one as it is a problem of data collection and statistical modeling.

2. *Neighborhood Schools.* It is important to examine the extent to which students in a particular school represent the community surrounding the school or some other community. We believe it is a mistake to always treat the school as if it represented a microcosm of the community in which it is located. One promising re-

search effort is a multilevel study designed to gather individual, situational, school, and community data in Philadelphia, including information on the communities surrounding schools as well as the communities from which students are drawn (Greene et al., 1993). Greene and his colleagues note that in Philadelphia, "at the middle and high school level, 'feeder' patterns suggest that students attending these schools come from a wider set of 'communities' than do students attending generally 'local' elementary schools" (p. 24). Lab and his colleagues (personal communication, June 1995) at Bowling Green University are also in the midst of a similar multilevel data collection effort in Ohio.

3. *Schools as Heterogenous Units of Analysis.* The school context itself exhibits a great deal of variation. Schools can be public or private; organized by grade and age of students (e.g., elementary vs. middle school, junior high vs. high school); vary in mission (e.g., college preparatory vs. vocational); and vary in location (e.g., urban vs. suburban vs. rural). One would expect these school differences to be relevant to an understanding of school violence and its relationship to family and neighborhood conditions. For example, there are conflicting data about whether big city high schools have more serious violence problems than big city junior high schools (see, e.g., Toby, 1995, p. 147). Although controversial, there is some suggestion that private city schools, particularly Catholic schools, are safer than public schools (Coleman & Hoffer, 1987). Gottfredson and Gottfredson (1985) also found that school resources, governance, and administration have independent influences on school violence in addition to the effects of community disorganization (see also Garbarino, 1978; Rutter et al., 1979). Researchers need to be more sensitive to wide variation of school contexts, particularly the social organization of the school and the classroom, and their effects on violence.

4. *Reciprocal Causation.* To our knowledge, there are no studies examining how school violence may influence community processes, which may in turn spawn more violence. Some evidence for such feedback effects can be gleaned from Roncek and Lobosco's (1983) study in San Diego of the influence of high schools on crime in their surrounding neighborhoods. Specifically, Roncek and Lobosco found that burglaries and auto thefts were higher in residential city blocks next to public high schools, but not next to private high schools. This finding held despite controlling for various social, housing, and demographic characteristics. (See also Roncek & Faggiani, 1985.)

5. *Need for Longitudinal Studies of Individual and Contextual Effects.* As we noted previously, most of the research in this area has been cross-sectional in design. Community change is an important consideration, but often ignored is individual change or development over time. Thus, as Farrington (1993) notes, a new generation of longitudinal studies is needed – studies that collect data not only for communities and families but for individuals over time. (See also Reiss, 1995.) Using dynamic, developmental models will allow us to begin to address the problem of how "exposure" to particular environments affects individual children, and of "feedback" effects between individual children and their social environments (Tienda, 1991). We believe such studies are essential for a full exploration of the interdependence of school violence with neighborhood and family conditions.

Policy Directions

The effective functioning of schools, especially schools free from violence, is largely dependent on the effective functioning of families and communities (see Coleman, 1991). Thus, context cannot be ignored in devising strategies for violence prevention and control. Strategies designed to address school violence must recognize the interdependence of school violence with neighborhood and family conditions. In general, community composition and family processes largely determine the student composition of the school, the extent of school resources, local norms, and the nature of peer group networks.

Clearly, approaches are needed to strengthen both the social organization of neighborhoods and parents' support networks (see National Research Council, 1993). In other words, efforts are needed to develop social capital. More generally, strong families and socially organized neighborhoods not only affect the student composition of schools, but also influence the infrastructure of schools as well. For example, parents with social capital may volunteer to support the school in many ways. Teachers want to work in a school with strong parental involvement, and because the parents help the school to develop a sense of mission, this often produces high morale and high expectations of achievement for students.

Schools can also take steps to involve parents with their children's education (Coleman, 1991). For example, schools can involve parents in academic work, such as homework. Parents can be informed of the school's expectations regarding homework and how they can best assist their children to succeed in school. In this regard the school can play an important role in the building of social capital in the family and in the community at large. (See also Coleman & Hoffer, 1987.)

Initiatives that "rebuild and strengthen" families and neighborhoods, such as "community development corporations," should also be considered (National Research Council, 1993). Neighborhood-based partnerships between direct service practitioners and community organizers, and between professionals and parents, seem especially worthwhile. The school can play an important role in these strategies by serving as multi-service centers, providing young people at risk and their families with services not available elsewhere in the community. For example, Dryfoos (1994) reports on the growing movement nationwide to bring services to where troubled teens and their families can most often be found. By putting health, counseling, and recreational programs under one roof, keeping schools open into the evening so that needy families can receive a "package of interventions" in one location, the conditions which make it difficult for adolescents from high-risk settings to achieve in school can be more effectively addressed (National Research Council, 1993, p. 223).

Conclusion

Although we must avoid oversimplifying the relationship between school violence and neighborhood and family conditions, our review of the research literature shows school violence is largely dependent on neighborhood and family conditions. In addition, the manner in which schools are organized and managed does have an effect on school violence. Thus, a multipronged approach that includes the community, the family, and the school itself is the most promising strategy for both understanding and controlling school violence.

Notes

1. For a general overview of school violence, the interested reader is directed to Toby (1995) and Lab and Whitehead (1992).
2. Our concern here is with aggregate and individual levels of explanation. Using violence as an example, an aggregate level of explanation accounts for variation in the rates of violence across a given type of social context (e.g., neighborhoods and schools) using characteristics of that context as explanatory variables. An individual level of explanation uses characteristics of individuals to explain variation in individual involvement in violence.

   For example, the higher the rate of population turnover (i.e., mobility) in a neighborhood, the higher the rate of violence; hence, neighborhood mobility is said to "explain" variation in neighborhood violence. But the neighborhood-level finding that high mobility explains violence does not logically require in a parallel finding at the individual level. It may or may not be the case that individuals who have moved most often are more likely to commit violent offenses. To determine if this is true requires a separate investigation of data on individuals' mobility and offense involvement. If the aggregate level relationship was found to be significant while the individual level was not, it would suggest a more complex picture of different effects of mobility on violence. Neighborhoods with high levels of turnover may be places in which residents, regardless of their own mobility, are at greater risk for violence. A full understanding of the conditions leading to violent behavior thus requires both aggregate and individual levels of analyses.
3. Land, McCall, and Cohen (1990) provide a summary of similar analyses at higher levels of aggregation (e.g., city and Standard Metropolitan Statistical Area [SMSA]). Specifically, Land et al. examined variation in homicide rates among SMSAs and cities during a 30-year period and found that resource deprivation (as determined by a composite measure of poverty concentration and income stratification) had the largest effect on the homicide rate. Specifically, cities with a large poor population and a high percentage of African Americans, in conjunction with a high percentage of single-parent families and high divorce rates, had a disproportionately high homicide rate. These predictors were more powerful for the 1970–1980 period, suggesting that increasing the concentration

of disadvantaged persons within stratified neighborhoods has contributed to the recent increase in violent crime (see also Chow & Coulton, 1992).

4. Brooks-Gunn and her colleagues (1993) point out that the number of neighborhood relationships enjoyed by individual children depends on the age of the child. Because adolescents have more immediate, direct, and intense interactions with institutions other than the family and with individuals outside their immediate family than do young children, neighborhood characteristics will have a greater effect on individual children during late adolescence than during early childhood. Consistent with this view, Aber et al. (1992) found more association between neighborhood impoverishment and adolescent outcomes (e.g., mental health and school achievement) for older students (i.e., junior high school students, grades 8 and 9) than for younger students (i.e., late elementary school students, grades 5 and 6).

5. For an excellent overview of the various ways neighborhoods might affect child development, see Jencks and Mayer (1990).

6. Duncan (1994) found the presence of affluent neighbors appeared to confer benefits on white males and on both African American and white females, even when family-level factors such as parental income, maternal education, and family structure are taken into account. Duncan also found the racial composition of the neighborhood mattered only for African Americans, not whites. In fact, African Americans did worse in neighborhoods with a high concentration of African Americans. However, affluent neighbors appeared to benefit African American males only if the affluent neighbors were African American themselves (see also Connell et al., 1995).

7. An alternative, but not inconsistent, interpretation of the relationship between neighborhood family composition and crime and violence comes from the "routine activities" theory of crime (Cohen & Felson, 1979). This perspective seeks to examine the circumstances under which criminal events are most likely to occur. Felson and Cohen (1980) have shown that U.S. crime rate trends from 1950–1972 were significantly affected by overall changes in the percentage of single adult heads of households. They and others have found that never married, separated, and divorced persons are at greater risk for personal violence than are married persons. This pattern may be a function of decreased guardianship (i.e., one person alone is generally more vulnerable than two), or it may reflect increased interpersonal conflict surrounding those adult relationships.

8. Steinberg et al. (1991) examined whether the ecological context in which adolescents live – defined by their ethnicity, socioeconomic status, and family structure – moderated the strong relationship previously observed between parental "authoritativeness" (i.e., firmness, blended with warmth and democratic attitudes) and adolescent behavior and adjustment. These authors found the positive correlation between parental authoritativeness and adolescent adjustment appeared to transcend context (i.e., ethnicity, socioeconomic status, and family structure). Adolescents whose parents were warm, firm, and democratic enjoyed psychological and behavioral advantages over their peers. However, the relationship between authoritativeness and school performance was stronger among white and Hispanic adolescents than among their African American and Asian American counterparts.

9. This research employed a macrolevel analysis with schools as the unit of analysis. (For more details see Gottfredson & Gottfredson, 1985.)
10. Pearson and Toby (1991) found a strong relationship between fear of attack going to and from school and mode of transportation. In the inner city, students who walked to school or took public transportation reported the highest percentages of fear of attack. Pearson and Toby suggest the absence of capable guardians on the walk route and on public transportation may account for these findings.
11. In a study of schools and delinquency in London, Rutter and his colleagues (1979) found the "intellectual balance" of the student body was more important than its socioeconomic composition in explaining the level of delinquency in the school. Similar results were reported by Lindstrom (1995) in his study of schools in Stockholm, Sweden.
12. This percentage varies by neighborhood and race. In one high school in a predominantly white neighborhood, the percentage of African American students and white students bused is 88% and 15% respectively. In another high school in a more racially heterogenous neighborhood, 27% of the African American students are bused, compared with 63% of the white students.

References

Aber, J., Mitchell, C., Garfinkel, R., Allen, L., & Seidman, E. (1992). *Indices of neighborhood impoverishment: Their association with adolescent mental health and school achievement.* New York: Columbia University School of Public Health, National Center for Children in Poverty.

Block, R. (1979). Community, environment, and violent crime. *Criminology, 17,* 46–57.

Bronfenbrenner, U. (1979). *The ecology of human development.* Cambridge, MA: Harvard University Press.

Brooks-Gunn, J., Duncan, G., Klebanov, P., & Sealand, N. (1993). Do neighborhoods influence child and adolescent development? *American Journal of Sociology, 99,* 353–395.

Bursik, R. (1986). Ecological stability and the dynamics of delinquency. In A. J. Reiss, Jr. & M. Tonry (Eds.), *Communities and crime* (pp. 35–66). Chicago: University of Chicago Press.

Bursik, R. (1988). Social disorganization and theories of crime and delinquency: Problems and prospects. *Criminology, 26,* 519–552.

Bursik, R., & Grasmick, H. (1993). *Neighborhoods and crime: The dimensions of effective community control.* New York: Lexington.

Chow, J., & Coulton, C. (1992). *Was there a social transformation of urban neighborhoods in the '80s? A decade of changing structure in Cleveland, Ohio.* Cleveland, OH: Case Western Reserve University, Center for Urban Poverty and Social Change.

Cohen, L., & Felson, M. (1979). Social change and crime rate trends: A routine activities approach. *American Sociological Review, 44,* 588–607.

Coie, J., & Jacobs, M. (1993). The role of social context in the prevention of conduct disorder. *Development and Psychopathology, 5,* 263–275.

Coleman, J. (1990). *Foundations of social theory.* Cambridge, MA: Harvard University Press.

Coleman, J. (1991). *Parental involvement in education.* Washington, DC: U.S. Government Printing Office.

Coleman, J., & Hoffer, T. (1987). *Public and private high schools: The impact of communities.* New York: Basic Books.

Connell, J., Halpern-Felsher, B., Clifford, E., Crichlow, W., & Usinger, P. (1995). Hanging in there: Behavioral, psychological, and contextual factors affecting whether African American adolescents stay in high school. *Journal of Adolescent Research, 10,* 41–63.

Curry, D., & Spergel, I. (1988). Gang homicide, delinquency, and community. *Criminology, 26,* 381–406.

Dryfoos, J. (1994). *Full-service schools: A revolution in health and social services for children, youth, and families.* San Francisco: Jossey-Bass.

Duncan, G. (1994). Families and neighbors as sources of disadvantage in the schooling decisions of white and black adolescents. *American Journal of Education, 103,* 20–53.

Elliott, D., Wilson, W. J., Huizinga, D., Sampson, R., Elliott, A., & Rankin, B. (1996). The effects of neighborhood disadvantage on adolescent development. *Journal of Research in Crime and Delinquency, 33,* 389–426.

Fagan, J., & Browne, A. (1994). Violence between spouses and intimates: Physical aggression between women and men in intimate relationships. In A. J. Reiss, Jr. & J. A. Roth (Eds.), *Understanding and preventing violence: Social influences* (Vol. 3) (pp. 115–292). Washington, DC: National Academy Press.

Farrington, D. (1993). Have any individual, family, or neighborhood influences on offending been demonstrated conclusively? In D. Farrington, R. Sampson, & P. O. Wikstrom (Eds.), *Integrating individual and ecological aspects of crime* (pp. 7–37). Stockholm: National Council on Crime Prevention.

Felson, M., & Cohen, L. (1980). Human ecology and crime: A routine activity approach. *Human Ecology, 8,* 389–406.

Felson, R., Liska, A., South, S., & McNulty, T. (1994). The subculture of violence and delinquency: Individual vs. school context effects. *Social Forces, 73,* 155–173.

Furstenberg, F. (1990, August). *How families manage risk and opportunity in dangerous neighborhoods.* Paper presented at the annual meeting of the American Sociological Association, Washington, DC.

Garbarino, J. (1978). The human ecology of school crime: A case for small schools. In E. Wenk & N. Harlow (Eds.), *School crime and disruption* (pp. 115–167). Davis, CA: Responsible Action.

Garbarino, J., & Crouter, A. (1978). Defining the community context for parent-child relations: The correlates of child maltreatment. *Child Development, 49,* 604–616.

Garbarino, J., & Kostelny, K. (1992). Child maltreatment as a community problem. *Child Abuse and Neglect, 16,* 455–464.

Garbarino, J., & Sherman, D. (1980). High-risk neighborhoods and high-risk families: The human ecology of child maltreatment. *Child Development, 51,* 188–198.

Garofalo, J., Siegel, L., & Laub, J. (1987). School-related victimizations among adolescents: An analysis of national crime survey narratives. *Journal of Quantitative Criminology, 3,* 321–338.

Gold, M., & Moles, O. (1978). Delinquency and violence in schools and the community. In J. Inciardi & A. Pottieger (Eds.), *Violent crime: Historical and contemporary issues* (pp. 111–124). Beverly Hills, CA: Sage.

Gottfredson, G., & Gottfredson, D. (1985). *Victimization in schools.* New York: Plenum.

Gottfredson, D., McNeil, R., & Gottfredson, G. (1991). Social area influences on delinquency: A multilevel analysis. *Journal of Research in Crime and Delinquency, 28,* 197–226.

Greene, J., Jenkins, P., Welsh, W., & Yancey, W. (1993). *Building a culture and climate of safety in public schools: School-based management and violence reduction in Philadelphia*. Philadelphia: Temple University, Center for Public Policy.

Hellman, D., & Beaton, S. (1986). The pattern of violence in urban public schools: The influence of school and community. *Journal of Research in Crime and Delinquency, 23,* 102–127.

Hunter, A. (1974). *Symbolic communities*. Chicago: University of Chicago Press.

Jencks, C., & Mayer, S. (1990). The social consequences of growing up in a poor neighborhood. In L. E. Lynn, Jr., & M. G. H. McGreary (Eds.), *Inner-city poverty in the United States* (pp. 111–186). Washington, DC: National Academy Press.

Jessor, R. (1993). Successful adolescent development among youth in high-risk settings. *American Psychologist, 48,* 117–126.

Kornhauser, R. (1978). *Social sources of delinquency*. Chicago: University of Chicago Press.

Lab, S., & Whitehead, J. (1992). *The school environment and school crime: Causes and consequences*. Washington, DC: National Institute of Justice, Final Report (Report No. 91-IF-CX-0005).

Land, K., McCall, P., & Cohen, L. (1990). Structural covariates of homicide rates: Are there any invariances across time and space? *American Journal of Sociology, 95,* 922–963.

Lindstrom, P. (1995). *School context and delinquency* (Project Metropolitan Report No. 41). Stockholm: University of Stockholm, Department of Sociology.

Loeber, R., & Stouthamer-Loeber, M. (1986). Family factors as correlates and predictors of juvenile conduct problems and delinquency. In M. Tonry & N. Morris (Eds.), *Crime and justice: An annual review of research* (Vol. 7) (pp. 29–150). Chicago: University of Chicago Press.

Mayer, S. (1991). *The effect of school and neighborhood social mix on adolescents' transitions to adulthood*. Paper prepared for the Panel on High-Risk Youth, Commission on Behavioral and Social Sciences and Education. Washington, DC: National Research Council.

McDermott, J. (1983). Crime in the school and in the community: Offenders, victims, and fearful youths. *Crime and Delinquency, 29,* 270–282.

Menacker, J., Weldon, W., & Hurwitz, E. (1990). Community influences on school crime and violence. *Urban Education, 25,* 68–80.

Messner, S., & Tardiff, K. (1986). Economic inequality and levels of homicide: An analysis of urban neighborhoods. *Criminology, 24,* 297–318.

National Institute of Education. (1978). *Violent schools – Safe schools: The Safe School Study report to the Congress*. Washington, DC: U.S. Government Printing Office.

National Research Council. (1993). *Losing generations: Adolescents in high risk settings*. Washington, DC: National Academy Press.

Patterson, G. (1980). Children who steal. In T. Hirschi & M. Gottfredson (Eds.), *Understanding crime: Current theory and research* (pp. 73–90). Beverly Hills, CA: Sage.

Pearson, F. S., & Toby, J. (1991). Fear of school-related predatory crime. *Sociology and Social Research, 75,* 117–125.

Peeples, F., & Loeber, R. (1994). Do individual factors and neighborhood context explain ethnic differences in juvenile delinquency? *Journal of Quantitative Criminology, 10,* 141–157.

Ralph, J., Colopy, K., McRae, C., & Daniel, B. (1995). *Gangs and victimization at school*. Washington, DC: National Center for Education Statistics.

Reiss, A. J., Jr. (1995). Community influences on adolescent behavior. In M. Rutter (Ed.), *Psychosocial disturbances in young people: Challenges for prevention* (pp. 305–332). New York: Cambridge University Press.

Reiss, A. J., Jr., & Roth, J. (1993). *Understanding and preventing violence.* Washington, DC: National Academy Press.

Robins, L. (1966). *Deviant children grown up.* Baltimore: Williams and Wilkins.

Roncek, D. (1981). Dangerous places: Crime and residential environment. *Social Forces, 60,* 74–96.

Roncek, D., & Faggiani, D. (1985). High schools and crime: A replication. *Sociological Quarterly, 26,* 491–505.

Roncek, D., & Lobosco, A. (1983). The effect of high schools on crime in their neighborhoods. *Social Science Quarterly, 64,* 598–613.

Rutter, M., Maughan, B., Mortimore, P., Auston, J., & Smith, A. (1979). *Fifteen thousand hours: Secondary schools and their effects on children.* Cambridge, MA: Harvard University Press.

Sampson, R. (1983). Structural density and criminal victimization. *Criminology, 21,* 276–293.

Sampson, R. (1985). Neighborhood and crime: The structural determinants of personal victimization. *Journal of Research in Crime and Delinquency, 22,* 7–40.

Sampson, R. (1986). Neighborhood family structure and the risk of criminal victimization. In A. J. Reiss, Jr., & M. Tonry (Eds.), *Communities and crime* (pp. 271–311). Chicago: University of Chicago Press.

Sampson, R. (1988). Community attachment in mass society: A multi-level systemic model. *American Sociological Review, 53,* 766–779.

Sampson, R. (1992). Family management and child development: Insights from social disorganization theory. In J. McCord (Ed.), *Facts, frameworks, and forecasts: Advances in criminological theory* (Vol. 3) (pp. 63–93). New Brunswick, NJ: Transaction.

Sampson, R., & Groves, W. B. (1989). Community structure and crime: Testing social disorganization theory. *American Journal of Sociology, 94,* 774–802.

Sampson, R., & Laub, J. (1993). *Crime in the making: Pathways and turning points through life.* Cambridge, MA: Harvard University Press.

Sampson, R., & Lauritsen, J. (1994). Violent victimization and offending: Individual-, situational-, and community-level risk factors. In A. J. Reiss, Jr., & J. A. Roth (Eds.), *Understanding and preventing violence: Social influences* (Vol. 3) (pp. 1–114). Washington, DC: National Academy Press.

Shaw, C., & McKay, H. (1942/1969). *Juvenile delinquency and urban areas.* Chicago: University of Chicago Press.

Sheley, J., McGee, Z., & Wright, J. (1992). Gun-related violence in and around inner-city schools. *American Journal of Diseases of Children, 146,* 677–682.

Sheley, J., McGee, Z., & Wright, J. (1995). *Weapon-related victimization in selected inner-city high school samples.* Washington, DC: National Institute of Justice.

Skogan, W. (1986). Fear of crime and neighborhood change. In A. J. Reiss, Jr., & M. Tonry (Eds.), *Communities and crime* (pp. 203–229). Chicago: University of Chicago Press.

Smith, D., & Jarjoura, G. R. (1988). Social structure and criminal victimization. *Journal of Research in Crime and Delinquency, 25,* 27–52.

Spergel, I. A. (1990). Youth gangs: Continuity and change. In M. Tonry & N. Morris (Eds.), *Crime and justice* (pp. 171–275). Chicago: University of Chicago Press.

Steinberg, L., Mounts, N., Lamborn, S., & Dornbusch, S. (1991). Authoritative parenting and adolescent adjustment across varied ecological niches. *Journal of Research on Adolescence, 1,* 19–36.

Stern, S., & Smith, C. (1995). *Family processes and delinquency in an ecological context.* Rochester Youth Development Study, Working Paper No. 20, University of New York at Albany, NY.

Taub, R., Taylor, D. G., & Dunham, J. (1984). *Paths of neighborhood change: Race and crime in urban America.* Chicago: University of Chicago Press.

Taylor, R., & Covington, J. (1988). Neighborhood changes in ecology and violence. *Criminology, 26,* 553–590.

Taylor, R., & Gottfredson, S. (1986). Environmental design, crime, and prevention: An examination of community dynamics. In A. J. Reiss, Jr. & M. Tonry (Eds.), *Communities and crime* (pp. 387–416). Chicago: University of Chicago Press.

Taylor, R., Gottfredson, S., & Brower, S. (1984). Block crime and fear: Defensible space, local social ties, and territorial functioning. *Journal of Research in Crime and Delinquency, 21,* 303–331.

Tienda, M. (1991). Poor people and poor places: Deciphering neighborhood effects on poverty outcomes. In J. Huber (Ed.), *Macro-micro linkages in sociology* (pp. 244–262). Newbury Park, CA: Sage.

Toby, J. (1986). [Review of the book *Victimization in schools*]. *Journal of Criminal Law and Criminology, 77,* 266–269.

Toby, J. (1995). The schools. In J. Q. Wilson & J. Petersilia (Eds.), *Crime* (pp. 141–170). San Francisco: ICS Press.

Verhovek, S. H. (1994, December 9). Where time on road beats time at class. *The New York Times,* p. A31.

Widom, C. (1989). The intergenerational transmission of violence. In N. Weiner & M. Wolfgang (Eds.), *Pathways to criminal violence* (pp. 137–201). Beverly Hills, CA: Sage.

Wilson, J. Q., & Kelling, G. L. (1982, March). Broken windows. *The Atlantic Monthly,* pp. 29–38.

Wilson, W. J. (1987). *The truly disadvantaged: The inner city, the underclass, and public policy.* Chicago: University of Chicago Press.

III. School-Based Interventions

6. Preventing Firearm Violence in and Around Schools

JAMES A. MERCY & MARK L. ROSENBERG

Introduction

Children are the witnesses, victims, and perpetrators of violence that has become increasingly lethal in our society. Over the past decade homicide rates among adolescents have increased dramatically and at a pace exceeding that of nonfatal assaultive behavior (Centers for Disease Control and Prevention, 1994; U.S. Department of Justice, 1992). Moreover, suicide rates among adolescents have more than tripled since the early 1950s (Centers for Disease Control and Prevention, 1995; Hollinger & Offer, 1981). Younger and younger children are represented among the perpetrators and the victims of these events (U.S. Department of Justice, 1990, 1992). Firearms are involved in an increasing proportion of interpersonal and self-directed violence affecting children. These trends have had a direct impact on schools for violence and its consequences, and the implements of violence have spilled into classrooms, school hallways, and playgrounds. With guns and their associated lethal violence increasingly finding their way into the lives of school-age children, the traditional view of schools as safe havens from violence can no longer be sustained.

In this chapter we describe the problem of firearm injuries and violence among school-age children; discuss prevention strategies; suggest a scientific, research-based process for identifying effective solutions; and public health policies for moving forward. A major theme is that no school is an island: What happens to children inside and on the way to and from school reflects what is happening in surrounding communities. Thus, if we are to understand the problem of guns and gun violence in schools we must first understand this problem in its larger societal context. Figure 6.1 illustrates the overlap among the domains of children, guns, and schools and how the components of this problem are embedded in the surrounding community. All three of these domains can contribute to the problem of gun violence

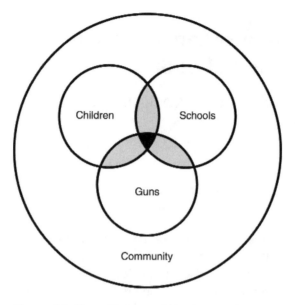

Figure 6.1. Venn diagram of the intersection among children, guns, and schools within a community.

in and around schools. First, the behavior of children in and around schools is strongly influenced by social and psychological influences that occur outside of school. Second, the availability of and attitudes toward firearms within children's families and the community are likely to be an important influence on the firearm violence problem in and around schools. Third, the policies and actions schools take can have an influence on this problem. Fourth, the demographic and socioeconomic characteristics of communities themselves can influence all these domains. Finally, this picture can become even more complicated when communities with different demographic and socioeconomic characteristics send their children to a common school. But although this is a complex problem, it is not insoluble: in each domain there are policies and interventions that can help.

The Prevalence of Violence

Firearm injuries and firearm violence in and around schools are a part of the larger problems of violence and firearm injuries facing society in the United States. In this section, we review information from official data sources and the research literature from multiple disciplines to place this

Table 6.1. *Number and rate of fatal and nonfatal firearm-related injuries among 5–19-year olds in the United States, 1992*

Injury circumstance	Nonfatal firearm injuries*		Fatal firearm injuries		Nonfatal/fatal injury ratio
	Number	Rate	Number	Rate	
Interpersonal violence	13,948	26.1	3,282	6.1	4.2
Unintentional circumstances	4,938	9.2	465	.9	10.6
Suicidal behavior	598	1.1	1,426	2.7	.4
Unknown	3,683	6.9	89	.2	41.4
Totals	23,167	43.3	5,262	9.8	4.4

* The number and rate of nonfatal firearm injuries are national estimates of firearm injuries treated in emergency departments for the period from June 1, 1992, through May 31, 1993. See Annest et al. (1995) for estimation procedures. *Data Sources:* National Center for Injury Prevention and Control, 1995; Annest, Mercy, Gibson, & Ryan, 1995.

problem in the context of these broader issues. We begin by describing the impact of firearm injuries and violence on school-age children and then review information about exposure and access to firearms by children. We conclude our description of the problem by reviewing what is known about the magnitude and nature of firearm injuries and violence in and around schools.

Firearm-Related Injuries and Violence among School-Age Children

Firearm injuries are a significant public health problem for children in the United States. As illustrated in Table 6.1, in 1992, 5,262 children and adolescents (in the age range 5–19 years) died from gunshot wounds: 62% by homicide, 27% by suicide, 9% by unintentional injuries, and 2% by undetermined circumstances (National Center for Injury Prevention and Control, 1995a). When the number of firearm-related homicides, suicides, and unintentional injuries are added together, firearm injuries rank as the fifth leading cause of death for 5- to 9-year-old children, and the second leading cause of death for children ages 10 to 14 and 15 to 19 in 1992 (National Center for Injury Prevention and Control, 1995b). An estimated 23,167 school-age children suffered nonfatal firearm injuries that were treated in hospital emergency rooms from June 1992 through May 1993 (Annest, Mercy, Gibson, & Ryan, 1995). Of these 23,167 nonfatal firearm injuries, an estimated 60% are attributable to interpersonal violence; 3% to suicidal behavior; 21% to unintentional injuries; and in 16%, the circumstances were undetermined.

As children grow older the number and rate of both nonfatal and fatal firearm-related injuries increases, regardless of the context in which the injury occurs. Additionally, male school-age children are at 7.3 times greater risk of fatal, and at 6.0 times greater risk of nonfatal, firearm injuries than are females. This gender gap in the risk of firearm-related fatalities increases with age. Approximately 4.4 nonfatal firearm-related injuries to school-age children are treated in emergency rooms for every fatality; however, this ratio differs by the circumstances under which the injury occurs. For firearm-related injuries occurring in the context of interpersonal violence, nonfatal firearm injuries outnumber fatalities by a ratio of 4.2, compared with 10.6 for those resulting from unintentional circumstances and 0.4 for those associated with suicidal behavior.

The lethality of violence among children has increased over time, and this increase is associated with the use of firearms. Scientific evidence clearly indicates that the presence of a gun in a violent interaction dramatically increases the likelihood that one or more of the participants will be killed (Cook, 1991). Firearms are associated with a high proportion of deaths related to interpersonal violence and suicide attempts. In 1992, among 5- to 19-year-old victims, 84% of the homicides (N = 3,889) and 66% of the suicides (N = 2,161) were committed with firearms (National Center for Injury Prevention and Control, 1995a). The question of whether violence is becoming more lethal, however, can be directly examined only in the context of interpersonal violence, because historical data on suicide attempts in the United States are insufficient.

The graph in Figure 6.2 shows the dramatic increase in the number of homicides per 100,000 violent events among adolescents from 1973–1991. These figures clearly indicate the lethality of interpersonal violence. Although there is substantial variation in lethality over the 20-year period, after the early 1980s the lethality of interpersonal violence increased substantially among 16- to 19-year-olds, whereas among 12- to 15-year-olds the increase was more gradual. Other evidence indicates quite clearly that recent increases in youth homicide and suicide are almost entirely attributable to increases in homicides and suicides involving firearms (Boyd & Moscicki, 1986; Centers for Disease Control and Prevention, 1994). The beginning of this increase in the rate and lethality of interpersonal violence is associated with the widespread introduction of crack cocaine in the inner cities. It has been theorized that the recruitment of children and ado-

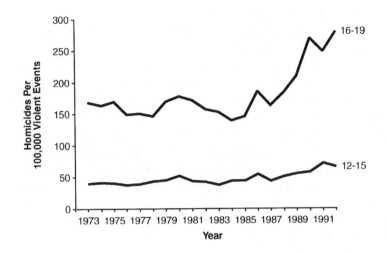

Figure 6.2. Homicides per 100,000 violent events among U.S. children, ages 12–15 and 16–19, 1973–1991. *Data Sources:* Centers for Disease Control and Prevention, National Center for Health Statistics, Vital Statistics Systems, 1973–1992; Bureau of Justice Statistics (1992, 1993).

lescents into the distribution of crack increased their access to guns and accelerated more widespread use of guns by a much wider group of children and adolescents (Blumstein, 1995).

The serious impact of firearm injuries and violence on children is also reflected in their self-reports of victimization and the extent to which they witness firearm violence. In a survey representative of U.S. students in the sixth through twelfth grades, 13% of respondents said someone else had seriously threatened to shoot them (LH Research, Inc., 1993). Other research indicates children are witnessing gun violence, and such direct exposure can cause severe psychological trauma (Groves, Zuckerman, Marans, & Cohen, 1993). In a recent study, one in ten children at an inner city (Boston) pediatric primary care clinic had witnessed a stabbing or shooting in their home or on the street before the age of 6 (Taylor, Zuckerman, Harik, & Groves, 1992). In another study of urban children in the fifth, seventh, and ninth grades, 89% of respondents said they had heard guns being fired in their neighborhood, and 41% said they themselves had seen someone get shot (Shapiro & Burkey, 1992). It has been estimated between 10–20% of the homicides that occur in Los Angeles are witnessed by children (Pynoos & Eth, 1985).

These data support several conclusions about the impact and nature of the problem of firearm-related injuries and violence among school-age children. First, the primary context for firearm injuries is interpersonal violence, which accounts for about 60% of both fatal and nonfatal firearm injuries among children and adolescents. Second, the problem has a disproportionate impact on male children and adolescents, and the risk of injury increases with age. Third, firearms are involved in a high proportion of the lethal violence that affects school-age children, and appear to play a significant role in the increasing lethality of interpersonal violence among adolescents during the past decade. Most researchers attribute the increased lethality to a greater access to firearms and a greater willingness to use firearms on the part of children and their assailants; however, the relative importance of each factor is unknown. Fourth, children who witness firearm violence can suffer psychological trauma, and this impact of firearm injuries on children can adversely effect individual development and the educational climate in schools.

Exposure and Access to Firearms by School-Age Children

Numerous studies in recent years have documented the unsettling frequency with which children have access to and carry guns in their homes, communities, and schools. Exposure and access depend in large measure on the supply of guns in a community and the demand for guns by children. Supply depends on how many guns there are, their price, their distribution, and how they are circulated and shared. The demand for guns includes how strongly children feel they need guns and why they want them. Understanding the patterns of supply and demand for firearms and the reasons for these patterns, therefore, is critical to identifying prevention strategies.

There are many guns in this country; their numbers appear to be increasing, and many children can easily obtain them. The U.S. Bureau of Alcohol, Tobacco, and Firearms (1991) estimates that in 1990 there were at least 200 million guns in circulation in the United States. Various surveys place the fraction of all households owning any type of gun somewhere between 40–50% (Cook 1991; Davis & Smith, 1986). One study estimated that in 1985 there were firearms in 44% of the 18.6 million households in the United States with children between the ages of 5 and 17 (Lee & Sacks, 1990). In a 1985 national survey of eighth and tenth grade students, 33% of respondents reported they could obtain a handgun (American School Health Association, Association for the Advancement of Health Education, & Society for Public Health Education, 1989). More recently, in a 1993 poll of students in the sixth through twelfth grades, 59% of respondents said they could obtain a handgun if they needed one. Among those who said they could, two of three said they could obtain the handgun within 24 hours (LH Research, Inc., 1993).

Many adolescents, particularly (but not exclusively) those who reside in inner cities, can easily and inexpensively obtain high-quality and powerful firearms. In an extensive study of gun acquisition and possession among selected juvenile samples, Sheley and Wright (1993) surveyed male inmates in juvenile correctional facilities and male students at nearby inner city high schools. In this study, 84% of the inmates (prior to incarceration) and 22% of the students said they possessed guns. The preferred type of firearms, among both inmates and students, was high-quality, powerful revolvers, followed by automatic or semiautomatic handguns and then shotguns. Both the inmates and students thought it easy to acquire guns. Seventy percent of inmates and 41% of students said they could acquire a gun with no trouble at all. For inmates, the most likely source for obtaining a gun was "off the street," while students reported their most likely source of acquiring a gun was to borrow it from a family member or friend. Sheley and Wright surmise the ultimate source of many of the guns obtained by male adolescents in this study was theft and burglary. Among respondents who had purchased firearms for cash, 65% of inmates and 74% of students had paid $100 or less for their most recently purchased handgun, and these guns could be acquired more cheaply through informal networks than from retail establishments. In a related study among inner city male and female students, Sheley, McGee, and Wright (1992) found 23% of the student respondents felt guns were easily accessible within the neighborhoods in which they lived. In a study of firearm possession and carrying among suburban high school students in Jefferson Parish, Louisiana, 18% of respondents said they owned or possessed a handgun. Of these, 9% claimed they owned or possessed an automatic or semiautomatic handgun (Sheley & Brewer, 1995). Male students were only slightly more likely to own or possess a handgun than female students in Jefferson Parish.

A surprisingly large proportion of adolescents reported they routinely carry guns and bring them to school. Results from studies of gun carrying are difficult to compare, however, because various studies use different time frames and differently worded questions. For example, it is difficult to compare findings on the prevalence of gun carrying when one survey asks about this behavior in the past 30 days and others ask if the respondents have ever carried a gun. The Youth Risk Behavior Survey (YRBS) conducted by the U.S. Centers for Disease Control and Prevention and by state and local education agencies is being used to establish and track trends in a broad range of risk behaviors among high school students, including gun carrying (Kann, Warren, Harris, et al., 1995). In 1993, 7.9% of students nationwide reported they had carried a gun during the 30 days preceding the survey (see Table 6.2). For all racial/ethnic groups and grades, male students were significantly more likely than female students to have carried a gun. Black male and female students were significantly more likely to carry guns than white male and female students. Similarly, in a survey conducted in New York City high schools in 1992, 7% of students reported carrying a handgun during the 30 days preceding the survey (Centers for Disease Control and Prevention, 1993). Among juvenile inmates, 84% reported carrying a gun "now and then" prior to incarceration, as did 23% of inner city male high school students (Sheley & Wright, 1993). In a related study, 11% of female inner city high school students reported carrying a gun outside of school (Sheley, McGee, & Wright, 1992). In a study of students at two inner city junior high schools, 25% of males reported having ever carried a gun for protection or to use in a fight, and 16% of these carried a gun routinely (i.e., 8 to 14 days of the preceding two weeks) (Webster, Gainer, & Champion, 1993). Among suburban high school students in Jefferson Parish, Louisiana, 28% of boys and 18% of girls reported carrying a gun (Sheley & Brewer, 1995).

Among studies examining the carrying of guns to, from, or at schools, a 1985 survey of eighth and tenth grade students found 2% of students reporting they had carried a handgun at school during the preceding year (American School Health Association, Association for the Advancement of Health Education, & Society for Public Health Education, 1989). According to this report, males were three times as likely to have carried a handgun to school as females. In New York City high schools, during the 30 days preceding one survey, 4% of respondents reported carrying a handgun when going to or from school and 4% reported carrying a handgun in school (Centers for Disease Control and Prevention, 1993). Among male and female inner city high school students, 6% reported carrying a gun at school at least "now and then" (Sheley, McGee, & Wright, 1992, p. 679).

The primary reason given by adolescents for obtaining or carrying guns is self-protection, but motivations for gun use are also associated with a propensity for violence and involvement in delinquent activities. At least one study suggests a substantial proportion of students believe that carrying a gun provides protection against victimization (Price, Desmo, & Smith, 1991). In Sheley and Wright's (1993) study of male juvenile inmates and inner city high school students, the primary reasons given for purchasing a

Table 6.2. *Percentage of high school students who carried a gun on ≥1 of the 30 days preceding the survey, by sex and race/ethnicity, in the United States, 1993*

Race/ethnicity	Male			Female			Total		
	%	95% confidence interval	N	%	95% confidence interval	N	%	95% confidence interval	N
White, non-Hispanic	12.0	(9.4–14.6)	3,225	1.2	(0.7–1.7)	3,331	6.8	(5.4–8.2)	6,575
Black, non-Hispanic	20.9	(17.9–24.0)	1,708	3.8	(2.6–5.0)	1,906	12.3	(10.8–13.8)	3,617
Hispanic	17.0	(13.0–20.9)	2,295	3.11	(1.8–4.4)	2,357	10.1	(8.1–12.0)	4,656
Other	14.2	(10.7–17.7)	637	.6	(0.5–2.7)	578	8.4	(6.2–10.6)	1,219
Total	13.7	(11.5–15.9)	7,888	1.8	(1.3–2.2)	8,202	7.9	(6.6–9.2)	16,129

(Weighted data)
Data Source: Kann, Warren, Harris, et al., 1995.

gun, in both groups, were for protection and to arm oneself against enemies. The researchers found little support for the notion that these adolescents carried a gun to command respect from peers or primarily for the purpose of using them in crime (cf. Chapter 3 of this volume). Sheley and Wright found evidence for one exception to this last finding, noting that among those students and inmates involved in drug dealing, firearm possession and use were much greater than among peers not involved in drug dealing.

Webster, Gainer, and Champion (1993) studied the association between beliefs and experiences and gun carrying and also found some evidence that gun carrying was related to involvement in crimes. In a multifactor analysis, they found gun carrying among inner city junior high school students to be associated with having been arrested, knowing more victims of violence, starting fights, and being willing to justify shooting someone. They concluded that "the image of otherwise law-abiding youth carrying guns solely for protection" was incorrect (p. 1607). Rather, gun carrying was more typically found in students who harbored extremely aggressive attitudes and behaviors. In a study of attitudes toward guns and violence in third through twelfth grade students, a multiple-factor analysis was used to identify those clusters of attitudes and beliefs that help explain the motivational components of attraction toward guns and violence (Shapiro, Dorman, Burkey, Welker, & Clough, 1997). The results suggested adolescents are likely to want a gun if: (1) they find guns exciting and stimulating; (2) they feel guns provide power and safety; (3) they feel comfortable with physical aggression; and (4) if offended, they can recover their pride only by fighting. Overall, these studies indicate gun use among children is more complex than simply a defensive reaction to a hostile environment.

The research on childhood exposure and access to firearms confirms that many school-age children in American society can easily obtain a firearm if they wish, even though laws forbid the sale of firearms to minors. Moreover, among inner city adolescents, theft and "straw" purchases (i.e., where a person who can legally purchase a gun buys one for a person who cannot legally purchase one) may be important sources for obtaining guns. The research also suggests that the use of firearms by school-age youths is much greater among those who live in the inner city. Several factors may contribute to this. First, these adolescents may perceive the need to use a gun for self-protection because they live in a world that is hostile and violent (Sheley & Wright, 1993). Second, handguns may be more readily available at low prices to adolescents in the inner city. Third, poverty and limited resources and neighborhood disorganization, which contribute to a greater prevalence of violent behavior among inner city adolescents, are also associated with gun use. Although the most popular explanation for why children obtain and carry guns is self-protection, the available research suggests this is an oversimplification. It appears that although self-protection is a critical motivation for gun carrying, involvement in delinquent activities such as drug dealing and a propensity for violent behavior may be key motivational factors as well. The supply of guns and demand for guns among adolescents appear to be substantial. Both must be addressed if we are to reduce current levels of gun violence. (See Chapter 3 of this volume for another discussion of this issue.)

Firearm Violence in and Around Schools

The *impact* of firearm violence on children as they travel to and from school and engage in activities in and around schools has not been researched extensively. This impact can be measured in terms of physical injury and death, psychological trauma to victims and witnesses, and disruption of the school learning environment. In an investigation of firearm violence in and around schools from 1986–1990, the Center to Prevent Handgun Violence (1990) identified 65 firearm-related fatalities and 186 nonfatal firearm injuries involving students. The accuracy and completeness of the information on the circumstances of these cases was limited, however, since the investigation relied on published newspaper accounts only. The main findings were that male teenagers (ages 14–17) were the primary offenders and victims, handguns were the most frequent type of weapon used, and incidents were twice as likely to occur near high schools as near junior high or elementary schools. In addition, shootings associated with interpersonal violence were four times as common as those associated with suicidal behavior or unintentional circumstances. The most common contexts in which these events occurred included gang/drug activity, longstanding disagreements, disagreements involving romantic relationships, and playing with or cleaning guns.

More recently a study of school-associated violent deaths (not necessarily by firearms) in the United States found 105 such deaths between 1992–1994. Data were derived from the National School Safety Center, the U.S. Department of Education, and a systematic search of two computerized newspaper and broadcast media databases (Kachur, Stennies, Powell, et al., 1996). Details on the circumstances of these events were obtained through a systematic review of police and medical examiner reports and interviews with police and school officials. Homicides accounted for 81% of these violent fatalities and suicide the remaining 19% of the cases. Firearms were the weapon used in the great majority (77%) of these incidents, and among those incidents in which the firearm type could be determined, handguns were the most frequently used type of gun (89%). Most, but not all, of the victims were students (72%), and less than half of the cases (44%) occurred during official school-sponsored activities. The risk of a school-associated violent death for students was determined to be low, only .09 deaths per 100,000 students, but students in secondary grades had a risk 13 times greater than students in elementary grades. In addition, although these violent deaths occurred in all types of communities, students in urban school districts were found to be at twice the risk of a school-associated violent death as students in suburban districts, and at nine times the risk of students in rural school districts. Based on a total of 75 violent deaths among students (63 homicides and 12 suicides) over the study period, it was determined that less than 1% of all homicides and suicides among school-age children in 1992 were school-associated.

Although this study showed fatalities were rare, 23% of students in a study of gun-related interpersonal violence among inner city high school students reported they had been victims of gun-related violence while in school or on the way to or from school in the preceding few years (Sheley, McGee, & Wright, 1992). Twenty percent of students said they had been threatened with a gun, and 12% said they had been shot at with a firearm. Male students were twice as likely as female students to have been threatened with a gun, and three times as likely to have been fired upon. Results of this study suggest the level of gun-related victimization experienced by inner city students in and around schools is substantially greater than for the country as a whole (Bastian & Taylor, 1991). This study also used a regression analysis to examine risk factors for gun-related victimization (i.e., being threatened or shot at with a gun) in and around schools. The basic finding from this analysis was that this type of victimization derives from factors external to schools. Male youths, children from large families, youths from families in which males carried guns routinely, youths who carried guns, and youths who used or sold drugs were at significantly greater risk of gun-related victimization independent of other factors addressed in the study.

The psychological impact of exposure to firearm violence in and around schools has not been directly studied. However, substantial evidence indicates exposure to such violence can adversely affect childhood development and the ability to function in school (Groves, Zuckerman, Marans, &

Cohen, 1993; Pynoos & Nader, 1990). Children who witness violence may exhibit symptoms associated with post-traumatic stress disorder, such as diminished ability to concentrate in school, sleep disturbances, flashbacks, and a fatalistic orientation toward the future (Lyons, 1987). Available evidence suggests the severity of a child's response to trauma is related to the physical distance between the child and the violent event, the victim's relationship with the child, and the presence of a parent or caretaker to help mediate the impact of the event on the child (Pynoos, Frederick, Nader, et al., 1987).

It is important to note that while gun-related injury and trauma have increased in and around American schools during the past decade, death and serious injuries from firearm violence are a much less common problem in and around schools than in the streets and neighborhoods in which children live (Center to Prevent Handgun Violence, 1990). Nevertheless, the impact of even one such death or injury can extend far beyond those directly involved, through psychological trauma to friends, acquaintances, and witnesses, and by severely disrupting the learning environment (Collison, Bowden, Patterson, et al., 1987). Even the threat posed by the presence of a gun without any injury occurring is very disruptive. Interpersonal violence is the primary context for firearm violence in and around schools, and firearm violence there primarily involves older adolescent males. The problem appears to be much greater for students in urban school districts than elsewhere. The available scientific evidence clearly suggests that many of the risk factors for being a victim of firearm violence derive from behavioral and environmental factors external to the school environment; however, this issue deserves much more study. Likely risk factors for victimization among children include attending school in an urban community, exposure to family role models who engage in gun carrying, and involvement in high-risk behaviors such as gun carrying or drug dealing (cf. Chapter 5 of this volume). There is no specific research to date that we know of identifying risk factors for the perpetration of firearm violence among children or adolescents.

A Process for Finding Effective Solutions

We must use science to help prevent the problem of firearm violence in and around schools. Although we know a great deal about the causes of violence in general, the particular nexus of firearm injuries to children in and around schools and outside the school environment is only beginning to be studied. The public health approach described in Figure 6.3 provides a

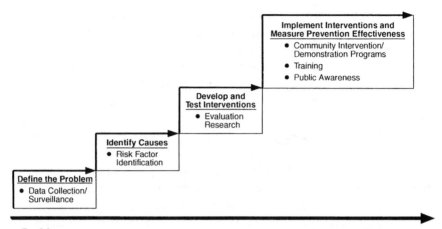

Figure 6.3. Public health model of a scientific approach to violence prevention. *Source:* Mercy, J. A., Rosenberg, M. L., Powell, K. E., Broome, C. V., & Roper, W. L. (1993, Winter). Public health policy for preventing violence. *Health Affairs, 12*(4), 7–29.

multidisciplinary, scientific approach explicitly directed toward identifying effective approaches to prevention (Mercy, Rosenberg, Powell, Broome, & Roper, 1993). This approach begins with defining the problem and progresses to identifying risk factors and causes, developing and implementing interventions, and evaluating intervention programs. Although Figure 6.3 suggests a linear progression from the first step to the last, in reality many of these steps are likely to occur simultaneously. In addition, the kind of information and data collection systems used to define the problem may also be useful in evaluating programs. Similarly, information gained in program implementation and evaluation may lead to new and promising interventions.

Defining the Problem

The first step in this approach, defining the problem, includes delineating incidents of firearm violence in or around schools and related mortality and morbidity, but goes beyond simply counting cases. This step includes obtaining information on, for example, the demographic characteristics of the persons involved, the temporal and geographic characteristics of the incident, the victim/perpetrator relationship, and the severity and cost of the injury. The information collected should be useful for answering questions such as these: How often does gun violence occur in or around schools? When and under what circumstances? Who has been involved or witnessed the event? Were drugs or alcohol involved? These additional factors may be important in defining discrete subsets of firearm violence for which various specific interventions may be appropriate. Each school and school district is unique, and it is important to collect information that will give an accurate picture of gun violence and the related problems in specific schools. Information can be collected from focus groups, incident reports, and surveys. Most of the descriptive information that has been collected so far pertains to inner city schools and children, but we need to know much more about suburban and rural children and schools. This information should be collected in advance of any crisis; in fact, having this information on hand will make it easier to respond appropriately when an incident of violence does occur, and may make it possible to avert a more serious crisis.

We need more descriptive studies of the patterns of firearm violence among children in and around schools. There are several priorities for descriptive studies. First, studies are needed to determine the validity and reliability of survey questions employed in questionnaires concerning gun use among adolescents. This information can then be used to develop better questionnaires about gun carrying and use. At present the diversity of methods used to inquire about these behaviors makes it difficult to interpret results across studies. Second, studies are needed to accurately quantify the nature and magnitude of firearm violence and related mortality and morbidity in and around schools. At present there are fewer than five studies in this area and each has significant limitations. Third, the current understanding of exposure to and use of firearms by school-age children is based on studies of inner city children. Although the study of this problem among inner city children should remain a priority, we need additional research on patterns of exposure to and use of firearms by children who live in suburban and rural communities. Fourth, firearm use among female students should be more closely examined, given the suggestion in the research literature that the prevalence of gun carrying among females is not insignificant. Fifth, although we know the problem of firearm violence has gotten worse in society in general, we need to discover whether it has gotten worse in and around schools or whether any progress has been made in this regard.

One method for better defining the problem and gathering data on trends is to create a surveillance system for the ongoing and systematic collection, analysis, and interpretation of data on firearm violence and firearm

use in and around schools. Such data could be helpful to school administrators in determining the extent of the problem, developing appropriate
preventive responses, and evaluating progress toward reducing the problem. It would probably be unreasonable to establish such a system for
firearm violence and firearm use alone; rather, such information could be
derived from a more general surveillance system focused on gathering
data on all violence in and around schools. Among the barriers to schools
collecting this sort of information is school administrators' valid concern
that such data may be used by the media or critics to unfairly and unfa-
vorably characterize their schools. However, procedures could be developed to protect the anonymity of schools while preserving their ability to
use the information to improve their response to this problem.

Identifying Causes

The second step in the public health approach involves identifying causes.
Whereas the first step examines who, when, where, what, and how, the second step explores why. This step may also be used to define populations
at high risk and to suggest specific interventions. Risk factors can be identified by a variety of scientific research methodologies including rate cal-
culations, cohort studies, and case-control studies.

The total volume of analytic research specifically focused on the causes
or risk factors for firearm violence in and around schools is very limited.
We need further research on questions such as: Why do children want guns
and why do they carry them? What is the relationship between guns and
other violence in and around schools? What social, community, and environmental factors account for variations among schools in the magnitude
of firearm violence? Are increases in youth homicide and suicide primarily
a function of greater access to firearms or a greater willingness to use
firearms?

Developing and Testing Interventions

The next step is to develop interventions based, in large part, on information obtained from the previous steps and to test these interventions. This
step includes evaluating the efficacy of programs, policies, or interventions
already in place. Methods for testing include prospective randomized controlled trials; comparisons of intervention and comparison populations for
occurrence of health outcomes; time series analysis of trends in multiple
areas; and observational studies, such as case-control studies.

Very little is known about the effectiveness of most interventions to prevent gun violence, therefore it is necessary to initiate programs based on our best knowledge of what is likely to work. Two principles follow from this. First, we must strive to complete rigorous evaluations of existing intervention programs. Second, we must continually assess and improve intervention programs based on these evaluations. There is a critical need to ensure that interventions are evaluated before they are adopted on a wide scale.

Implementing Interventions and Measuring Prevention Effectiveness

The final stage is to implement proven interventions or those that are highly likely to be effective. In both instances, it is important that data be collected to evaluate the program's effectiveness, particularly since an intervention that has been found effective in a clinical trial or an academic study may perform differently at the community or state level. Another important component of this fourth stage is determining the cost-effectiveness of such programs. Balancing the costs of a program against the cases prevented by the intervention can be helpful to policy makers in determining optimal public health practice.

Another important facet of the implementation phase is to develop guidelines and procedures for putting effective programs in place. For example: How does one involve parents and students in programs designed to prevent firearm violence in and around schools? How does one build effective coalitions across traditionally separate sectors such as criminal justice, education, and public health? How does one continuously assess and improve the programs put into place? This is especially important because so far there is little information about which programs work on a large scale. How does one adopt interventions for particular community values, cultures, and standards and, at the same time, allow for and benefit from racially/culturally diverse participation from all segments of the community?

Prevention Strategies

In light of the previous discussion of risk and protective factors associated with firearm violence, any prevention strategy that reduces violence generally in the community should also reduce gun-related violence in schools. These broad, community-level interventions are discussed in other chapters. In our discussion of prevention strategies, we focus more narrowly on

Table 6.3. *Strategies for preventing firearm injuries*

Strategies	Interventions
Controlling access to firearms	Permissive licensing (e.g., all but felons, minors, the mentally ill, etc.)
	Restrictive licensing (e.g., only police, military, guards, etc.)
	Waiting periods
	Forbid sales to high-risk purchasers
	Disrupt illegal gun markets
	Combination/electronic locks on guns
	Promotion of safe storage of guns
Changing how firearms are used	Restriction of gun carrying in public
	Mandatory sentences for gun use in crimes
	Owner liability for damage by guns
	Safety education
	Metal detectors
	Gun-free school zones
Reducing the lethality of firearms/ ammunition	Develop "safe" guns
	Reduction of magazine size
	Ban dangerous ammunition

prevention and intervention strategies designed specifically to address gun-related violence in the school context. We review only those interventions related directly to the role of firearms in violence or key risk factors for firearm violence in and around schools. We consider interventions that affect access to and use of firearms by school-age children, and strategies that can be applied at all jurisdictional levels (i.e., national, state, and local).

Table 6.3 summarizes a range of strategies and associated interventions that have the potential to reduce firearm violence among school-age children, both within and outside the school environment (Reiss & Roth, 1993). The three broad strategies include controlling access to firearms, changing how firearms are used, and reducing the lethality of firearms. Few of these interventions have been rigorously evaluated, and none have been evaluated to assess their impact on firearm injuries and violence specifically among school-age children. The interventions associated with these strategies have been implemented in various jurisdictions, ranging from the local to the national level. Many of these interventions are already reflected in current law, and often what is required is better enforcement of existing regulations. An important assumption is that the prevention of firearm violence in and around schools cannot be achieved through interventions targeted solely at the school environment. What will be needed is a comprehensive strategy combining socially acceptable and effective interventions across school, community, state, and national jurisdictions.

Controlling Access to Firearms

Inevitably, people who should not have guns have access to them. Some are people who intend to commit crimes. Others are people with impaired judgment, such as alcohol or drug abusers. Keeping firearms out of the hands of children and adolescents in the absence of adult supervision should be an especially high priority.

Since, for the most part, the avenues through which adolescents obtain guns are already illegal, greater enforcement of existing laws regulating the illegal transfer of guns may have a high return in reducing firearm violence among school-age children (Sheley & Wright, 1993). Law enforcement agencies might focus on disrupting illegal local and interstate gun markets in a fashion analogous to anti-drug efforts (Cook & Moore, 1994). Virginia has enacted a law restricting handgun purchases to one per month per individual, thus indirectly disrupting illegal interstate transfer of handguns by undermining the economic incentive. Criminals frequently purchase large quantities of guns in states with low retail prices and sell them in states that have much higher street prices due to restrictive gun laws (Weil & Knox, 1995). An evaluation of Virginia's law found that after it was passed the odds that guns used in crimes in states outside of Virginia could be traced back to a Virginia gun dealer rather than a dealer in another southeastern state were substantially reduced. However, it is not known whether the gun purchases that would have been made in Virginia were displaced to other states, or if this law actually reduced firearm deaths and injuries. Unfortunately, there is only limited research on the effectiveness of this approach to reducing gun-related violence. It may or may not be a cost-effective strategy for reducing adolescent access to firearms.

A type of intervention that holds promise for having an immediate impact on firearm injuries and violence among school-age children is requiring and promoting the safe and secure storage of firearms. This approach may limit the access of both children and burglars to guns. Theft is a major source of guns for illegal markets, and theft and burglary are the ultimate, although not always immediate, source through which juveniles obtain guns (Cook & Moore, 1994; Sheley & Wright, 1993). An estimated 400,000 firearms are stolen from households each year, and this figure excludes thefts from commercial establishments (Cook & Moore,

1994). Interventions promoting safe and secure gun storage through public education, or that impose requirements for safe and secure storage on owners or dealers, could help to reduce the supply of firearms to the illegal markets in which adolescents often obtain these weapons.

A longer-term strategy for reducing theft as a source of guns for adolescents would be to advance the technological research of developing "smart" guns that are rendered useless if attempted to be used by anyone other than the owner (e.g., a law enforcement officer). "Smart" guns might operate by recognizing the owner's palm print, or by being operational only in close proximity to a holster or special ring.

Some other interventions designed to control access to guns that have been evaluated include restrictive licensing laws and efforts to prohibit sales to convicted felons and to minors. The 1968 Federal Gun Control Law, among many other provisions, prohibits sales to certain classes of individuals including minors, convicted felons, drug users, and persons with mental illness (Zimring, 1975). In an extensive evaluation of the administration and impact of this law, it was discovered that little was done to enforce its provisions. Although the prosecution of these types of illegal transactions increased, the sheer volume of transactions that required policing far exceeded the capacity of the U.S. Bureau of Alcohol, Tobacco, and Firearms (ATF), which was given the administrative responsibility for enforcing this law, to perform its task. Whether this type of legal provision can be effective with adequate enforcement capabilities remains to be seen. In 1977, Washington, D.C., passed a restrictive licensing law prohibiting handgun ownership by everyone but police officers, security guards, and previous gun owners. Immediately, firearm suicides and homicides declined by 25% (Loftin, McDowall, Wiersema, & Cottey, 1991). The impact of this law on reducing firearm violence specifically among school-age children has not yet been studied.

Change How Firearms Are Used

A comprehensive strategy to prevent firearm injuries should be designed not only to limit access by people who should not have guns, but also to prevent those people who do gain possession of firearms from using them unlawfully. Among the interventions included within this strategy are laws prohibiting the carrying of guns in public and imposing a mandatory sentence for crimes perpetrated with a firearm. These laws have been found to have small but positive effects in reducing firearm homicides (McDowall, Loftin, & Wiersema, 1992; Pierce & Bowers, 1981; Rossman,

Paul, Pierce, McDevitt, & Bowers, 1980). Easing of laws prohibiting the carrying of a concealed firearm, a form of permissive licensing, has been found to be associated with modest increases in firearm homicide (McDowall, Loftin, & Wiersema, 1995).

Enforcement of existing laws regulating firearm carrying may also be an effective way to prevent firearm violence among school-age children, given their reported prevalence of gun carrying. In an experiment conducted in Kansas City, police used directed patrols to increase enforcement of laws against carrying concealed weapons in a specific target area. Researchers compared the impact of this strategy with a similar, nonadjacent beat in which the strategy was not used (Sherman, Shaw, & Rogan, 1995). The results indicated directed police patrols in gun crime "hot spots" can reduce gun crime by increasing seizures of illegally carried guns. Gun crimes declined by 49% in the target beat while remaining unchanged in the control beat, and there was no measurable displacement of gun crimes to surrounding beats. The specific impact of this strategy on gun crimes involving school-age children has not yet been studied. A similar approach to enhanced enforcement of laws against concealed and illegally carried weapons could be applied to areas around schools. Although a federal law banning guns within one thousand feet of schools was recently overturned by the Supreme Court, local jurisdictions may be able to pass and enforce similar laws, since their ability to do this does not depend on the commerce clause of the Constitution.

Metal detector programs are among the most popular and controversial of school-based strategies for reducing gun carrying and storage in schools. As of the late 1980s, approximately one-fourth of large urban school districts in the United States had metal detector programs (National School Safety Center, 1990). A study of violence-related attitudes and behaviors among students in New York City high schools found students who attended schools with metal detector programs were equally likely as those who attended schools without metal detector programs to have carried a weapon outside of school, but were less likely to have carried a weapon inside the school building or going to or from school (Centers for Disease Control and Prevention, 1993). The decrease in school-related weapon carrying reflected reductions in the carrying of both knives and handguns. No studies have yet been done to determine whether the programs reduced the incidence of firearm violence in the schools.

Some schools have also used strategies other than metal detectors for reducing gun carrying in schools. For example, some have tried to make it harder to carry or store guns undetected, including random locker searches, closing and/or removing lockers, limiting the size and concealability of book bags, and encouraging students to report weapon violations to school officials (Office of Juvenile Justice and Delinquency Prevention, 1989). Clear school policies prohibiting weapon carrying, though they are a prerequisite for keeping guns out of schools, are not sufficient in and of themselves. The National School Safety Center (1990) recommends that schools enhance campus security by taking responsibility for implementing security measures; establishing a school security committee; developing a crisis management plan; developing a communications network linking the front office, classrooms, and the schoolyard; regularly updating staff on security issues; using parent and community volunteers to help patrol surrounding neighborhoods and supervise the campus; limiting and monitoring access points to school grounds; and encouraging students to report suspicious individuals or activities. Each of these measures is described in detail in Chapter 9 of this volume.

Gun safety education is being provided to students in some school districts. The contents of these curricula vary from community to community. In some curricula the focus is on avoiding firearms altogether, while in others the primary emphasis is on safe handling of firearms (National Center for Injury Prevention and Control, 1993). For example, a program called Kids + Guns = A Deadly Equation was designed by the Dade County, Florida, Public Schools, the Center to Prevent Handgun Violence, and Youth Crime Watch of Dade to teach students from kindergarten through high school about the dangers of playing with or carrying guns (Northrop & Hamrick, 1990). This program includes classroom instruction and schoolwide activities that center on helping students to: recognize unsafe situations, react appropriately when encountering guns, resist peer pressure to play with or carry guns, and distinguish between real-life and media gun violence. The National Rifle Association (NRA) has also developed gun safety curricula (Northrop & Hamrick, 1990). One such program is targeted at children in kindergarten through second grade and features a cartoon character, Eddie the Eagle. Eddie delivers the message that children encountering a gun should "Stop. Don't Touch. Leave the Area. Tell an Adult." The efficacy of gun safety educational programs has not been determined.

Creating safe routes for children going to and from school may decrease students' perceived level of danger and, in doing so, may decrease the degree to which they feel a need to carry weapons to and from school for self-defense. In the East Harlem section of New York City, a program called Safe Routes/Safe Havens was established for students in two junior high schools (Battelle Institute, 1995). The New York City Department of Health worked with the police department, a local community board, and schools to establish a predetermined route for students to follow to school, to recruit merchants to serve as "islands of safety" where students could go if they felt threatened or harassed, and to increase police presence along the safe route. A preliminary evaluation indicated knowledge of the program was low among students and parents, and, therefore, greater effort was needed to promote awareness of the program. Nevertheless, the creation of safe environments for children in and around schools must be an important priority, given the association between perceptions of safety and gun carrying among youth.

Reducing the Lethality of Firearms/Ammunition

Firearms and their ammunition are consumer products and, as such, can be designed with greater safety in mind (Christoffel, 1991; Hemenway & Weil, 1990). The premise underlying this approach is that modification of firearms or ammunition can provide a measure of protection not dependent on the behavior of the user or a potential victim. Design modifications such as loading indicators or minimum standards for trigger-safety mechanisms could reduce the likelihood of unintended discharges, thereby reducing unintentional firearm injuries, particularly to children (Christoffel, 1991; Hemenway & Weil, 1990). Even more speculative is the possibility that guns or ammunition could be developed that would be useful for self-protection, but be substantially less lethal, through the use of advanced electronics or pharmacologic agents (Hemenway & Weil, 1990).

Conclusion

In this country, we believe we should and can provide schools where it is safe for our children to learn and our teachers to teach. This is an important and attainable goal. It will require attention to the problem of children and violence in homes and communities as well as in schools. And it will require a serious investment and sustained commitment to change. The degree to which the debate in the United States about firearm violence has been polarized is no small part of the problem. We must move forward and find common ground. We believe the public debate about firearms should be reframed, evolving from a gridlocked political and philosophical debate to an informed discussion based on scientifically documented information about patterns, costs, and benefits of firearm ownership and access. Some of this information is available, but much remains to be developed. If we do this, we can move forward to save lives and prevent injuries. This section summarizes a framework for the development of public policies that draws upon the knowledge base reviewed in this chapter. The following recommendations are offered as guidelines for making progress in preventing firearm injuries among children that can be applied both nationally and within local school districts:

1. *Establish School-Based Surveillance Systems for Violent Behavior.* Systems should be established to routinely gather information on the frequency and key characteristics of violence as it occurs in and around schools and on the way to and from schools. As part of this system information should be collected to quantify the nature and magnitude of firearm availability and violence. Since the nature and characteristics of violence may differ from community to community, each school should collect its own data. These data, collected for local analysis and response development, should, at a minimum, describe the demographic characteristics of persons involved, characteristics of incidents, types of weapons involved, victim/ perpetrator relationship, and severity and cost of the injuries.

2. *Use Science to Guide Action.* Science is a critical tool for developing effective solutions to the problem of violence among children and adolescents. Local colleges and universities can be a valuable source of expertise in assisting local school districts in acquiring knowledge about the causes of violence, establishing surveillance systems, and evaluating the effectiveness of prevention programs. Nationally, a research agenda is needed to focus funding organizations and researchers on the questions most critical to the development of effective policies. This agenda should be informed by the leading researchers in this field as well as leading educators. Some of the scientific priorities for addressing the role of firearms in violence affecting children and adolescents in and around schools include:

- Assessment of the factors that affect the demand for and supply of firearms to children and adolescents.
- Research into the exposure to and use of firearms by children and adolescents who live in suburban and rural communities.
- Determination of the validity and reliability of survey questions concerning gun use among adolescents, and developing standard and reliable methods for asking about these behaviors and attitudes.
- Disentangling whether increases in adolescent homicide and suicide are a function primarily of greater access to firearms or a greater willingness to use firearms.
- Rigorous evaluation of the effectiveness of programs, interventions, and policies to prevent firearm violence in and around schools.

3. *Adopt a Learn-As-We-Go Approach.* In order to prevent violence and the associated use of firearms we must act. However, because our knowledge of what works in preventing violence in and around schools is still limited, it is important to rigorously evaluate these actions. We must develop programs which acknowledge both the importance of proceeding scientifically while simultaneously doing something now to deal with the urgency of this problem. There are several measures relating to firearm-related violence involving children in and around schools that could be immediately adopted and simultaneously evaluated:

- Enhancement of school security through improved planning, organization, and communication.

- Provision of information about gun safety and safety training programs.
- Creation of safe routes for children to and from school to decrease students' risk and perceived level of danger.
- Limiting the carrying of weapons to school with control measures such as the use of metal detectors, lockers accessible for inspection, and book bags that cannot conceal weapons.
- Establishment of a crisis response plan that focuses on reducing the extent of the violence and disruption of the school environment after a violent act, both in the immediate situation and the long-term impact of violence on witnesses and victims.

4. *Emphasize Coordinated Action.* The complexity of violent behavior defies a single simple solution. Multiple, complementary activities are required to effectively prevent violence, and they will demand the involvement of a broad spectrum of participants including citizens, local officials, businesses, grassroots organizations, and a variety of governmental agencies including justice, education, health, labor, and housing. The success of efforts to address violence and firearm injury to children in and around schools will depend, in no small part, on the ability of a community to coordinate its violence prevention activities across various sectors.

5. *Stress the Importance of Changing the Social Environment.* In addressing the problem of violence and firearm injuries to children, we must broaden the range of solutions to include changes in the social environment. Recent research points to numerous dimensions of economic deprivation, for example, associated with high community rates of violence: high concentrations of poverty; high population mobility; family disruption; crowded housing; weak local social structure (e.g., low organizational participation in community life, weak intergenerational ties in families and communities, low density of friends and acquaintances); and the presence of dangerous commodities or opportunities associated with violence (e.g., drug distribution networks) (Levine & Rosich, 1996; Reiss & Roth, 1993). In the final analysis, if we are to prevent violence, these fundamental societal issues must be addressed at the same time that we take all possible immediate actions to prevent violence. In addressing violence to children in and around schools, we must recognize the need to reinvest in social capital and address poverty, discrimination, lack of jobs, lack of education, and lack of hope (cf. Chapter 5 of this volume).

6. *Rigorously Enforce Existing Laws.* Many laws already exist that are directed at limiting inappropriate access to or use of guns by children. What is needed is renewed commitment to and innovative strategies for enforcing these laws. The types of law enforcement approaches that hold promise in helping to more rigorously enforce existing laws and, thereby, reduce inappropriate access of children to guns include:

- Directed police patrols to increase enforcement of laws prohibiting the carrying of concealed firearms.
- Disruption of illegal markets which sell firearms to children and youth or to persons who sell firearms to children and youth.

7. *Explore New Technologies that Will Enhance Enforcement Capabilities and Gun Safety.* New technology can potentially help in addressing this problem in two ways. First, technology is being developed to enable more accurate and less intrusive detection of illegally carried or concealed weapons and to help keep firearms off school property and out of the hands of children. Second, there is the potential to use technology to manufacture firearms that cannot be operated by young children or others not authorized to use them. Continued investment in and testing of

these new technologies may provide substantial benefits to preventing firearm injuries among children and youth.

Through adherence to this framework and other actions detailed in this volume we can make progress in reducing violence to children and youth both within and outside of the school environment. A sustained and coordinated effort to prevent violence and the associated firearm injuries will be necessary at all levels of society to address this complex and deeply rooted problem. But this is a problem we can solve.

References

American School Health Association, Association for the Advancement of Health Education, & Society for Public Health Education (1989). *The national adolescent health survey: A report on the health of America's youth.* Oakland: CA: Third Party.

Annest, J. L., Mercy, J. A., Gibson, D. R., & Ryan, G. W. (1995). National estimates of nonfatal firearm-related injuries: Beyond the tip of the iceberg. *Journal of the American Medical Association, 273*(22), 1749–1754.

Bastian, L. D., & Taylor, B. M. (1991). *School crime: A national crime victimization survey report.* Washington, DC: U.S. Department of Justice.

Battelle Institute. (1995). *Reducing the burden of injury; An evaluation of CDC's injury grant program: A report to the Centers for Disease Control and Prevention, National Center for Injury Prevention and Control.* Arlington, VA: Author.

Blumstein, A. (1995). Youth violence, guns, and the illicit-drug industry. *The Journal of Criminal Law and Criminology, 86*(1), 10–36.

Boyd, J. H., & Moscicki, E. K. (1986). Firearms and youth suicide. *American Journal of Public Health, 76,* 1240–1242.

Bureau of Justice Statistics. (1992). *Criminal victimization in the United States, 1991* (Report No. NCJ-139563). Washington, DC: U.S. Department of Justice, Office of Justice Programs, Bureau of Justice Statistics.

Bureau of Justice Statistics. (1993). *Criminal victimization in the United States, 1992* (Report No. NCJ-145125). Washington, DC: U.S. Department of Justice, Office of Justice Programs, Bureau of Justice Statistics.

Centers for Disease Control and Prevention. (1993). Violence-related attitudes and behaviors of high school students: New York City, 1992. *Morbidity and Mortality Weekly Report, 42*(40), 773–777.

Centers for Disease Control and Prevention (1994). Homicide among 15–19-year-old males. *Morbidity and Mortality Weekly Report, 43*(40), 725–727.

Centers for Disease Control and Prevention. (1995). Suicide among children, adolescents, and young adults: United States, 1980–1992. *Morbidity and Mortality Weekly Report, 44*(15), 289–291.

Center to Prevent Handgun Violence. (1990). *Caught in the crossfire: A report on gun violence in our nation's schools.* Washington, DC: Author.

Christoffel, K. K. (1991). Toward reducing pediatric injuries from firearms: Charting a legislative and regulatory course. *Pediatrics, 88*(2), 294–305.

Collison, B. B., Bowden, S., Patterson, M., Snyder, J., Sandall, S., & Wellman, P. (1987). After the shooting stops. *Journal of Counseling and Development, 65*(7), 389–390.

Cook, P. J. (1991). The technology of personal violence. In M. Tonry (Ed.), *Crime and justice: A review of research* (Vol. 14). Chicago: University of Chicago Press.

Cook, P. J., & Moore, M. H. (1994). *Gun control policy* [working paper]. Durham, NC: Duke University, Institute of Policy Sciences and Affairs.

Davis, J. A., & Smith, T. W. (1986). *General social surveys, 1972–1986: Cumulative codebook.* Chicago: National Opinion Research Center.

Groves, B. M., Zuckerman, B., Marans, S., & Cohen, D. J. (1993). Silent victims: Children who witness violence [commentary]. *Journal of the American Medical Association, 269*(2), 262–264.

Hemenway, D., & Weil, D. (1990). Phasors on stun: The case for less lethal weapons. *Journal of Policy Analysis and Management, 9*(1), 94–98.

Hollinger, P. C., & Offer, D. (1981). Perspectives on suicide in adolescence. In J. R. Greenley (Ed.), *Research in community and mental health* (Vol. 2) (pp. 139–157). Greenwich, CT: JAI Press.

Kachur, S. P., Stennies, G. M., Powell, K. P., Modzeleski, W., Stephens, R., Murphy, R., Kresnow, M., Sleet, D., & Lowry, R. (1996). School-associated violent deaths in the United States, 1992 to 1994. *Journal of the American Medical Association, 275*(22), 1729–1733.

Kann, L., Warren, C. W., Harris, W. A., Collins, J. A., Douglas, K. A., Collins, M. E., Williams, B. I., Ross, J. G., & Kolbe, L. J. (1995) Youth risk behavior surveillance: United States, 1993. In *CDC Surveillance Summaries,* March 24, 1995. *Morbidity and Mortality Weekly Report, 44*(No. SS-1), 1–56.

Lee, R. K., & Sacks, J. J. (1990). Latchkey children and guns at home [letter to the editor]. *Journal of the American Medical Association, 264*(17), 2210.

Levine, F. J., & Rosich, K. J. (1996). *Social causes of violence: Crafting a science agenda.* Washington, DC: American Sociological Association.

LH Research, Inc. (1993, June). *A survey of experiences, perceptions, and apprehensions about guns among young people in America* (Report to the Harvard School of Public Health). New York: Author.

Loftin, C., McDowall, D., Wiersema, B., & Cottey, T. J. (1991). Effects of restrictive licensing of handguns on homicide and suicide in the District of Columbia. *The New England Journal of Medicine, 325,* 1615–1620.

Lyons, J. A. (1987). Post-traumatic stress disorder in children and adolescents: A review of the literature. In S. Chess & A. Thomas (Eds.), *Annual progress in child psychiatry* (pp. 451–467). New York: Brunner Mazel.

McDowall, D., Loftin, C., & Wiersema, B. (1992). A comparative study of the preventive effects of mandatory sentencing laws for gun crimes. *Journal of Criminal Law and Criminology, 83,* 378–394.

McDowall, D., Loftin, C., & Wiersema, B. (1995). Easing concealed firearm laws: Effects on homicide in three states. *Journal of Criminal Law and Criminology, 86*(1).

Mercy, J. A., Rosenberg, M. L., Powell, K. E., Broome, C. V., & Roper, W. L. (1993, Winter). Public health policy for preventing violence. *Health Affairs, 12*(4), 7–29.

National Center for Injury Prevention and Control. (1993). *The prevention of youth violence: A framework for community action.* Atlanta, GA: U.S. Department of Health and Human Services, Public Health Service, Centers for Disease Control and Prevention, National Center for Injury Prevention and Control.

National Center for Injury Prevention and Control. (1995a). *Injury mortality: National summary of injury mortality data, 1986–1992.* Atlanta, GA: Centers for Disease Control and Prevention.

National Center for Injury Prevention and Control. (1995b). *1992: 10 leading causes of death.* Atlanta, GA: Centers for Disease Control and Prevention.

National School Safety Center. (1990). *Weapons in schools* [NSSC resource paper]. Malibu, CA: Author.

Northrop, D., & Hamrick, K. (1990). Weapons and minority youth violence. *Proceedings of the 1990 Forum on Youth Violence in Minority Communities.* Boston: Education Development Center.

Office of Juvenile Justice and Delinquency Prevention. (1989). *Weapons in schools* [OJJDP juvenile justice bulletin]. Washington, DC: U.S. Department of Justice, Office of Juvenile Justice and Delinquency Prevention.

Pierce, G. L., & Bowers, W. (1981). The Bartley-Fox gun law's short-term impact on crime in Boston. *Annals of the American Academy of Political and Social Sciences, 455,* 120–137.

Price, J. H., Desmo, S. M., & Smith, D. (1991). Inner city adolescents' perceptions of guns: A preliminary investigation. *Journal of School Health, 61,* 255–259.

Pynoos, R. S., & Eth, S. (1985). Children traumatized by witnessing acts of personal violence: Homicide, rape or suicidal behavior. In S. Eth & R. S. Pynoos (Eds.), *Post-traumatic stress disorder in children* (pp. 19–43). Washington, DC: American Psychiatric Press.

Pynoos, R. S., Frederick, C., Nader, K., Arroyo, W., Steinberg, A., Eth, S., Nunez, F., & Fairbanks, L. (1987). Life threat and post-traumatic stress in school-age children. *Archives of General Psychiatry, 44,* 1057–1063.

Pynoos, R. S., & Nader, K. (1990). Children's exposure to violence and traumatic death. *Psychiatric Annals, 20,* 334–344.

Reiss, A. J., & Roth, J. A. (Eds.). (1993). *Understanding and preventing violence.* Washington, DC: National Academy Press.

Rossman, D., Paul, F., Pierce, G. L., McDevitt, J., & Bowers, W. (1980). Massachusetts' mandatory minimum sentence gun law: Enforcement, prosecution, and defense impact. *Criminal Law Bulletin, 61,* 150–163.

Shapiro, J. P., & Burkey, W. M. (1992). *Development of the gun-proneness questionnaire: A measure of attitudes towards guns and violence among urban youth.* Final report for the Gun Safety Institute, Cleveland, OH.

Shapiro, J. P., Dorman, R. L., Burkey, W. M., Welker, C. J., & Clough, J. B. (1997). Development and factor analysis of a measure of youth attitudes toward guns and violence. *Journal of Clinical Child Psychology, 26*(3), 11–320.

Sheley, J. F., & Brewer, V. E. (1995). Possession and carrying of firearms among suburban youth. *Public Health Reports, 110*(1), 16–26.

Sheley, J. F., McGee, Z. T., & Wright, J. D. (1992). Gun-related violence in and around inner-city schools. *American Journal of Diseases of Children, 146,* 677–682.

Sheley, J. F., & Wright, J. D. (1993). *Gun acquisition and possession in selected juvenile samples* [research in brief]. Washington, DC: U.S. Department of Justice.

Sherman, L. W., Shaw, J. W., & Rogan, D. P. (1995). *The Kansas City gun experiment* [research in brief]. Washington, DC: U.S. Department of Justice, Office of Justice Programs, National Institute of Justice.

Taylor, L., Zuckerman, B., Harik, V., & Groves, B. (1992). Exposure to violence among inner city parents and children. *American Journal of Diseases of Children, 146,* 487.

U.S. Bureau of Alcohol, Tobacco, and Firearms. (1991, May 22). How many guns? [press release]. *BATF News.* Washington, DC: Author.

U.S. Department of Justice. (1990). *Age-specific arrest rates and race-specific arrest rates for selected offenses, 1965–1988.* Washington, DC: U.S. Department of Justice, Federal Bureau of Investigation.

U.S. Department of Justice. (1992). *Criminal victimization in the United States: 1973–90 trends* (Report No. NCJ-139564). Washington, DC: U.S. Department of Justice, Bureau of Justice Statistics.

Webster, D. W., Gainer, P. S., & Champion, H. R. (1993). Weapon carrying among inner-city junior high school students: Defensive behavior vs. aggressive delinquency. *American Journal of Public Health, 83,* 1604–1608.

Weil, D. S., & Knox, R. (1995). *Evaluating the impact of Virginia's one-gun-a-month law.* Washington, DC: Center to Prevent Handgun Violence.

Zimring, F. E. (1975). Firearms and federal law: The Gun Control Act of 1968. *Journal of Legal Study, 4*(1), 133–198.

7. Reducing Violence through the Schools

J. DAVID HAWKINS, DAVID P. FARRINGTON,
& RICHARD F. CATALANO

Introduction

Concern about adolescent violence is not new, nor is a focus on the role of schools in reducing violence (McPartland & McDill, 1977). As a society, we are quick to jump to solutions: a violence prevention curriculum for the classroom, a conflict resolution team for the hallways and school grounds, hallway monitors and hallway patrols, visitor sign-ins, metal detectors, or school uniforms. In our view, these are partial solutions that miss a fundamental fact: Effective schools prevent violence. Schools that promote prosocial, cooperative behavior, and a culture of learning, are central to preventing violence.

To design effective strategies for violence prevention in schools, one needs to use what one knows about where violence comes from: what factors contribute to the risk of violent behavior, and what factors protect children against becoming either violent offenders or victims of violence. One also needs to use research evidence regarding effective interventions that reduce risk for and enhance protection against violence.

Given the multiplicity of risk and protective factors for violence, preventive interventions should be guided by theory that suggests the causal mechanisms that link these factors to future violence. Theory plays a critical role in specifying how different risk and protective factors interrelate, and how and when they should be addressed through intervention (Kazdin, 1990).

Risk Factors for Violence

Extensive research has identified risk factors for violence across the life span (American Psychological Association, 1993; Brewer, Hawkins, Catalano, & Neckerman, 1995; Reiss & Roth, 1993; Sampson & Lauritsen, 1994).

Individual and environmental factors interact to promote or inhibit violent behavior. Exposure to multiple risk factors during childhood appears to increase significantly the likelihood of later violence (Huizinga, Loeber, & Thornberry, 1995).

From conception to age six, risk factors for violence include perinatal difficulties (e.g., preterm delivery, low birthweight, and anoxia or oxygen deprivation), physical trauma to infants, minor physical abnormalities and brain damage (e.g., from infectious disease; traumatic head injury; or exposure to toxins such as heavy metals, alcohol, tobacco, or cocaine) (Brennan, Mednick, & Kandel, 1991; Michaud, Rivara, Jaffe, Fay, & Dailey, 1993). Some of these factors may impair reasoning and impulse control in the developing child, leading both to later academic and behavioral difficulties in school and to increased risk of violent behavior in stressful situations.

Males engage in more violent behavior in and out of school than females. This holds for both fighting and bullying (Farrington, 1993). For some boys, violence begins early in life in the form of physically aggressive behavior and continues as a violent behavior pattern well into adulthood (Farrington, 1991; Loeber, 1988; Moffitt, 1993). Much aggressive behavior by males, particularly fighting, begins at or near school. And early fighting predicts later conduct disorders (Loeber, Green, Keenan, & Lahey, 1995). Those boys rated by their teachers as "aggressive" in early grades are at significantly greater risk of engaging in later violent behavior as teenagers than are boys rated "nonaggressive" (Farrington, 1991). Similarly, boys who exhibit bullying behavior in early grades are more likely to be involved in violent crime when they are adolescents (Farrington, 1993).

Within the family, poor family management practices increase the risk for violence by children. Such practices include parents' failure to set clear expectations for their children's behavior; failure to supervise and monitor children's behavior; and excessively severe, harsh, or inconsistent punishment (Yoshikawa, 1994). Physically abusive or neglectful parents are more likely to raise violent children (Widom, 1989). In addition, violent disputes between adults in the family increase the risk of later violent behavior by the children (Yoshikawa, 1994). Children whose parents are violent and who witness or are victims of violence in the home are more likely to engage in violence themselves in adolescence and young adulthood (Farrington, 1991; McCord, 1988; Patterson, Capaldi, & Bank, 1991; Salzinger, Feldman, Hammer, & Rosario, 1993).

As children approach adolescence, rebelliousness, association with peers engaged in violence (Cairns, 1996; Elliott & Menard, 1996; Thornberry, 1996), favorable attitudes toward the use of violence (Jessor & Jessor, 1977), and early initiation of violent behavior all predict later violence (Farrington, 1991; Patterson, 1996; Robins, 1978).

More broadly, community contexts also contribute to the risk for violence. Children who live in economically deprived urban neighborhoods characterized by extreme poverty, poor living conditions, and high unemployment are more likely to engage in violent behavior and be victims of violence than are children who live in less deprived areas (Bursik & Grasmick, 1993; Farrington, 1991; Gottfredson & Gottfredson, 1985; Mansfield, Alexander, & Farris, 1991; Yoshikawa, 1994). Children who reside in socially disorganized neighborhoods with high rates of crime and violence, high population density, high residential mobility, physical deterioration, lack of natural surveillance of public places, and low levels of attachment to the neighborhood are at elevated risk for violent behavior (Bastian & Taylor, 1991; Farnworth, 1984; Sampson, 1994).

To some degree, schools reflect their communities. Schools in urban, socially disorganized areas, for example, experience higher rates of victimization than do other schools (Gottfredson & Gottfredson, 1985). Yet schools can contribute to risks for violence or can, by their arrangements and actions, inhibit violent behavior. Specific characteristics of schools have been found to be related to the amount of violence experienced by students (Office of Educational Research and Improvement, 1992). A lack of clear rules governing student behavior, failure to enforce school rules and policies, and ineffective academic instruction all contribute to the development of antisocial behavior within schools (Mayer, 1995; Walker, Colvin, & Ramsey, 1994). A strong academic mission, clear nonviolent and prosocial behavioral norms, consistent and fair rule enforcement, and a climate of emotional support appear to reduce school disorder (Gottfredson & Gottfredson, 1985; Lab & Clark, 1996; Office of Educational Research and Improvement, 1992). Mortimore (1995) provided an excellent review of how differences in schools are associated with a wide range of outcomes for children, including behavior.

During the years of school attendance, students who experience academic failure are at increased risk for involvement in crime, including violence (Maguin & Loeber, 1995). To the extent that schools ensure academic success for all students, they are likely to reduce the students' risk for violence. A lack of commitment to learning has also been found to be predictive of juvenile crime (Hawkins, Catalano, Jones, & Fine, 1987; Yoshikawa, 1994). Schools that instill a commitment to learning and academic achievement in all students promote academic success, and they are likely to reduce the risk for violent behavior as well (Hawkins, Kosterman, Catalano, Abbott, & Hill, 1996).

This is true even for students who have a propensity for violence, as evidenced by aggressive behavior in the elementary grades. For example, O'Donnell, Hawkins, and Abbott (1995) found levels of bonding to school contributed to determining whether boys who had been rated as aggressive by teachers at ages 10 and 11 were engaged in seriously delinquent behavior (including violence) at ages 13 and 14. Even among those at greatest risk of violent behavior by virtue of early aggressiveness, bonding to school was found to be an important protective factor against later violence.

Clearly, then, multiple risk factors in a number of domains, including the individual, family, peer group, community, and the school itself can contribute to risk for violence (Brewer et al., 1995). By creating a community of learning, schools can play a part in violence prevention. But they should not be expected to reduce levels of community violence significantly unless other interventions are initiated to address the sources of violence within families, peer groups, and communities. Although this chapter focuses on what can be done in schools to reduce violence, we assume that better results will be achieved if school-based interventions are nested within a coordinated, well-designed prevention system involving the entire community (Farrington, 1996; Hawkins, Catalano, & Associates, 1992).

Social Development Model: A Theory of Violence Prevention in Schools

The "social development model" is a theory of behavior that seeks to explain why both prosocial and antisocial behaviors emerge over the course of a child's development. It incorporates the risk factors we have just identified and hypothesizes that school environments can contribute to either prosocial or antisocial behavior. The model is briefly presented below, as it bears on the processes of schooling; a more complete version is presented in Catalano and Hawkins (1996).

The social development model views both antisocial (i.e., criminal) and prosocial behaviors as products of the interaction between the individual and the environment (Hawkins & Weis, 1985). It specifies generic processes of social development that recur in different environments over the life course of the developing individual. From ages 6 to 18, the period during which involvement in violent behavior usually emerges and peaks, schools are a major social environment experienced by most children. Children who develop a commitment to succeed in school and who feel attached or bonded to the school community – to teachers and fellow students – are more successful academically than other children. They are also less likely to engage in serious crime, including violent behavior. Bonding to school (as measured by attachment to the school community and commitment to schooling) and academic success help to protect against violent behavior during adolescence.

Social Bonding and Academic Achievement

Bonding to school is the result of an interaction between the developing child and the school environment. The level of bonding between the individual and the school depends, in part, on the degree to which the school provides opportunities to the developing child for active involvement in the educational process (Mortimore, 1995). Opportunities for active participation should be developmentally appropriate to the child's current level of skills, in order to motivate the child to engage in the learning process (Csikszentmihalyi & Larson, 1980).

The development of individual skills or competencies is a second element in the interactive process by which bonding develops. Individuals vary greatly in intellectual skills (Herrnstein & Murray, 1994), but skills vary on a number of dimensions (Gardner, 1993; Goleman, 1995). To the extent that an individual child possesses and uses behavioral, cognitive, emotional, and interpersonal skills in confronting a particular opportunity in school, that child is more likely to experience the opportunity as positive, both as a result of the internal satisfaction derived from an awareness of competence (Csikszentmihalyi & Larson, 1980) and as a result of external reinforcement in the form of praise and approval from teachers and students. In the social development model, reinforcement, rewards, or recognition for skillful involvement is the third element in the process by which bonding to school develops (Mortimore, 1995).

Since Plato set out to train youths to find pleasure in actions which strengthen the bonds of human society rather than weaken them, the creation of social bonding has, itself, been a goal of education (Csikszentmihalyi & Larson, 1980). School personnel, especially teachers, have a great deal of influence over the degree to which children develop a bond to the school community. Teachers, through their selection of curricular materials, choice of classroom management methods, and choice of instructional methods, control the opportunity structure for children at school. Teachers also control many of the reinforcements experienced by students through the methods of classroom management and instruction they use. One of the jobs of the teacher is to provide an opportunity and reinforcement system that promotes the development of desired skills in children. Success in that endeavor creates strong bonding to schools among students.

In thinking about how to promote social bonding to schools, we must bear in mind a crucial fact: The school is only one of many groups in a child's social environment to which bonding may occur. Opportunities for active involvement, skills for participation, and reinforcement for skillful participation are elements in the process by which bonding develops to any social group, whether that group is a school, a class, a family, or a group of peers, such as a delinquent gang. This process can occur, developing a bond between a child and a group, regardless of whether the group holds norms favorable or unfavorable to violent behavior.

The extent to which individuals engage in violent behavior is determined, in part, by the relative balance of opportunities, skills, and reinforcements they experience during development. To the extent that individuals develop bonds of commitment and attachment to other individuals and social groups who do not condone violence, their violent behavior will be inhibited. To the extent that they do not develop such bonds, they are less constrained from violent behavior. They may, in fact, as a result of opportunities and reinforcements experienced in social groups that model, condone, or approve of violent behavior, be encouraged to engage in violence (Bourgois, 1995).

This theoretical view of the etiology of violence has direct implications for violence prevention through the schools. It suggests that the development of a social bond of commitment and attachment to the school on the part of students is, in part, a responsibility of schools. This is accomplished through the provision of appropriate opportunities for active participation and skill development and the use of appropriate reinforcement for skillful performance both inside and outside the classroom. The development of bonds to schools is essential both to ensure successful academic achievement and to create the motivation to live and learn according to norms or standards for nonviolent behavior.

In the school context, violence prevention is more fundamental than a new curriculum taught in addition to the "three Rs" or the installation of a metal detector in a hallway. Violence prevention is a function of the social environment of the school as a whole: of the policies and practices of school administrators that support and encourage a positive learning environment, and of the way teachers manage and teach in classrooms and on playgrounds. Schools that fail to generate strong bonds to school in their students will be unable to counteract the competing influence of gangs and other social groups that reinforce violent behavior, often in schools serving disorganized neighborhoods in poverty.

Promoting Norms of Nonviolence

The explicit development and promotion of norms of nonviolence is a second essential responsibility of schools. Schools that attempt to create the conditions for bonding while condoning violent behavior do not inhibit violence; instead, they unwittingly promote violence. The promotion of norms of nonviolence in schools must include, but go beyond, the specification of formal rules of conduct. It must include influencing the informal norms and expectations for behavior that exist among the students themselves.

The task is difficult. In some neighborhoods, norms endorsing violence are widely accepted and form part of children's environment from birth. Association with groups in which the individual hears violence advocated as acceptable behavior increases the risk of violence. Davies (1982) reported that children sometimes fight to create a good impression on their peers. Fighting "gives you a reputation as someone to be respected and taken into account" (p. 40); "on some occasions children fight not because they are angry per se but because of status considerations, especially to be seen as tough or 'hard'" (Boulton, 1993, p. 28). Coie, Dodge, Terry, and Wright (1991) reported that children who did not stand up for themselves by fighting when it was justified tended to be rejected by their peers.

Many students' families endorse a belief in the need for violence. Ginsberg and Loffredo (1993) found that, in New York City, students who had been involved in physical fights in school were more likely than those who had not to believe their families would want them to hit back if someone hit them first. Families' acceptance of the need for violence is a part of the normative context of childhood that must be confronted. Belief in the principle of reciprocation, or "paying someone back" for an injury, as Davies (1991) pointed out, is widespread: "The rule of negative reciprocation seems to be a very basic law within childhood culture" (p. 257). Boulton (1993) also found similar evidence, even among children who are friends. As stated by one male subject, "Well, if someone hurts you, you've got to get them back, otherwise you're a wimp" (p. 34).

Not fighting can jeopardize a boy's status in childhood and early adolescence. Most boys believe it is important to fight if challenged, to avoid being perceived as a coward: "a constant theme that occurred during many of the interviews was that children felt coerced into fighting by peers who would ridicule them if they backed down in a cowardly way" (Boulton, 1993, p. 35).

Ritualized fighting among boys is part of typical middle school behavior. A boy without status or a stake to lose can enter the "gladiatorial ring" and become recognized by many as a "tough guy." A small number of boys get status from fighting and being perceived as "hard." More fight when they "have to," so as not to "lose face." These group norms are internalized by those who get into fights. Boys who fight are less likely to believe that apologizing and walking away from someone who wants to fight are effective ways to avoid a physical fight (Ginsberg & Loffredo, 1993).

Changing the norms of developing children and adolescents regarding fighting and violent behavior is a major challenge for schools. Fortunately, there are precedents that suggest that it can be done. For example, adolescent norms regarding substance abuse have been successfully modified using school curricula. School-based prevention programs have portrayed drug use as socially unacceptable, identified short-term negative consequences of drug use, provided evidence that drug use is less prevalent among their contemporaries than children may think, encouraged children to make public commitments to remain drug-free, and often engaged peer leaders to teach the curricula. These interventions have produced modest but significant reductions in the onset and prevalence of cigarette smoking, alcohol use, and marijuana use (Ellickson & Bell, 1990; Hansen & Graham, 1991; Perry, 1986). They suggest that a focus on changing child and adolescent norms regarding violent behavior could change the prevalence of violence during ages when violent behavior is most common.

Teaching Skills for Living According to Nonviolent Norms

The social development model emphasizes the importance of teaching skills both for taking advantage of opportunities for prosocial involvement and for avoiding violent behavior. Schools can teach skills for living according to nonviolent norms. Conflict resolution and violence prevention curricula have been designed and implemented to improve students' emotional self-regulation (Greenberg & Kusche, 1993), problem-solving skills (Shure & Spivack, 1982), and anger management skills (Prothrow-Stith, 1987). Directly teaching these skills in school is an important component of violence prevention (Grossman et al., 1997). Unfortunately, as we have noted, this has sometimes been viewed as the only way for schools to contribute to the prevention of violence.

Eliminating Weapons/Firearms

The availability of firearms increases the risk that fighting will result in serious injury or death (see Chapter 6 of this volume). In 1989, 2% of students nationally reported they had taken a weapon of some kind to school to protect themselves during the previous six months (Bastian & Taylor, 1991). By 1993, 13% of a national sample of secondary school students reported bringing weapons to school (Metropolitan Life Insurance Company, 1993). In 1991, the national Youth Risk Behavior Survey found 26% of students in grades 9–12 reported carrying a weapon at least once during the 30 days prior to the survey (as cited in Ginsberg & Loffredo, 1993).

Gun carrying and gun victimization appear most prevalent in inner cities. Among inner city high school students in five cities surveyed in 1991 by Sheley and Wright (1993), 22% said they owned a gun; 12% said they carried a gun most or all of the time; and 9% said they carried a gun to school. Sheley, McGee, and Wright (1992) reported that 20% of inner city high school students surveyed in five cities had been threatened with a gun and 12% had been shot at, with males being three times as likely to be fired upon as females.

Becoming a victim of firearm violence is strongly linked to carrying guns and associating with people who carry guns, as well as with drug use and drug dealing (Sheley et al., 1992). Only one in ten gun victimizations in the study by Sheley and his colleagues was not linked to one or more of these factors. In short, carrying guns and associating with those who do increases the risk of becoming a victim of firearm violence.

In spite of this evidence, Ginsberg and Loffredo (1993) found that students who carried a weapon inside a school building were more likely to believe that threatening to use and carrying a weapon were effective ways to avoid a physical fight than were New York City students in general. Weapon-carrying students were also more likely to feel safer during a fight if they had a knife or handgun. In sum, there are young people who think that arming themselves will make them safer, while the evidence suggests that, in fact, it increases their risk of being injured or killed by a gun.

Interventions

We have identified four ways in which schools can inhibit violent behavior: (1) by the use of management and instructional practices in classrooms and on playgrounds that promote the development of social bonding (i.e., commitment and attachment) to school and academic success; (2) by the promotion of norms antithetical to violent behavior; (3) by teaching skills to resolve conflicts nonviolently; and (4) by minimizing the availability and acceptance of weapons and their use. In addition, some efforts have focused on changing an entire school to make it more protective against violence or risks for violence. We turn now to a review of the empirical evidence regarding the effectiveness of school-based interventions that seek to achieve these aims.

Promoting School Bonding and Academic Achievement

Although not typically considered violence prevention strategies, efforts to change the opportunity and reward structure of schooling have the potential to prevent violent behavior in at least two ways. First, to the extent that these interventions provide explicit reinforcement for nonviolent behavior, they may help to decrease violent behavior. Second, as we have seen, interventions in schools that positively affect the opportunity and reward structure of the educational experience have the potential to promote school bonding and commitment to learning.

A number of different strategies with potential for changing the opportunity and reward structures of schools have been tried (Mortimore, 1995). Reductions in class size have been widely advocated as a way to provide greater opportunities for students to learn effectively in classrooms. But in fact, reductions in class size have been shown to be effective in improving student achievement only for the earliest school grades (i.e., kindergarten and first grade). Reduced class sizes have not produced positive results in achievement for students in later grades (Slavin, 1990).

Similarly, though the provision of teacher aides who assist with instructional, clerical, and custodial activities has been advocated to free teachers' time for greater involvement with students, the use of teacher aides has not consistently led to the increased achievement of students (Slavin, 1994).

Behavior Management to Alter Reinforcements

In contrast, improvements in teachers' methods of classroom management and instruction have shown consistent positive effects on several predictors of violent behavior in multiple studies conducted by different investigators. Behavioral techniques for classroom management have long been recognized as effective in promoting positive classroom behavior and reducing disruptive behavior (O'Leary & O'Leary, 1977). For example, Kellam's experimental test of the "Good Behavior Game" in Baltimore, Maryland

(Kellam, Rebok, Ialongo, & Mayer, 1994) showed significant reductions in aggressive behavior among boys that used this behavioral reinforcement game. In the game, three heterogeneous teams of children were created within the class, with aggressive children spread across the teams. During the game, teachers assigned checkmarks on the chalkboard to a team when a student on the team engaged in disruptive behaviors. At the end of the game period, teams with fewer than five checkmarks earned a reward. Teams that won the most games during the week received special recognition. Over time, tangible rewards were replaced with less tangible rewards, and rewards were delayed until the end of the day or week.

In the Baltimore experiment, the game was used by teachers in grades one and two. Tested with a 65% African American sample, the game showed reductions in teacher-rated aggressiveness after one year and enduring effects at grade 6 in reducing the aggressive behavior of boys who had been rated most aggressive by their teachers in grade one, though not in reducing overall rates of aggression in classrooms (Kellam et al., 1994).

A number of other studies have shown that changes in the opportunity and reward structures of the school outside the classroom can reduce aggressive behavior and crime (Brewer et al., 1995). For example, two studies have shown that creating opportunities for structured group play on the playground in elementary school can reduce fighting and other forms of aggressive behavior. O'Rourke (1980) found if adults set up activities for children when they entered the playground for recess and then left them on their own after eight to ten minutes, levels of fighting and rule breaking were significantly reduced. Murphy, Hutchinson, and Bailey (1983) found that adult-organized games decreased the frequency of aggression, property abuse, and rule violations among 5- to 7-year-old children on the playground prior to the start of the school day.

Bry (1982) showed beneficial effects of altering the reward structure of schooling for low achieving, disruptive students who had low bonding to their families. In an experiment involving both African American and white seventh grade students from urban and suburban schools, students involved in the experiment earned points for positive weekly ratings by teachers on class attendance, preparedness, performance, and prosocial behavior; for lack of disciplinary referrals; and for not behaving inappropriately in weekly small group sessions to review their school behavior. Participants could use the points they accumulated during the school year to qualify for an extra school trip of their choosing. Parents were contacted periodically regarding their children's progress. The two-year intervention was followed by one year of biweekly small group booster review sessions with participants.

In the booster year, students in the experiment displayed significantly fewer problem behaviors at school (e.g., suspensions, academic failure, poor attendance, and tardiness) than did students not in the program (i.e., the control group). In the 18 months following the intervention, students in the program self-reported significantly less illegal drug use and significantly less criminal behavior. Five years after the intervention, youths who had been in the experimental group were 66% less likely than students in the control group to have a juvenile criminal record (Bry & George, 1979, 1980).

Early Childhood Education

Early childhood education programs emphasizing language development advance children's development of cognitive and social skills important to academic success (Yoshikawa, 1994). Three major controlled studies of early childhood education programs supplemented with home visitation have followed participants well into adolescence. Children who received these interventions did better academically in school and later had lower rates of violence and crime.

The Perry Preschool program is one example (Berrueta-Clement, Schweinhart, Barnett, Epstein, & Weikart, 1984). The program used the High/Scope Cognitively Oriented Curriculum to foster social and intellectual development in children ages three to four years. Disadvantaged African American children from a poor neighborhood in Ypsilanti, Michigan, were assigned to experimental or control groups. The children in the experimental group attended a daily preschool program supplemented by weekly home visits. A follow-up study to age 27 showed the experimental group had accumulated only half as many arrests as the control group (Schweinhart, Barnes, & Weikart, 1993). They also had significantly higher earnings and were more likely to be homeowners. More of the women in the experimental group were married, and fewer of their children had been born out of wedlock. Also, they were more likely to have graduated from high school and to have received college or vocational training. This preschool program led to greater academic achievement and to decreases in offending.

The Houston Parent-Child Development Center program of home visitation services during the first year of a child's life, followed by center-based educational nursery school and parent effectiveness training, produced reductions in childhood fighting and disruptive, impulsive, and restless behavior in school through age 11 (Johnson & Walker, 1987). A similar combination of early home visitation, parent training, center-based educational child care, and a parent organization during the preschool years for families in poverty, tested in the Syracuse Family Development Research Program, led to significant reductions by age 15 in official juvenile court records (6% among children in the intervention group, compared with 22% of children in the control group), and fewer and less serious offenses among those who did have records (Lally, Mangione, & Honig, 1988).

Results from these studies become more compelling when viewed in the context of ten other early childhood education projects identified by the Consortium for Longitudinal Studies (1983), and other early childhood interventions such as the Carolina "Abecedarian" Project, which began at age three months (Horacek, Ramey, Campbell, Hoffman, & Fletcher, 1987). With quite impressive consistency, all these studies have shown that preschool intellectual enrichment programs for children from cultures of poverty have long-term beneficial effects on school success, especially in increasing the rate of high school graduation and decreasing the rate of special education placement. The consistency of the school success results in these projects suggests the effects on offending might also be replicable if these studies measured this outcome.

Instruction and Tutoring

Success in school is a form of reinforcement that strengthens commitment to education and, hence, increases protection against violent behavior. Numerous evaluations have shown three specific methods of instruction to be consistently effective in increasing academic success for students at risk of failure: continuous progress instructional methods, cooperative learning methods, and tutoring.

In continuous progress instructional programs, students proceed in a given subject through a defined hierarchy of skills and are tested at each level to assess their readiness to advance. Corrective instruction and tutoring are provided for those who need this assistance to achieve mastery of a skill. Teachers deliver most instruction to groups of students at the same level. Evaluations of seven different continuous progress instructional programs have shown positive effects on academic achievement (Slavin & Madden, 1989).

In cooperative learning, after the teacher has provided instruction to the larger group, students work in learning teams of four to five members of mixed skill levels to help each other master material. Students are tested individually but contribute to team recognition if their scores show increasing mastery, thereby increasing motivation to help their teammates learn. Positive effects of cooperative learning on achievement have been shown in both short- and long-term experimental tests in elementary schools, and in short-term tests in secondary schools (Slavin & Madden, 1989).

Academic achievement is also positively affected by one-to-one tutoring of elementary school students. Tutoring by older students, adult community volunteers, trained paraprofessionals, and certified teachers has produced substantial long-term improvement in students' achievement in reading and mathematics (Wasik & Slavin, 1994). Positive results of tutoring have been found regardless of whether the tutoring was preventive or remedial, or structured or unstructured in design. Tutoring provided by other students has positive effects on both the tutors' and tutees' academic achievement and attitudes toward the subject covered, across all achievement levels (Cohen, Kulik, & Kulik, 1982). Tutoring of elementary school students has been shown to affect achievement positively for two years following the tutoring (Coie & Krehbiel, 1984; Greenwood, Terry, Utley, Montagna, & Walker, 1993).

Multicomponent Approaches

Slavin and his colleagues have combined a number of these elements into the Success for All program, tested initially in Baltimore, Maryland, in an inner city elementary school (Slavin, Madden, Karweit, Livermon, & Dolan, 1990). Now disseminated widely, the program has been implemented most frequently in schools eligible for federal Chapter One funds. It seeks to bring all children up to grade level in basic skills by the third grade. The program uses one-to-one tutoring, a research-based reading instructional program involving continuous progress instruction as described above, and regrouping for instruction, plus frequent assessment, enhanced preschool and kindergarten programs, and family support interventions. Evaluations of Success for All in 15 schools in 7 cities have produced very consistent positive effects on reading achievement. Positive effects on attendance and reduction in grade retention (i.e., failure to pass) have also been found (Slavin, Madden, Dolan, Wasik, Ross, & Smith, 1994).

The Seattle Social Development Project, a multicomponent intervention designed to prevent delinquency, violence, and other problem behaviors, employed a package of classroom management and instructional methods in the elementary grades, including cooperative learning, proactive class-room management, and interactive teaching (Hawkins, Catalano, Morrison, et al., 1992; O'Donnell, Hawkins, Catalano, Abbott, & Day, 1995). A proactive classroom management method was used, consisting of establishing expectations for classroom behavior; using methods of maintaining classroom order that minimized interruptions to instruction and learning; and giving frequent, specific, and contingent praise and encouragement for student effort and progress. Interactive teaching involved the clear specification of learning objectives, continuous monitoring of student progress, and remediation. Students were expected to master specific learning objectives before proceeding to more advanced work. Structured cooperative learning groups were used in experimental classrooms from grades 2–6. In the experimental intervention, teachers of the elementary grades were trained to use these three methods of instruction. These methods were tested in combination with a social competence curriculum and parent training over the six years of elementary school.

The intervention was tested with a multiethnic urban sample. By the end of grade 2, boys in intervention classrooms were rated as significantly less aggressive than boys in control classrooms (Hawkins, Von Cleve, & Catalano, 1991). By the beginning of grade 5, students in experimental classrooms were significantly less likely to have initiated delinquent behaviors and alcohol use than students in control classrooms (Hawkins, Catalano, Morrison, et al., 1992). By the end of grade 6, boys in intervention classrooms from low-income families had significantly greater academic achievement, better teacher-rated behavior, and lower rates of delinquency initiation than did boys from low-income families in control classrooms (O'Donnell, Hawkins, Catalano, et al., 1995). A six-year follow-up study at age 18 found significantly higher academic achievement and lower rates of lifetime violent delinquent behavior among children exposed to the full intervention compared with those in the control group (Hawkins, Kosterman, et al., 1996).

Several researchers have suggested that if school failure causes offending, sending aggressive children to alternative schools where failure experiences are minimized might lead to a decrease in their offending. Gold and Mann (1984) studied three alternative schools in Detroit, Michigan, for disruptive and delinquent juveniles that aimed to increase their success experiences through individualized curricula and grading based on a student's own progress (not judged in relation to other students' progress). They found students assigned to the alternative schools showed less disruptive behavior than those in a control group assigned to regular high schools.

Similarly, Gottfredson (1987) evaluated several alternative school projects and found that some led to decreases in offending.

In summary, there is evidence from multiple, well-designed, and well-implemented studies showing intentionally changing schools to increase opportunities and rewards for prosocial involvement can enhance student achievement and commitment to schools, and reduce delinquent and violent behavior, both within and beyond the school setting.

Promoting Norm Change and Conflict Management Skills

Numerous school curricula have been developed to promote the acceptance of norms against violent behavior and to help students develop social, problem-solving, and anger management skills to avoid violence. Some of these are social competence and emotional competence curricula that aim to counteract and prevent early antisocial behavior by teaching basic interpersonal skills. Two examples of effective interventions of this type for early elementary grades are the Interpersonal Cognitive Problem-Solving (ICPS) curriculum and the Positive Alternative Thinking Strategies (PATHS) curriculum.

The ICPS curriculum consists of daily lessons in the form of games for preschool and kindergarten children, focused on generating alternative solutions to interpersonal problems, consequential thinking, and recognizing and being sensitive to others' feelings. In tests with children from low-income urban families, the program produced significant and durable effects on behavior, including aggressive and antisocial behavior (Shure & Spivack, 1980, 1982, 1988). The PATHS curriculum enhances instruction by integrating emotional, cognitive, and behavioral skill development in young children. It was first shown to be effective in reducing behavior problems among deaf children (Greenberg & Kusche, 1993). Randomized controlled trials of PATHS in regular education and special needs classes have shown significant effects on teacher- and self-reported conduct problems and teacher ratings of adaptive behavior (Weissberg & Greenberg, 1997).

Conflict resolution and violence prevention curricula seek to improve students' social, problem-solving, and anger management skills and to promote beliefs favorable to nonviolence. These curricula typically teach skills of empathy, appropriate social behavior, interpersonal problem solving, and anger management using discussion, modeling, and role-play methods to ensure skill acquisition. Topics and sessions are developmentally adjusted for the grades and ages of the students and vary in duration from 10 to 30 sessions and in length from 30 minutes to 1 hour per session.

Of four quasi-experimental studies that investigated the effects of conflict resolution and violence prevention curricula on attitudes toward or norms concerning violence, only one study appeared to demonstrate a positive impact on these norms (Gainer, Webster, & Champion, 1993). This curriculum for students in grades 5–9 reviewed risk factors for violence, including drug use and selling, alcohol use, weapon carrying, anger/arguments, and poverty, and explicitly discussed the relationship between drugs and violence. Half of the curriculum sessions focused on skills for solving social problems. Individual students in the program also contracted with an adult not involved with drugs, alcohol, or weapons to help the students resolve conflicts nonviolently.

In the program, instructors with firsthand experience of the consequences of youth violence (e.g., a trauma nurse, an emergency medical technician, a former drug dealer who was shot and became a paraplegic, and an attorney) taught different sessions of the curriculum. The curriculum consisted of fifteen 50-minute sessions conducted on consecutive days over three weeks with fifth and seventh grade students in schools serving high-crime areas of Washington, D.C.

The study yielded mixed results. Following intervention, students exposed to the curriculum listed more negative consequences of using violence and were less likely to legitimize violence in discussing it than students in a comparison group. However, they were significantly less likely to provide nonviolent solutions in hypothetical conflict situations, and actually perceived less risk of violence associated with drug dealing than did comparison students. The effects of the intervention on attitudes and perceptions of violence were inconsistent, and there was no attempt to assess the program's effect on violent behavior.

Perhaps the best evidence of the effectiveness of a violence prevention curriculum comes from a randomized controlled trial of the Second Step curriculum with second and third grade students that found significant decreases in observed physically aggressive behavior, and increases in observed prosocial behavior, following intervention (Grossman et al., 1997). More rigorous evaluations of conflict resolution and violence prevention curricula are needed (see Chapter 8 of this volume).

Peer mediation programs, sometimes operated in conjunction with conflict resolution curricula, are another curricular approach to preventing violence. These programs, unlike the others discussed so far, address disputes between students with the potential to result in violence and injury. If students who are involved in a personal dispute request help, they agree to use a trained peer mediator to help them resolve the dispute. The peer mediator helps the disputants examine various aspects of the problem, recommends compromises, and assists in developing a mutually agreeable, nonviolent solution. Peer mediators are trained in problem solving, active listening, communication skills, taking command of adversarial situations, identifying points of agreement, and maintaining confidentiality and a nonjudgmental stance (Goleman, 1995).

Two quasi-experimental evaluations of peer mediation programs that operated in tandem with conflict resolution curricula have shown desirable effects on attitudes toward conflict and violence (Benenson, 1988; Jenkins & Smith, 1987). However, only one study indicated a decrease in aggressive behavior associated with peer mediation (Tolson, McDonald, & Moriarty, 1992). That study found high school students who participated as disputants in peer mediation were less likely to be referred to school officials for interpersonal conflicts during a two and one-half month follow-up period than were students in the control group.

Peer counseling (also called guided group interaction, peer culture development, or positive peer culture) has also been implemented in schools as a strategy for preventing or reducing violent and other delinquent behavior. Peer counseling typically involves an adult leader guiding group discussions in which participants are encouraged to recognize problems with their behavior and attitudes. The approach seeks to shift participants' attitudes or norms so they become unfavorable to antisocial behavior, and to provide peer group support for this shift. Peer counseling has been used in elementary and secondary schools as a preventive intervention and frequently involves mixing students at high risk for delinquency and violence in the same group with prosocial student leaders and others. Unfortunately, the available evidence indicates peer counseling in schools has no positive effects and may even encourage involvement in delinquency and attitudes favorable toward violence (Gottfredson, 1987). In short, while peer counseling attempts to change norms, it does not appear to be an effective strategy for doing so.

In summary, there is evidence that schools can promote the development of skills to avoid violent behavior through the use of classroom curricula that seek to promote social competence (Goleman, 1995) and teach skills for anger management, impulse control, and empathy (Grossman et al., 1997). There is less evidence to date that conflict resolution curricula can positively affect students' skills for resolving conflict situations nonviolently, or reduce involvement in violent behavior. There is limited evidence that peer mediation programs can encourage the development of norms against violent solutions to conflict situations. More rigorous evaluations of peer mediation, conflict resolution, and violence prevention curricula are needed (Hausman, Spivak, Prothrow-Stith, & Roeber, 1992). In contrast, the evidence suggests that peer counseling as a strategy for developing norms of nonviolence or reducing violent behavior may reinforce violent norms and is not an effective violence prevention approach.

Reducing the Availability of Weapons in Schools

If weapons contribute to the risk of injury and death from violence, metal detectors in schools may help to reduce this risk in and around schools. Ginsberg and Loffredo (1993) found that, although metal detectors had no apparent effect on the prevalence of threats of violence and physical fights in schools, they were associated with lower rates of carrying a weapon inside schools or while going to and from schools in a comparison of New York City schools with and without metal detectors. However, it is not known whether metal detectors actually reduce violence-related injuries or deaths in schools. They are situational prevention tools that are not likely to reduce weapon carrying outside of schools, or threats and physical fighting in or out of schools (Ginsberg & Loffredo, 1993). Yet the absence of weapons in fights should reduce the levels of injury and lethality of fights. This fact reinforces the importance of schools' efforts to promote norms against violent behavior, including carrying weapons. (For a more detailed discussion of this approach, see Chapter 6 of this volume.)

Whole-School Programs

Building on the evidence that certain characteristics of schools themselves are associated with levels of disorder and violence among students, some investigators have worked to change the social organization of schools. These efforts have focused on various goals, but generally have endeavored to create a community of learning in the school and to eliminate risk factors for violence.

Comer (1988) developed a comprehensive elementary school intervention involving four components: (1) a social calendar that integrated arts and athletic programs into school activities; (2) a parent program in support of school academic and extracurricular activities that fostered interaction among parents, teachers, and other school staff; (3) a multidisciplinary mental health team that provided consultation for school staff in managing student behavior problems; and (4) a representative governance and management team, composed of school administrators, teachers, support staff, and parents, that oversaw the implementation of the other three program components. The intervention was originally implemented in two New Haven, Connecticut, inner city elementary schools serving predominantly African American children from families in poverty. Before the intervention, these schools were characterized by poor attendance, low academic achievement, discipline problems, and high teacher turnover.

A study conducted when these children entered middle school found students from the intervention elementary schools had significantly better middle school grades, academic achievement test scores, and self-rated social competence than did students matched on age and gender from schools that did not receive the intervention program (Cauce, Comer, & Schwartz, 1987; Comer, 1988). Because of small sample sizes and questions about the appropriateness of the comparison group, this evidence is not very compelling. However, many schools across the country have adopted the intervention, and results of a large experimental study of this intervention should soon be reported (Cook et al., 1997).

In Charleston, South Carolina, Gottfredson (1986) tested an intervention for changing the social organization of secondary schools, called the PATHE (Positive Action through Holistic Education) program. The main elements included teams composed of teachers, other school staff, students, parents, and community members that designed and implemented school improvement programs; curriculum and discipline policy review and revision, including student participation in the development of school and classroom rules; inservice training for classroom teachers in the kinds of positive instructional and classroom management practices described previously in this chapter; increasing the academic competence of students through teaching study skills and the use of cooperative learning techniques; improving the school climate (e.g., through a "school pride" program); career preparation programs, including a job-seeking skills program and a career exploration program; and special academic and counseling services for low achieving and disruptive students.

The evaluation of the program involved four middle schools and four high schools serving students from predominantly low-income African American neighborhoods and reported changes in outcomes over time for intervention and nonintervention schools separately. There was no direct comparison of pre- and post-outcomes for intervention and control schools. Over the course of the program, students in experimental schools reported small but significant decreases in delinquency and school suspensions, while students in comparison schools did not show such improvements. A similar program was also implemented successfully in a school in Baltimore, Maryland (Gottfredson, 1987).

Whole-school programs designed to reduce bullying in schools can be targeted at bullies, victims, or schools, or at some combination of the three. For example, Lowenstein (1991) proposed making bullies aware of victims' feelings, punishing bullies, providing opportunities for bullies to behave positively, and rewarding desirable behavior by bullies (e.g., using tokens that could be exchanged for extrinsic rewards such as candy and privileges). Herbert (1989) aimed to improve the social skills of victims, including holding conversations, asking for help, coping with feelings, negotiating, and responding to teasing. However we will focus on programs targeted at schools, partly because these have been evaluated more adequately. Most were primarily targeted at school norms.

The most important evaluation of a whole-school anti-bullying program was conducted in Bergen (Norway) by Olweus (1991). This program aimed to increase awareness and knowledge of bullying by teachers, parents, and students. Booklets were distributed to schools and parents describing what was known about bullying and what steps could be taken to reduce this behavior. Students completed anonymous self-report questionnaires about the prevalence of bullies and victims. The results were discussed in a specially arranged school conference day. Teachers were encouraged to develop explicit rules about bullying (e.g., "Bullying will not be tolerated"; "Tell someone when bullying happens"; and "Try to help victims"), and to discuss bullying in their classes using videotape and role play exercises. Also, teachers were encouraged to improve monitoring and supervision of children, especially on the playground.

The success of the program was evaluated using before and after measures of bullying and victimization of children at each age. For example, the self-reported prevalence of bullies and victims among 13-year-olds before the program was compared with the prevalence of bullies and victims among (different) 13-year-olds 20 months after the program. Generally, the percentage of students reporting being bullied or bullying others decreased by 50% or more in most comparisons (Olweus, 1994). Hence, the program seemed to be successful in reducing school bullying.

A similar program was implemented in 23 Sheffield, England, schools by Smith and Sharp (1994). The core program involved establishing a whole-school anti-bullying policy, increasing awareness of bullying, and clearly defining roles and responsibilities of teachers and students, so that everyone knew what bullying was and what they should do about the behavior. In addition, there were optional interventions tailored to particular schools: curricula work (e.g., reading books, watching videotapes), direct work with students (e.g., assertiveness training for victims), and playground work (e.g., training lunchtime supervisors). This program was successful in reducing bullying among younger children but had relatively small effects on older children.

Gangs are a significant contributor to violence in some schools (Kodluboy & Evenrud, 1993). Whole-school strategies have been proposed to reduce gang activity, including a gang prevention curriculum; a dress code or school uniform (which in effect prohibits gang clothing and insignia); a gang reporting hot line; support and protection for victims of gang violence; parent notification of gang activity; and school visitor screening (Stephens, 1993).

Unfortunately, the effectiveness of most of these measures in reducing violence in schools has not yet been established. For example, rigorous studies of the effectiveness of other whole-school interventions, such as the use of dress codes or school uniforms, remain to be conducted. However, Thompson and Jason (1988) evaluated the combination of a gang prevention curriculum and after-school recreation activities provided to eighth grade students in lower-income neighborhoods in Chicago with high gang activity. The 12-session curriculum included classroom sessions on gang violence, gang substance abuse, gang recruitment and methods of resisting recruitment, consequences of gang membership, and values clarification in three middle schools. After the curriculum was taught, youths considered to be at high risk for joining a gang were invited to participate in after-school recreation activities, including organized sports clinics, job skills/training workshops, educational assistance programs, and social activities.

A comparison group of three other middle schools, each matched in a pair with one of the intervention schools on the basis that the same gang actively recruited members from both schools, was used to evaluate this program. Youths in the intervention schools were less likely to become gang members over the course of the eighth grade. Unfortunately, the evaluation was limited by the short follow-up period and a relatively small sample size, given the low prevalence of gang membership. Of the 43 comparison group youths at risk in the study, four had joined gangs by the end of the school year, compared with one of the 74 youths at risk in the intervention schools.

Conclusion

There is growing evidence that changing the opportunity and reward structure of classrooms and schools can promote academic achievement, promote commitment and attachment, (i.e., bonding) to schools, and reduce misbehavior including violent behavior. Unfortunately, those concerned about youth violence often do not focus on changing the opportunity and reward structures of classrooms or the larger schools. More typically, schools add a violence prevention curriculum, peer mediation, or peer counseling program that seeks to deal with aggressive and violent behavior directly. While these approaches show promise, they are only part of an effective strategy for violence prevention in schools.

In this chapter we have attempted to identify empirically and theoretically grounded components fundamental to the prevention of violence through the schools. Schools should not be expected to confront the problems of youth violence alone. School personnel, parents, neighborhood residents, health and human service providers, law enforcement, other community groups, and governmental and nongovernmental organizations must work together to implement comprehensive strategies to reduce risks of violence that characterize each community and to enhance protection against violence (Hawkins, Catalano, & Associates, 1992).

But schools must be involved. They are places that concentrate children and adolescents together during the ages when aggressive behavior develops into violence and peaks in prevalence. Moreover, K-12 public schools receive more than 80% of the public resources spent on children, youth, and families in the United States (Holmes, Gottfredson, & Miller, 1992). These resources must be leveraged to reduce risks of and increase protection against violence.

We have identified key ways in which schools can contribute to the prevention of violence, such as ensuring that schools are environments of opportunity and reward for academic achievement and prosocial behavior for all students, regardless of their ability, race, gender, or socioeconomic class. In short, by doing their primary job of motivating and educating all the students who attend, schools contribute to violence prevention. Schools also can prevent violence by promoting norms of nonviolence among students and by ensuring that students develop behavioral, cognitive, emotional, and interpersonal skills to live and learn nonviolently. In addition, where necessary, schools can reduce the negative consequences of violence by taking steps to reduce the availability of weapons in schools. The existing evidence suggests promising directions for achieving all of these outcomes.

References

American Psychological Association. (1993). *Violence and youth: Psychology's response*. Washington, DC: Author.

Bastian, L. D., & Taylor, B. M. (1991). *School crime: A national crime victimization survey report* (NCJ-131–645). Washington, DC: U.S. Department of Justice.

Benenson, W. (1988). "Assessing the effectiveness of a peer based conflict management program in elementary schools." Unpublished doctoral dissertation, University of Idaho, Boise.

Berrueta-Clement, J. R., Schweinhart, L. J., Barnett, W. S., Epstein, A. S., & Weikart, D. P. (1984). *Changed lives: The effects of the Perry Preschool Program on youths through age 19 (High/Scope Educational Research Foundation, Monograph 8).* Ypsilanti, MI: High/Scope Press.

Boulton, M. J. (1993). Aggressive fighting in British middle school children. *Educational Studies, 19*(1), 19–39.

Bourgois, P. (1995). *In search of respect: Selling crack in El Barrio.* Cambridge, England & New York: Cambridge University Press.

Brennan, P., Mednick, S., & Kandel, E. (1991). Congenital determinants of violent and property offending. In. D. J. Pepler & K. H. Rubin (Eds.), *The development and treatment of aggression* (pp. 81–92). Hillsdale, NJ: Lawrence Erlbaum.

Brewer, D. D., Hawkins, J. D., Catalano, R. F., & Neckerman, H. J. (1995). Preventing serious, violent, and chronic juvenile offending: A review of selected strategies in childhood, adolescence, and the community. In J. C. Howell, B. Krisberg, J. D. Hawkins, & J. J. Wilson (Eds.), *A sourcebook: Serious, violent, and chronic juvenile offenders* (pp. 61–141). Thousand Oaks, CA: Sage.

Bry, B. H. (1982). Reducing the incidence of adolescent problems through preventive intervention: One- and five-year follow-up. *American Journal of Community Psychology, 10,* 265–276.

Bry, B. H., & George, F. E. (1979). Evaluating and improving prevention programs: A strategy from drug abuse. *Evaluation and Program Planning, 2,* 127–136.

Bry, B. H., & George, F. E. (1980). The preventive effects of early intervention on the attendance and grades of urban adolescents. *Professional Psychology, 11,* 252–260.

Bursik, R. J., Jr., & Grasmick, H. G. (1993). *Neighborhoods and crime: The dimensions of effective community control.* New York: Lexington Books.

Cairns, R. (1996). "Social networks and the development of antisocial behaviors." Manuscript submitted for publication.

Catalano, R. F., & Hawkins, J. D. (1996). The social development model: A theory of antisocial behavior. In J. D. Hawkins (Ed.), *Delinquency and crime: Current theories* (pp. 149–197). New York: Cambridge University Press.

Cauce, A. M., Comer, J. P., & Schwartz, D. (1987). Long-term effects of a systems-oriented school prevention program. *American Journal of Orthopsychiatry, 57,* 127–131.

Cohen, P. A., Kulik, J. A., & Kulik, C. C. (1982). Educational outcomes of teaching. *American Education Research Journal, 19,* 237–248.

Coie, J. D., Dodge, K. A., Terry, R., & Wright, V. (1991). The role of aggression in peer relations: An analysis of aggression episodes in boys' play groups. *Child Development, 62,* 812–826.

Coie, J. D., & Krehbiel, G. (1984). Effects of academic tutoring on the social status of low-achieving, socially rejected children. *Child Development, 55,* 1465–1478.

Comer, J. P. (1988). Educating poor minority children. *Scientific American, 259,* 42–48.

Consortium for Longitudinal Studies. (1983). *As the twig is bent: Lasting effects of preschool programs.* Hillsdale, NJ: Lawrence Erlbaum.

Cook, T., Habib, F., Phillips, M., Settersten, R., Shagle, S., & Degirmencioglu, S. (1997). "The Comer School Development Program: An evaluation of the effectiveness of its theoretical assumptions." Unpublished manuscript. Evanston, IL: Northwestern University.

Csikszentmihalyi, M., & Larson, R. (1980). Intrinsic rewards in school crime. In K. Baker & R. J. Rubel (Eds.), *Violence and crime in the schools* (pp. 181–192). Lexington, MA: Lexington Books.

Davies, B. (1982). *Life in the classroom and playground: The accounts of primary school children*. London: Routledge & Kegan Paul.

Davies, B. (1991). Friends and fights. In M. Woodhead, P. Light, & R. Carr (Eds.), *Growing up in a changing society* (pp. 243–264). London: Routledge.

Ellickson, P. L., & Bell, R. M. (1990). Drug prevention in junior high: A multisite longitudinal test. *Science, 247,* 1299–1305.

Elliott, D. S., & Menard, S. (1996). Delinquent friends and delinquent behavior: Temporal and developmental patterns. In J. D. Hawkins (Ed.), *Delinquency and crime: Current theories* (pp. 28–67). New York: Cambridge University Press.

Farnworth, M. (1984). Family structure, family attributes, and delinquency in a sample of low-income minority males and females. *Journal of Youth and Adolescence, 13,* 349–364.

Farrington, D. P. (1991). Childhood aggression and adult violence: Early precursors and later life outcomes. In D. J. Pepler & K. H. Rubin (Eds.), *The development and treatment of childhood aggression* (pp. 5–29). Hillsdale, NJ: Lawrence Erlbaum.

Farrington, D. P. (1993). Understanding and preventing bullying. In M. Tonry (Ed.), *Crime and justice* (Vol. 17) (pp. 381–458). Chicago: University of Chicago Press.

Farrington, D. P. (1996). *Understanding and preventing youth crime*. York, England: Joseph Rountree Foundation.

Gainer, P. S., Webster, D. W., & Champion, H. R. (1993). A youth violence prevention program: Description and preliminary evaluation. *Archives of Surgery, 128,* 303–308.

Gardner, H. (1993). *Multiple intelligences: The theory in practice*. New York: Basic Books.

Ginsberg, C., & Loffredo, L. (1993). Violence-related attitudes and behaviors of high school students – New York City 1992. *Journal of School Health, 63,* 438–439.

Gold, M., & Mann, D. W. (1984). *Expelled to a friendlier place*. Ann Arbor, MI: University of Michigan Press.

Goleman, D. (1995). *Emotional intelligence*. New York: Bantam.

Gottfredson, D. C. (1986). An empirical test of school-based environmental and individual interventions to reduce the risk of delinquent behavior. *Criminology, 24,* 705–731.

Gottfredson, D. C. (1987). Examining the potential of delinquency prevention through alternative education. *Today's Delinquent, 6,* 87–100.

Gottfredson, G. D., & Gottfredson, D. C. (1985). *Victimization in schools*. New York: Plenum.

Greenberg, M. T., & Kusche, C. A. (1993). *Promoting social and emotional development in deaf children: The PATHS project*. Seattle, WA: University of Washington Press.

Greenwood, C. R., Terry, B., Utley, C. A., Montagna, D., & Walker, D. (1993). Achievement, placement, and services: Middle school benefits of classwide peer tutoring used at the elementary school. *School Psychology Review, 22,* 497–516.

Grossman, D. C., Neckerman, H .J., Koepsell, T., Asher, K., Liu, P. Y., Beland, K., Frey, K., & Rivara, F. P. (1997). Effectiveness of a violence prevention curriculum among children in elementary school. *Journal of the American Medical Association, 277*(20), 1605–1611.

Hansen, W. B., & Graham, J. W. (1991). Preventing alcohol, marijuana, and cigarette use among adolescents: Peer pressure resistance training versus establishing conservative norms. *Preventive Medicine, 20,* 414–430.

Hausman, A. J., Spivak, H., Prothrow-Stith, D., & Roeber, J. (1992). Patterns of teen exposure to a community-based violence prevention project. *Journal of Adolescent Health, 13,* 668–675.

Hawkins, J. D., Catalano, R. F., & Associates (Eds.). (1992). *Communities that care: Action for drug abuse prevention.* San Francisco: Jossey-Bass.

Hawkins, J. D., Catalano, R. F., Jones, G., & Fine, D. N. (1987). Delinquency prevention through parent training: Results and issues from work in progress. In J. Q. Wilson & G. C. Loury (Eds.), *From children to citizens: Families, schools, and delinquency prevention* (Vol. 3) (pp. 186–204). New York: Springer-Verlag.

Hawkins, J. D., Catalano, R. F., Morrison, D. E., O'Donnell, J., Abbott, R. D., & Day, L. E. (1992). The Seattle Social Development Project: Effects of the first four years on protective factors and problem behaviors. In J. McCord & R. Tremblay (Eds.), *The prevention of antisocial behavior in children* (pp. 139–161). New York: Guilford.

Hawkins, J. D., Kosterman, R., Catalano, R. F., Abbott, R. D., & Hill, K. G. (1996). "Promoting academic success and preventing crime in urban America: Six-year followup effects of the Seattle Social Development Project." Manuscript in preparation.

Hawkins, J. D., Von Cleve, E., & Catalano, R. F. (1991). Reducing early childhood aggression: Results of a primary prevention program. *Journal of the American Academy of Child and Adolescent Psychiatry, 30,* 208–217.

Hawkins, J. D., & Weis, J. G. (1985). The social development model: An integrated approach to delinquency prevention. *Journal of Primary Prevention, 6,* 73–97.

Herbert, G. (1989). A whole-curriculum approach to bullying. In D. Tattum & D. Lane (Eds.), *Bullying in schools.* Stoke-on-Trent, England: Trentham.

Herrnstein, R. J., & Murray, C. (1994). *The bell curve: Intelligence and class structure in American life.* New York: Free Press.

Holmes, A. B., Gottfredson, G. D., & Miller, J. Y. (1992). Resources and strategies for funding. In J. D. Hawkins, R. F. Catalano, & Associates (Eds.), *Communities that care: Action for drug abuse prevention* (pp. 191–210). San Francisco: Jossey-Bass.

Horacek, H. J., Ramey, C. T., Campbell, F. A., Hoffman, K. P., & Fletcher, R. H. (1987). Predicting school failure and assessing early intervention with high-risk children. *Journal of the American Academy of Child and Adolescent Psychiatry, 26,* 758–763.

Huizinga, D., Loeber, R., & Thornberry, T. P. (1995). The prevention of serious delinquency and violence: Implications from the program of research on the causes and correlates of delinquency. In J. C. Howell, B. Krisberg, J. D. Hawkins, & J. J. Wilson (Eds.), *Sourcebook on serious, violent, and chronic juvenile offenders* (pp. 213–237). Thousand Oaks, CA: Sage.

Jenkins, J., & Smith, M. (1987). *Mediation in the schools: 1986–87 program evaluation.* Albuquerque, NM: New Mexico Center for Dispute Resolution.

Jessor, R., & Jessor, S. L. (1977). *Problem behavior and psychosocial development: A longitudinal study of youth.* New York: Academic.

Johnson, D. L., & Walker, T. (1987). Primary prevention of behavior problems in Mexican-American children. *American Journal of Community Psychology, 15,* 375–385.

Kazdin, A. E. (1990, June). *Prevention of conduct disorder.* Paper presented to the National Conference on Prevention Research, National Institute of Mental Health (NIMH), Bethesda, MD.

Kellam, S. G., Rebok, G. W., Ialongo, N., & Mayer, L. S. (1994). The course and mal-leability of aggressive behavior from early first grade into middle school: Re-sults of a developmental epidemiologically-based preventive trial. *Journal of Child Psychology and Psychiatry, 35,* 259–281.

Kodluboy, D. W., & Evenrud, L. A. (1993). School-based interventions: Best prac-tices and critical issues. In A. P. Goldstein & C. R. Huff (Eds.), *The gang inter-vention handbook* (pp. 257–299). Champaign, IL: Research Press.

Lab, S. P., & Clark, R. D. (1996). *Discipline, control and school crime: Identifying effec-tive intervention strategies* (Grant No. 93-IJ-CX-0034). Washington, DC: National Institute of Justice.

Lally, J. R., Mangione, P. L., & Honig, A. S. (1988). The Syracuse University Family Development Research Program: Long-range impact on an early intervention with low-income children and their families. In D. R. Powell & I. Sigel (Eds.), *Advances in applied developmental psychology: Vol. 3. Parent education as early childhood intervention: Emerging direction in theory, research and practice.* Nor-wood, NJ: Ablex.

Loeber, R. (1988). Natural histories of conduct problems, delinquency, and associ-ated substance use: Evidence for developmental progressions. In B. B. Lahey & A. E. Kazdin (Eds.), *Advances in clinical child psychology* (Vol. 11) (pp. 73–124). New York: Plenum.

Loeber, R., Green, S. M., Keenan, K., & Lahey, B. B. (1995). Which boys will fare worse? Early predictors of the onset of conduct disorder in a six-year longitu-dinal study. *Journal of American Academy of Child and Adolescent Psychology, 34,* 499–509.

Lowenstein, L. F. (1991). The study, diagnosis and treatment of bullying in a ther-apeutic community. In M. Elliott (Ed.), *Bullying: A practical guide to coping for schools.* (pp. 154–165). Harlow, England: Longman.

Maguin, E., & Loeber. R. (1995). Academic performance and delinquency. In M. Tonry (Ed.), *Crime and justice: A review of research* (Vol. 20) (pp. 145–264). Chicago: University of Chicago Press.

Mansfield, W., Alexander, D., & Farris, E. (1991). *Teacher survey on safe, disciplined, and drug-free schools.* Washington, DC: National Center for Education Statistics.

Mayer, G. R. (1995). Preventing antisocial behavior in the schools. *Journal of Applied Behavior Analysis, 28,* 467–478.

McCord, J. (1988). Parental aggressiveness and physical punishment in long-term perspective. In G. T. Hotaling, D. Finkelhor, J. T. Kirkpatrick, & M. A. Straus (Eds.), *Family abuse and its consequences: New directions in research* (pp. 91–98). Newbury Park, CA: Sage.

McPartland, J. M., & McDill, E. L. (1977). *Violence in schools.* Lexington, MA: Heath.

Metropolitan Life Insurance Company. (1993). *Violence in America's public schools.* New York: Author.

Michaud, L. J., Rivara, F. P., Jaffe, K. M., Fay, G., & Dailey, J. L. (1993). Traumatic brain injury as a risk factor for behavioral disorders in children. *Archives of Physiological and Medical Rehabilitation, 74,* 368–375.

Moffitt, T. E. (1993). Adolescence-limited and life-course persistent antisocial be-havior: A developmental taxonomy. *Psychology Review, 100*(4), 674–701.

Mortimore, P. (1995). The positive effects of schooling. In M. Rutter (Ed.), *Psy-chosocial disturbances in young people: Challenges for prevention* (pp. 333–363). Cambridge, MA: Cambridge University Press.

Murphy, H. A., Hutchinson, J. M., & Bailey, J. S. (1983). Behavioral school psychol-ogy goes outdoors: The effect of organized games on playground aggression. *Journal of Applied Behavioral Analysis, 16,* 29–35.

O'Donnell, J., Hawkins, J. D., & Abbott, R. D. (1995). Predicting serious delinquency and substance use among aggressive boys. *Journal of Consulting and Clinical Psychology, 63,* 529–537.

O'Donnell, J., Hawkins, J. D., Catalano, R. F., Abbott, R. D., & Day, L. E. (1995). Preventing school failure, drug use, and delinquency among low-income children: Effects of a long-term prevention project in elementary schools. *American Journal of Orthopsychiatry, 65,* 87–100.

Office of Educational Research and Improvement. (1992). *Review of research on ways to attain Goal 6* [Working paper]. Washington DC: U.S. Department of Education.

O'Leary, K. D., & O'Leary, S. G. (1977). *Classroom management: The successful use of behavior modification* (2nd ed.). New York: Pergamon.

Olweus, D. (1991). Bully/victims problems among schoolchildren: Basic facts and effects of a school-based intervention program. In D. J. Pepler & K. H. Rubin (Eds.), *The development and treatment of childhood aggression* (pp. 411–448). Hillsdale, NJ: Lawrence Erlbaum.

Olweus, D. (1994). Bullying at schools: Basic facts and effects of a school-based intervention program. *Journal of Child Psychology and Psychiatry, 35,* 1171–1190.

O'Rourke, M. (1980). Patrol or participate in the playground? *Education, 1,* 29–30.

Patterson, G. R. (1996). "Differential histories and outcomes for early and late onset delinquency." Manuscript submitted for publication.

Patterson, G. R., Capaldi, D., & Bank, L. (1991). An early starter model for predicting delinquency. In D. Pepler & K. H. Rubin (Eds.), *The development and treatment of childhood aggression* (pp. 139–168). Hillsdale, NJ: Lawrence Erlbaum.

Perry, C. L. (1986). Community-wide health promotion and drug abuse prevention. *Journal of School Health, 56,* 359–363.

Prothrow-Stith, D. (1987). *Violence prevention curriculum for adolescents.* Newton, MA: Education Development Center.

Reiss, A. J., & Roth, J. A. (Eds.). (1993). *Understanding and preventing violence.* Washington, DC: National Academy Press.

Robins, L. N. (1978). Sturdy childhood predictors of adult anti-social behavior: Replications from longitudinal studies. *Psychological Medicine, 8,* 611–622.

Salzinger, S., Feldman, R. S., Hammer, M., & Rosario, M. (1993). The effects of physical abuse on children's social relationships. *Child Development, 64,* 169–187.

Sampson, R. J. (1986). Crime in cities: The effects of formal and informal social control. In A. J. Reiss & M. Tonry (Eds.), *Crime and justice: An annual review of research: Vol. 8, Communities and crime* (pp. 271–311). Chicago: University of Chicago Press.

Sampson, R. J. (1994, February). *Community-level factors in the development of violent behavior: Implications for social policy.* Paper presented at the Aspen Institute Conference on Children and Violence, Boca Raton, FL.

Sampson, R. J., & Lauritsen, J. L. (1994). Violent victimization and offending: Individual, situational, and community level risk factors. In A. J. Reiss & J. A. Roth (Eds.), *Understanding and preventing violence: Social influences, Vol. 3* (pp. 1–115). Washington, DC: National Academy Press.

Schweinhart, L. J., Barnes, H. V., & Weikart, D. P. (1993). *Significant benefits.* Ypsilanti, MI: High/Scope Press.

Sheley, J. F., McGee, Z. T., & Wright, J. D. (1992). Gun-related violence in and around inner-city schools. *American Journal of Diseases of Children, 146,* 677–682.

Sheley, J. F., & Wright, J. D. (1993). *Gun acquisition and possession in selected juvenile samples* [Research in brief]. Washington, DC: National Institute of Justice.

Shure, M. B., & Spivack, G. (1980). Interpersonal problem-solving as a mediator of behavioral adjustment in preschool and kindergarten children. *Journal of Applied Developmental Psychology, 1,* 29–44.

Shure, M. B., & Spivack, G. (1982). Interpersonal problem-solving in young children: A cognitive approach to prevention. *American Journal of Community Psychology, 10,* 341–356.

Shure, M. B., & Spivack, G. (1988). Interpersonal cognitive problem-solving. In R. H. Price, E. L. Cowen, R. P. Lorion, & J. Ramos-McKay (Eds.), *14 ounces of prevention: A casebook for practitioners* (pp. 69–82). Washington, DC: American Psychological Association.

Slavin, R. E. (1990). Class size and student achievement: Is smaller better? *Contemporary Education, 42,* 6–12.

Slavin, R. E. (1994). School and classroom organization in beginning reading: Class size, aides, and instructional grouping. In R. E. Slavin, N. L. Karweit, & B. A. Wasik (Eds.), *Preventing early school failure: Research, policy, and practice* (pp. 122–142). Boston: Allyn & Bacon.

Slavin, R. E., & Madden, N. A. (1989). Effective classroom programs for students at risk. In R. E. Slavin, N. L. Karweit, & N. A. Madden (Eds.), *Effective programs for students at risk* (pp. 23–51). Boston: Allyn & Bacon.

Slavin, R. E., Madden, N. A., Dolan, L. J., Wasik, B. A., Ross, S. T., & Smith, L. J. (1994, April). Whenever and wherever we choose: The replication of Success for All. *Phi Delta Kappan,* 639–647.

Slavin, R. E., Madden, N. A., Karweit, N. L., Livermon, B. J., & Dolan, L. (1990). Success for All: First-year outcomes of a comprehensive plan for reforming urban education. *American Educational Research Journal, 27*(2), 255–278.

Smith, P. K., & Sharp, S. (1994). *School bullying.* London: Routledge.

Stephens, R. D. (1993). School-based interventions: Safety and security. In A. P. Goldstein & C. R. Huff (Eds.), *The gang intervention handbook* (pp. 219–256). Champaign, IL: Research Press.

Thompson, D. W., & Jason, L. A. (1988). Street gangs and preventive interventions. *Criminal Justice and Behavior, 15,* 323–333.

Thornberry, T. P. (1996). Empirical support for interactional theory: A review of the literature. In J. D. Hawkins (Ed.), *Delinquency and crime: Current theories* (pp. 198–235). New York: Cambridge University Press.

Tolson, E. R., McDonald, S., & Moriarty, A. R. (1992). Peer mediation among high school students: A test of effectiveness. *Social Work in Education, 14,* 86–93.

Walker, H., Colvin, G., & Ramsey, E. (1994). *Antisocial behavior in school: Strategies and best practices.* Pacific Grove, CA: Brooks/Cole.

Wasik, B. A., & Slavin, R. E. (1994). Preventing early reading failure with one-to-one tutoring: A review of five programs. In R. E. Slavin, N. L. Karweit, & B. A. Wasik (Eds.), *Preventing early school failure: Research, policy, and practice* (pp. 143–174). Boston: Allyn & Bacon.

Weissberg, R. P., & Greenberg, M. T. (1997). School and community competence-enhancement and prevention programs. In W. Damon (Series Ed.), I. E. Sigel, & K. A. Renninger (Vol. Eds.), *Handbook of child psychology: Vol 5. Child psychology in practice* (5th ed.). New York: John Wiley & Sons.

Widom, C. S. (1989). The cycle of violence. *Science, 244,* 160–166.

Yoshikawa, H. (1994). Prevention as cumulative protection: Effects of early family support and education on chronic delinquency and its risks. *Psychological Bulletin, 115,* 28–54.

8. Evaluations of School-Based Violence Prevention Programs

FAITH SAMPLES & LARRY ABER

Introduction

As youth violence continues to rise in the United States, even when adult crime rates are falling (Blumstein, 1995), the search for effective youth violence prevention strategies becomes more urgent. Because of near-universal school attendance by American children (until some time in high school), schools are a common site for preventive interventions, including strategies to prevent youth violence. But despite the growing need for youth violence prevention and the logic and attractiveness of using schools as prevention sites, the literature on empirical evaluations of school-based violence prevention initiatives is scattered and thin. The primary purpose of this chapter is to begin to compile the scant existing systematic literature on violence prevention programs in schools. A second purpose is to provide a developmental and contextual framework within which to understand current school-based violence prevention efforts.

Finally, a third purpose of this chapter is to briefly raise two sets of issues based on the description and analysis of school-based youth violence prevention initiatives that, in our opinion, are critical to our nation's progress in preventing youth violence. They are: (1) how to begin to move from violence prevention programs to violence prevention policies, and (2) how to develop a prevention science for school violence adequate to the task of guiding prevention policy.

We begin this chapter by briefly presenting a developmental and contextual framework we use to understand preventive interventions in schools. This framework is the prevailing paradigm linking research on child development with thinking about the design, implementation, and evaluation of child and youth programs and policies (Aber, Brown, Chaudry, Jones, & Samples, 1996; Connell, Aber, & Walker, 1995). Because this framework is described in detail elsewhere (see Williams, Guerra, &

Elliott, 1996) and widely shared in the field, we will only briefly review the main features of the framework required to understand school-based violence prevention programs. These include the concepts of stage-salient (i.e., developmental) tasks and the school organizational (i.e., contextual) issues associated with aggressive/violent behavior.

We then present the heart of this chapter, which describes, by developmental stage, evaluations of violence prevention programs in schools. In addition to organizing the programs by developmental stage, we also characterize them as primary, secondary, or tertiary strategies and as targeted at individual and/or contextual factors.

Next, we briefly describe nonprogrammatic policies proposed to help create safe school environments. In this section, we emphasize the importance of differentiating violence prevention programs and policies. Then we highlight critical issues that must be faced in order to evolve from preventive interventions to prevention policies, and to develop the preventive intervention research necessary to support effective violence prevention policies. Throughout the chapter, we emphasize that while little is known about school-based youth violence prevention to date, much can be and should be learned soon.

Developmental and Contextual Framework for Understanding Preventive Interventions in Schools

As the next section will illustrate, despite the fact that youth violence is a growing national problem, there have been too few well-documented and evaluated efforts to prevent youth violence using schools as the sites for interventions. In this section, we briefly describe a theoretical rationale for why school-based preventive interventions are a strategically good idea. This same rationale provides a developmental and contextual framework within which to understand school-based youth prevention initiatives.

The keys to the developmental-contextual framework are the linked concepts of: (1) development as a series of stage-salient tasks to be mastered, and (2) the notion that the features of a child's environment that are critically important to developmental success change with the key tasks to be mastered at each stage of development.[1] Sroufe and his colleagues have spelled out the implications of this framework as it relates to early childhood development and the immediate caretaking environment (Sroufe, Cooper, DeHart, Marshall, & Bronfenbrenner, 1992).

For instance, Sroufe (1988) and others (Sroufe, Carlson, & Shulman, 1993) argue the most important stage-salient task of socioemotional development in infancy is the development of a secure, trusting attachment relationship with at least one primary caretaker. The corresponding key feature of the caretaking environment is the provision of sensitive, responsive caretaking, which is the key factor influencing security of attachment. This example illustrates several points. First, it illustrates that a stage-salient task is not a stage-specific task. While development of a secure attachment is especially salient in infancy, attachment to others remains a lifelong task. Second, successful adaptation to one stage-salient task increases the chances of success in adapting to later tasks, for example to the development of self-regulation in the preschool years or identity formation in adolescence. The context that promotes successful development obviously must change to promote adaptation to stage-salient tasks.

Others have begun to spell out the details of this perspective for older children and youth as well as for environments beyond parents and family, including schools and neighborhoods (Aber et al., 1996; Connell, Aber, & Walker, 1995). It is this expression of this framework offered by a host of researchers that is particularly relevant to this chapter on violence prevention programs in schools. They lead us to ask the following questions: (1) What are the key stage-salient tasks facing children during the school years relevant to the development of aggressive or violent behavior? and (2) What features of schools as contexts for development are especially related to these stage-salient tasks? While this section cannot offer an exhaustive discussion of these questions, it can provide an introduction to them which can serve as the framework for describing and analyzing school-based violence prevention efforts.

In the remainder of this section, we highlight violence-related stage-salient tasks during four major phases of the school years: early childhood (ages 2–5), middle childhood (ages 6–11), early adolescence (ages 12–14), and middle adolescence (ages 15–18). These stages also correspond to pre-school, elementary school, junior high/middle school, and senior high as organizational contexts for development. Hence, for illustrative purposes, we will also briefly identify one or two school organizational issues associated with aggressive-violent behavior in each of these four stages.

Early Childhood (Ages 2–5)

While serious violence is typically not exhibited until later in life and school proper doesn't generally begin until age six, early childhood is increasingly recognized as a key stage in the development of aggressive-violent behaviors (Keenan & Shaw, 1997; Miller, 1994). And the quality of a "school-like" child care, early education, and family support programs are viewed as affecting the probability of later aggression and violence (Galinsky, Howes, Kontos, & Shinn, 1994; Helburn, Culkin, Morris, et al., 1995; Yoshikawa, 1995; Zigler & Styfco, 1993). In both the developmental and program evaluation literatures, the development of self-regulation appears to be a key stage-salient task of the preschool years and one that is causally linked to other processes that lead to aggressive-violent behavior. From a contextual point of view, caregiver/child ratios (in child care settings) and the quality of caregiver/child interactions (sensitive/nurturing vs. insensitive/harsh-punitive) are key environmental influences on the development of self-regulation (Zigler, Styfco, & Gilman, 1993).

Middle Childhood (Ages 6–11)

Perhaps the stage of childhood development least explored for its potential for youth violence prevention is middle childhood. Yet the potential is great because several key developmental processes related to violent behavior are consolidated at this stage (Aber et al., 1996; Collins, 1984; Collins, Harris, & Susman, 1955). These include the development of children's normative beliefs about aggression (e.g., Is it all right to use aggression to resolve different kinds of disputes?) and the development of children's interpersonal negotiation strategies (Huesmann, Guerra, Miller, & Zelli, 1992; Selman, Beardslee, Schultz, Krupa, & Podoresky, 1986). A number of school contextual factors could influence development at this stage, including the nature of classmates (from whom students may learn particular beliefs and strategies); teachers' perceptions of children's aggression-related cognitions and behaviors; and the probability of exposure to antisocial youth, depending on staggered release times. That is, some schools experiencing problems of older students victimizing (and in that sense negatively socializing) younger students may release the younger students so they can get home unharassed before the older students are released. Thus, behavioral tracking and dismissal time policies can affect children in elementary school.

Early Adolescence (Ages 12–14)

A key stage-salient task of early adolescence is the development of a stable peer group. Whether that peer group is primarily prosocial or antisocial in orientation affects the probability of aggressive and violent behavior greatly (Allen, Weissberg, & Hawkins, 1989). Among the school-organizational characteristics in middle/junior high school and high school found to influence success are: (1) the practice of changing classes with their "homeroom" class (Felner, Brand, Adan, & Mulhall, 1993); and (2) being instructed in a smaller, more personalized classroom or "school within a school" (Comer, 1989). Both of these organizational factors may operate by affecting the nature and functioning of an early adolescent's peer group.

Middle Adolescence (Ages 15–18)

A key task of middle adolescence is the formation and consolidation of an identity, including a personal identity, racial/ethnic identity, etc. Identity processes are hypothesized to moderate the effects of psychosocial stressors on adolescent mental health (Allen, Leadbeater, & Aber, 1994). For instance, a positive racial/ethnic identity appears to buffer adolescents from the effects of racial minority status (in a school or neighborhood) on depression. Such processes may also moderate the impact of institutional racism on adolescent behavior and mental health (Allen et al., 1994).

How various violence prevention initiatives affect identity processes is a currently underexamined but potentially important issue in adolescence. For example, it appears that high-risk schools adopt widely divergent anti-violence strategies. A case in point is the tendency for some schools to use metal detectors as a seemingly aggressive approach to addressing the problem of weapon possession and violence on school grounds. Other schools, in contrast, choose to address the problem of violence through conflict resolution and peer mediation programs. It is the latter approach we wish to examine in this chapter.

Table 8.1 outlines the stage-salient tasks and school contextual factors just described briefly. This is not meant to be an exhaustive list of stage-salient tasks or school features associated with a trajectory toward youth violence; rather these tasks and factors are meant to illustrate what an adequate theoretical approach to the design and evaluation of school-based violence prevention programs might look like.

Violence Prevention Programs

The importance of reviewing violence prevention programs from developmental and contextual perspectives should not be underestimated in light of the consistently younger ages when and the multiple ecologies in which children of increasingly younger ages are exposed to and become

Table 8.1. *Elements of a developmental-conceptual framework to understand school-based violence prevention strategies*

Stage/age	Developmental tasks	Organizational issues
Early childhood (ages 2–5)	Development of self-regulation	Quality of caretaking Caretaker/child ratios
Middle childhood (ages 6–11)	Development of normative beliefs about aggression Development of interpersonal negotiation strategies	Nature of classmates Teachers' perceptions Early release policies for younger students
Early adolescence (ages 12–14)	Development of stable, prosocial (vs. antisocial) peer group	Changes classes with "homeroom" class Instruction in smaller classrooms
Middle adolescence (ages 15–18)	Identity formation	Metal detectors vs. conflict resolution or peer mediation

victims of violence. Escalating rates of violence in American communities are having detrimental effects on the healthy growth and development of youth. There is evidence to suggest that early childhood interventions may help reduce violence (Yoshikawa, 1995). To the extent that these programs employ an ecological approach to enhancing child development, by promoting overall social competence, they provide hope for improving children's competencies in other areas. This, in turn, may reduce the risk of children engaging in violence-related behaviors as they grow older.

In this section we review a number of school-based violence prevention programs that have been or are being evaluated using an appropriate empirical methodology. These programs are categorized as primary, secondary, and tertiary prevention efforts and assessed from a developmental perspective. It should be noted that several programs included herein serve multiple populations at differing developmental stages. When evaluations have been or are being conducted on selected age groups, discussion of those programs will be specific to the developmental stage of the sample. Otherwise, discussion of multipopulation programs will be based on the earliest developmental stage covered. The list of programs presented is by no means exhaustive; rather, it represents programs about which sufficient printed information was available. A summary of the programs reviewed in this section, including the age of the target children, the nature and intensity of the intervention, and the design of the evaluation research and outcomes, is then provided in Table 8.2.

Early Childhood (Ages 2–5)

Relatively few programs have been designed specifically to prevent violence by targeting interventions for young children. In fact, only in recent years has attention been paid to the meaning of violence for infants and toddlers. Thus, school-based preventive interventions for young children are quite rare. Prevention programs have generally been targeted at behavior change within adolescent populations by focusing on specific risk behaviors or settings. The need to provide preventive interventions at relatively early ages has resulted in one program, Second Step, that extended its violence prevention efforts to the classrooms of pre-kindergarten and kindergarten children as a means of delaying or eliminating the onset of antisocial or deviant behavior.

However, programs like Second Step are not the norm. The more common approach to behavior change has been the use of early intervention programs that combine childhood education and family support. Because these early intervention efforts could be implemented via the schools, they are also reviewed here for their potential relevance to school-based prevention efforts.

Recent reviews of such programs suggest they may serve as primary prevention strategies for risk factors resulting in later delinquency and antisocial behavior (Yoshikawa, 1995; Zigler, Taussig, & Black, 1992). Yoshikawa (1995) reported programs that targeted multiple risk factors and showed cumulative effects for buffering children against later antisocial and aggressive behaviors. Although they are not specifically designed to target child behavior problems, researchers (e.g., Johnson & Breckenridge, 1982) have suggested the need to examine early intervention programs for possible primary prevention effects. For purposes of this chapter, however, the early intervention programs presented following Second Step are classified as secondary prevention initiatives since their primary focus and early findings were on the ability of such programs to enhance high-risk children's social and intellectual competencies rather than the long-term effects on behavior problems.

Second Step. The Second Step program is one of the few programs that offer a school-based violence prevention curriculum to children as young as three years old (Moore & Beland, 1992). The curriculum is designed to serve children from preschool through ninth grade. The intervention consists of classroom-based lessons, divided into three units (empathy training, impulse control, and anger management), conducted with children up to three times weekly. The goal of the program is to reduce impulsive and aggressive behaviors and to increase overall social competence among children. The program's focus on the reduction of aggressive and impulsive behavior among all children makes Second Step a primary prevention initiative.

Summary results of Second Step's pilot studies suggested that involvement in the program produced positive behavioral change (Sylvester & Frey, 1994). Teacher ratings of children's behavior were generally positive, indicating that children used curriculum concepts and vocabulary, as well as applied problem-solving and anger management strategies (usually following a teacher prompt) more frequently than their peers who did not receive training in the program. Additionally, children were shown to recognize the emotional states of others, to negotiate with others, and to manage their anger more effectively than nonprogram children (Moore & Beland, 1992).

Encouraging results of a study of second and third grade students in 12 schools were recently released (Grossman, Neckerman, Koepsell, & Rivara, 1997). Intervention consisted of two to three aggression prevention curriculum lessons per week for 16–20 weeks. Using a randomized trial, Grossman and colleagues evaluated children's behavior in school before the program began, two weeks after completion, and at six months postintervention. Results at final evaluation showed fewer acts of aggressive behavior from the experimental group than the control group. As compared with the control group, the experimental group exhibited approximately 30 fewer acts of aggression per day. Rates of aggressive behavior (including kicking, hitting, and shoving) among children who did not participate in the program were also found to increase over time.

High/Scope Perry Preschool Project. The High/Scope Perry Preschool Project was among the first longitudinal studies designed to assess the impact of an early childhood education program on the lives of poor children and their families, as well as the quality of their communities (Berrueta-Clement, Schweinhart, Barnett, Epstein, & Weikart, 1984). The central focus was on high-risk children's intellectual development, school achievement patterns, and social maturity, making it a secondary prevention initiative. Data were collected annually on a sample of 123 poor 3- and 4-year-old African American youths while they were between the ages of 3 and 11, who were randomly assigned to program and no-program groups. Data were collected again when the children were 14, 15, 19, and 27 years of age (Schweinhart & Weikart, 1989). The intervention consisted of a seven and one-half month early childhood education program, with 12.5 hours of weekly instruction over a one- to two-year period plus weekly home visits with parents and children.

Involvement in a high quality early childhood education program was found to positively affect the rate of misconduct, crime, and delinquency among children in the program group. Data drawn from self-reports and official police or court records showed that early childhood education reduced antisocial behavior and misconduct from the elementary school years, as well as at age 15 (Schweinhart & Weikart, 1980). Teacher ratings of personal and school misconduct, when study participants were 6 to 9 years old, were reportedly significantly lower for the program group as compared with the no-program group. The researchers also found a reduction in after-school detentions and in the frequency of self-reported misconduct and delinquency at age 15. Results at age 19 indicated program participants were less likely to have ever been arrested and more likely to have a lower total arrest rate (Berrueta-Clement et al., 1984). Similarly, children in this group had fewer offenses as adults and rated themselves lower on a measure of the frequency of serious delinquent events (Schweinhart & Weikart, 1989).

Rates of delinquency and crime continued to be higher for the no-program group as compared with the program group through adulthood, as reported by Schweinhart, Barnes, and Weikart (1993). According to police or court records, the program group had a significantly lower number of lifetime criminal (2.3 vs. 4.6) and adult (1.8 vs. 4.0) arrests; were significantly less likely to be frequent offenders over their lifetimes (7% vs. 35%) or as adults (7% vs. 31%); and were sentenced to significantly fewer months of probation and parole (3.2 vs. 6.6 months). Self-reported measures of misconduct yielded similar results, albeit not significant. In contrast to the no-program group, the program group rated themselves lower on acts of misconduct, arrests by police, and time spent on probation by age 27 (Schweinhart et al., 1993).

Houston Parent-Child Development Center (PCDC). Long-term effects on antisocial behavior and delinquency have also been assessed by several other early childhood programs. The Houston Parent-Child Development Center, or PCDC, was a two-year, parent/child education program designed to promote social and intellectual competence among low-income, Mexican

American families with children ages one to three (Johnson & Breckenridge, 1982). Random assignment was used to divide families into program and control groups. Program participation involved 25 sessions of 1.5 hours each. Weekend sessions were incorporated to include the entire family in discussions of topics related to family management and communication. Year one of the program was delivered in the home, with a focus on parent-child interactions, child development, and parenting skills. During year two, the mothers were required to attend classes to learn more about child development, communication, family management, and other family-related topics.

Results showed a decline in the frequency of behavior problems favoring program children. A follow-up study revealed that when compared with program children, the control group children were rated by their mothers as more destructive, resistant, and restless, and more prone to negative attention seeking. Teacher ratings of classroom behavior, at five to eight years post-intervention, showed fewer aggressive, acting-out behaviors among program children than among their control group peers (Johnson & Walker, 1987). Teachers rated program children as more considerate and less hostile. Control group children, on the other hand, were rated as more disruptive, impulsive, obstinate, restless, and involved in more fights.

Yale Child Welfare Project. Evidence of long-term effects on delinquency and antisocial behavior were found with the Yale Child Welfare Project, which provided medical and social services to a predominantly African American sample of low-income, first-time mothers (Seitz, Rosenbaum, & Apfel, 1985). A comprehensive set of services, including 28 home visits, routine well-baby care, developmental screening, and an average of 13.2 months of child care, was provided to strengthen the caregiving and self-sufficiency abilities of families. Ten-year follow-up results using a quasi-experimental design found program children to be more socially competent and at less risk for delinquency. Results were significant only for boys and revealed more negative ratings on classroom behavior for control boys than for program boys. As compared with program boys, control boys were rated by their teachers as being disobedient and as having problems getting along with other children. Parental reports supported these findings, indicating control boys were more likely to steal, violate curfew, and be expelled from school for fighting than their program counterparts (Seitz, Rosenbaum, & Apfel, 1985).

Syracuse Family Development Research Program (FDRP). The efficacy of family support and early childhood education as a means of reducing the risk for future delinquent behavior can also be evidenced by the Syracuse Family Development Research Program (FDRP). The FDRP attempted to enhance family and child functioning through parent contact and supplementary child care through the first five years of life. A largely African American sample of first-time mothers from impoverished communities was recruited and provided with an array of health and human service resources (Lally, Mangione, & Honig, 1987; Lally, Mangione, Honig, & Wittner, 1988). Weekly home visits were designed to encourage quality family interactions and cohesiveness, with home visitors serving to bridge the gap between the home and child care environments. Children between the ages of 6 and 15 months attended day care 50 weeks per year, five days per week, for half a day. Children between 15–18 months of age were transitioned to full-time care which continued until they reached school age.

A longitudinal follow-up at ten years (post-intervention) showed the strongest effects of the program in the domain of social deviance and functioning in the community (Lally et al., 1988). Program children were found to differ dramatically from their control group peers (Lally et al., 1987). For example, county probation records showed in the follow-up that 22% of the control children, as compared with only 6% of program children, had been placed on probation. Data also revealed control group children committed more severe offenses and were more likely to be chronic offenders. Moreover, the cost of handling cases through the courts and probation departments were far more extensive for control children than for their counterparts in the program group (Lally et al., 1987).

Summary. These programs, which were evaluated using truly experimental and quasi-experimental designs, clearly show evidence of the potential for early childhood education programs to function as primary prevention initiatives for later delinquent and antisocial behavior. Findings from these studies show a connection between improvements in family functioning and parenting behavior and lasting, positive effects on child behavior. Essentially, the research suggests the experiences of young children are shaped by the coping strategies employed by their parents or caregivers. Combined with the need to begin interventions as early in a child's life as possible is the need to involve parents in preventive interventions designed for young children. The most effective approach appears to be an intervention program that engages the multiple and diverse systems in which children exist in targeting individual risk factors that predict later violence and violence-related behaviors.

Middle Childhood (Ages 6–11)

Most violence prevention efforts have responded to behavior problems following children's exposure to violence. This is evidenced by the proliferation of conflict resolution and violence prevention programs targeted at high-risk youth. In more recent years, the focus has shifted from the need to repair damage caused by exposure to violence to the emphasis on earlier and more preventive measures aimed at delaying or eliminating the onset of behavior problems. Practitioners have responded to the call for more preventive interventions by developing and implementing programs that address the needs of children at the elementary and middle/junior high school levels.

The likelihood that children will be involved in a school-based violence prevention program of some sort increases dramatically as children approach transitional school age. With the increasing interest in the primary prevention of youth violence, practitioners have begun to create programs that teach younger children more effective ways of dealing with conflicts and that attempt to change the overall climate of the school. Although relatively few in number to date, it appears the trend toward preventive interventions with elementary school children is becoming more popular. Unfortunately, many of these programs have not undergone rigorous scientific examination or results of empirical investigations have not yet become available. Programs for which some outcome data were available are discussed following.

Resolving Conflict Creatively Program (RCCP). The Resolving Conflict Creatively Program (RCCP) is one of the largest and longest running school-based primary violence prevention efforts in the country. The RCCP provides K-12 curricula for elementary, secondary, and special education. The program seeks to encourage all children to experiment with new and different ways of handling conflicts with others by using: (1) a 51-lesson curriculum; (2) a peer mediation program; and (3) parental involvement and support for resolving conflicts nonviolently outside of school.

A quasi-experimental process and outcome evaluation of the RCCP has recently been designed and data collection has been completed (Aber, Brown, Chaudry, Jones, & Samples, 1996). The study follows more than 8,000 children and their teachers in second through sixth grades from 15 New York City public elementary schools. Participating schools were selected to represent four groups of varying levels of intervention: no intervention (year one); beginning level; consolidation; and saturation. Children were exposed to the program through multiple components (including 25 hours of introductory teacher training, RCCP classroom lessons, staff development support, administrator training, parent training, and peer mediation) for a period of two years.

Final results of the evaluation are not yet available; however, preliminary findings based on the first year of the study data reveal positive effects of the RCCP when a large number of lessons (i.e., ten or more) are provided to students (RCCP Research Group, 1997). Generally, it was found that irrespective of program participation, all the children developed more aggressive fantasies, more hostile attributional biases, more aggressive interpersonal negotiation strategies, and more conduct problems over the course of the school year and as grade level increased. In addition, children's levels of prosocial fantasies and competent interpersonal negotiation strategies decreased over time and with grade level. However, longitudinal analyses (over year 1) indicated the rates of growth in children's aggressive fantasies, hostile attributional bias, and aggressive problem-solving strategies were all slowed when given a large number of RCCP lessons. Conversely, the more lessons the children received, the slower their decrease over time in prosocial fantasies and the use of a competent strategy to resolve potential conflicts with peers. Thus, children's developmental trajectories were improved by receiving more classroom instruction in conflict resolution and related skills by RCCP.

Interaction effects were also found, suggesting a combination of factors determined program impact. For instance, results showed the slowest rate of decrease in children's use of competent strategies in classrooms in which teachers received the most training in the program and in which the students of these teachers received a high number of lessons. The rate of increase in children's use of aggressive strategies was slowest in classrooms with high teacher contact with the RCCP and when the number of lessons provided exceeded ten (RCCP Research Group, 1997). Results based on the second year of data collection will be available in 1998.

Peace Builders. Peace Builders is a school-based primary prevention program that serves children in elementary schools exclusively, ranging from kindergarten to fifth grade. The focus of the program is broad in that it targets not only children but also parents, schools, and communities as a means of reducing physical and verbal aggression among children (Heartsprings, Inc., 1992). Specific principles of teaching children positive social skills both on and off school grounds, teaching parenting competence skills, and disseminating practical tools to improve school climate serve as the basis of this program.

As with the RCCP, a quasi-experimental study of the Peace Builders program has recently been designed and is being completed (Flannery, Vazsonyi, Embry, Powell, & Atha, 1997). The study has yielded promising results in favor of children in the program for more than one year. A sample of third to fifth grade children was divided into two groups: one that received the intervention for the two years (Wave 1) and another that received the intervention only in one year (Wave 2). Results showed improvements in the effect size of teacher-rated social competence and initial treatment effects for children. Both child and teacher ratings indicated the overall rate of problem behavior was highest for children who had been exposed to the program for only one year. Over time, teacher ratings of children's aggression and social competence showed the two-year intervention group to be less cruel or mean, less likely to bully and threaten others, and more likely to be obedient in school as compared with the one-year intervention group. Teachers' ratings showed both groups coping more effectively with aggression from others and fighting less after the intervention, although greatest improvement was seen among the two-year intervention group. Child self-reports were consistent with teacher ratings, showing decreasing rates of negative behavior over time for the two-year intervention group and increasing rates of aggressive behavior for their one-year intervention group peers (Flannery, Vazsonyi, & Vesterdal, 1997).

BrainPower. The BrainPower program was designed to reduce the tendency toward attributional bias and reactive aggression among children in elementary school. More specifically, it is one of the very few primary prevention efforts targeting aggressive African American boys in grades three through six. Program participation involves role playing, discussions of personal experiences, and training to interpret and categorize the behavioral cues of others in social settings. The goal of the program is threefold: (1) to strengthen the ability of young males to accurately detect intentionality through the interpretation of social cues; (2) to increase their understanding of ambiguously caused acts; and (3) to expound on the meaning of intentionality while linking appropriate behavioral responses to ambiguously caused, negative outcomes (Hudley, 1994).

Empirical studies using a truly experimental design have shown treatment effects for aggressive boys involved in the BrainPower program (e.g., Hudley 1994, 1995). The intervention consisted of 12 sessions of 60 minutes each over a six-week period. Children were randomly assigned to three treatment groups (experimental aggressive, attention-only aggressive, no attention aggressive), and compared to a group of nonaggressive controls. Baseline reports of children's behavior and social competence, provided by teachers, indicated the three groups of aggressive children were more aggressive overall, more prone to retaliation, and less likely to display prosocial behaviors toward their peers than their nonaggressive counterparts.

Findings from the 1994 study (Hudley, 1994), using fourth to sixth grade boys, showed a reduction in hostile attributional bias, anger, and retaliatory behavior among the experimental aggressive group. Moreover, ratings of these behaviors in ambiguous situations among the experimental aggressive group reached levels comparable to that of nonaggressive children at the end of the intervention. Furthermore, while remaining higher than that of the nonaggressive controls, the overall rate of decline in aggressive behavior and reactive aggression among the experimental aggressive group was double that of the other two treatment groups. Finally, a laboratory task conducted one week after completion of the program showed a decline in the tendency of the experimental aggressive children to infer hostile intent, to feel angry, and to engage in aggressive verbal behavior.

A second study of third to fifth grade boys yielded similar results on teacher ratings and provided support for an earlier trend that suggested the experimental aggressive group had fewer disciplinary referrals than their aggressive peers in the other two treatment groups (Hudley, 1995). One somewhat perplexing finding was the tendency for third grade experimental aggressive boys to increase their perceptions of hostile intent in hypothetical scenarios of ambiguous causation. Hudley suggested this finding might be explained by the difficulty some younger children have in applying new information to hypothetical tasks, or simply by the inability of the younger children to fully understand the instrument.

Washington Community Violence Prevention Program (WCVPP). The Washington Community Violence Prevention Program, or WCVPP, is a primary and secondary prevention program that uses a classroom-based approach as its key component to improve children's social problem-solving skills, their attitudes about aggression, and their knowledge of risk factors associated with violence. The emphasis is on prevention through the use of a multidisciplinary approach that focuses (among other things) on the motivation behind violence. The program is administered over a three-week period, using 15 50-minute sessions on consecutive weekdays.

An evaluation of the intervention (Gainer, Webster, & Champion, 1993) included a sample of fifth and seventh grade students who received a pre- and post-test measure within a four to five week interval. All fifth grade students in two elementary schools, and three classes of seventh grade students from a junior high school were included in the treatment group. The control group was selected from the same grades and schools one year after the intervention was introduced.

Program effects were found generally to favor the treatment group over the control group. Involvement in the program reduced the tendency for children to attribute hostile intent to an ambiguous cue. However, when controls for baseline data were introduced, it was found that fifth grade children in the control group were less likely than their treatment group peers to provide violent and hostile solutions in problem-solving situations. Treatment group children were found to support the notion of the legitimacy of aggression less often than children in the control group. Control group children were more likely to report violent solutions to hypothetical social problems, to associate negative consequences to violent responses, and to provide hostile solutions to a problem at baseline. There was no reported change in their knowledge of risk factors, and they were more likely than their treatment group peers to believe that aggression was an appropriate response under certain circumstances (Gainer et al., 1993).

Early and Middle Adolescence (Ages 12–18)

As the evidence suggests, school-based violence prevention efforts have largely been targeted at youth in this key developmental stage. Adolescent peer relationships become profoundly important during this stage of development, increasing the possibility of learned antisocial behaviors. Data clearly show that adolescents are at the greatest risk for violence, both as perpetrators and as victims. This is particularly true for African American males who live in poor, inner city communities (Hammond & Yung, 1991). The following programs were designed and implemented to address the needs of adolescents by teaching them effective ways to manage conflicts and disputes.

Positive Adolescent Choices Training (PACT). The Positive Adolescent Choices Training (PACT) program is a model for primary violence prevention designed specifically for African American youth ages 12–15. PACT is a three-part training approach used to educate adolescents about the risks associated with violence; to teach skills in anger management; and to teach prosocial skills. Youths participated in approximately 38 biweekly training sessions in the schools involving peer-based videotaped vignettes, role plays, psychodramas, and discussions. Skill training was conducted in six areas, including giving positive feedback, giving negative feedback, accepting negative feedback, resisting peer pressure, solving problems, and negotiating (Hammond, 1990).

In a quasi-experimental study of the program, results revealed improvement in all target areas as rated by teachers and outside observers (Hammond & Yung, 1991). The individual skill gain of 12 PACT participants was 30.4%, compared to a skill loss of 1.1% in a comparison group of seven untrained students. Seventy-five percent of PACT students showed skill improvement, whereas only 43% of controls gained in skills. The proportion of skill loss was also significantly less for PACT students (17%) as compared with the no-program controls (57%). Youth self-reports and school records also showed positive results, with students reporting overall improvement in skills and school records indicating less involvement in violence-related school behaviors.

Bully/Victim Program. The Bully/Victim Program represents a line of research designed to limit conflict in schools and change the climate of schools in Norway (Olweus, 1994, 1995). Program goals were to reduce existing bully/victim problems and prevent the future occurrence of new problems, thus qualifying it as both a primary and secondary prevention program. Typical bullies were identified as engaging in aggressive reaction behavior patterns (in the case of boys), with physical strength. Additionally, these children were viewed as having more problems with conduct disorder and as displaying more antisocial and rule breaking behavior patterns. Participation involved schoolwide communication campaigns that redefined aggressive behavior as inappropriate. The intervention targeted students in grades four through seven, ranging in age from 11–14. Children were divided into grade level groups, and baseline data was used as a basis for comparison after children had been involved in the program for one to two years.

A test of the intervention showed not only a reduction in the number of new victims of bullying but also showed a marked decline in antisocial behavior among the children. More directly, studies showed a 50% reduction in bullying after both 8 and 20 months of intervention. Declines in the rates of antisocial behavior (e.g., fighting, pilfering, and truancy), and improvements in general classroom order and discipline were also found. Finally, children were rated as having more positive social relationships after being involved in the program.

Viewpoints. While not specifically a school-based prevention program, the Viewpoints training program is included here because of its potential applicability to school settings. Based on a model of social-cognitive development, Viewpoints seeks to remediate cognitive factors related to youth behavior problems (Guerra & Slaby, 1990). The objective of this primary prevention program is to teach the skills necessary to help adolescents avoid aggression, violence, and other problem behaviors. Participation in the intervention involves 12 one hour-long sessions, which occurred in a classroom-type environment within a juvenile detention center. The objective was to change adolescents' attitudes and beliefs about the legitimacy of violence. Using a sample of 15- to 18-year old aggressive, incarcerated juvenile offenders randomly assigned to a treatment group, an attention control group, or a no-treatment control group, the authors found a decrease in the endorsement of beliefs supporting the legitimacy of aggression among the treatment group only. Ratings of overall behavioral adjustment, indicating reductions in aggressive, impulsive, and inflexible behavior, were also lower for the treatment group than the comparison groups.

Responding in Peaceful and Positive Ways (RIPP). The Responding in Peaceful and Positive Ways (RIPP) program is a 25-session sixth grade primary prevention curriculum grounded in social-cognitive learning theory (Meyer & Farrell, in press). It targets the interactive influences of behaviors, intrapersonal attributes, and environmental factors by employing adult role models to teach students knowledge, attitudes, and skills that promote nonviolence and foster positive communication. Children were randomly assigned to treatment and no-treatment control groups, and participation in the intervention involved weekly sessions of 25–50 minutes for seven to eight months.

A study of program effectiveness (Farrell & Meyer, 1997a) revealed a reduction in the number of school discipline code violations and a decline in rates of in-school suspension and fight-related injuries among the treatment group by the end of the intervention. Using student self-reports and school disciplinary data, the authors examined the prevalence of code violations for fighting, assaults, and bringing weapons to school, as well as for in- and out-of-school suspensions. Prevalence rates of these behaviors were not found to differ significantly between the two groups during the first three quarters of the school year. However, data from the fourth quarter showed the percentage of youths in the control group charged with fighting to be more than twice that of their treatment group peers. Additionally, youths in the control group were nearly four times more likely than those in the treatment group to be charged with bringing a weapon to school. Moreover, the rate of in-school suspensions was also higher among controls than among the treatment group. Consistent with school code violation data, results from student self-reports revealed significantly lower frequencies of fighting among youths in the treatment group as compared with youths in the control group. Finally, relative to the control group, youths in the treatment group reported significantly fewer fight-related injuries.

Results on treatment effects at six months post-intervention have recently been studied (Farrell & Meyer, 1997b). Preliminary findings, based on student self-reported data, suggest positive effects on youths involved in the RIPP intervention group as compared with their control group counterparts. Analyses of school code violations have also shown significantly fewer in-school and out-of-school suspensions among the treatment group than among the control group.

Adolescent Transitions Program (ATP). The Adolescent Transitions Program (ATP) evolved from a parent-focused program, based on social learning theory, that proved successful in reducing antisocial behavior in pre-delinquent young children. As with Viewpoints, the program is included because of the potential ability to apply it to the school setting. ATP is both a primary and secondary prevention program.

ATP uses a combination of parent and adolescent training to achieve the same goal as other programs targeted at adolescents, but with high-risk youth (Dishion & Andrews, 1995). Adolescents are provided strategies for improving self-regulation and prosocial behavior in 12 weekly sessions of 90 minutes each over the course of three to four months. Sessions are based on curriculum instruction and videotapes, role playing, and discussions. Parents are engaged in an equal number of two-hour sessions that focus on family management practices and communication skills (Dishion & Andrews, 1995).

A randomized trial of 10- to 14-year-olds, using four treatment conditions (parent focused, teen focused, parent-teen focused, and self-directed change), showed short-term program effects. Immediate beneficial effects were found for the parent focused group, indicating that families in this group had fewer reports of behavior problems at the end of the program. Likewise, results showed immediate positive effects for the parent-teen focused group, suggesting a reduction in observed and reported family conflict. However, one-year follow-up results yielded no enduring effects of the program on antisocial behavior, and in fact suggested that grouping high-risk children together may accentuate their negative behaviors (Dishion & Andrews, 1995).

Summary

The programs included herein (and outlined in Table 8.2) are but some of the existing intervention strategies being used to combat the wave of violence sweeping our country. They range in focus to include emphases on children's social and cognitive processing, parent behavior, and children's prosocial behavior. While generally suggesting positive impacts on aggression and antisocial behavior, the paucity of rigorously evaluated programs makes it difficult to truly assess the broader effects of such programs on child behavior problems.

Several earlier researchers reviewed violence prevention and conflict resolution programs and concluded that the results on effectiveness were mixed. For instance, Webster (1993) reviewed several conflict resolution programs and argued that there is insufficient evidence of long-term effects on violent behavior. Moreover, he contends that in the absence of other supporting interventions, classroom-based curricula have generally failed to produce results that have sustainable effects on other health and social problems among youth. Gottfredson's (1996) review of violence prevention programs indicated that while some programs offer some of what schools, communities, and families need to mitigate the effects of violence with which they are confronted, there is still a need for more comprehensive programs to address the problem.

An important but largely unaddressed issue in all of these violence prevention interventions is that of safety and the degree to which children are safe in the context of the school environment or within their larger communities. Very few of the programs included addressed school safety issues as a focus of the intervention. Of those doing so, the approach was largely through anti-violence campaigns designed to create a culture of nonviolence in schools. (The next section of this chapter differentiates between program efforts to develop safe and protective environments for children and existing institutional policies that help to create safer settings in which children can learn.)

As reflected in this program review, there are encouraging results that suggest that school-based violence prevention efforts may serve as primary prevention for children. In contrast to some other reviews (e.g., Webster, 1993), the findings summarized here have generally been in support

Table 8.2. *Summary of school-based violence prevention programs*

Studies and program names	Age of children (sample size)	Nature and intensity of intervention	Research design	Outcomes	Special outcomes
Second Step (Grossman et al., 1997: Moore & Beland, 1992; Sylvester & Frey, 1994)	Pre-K to 8th grade (3–13 years)	28 sessions, 2–3 times/week for 2.5–6 months Primary prevention	Quasi-experimental design	Aggressive behavior (e.g., hitting, kicking, and shoving): E<C Social problem-solving behavior: E>C	Findings on aggressive behavior based on 6-month follow-up
High/Scope Perry Preschool Project (Berrueta-Clement et al., 1984; Schweinhart & Weikart, 1980, 1989)	3–5 years (3–4 years at enrollment)	Weekly home visits Preschool: 12.5 hours/week Secondary prevention	Randomized trial with control group	Antisocial behavior between ages 6–9: E<C Delinquent behavior at age 15: E<C Arrests at ages 19 and 27: E<C	
Houston PCDC (Johnson & Breckenridge, 1982; Johnson & Walker, 1987)	1–3 years at enrollment; 3–5 years at end of intervention	Year 1: 25 home visits Year 2: parent classes and 16 hours/week of preschool Secondary prevention	Randomized trial with control group	Aggressive behavior at 1–4 year and 5–8 year follow-ups: E<C Aggressive behavior at 8–11 year follow-up: E=C	

Table 8.2. (*cont.*)

Studies and program names	Age of children (sample size)	Nature and intensity of intervention	Research design	Outcomes	Special outcomes
Yale Child Welfare Project (Seitz et al., 1985)	Pregnancy to 30 months	28 home visits, well-baby care, developmental screening, and educational child care (13.2 months) Secondary prevention	Quasi-experimental design	Aggression and delinquency at 10-year follow-up (boys only): E<C	Direct applicability to a school setting is questionable, but some components may be transferable
Syracuse FDRP (Lally et al., 1987; Lally et al., 1988)	Birth to 5 years	Weekly home visits and day care (part-time: 6–14 months: full-time: 15 months to 5 years) Secondary prevention	Quasi-experimental design	Aggressive behavior in 1st grade: E>C Delinquency at 10-year follow-up: E<C	May be applied to a school setting
RCCP (Aber et al., 1996; RCCP Research Group, 1997)	K–12th grade	51-lesson curriculum; teacher, parent, and administrator training; and peer mediation Primary prevention	Quasi-experimental; selection cohort design	Aggressive cognitions and behaviors: E<C Prosocial cognitions and behaviors (with high number of lessons and high	Analyses based on 2nd–6th grade only

Program	Age/Grade	Description	Design	Results	Notes
Peace Builders (Flannery, Embry, Powell, & Atha, 1997; Flannery, Vazsonyi, & Vesterdal, 1997)	K–5th grade	1–2 years of integrated school-based program; parenting skills Primary prevention	Quasi-experimental; selection cohort design	teacher contact with program): E>C Aggressive behavior: W1>W2 Social competence: W1<W2	Analyses based on 3rd–5th grade only
BrainPower (Hudley, 1994, 1995)	3rd–6th grade	12 sessions, 60 minutes each, over six weeks Primary prevention	Randomized trial with aggressive (EC) and nonaggressive controls	Aggressive cognitions and behaviors: E<EC, E=C (by end of intervention)	1994 results based on 4th–6th graders; 1995 results based on 3rd–5th graders
WCVPP (Gainer, Webster, & Champion, 1993)	5th and 7th grades	15 50-minute sessions on consecutive weekdays for three weeks Primary and secondary prevention	Quasi-experimental design	Aggressive cognitions: E<C Problem solving: E>C (without baseline control)	Among 5th graders, on problem solving with baseline controls: C>E
PACT (Hammond & Yung, 1991)	12–15 years	38 biweekly sessions for 5–6 months (50 minutes each) Primary prevention	Quasi-experimental design	Social skills improvement: E<C Aggressive behaviors: E<C	

Table 8.2. (*cont.*)

Studies and program names	Age of children (sample size)	Nature and intensity of intervention	Research design	Outcomes	Special outcomes
Bully/Victim Program (Olweus, 1994, 1995)	4th–7th grade	Schoolwide communications campaign redefining bullying as wrong or inappropriate Primary and secondary prevention	Quasi-experimental; selection cohort design	Bully-victim problems: 50% reduction Antisocial behavior: general reductions over time	Reductions in negative behavior found with 8 and 20 months of intervention respectively
Viewpoints (Guerra & Slaby, 1990)	15–18 years	12 sessions of 1 hour each Primary prevention	Randomized trial with experimental and no-treatment controls	Aggressive behavior: E<EC Aggressive corrections: E<C and E<EC	Intervention administered at juvenile detention center but occurred in classroom context
RIPP (Farrell & Meyer, 1997a, 1997b; Meyer & Farrell, in press)	6th grade	25 sessions of 25–50 minutes, over 7–8 months Primary prevention	Randomized trial with experimental and no-treatment controls	Aggressive behaviors (i.e., fighting and carrying weapons): E<C Suspension (in-school): E<C (results at post-intervention and 6-month follow-up)	Findings based on student self-reports and school code violation data

| ATP (Dishion & Andrews, 1995) | 10–14 years | 12 weekly sessions, 90 minutes each, over 3–4 months Primary and secondary prevention | Randomized trial with experimental controls | Antisocial behavior: E<EC Parent-focused group=E | Immediate effects only; no differences at 1-year follow-up |

of children involved in preventive interventions as compared with their peers in no-treatment groups. However, for several reasons, both these data and our conclusions should be viewed with some caution.

One reason these data should be viewed with caution is that we know little about whether these programs apply equally well to children of diverse cultural backgrounds and social classes. Very often, African American and low-income children and families were overrepresented in sample populations of studies on early education interventions. In school-based programs for older children, there were far fewer studies that included largely African American samples. It raises the question of whether such programs would be as effective with different populations of children.

What seems quite clear from this review and from other studies as well (e.g., Posner, 1994) is that school-based violence prevention efforts offer the most hope for long-term effectiveness when they are integrated with other services that cater to the needs of schools on a comprehensive scale. In other words, when interventions target several key stage-salient developmental contexts, the probability of treatment efficacy appears to increase. Children do not exist in a vacuum, and what they learn in school must be reinforced in their homes and communities. The desire for comprehensive change requires preventive interventions that encompass the broader contextual environments in which children live.

Our conclusions should also be considered with caution because we did not assume the task of a detailed methodological critique of the existing research. While we limited ourselves to programs that included empirical evaluations based on a truly experimental or appropriate quasi-experimental design, we have not tried to specify how potential problems in design or analysis may limit the validity of these studies. Another review of these studies could judge whether they are flawed due to: lack of appropriate covariates (in the quasi-experimental studies); lack of sufficient statistical power to detect treatment effects; lack of control for multiple comparisons; and the like. We did not undertake this type of review for two reasons. First, not all the studies in their current forms contain sufficient information to address these issues. Second, and most important, we had a different goal in mind. We chose to present programs that have shown some potential for being effective, even though it might turn out that some of them are not effective, rather than risk rejecting programs that eventually will prove to be effective. On the whole, we believe the studies reviewed here support the thesis that school-based efforts can work. Of course, the next and more difficult questions are: Who do they work for (i.e., subgroups), under what conditions (i.e., context effects), and why (i.e., mediating processes)? These are the questions that must be addressed at the next stage of a prevention science for school-based strategies, and they will be addressed in more detail below.

Effects of Policies on Safe School Environments

The impact of violence on the psychosocial development of children has only recently come to the forefront of discussions among policy makers, researchers, and practitioners alike. According to Garbarino, Kostelny, and Dubrow (1991), escalating rates of violence experienced in some inner cities resemble those of war-torn countries. The increased risk of poor children in urban centers being exposed to violence on an almost daily basis has been cause for much concern regarding their psychological well-being. The consequences of children growing up in such environments raise questions about children's overall safety, but specifically as it relates to their safety at school and in their communities.

Violence prevention programs have begun to address the problem of school safety. Many researchers and practitioners now realize that "programs" are not enough to change the tide of violence on school grounds without changes in the way schools deal with the growing number of assaults and other violent incidents. School policies are institutionalized regulations that provide a sense of security to students and staff through measures ranging from early release policies to the installation of metal detectors. On the other hand, prevention programs providing safety components attempt to convey messages of nonviolence that hopefully translate into less hostile school environments over time. School policies, if viewed as institutional regulations incorporated to increase or improve the current level of safety, would presumably bring about more rapid change in a school's overall climate. The focus here is on the ability of institutionalized school policies to make schools safe havens for the nation's children.

Without question, the safety of children both in and out of school has raised concern among researchers. In a study conducted by Fick, Lewis, Osofsky, and Flowers (1995), children, parents, and police were asked about perceived safety at home, at school, traveling to and from school, and in the neighborhood. It was found that children and parents reported similar levels of safety at home but dramatically different perceptions were reported with respect to school safety. While 64% of students reported feeling "very safe" at school, less than half as many parents (31%) felt the same way about their children's schools. Both children and parents felt less safety outside of the confines of home and school, with 37% of children and more than half of parents (54%) reporting that children were "not safe at all" when walking to school or playing in their neighborhoods. When police and parents were asked what they thought would improve the safety of children at school, both responded that the need for better security was paramount.

The reasons for the lack of safety in schools across the country are numerous and varied. It is believed that specific causes of violence in and around schools have much to do with schools themselves. For example, some studies (Harootunian, 1986; U.S. Department of Health, Education, and Welfare, 1977) have suggested a number of factors believed to contribute to the hostile environment in most schools. Perhaps most important among them are inadequate school facilities and overcrowding. The list could well go on indefinitely, but the bigger problem of how to ensure that the educational process is not disrupted by violence would still be in need of resolution. The National School Safety Center (NSSC) was created for just this purpose as a result of a presidential directive in 1984. Likewise, a number of cities have developed school safety departments within their school districts.

Metal detectors are one of the most controversial ways of attempting to reduce school violence. Yet they have been purchased and used in some schools as a last-ditch effort to curb violence. In addition to being costly and impractical, some question their effectiveness since a great deal of violence occurs outside rather than inside schools. A metal detection program began in 1988 in five schools around the New York City area, with only periodic (unannounced) checks for weapons. The number of schools participating in the program has since grown, as has the frequency of screenings (New York City Department of School Safety, 1993). Students, school safety officials, and school administrators and staff there believe that metal detectors may act as a deterrent but agree they are not a foolproof way of keeping weapons out of city schools. Some argue for stricter punishment for students who are found with weapons, and continue their support for metal detectors. Due to the fact that metal detectors provide some element of safety, they are believed to be better than having no such system in place (New York City Department of School Safety, 1993).

According to Muir (1994), the disciplinary procedures currently in place are not effective enough to deal with the escalation of violence experienced on an almost daily basis. The United Federation of Teachers (UFT) complains of disciplinary codes that are too lax and rarely created to serve the best interests of teachers. Consequently, not only do children face the dangers of a more violent society, as reflected in more violence in their schools and communities; the adults to whom they look for support are also endangered in ways that jeopardize their ability to protect children or to assist them in coping with distress after experiencing a violent event. It is the inability of teachers to provide safety and protection to children that has policy makers, researchers, and practitioners alike concerned about the well-being of children.

Evolving from Preventive Interventions to Prevention Policies

Given the scope of the problem, the number of children and youth at risk for violence and the number of schools in contact with children and youth at risk for violence, it seems very unlikely to us that intervention programs alone will be adequate to the task of effective school-based prevention. Many of the prevention initiatives described in this chapter, while holding considerable promise as youth violence prevention programs, have not been designed to "go to scale," to be implemented in enough sites with enough intensity and devotion to fidelity to make a difference on the population of children and youth at risk.

Rather than view the majority of existing programs as models that could go to scale, we suspect it is more valuable to view them as efforts to identify and test "prevention principles" that can be drawn upon to develop prevention policies that are integrated into more general school reform efforts. The point we are trying to make is that for most of the programs reviewed, school systems have neither the resources nor the technical capability to attempt to solve the youth violence problem through progressive replication of these violence prevention programs. While we won't be sure until schools try to replicate initially efficacious programs and endeavor to gauge their cost-effectiveness, it seems very likely there are more effective and cost-effective ways to draw upon what is being learned in school-based violence prevention efforts to inform educational policies and day-to-day practice. Following we list some examples of how particular findings from school-based violence prevention programs could generate changes in policies and day-to-day practice that don't have the same costs as separate programs but hold the potential of reducing child and youth risk of violence.

Early Childhood Education Strategies to Prevent Violence

Perhaps the clearest implication of the rigorous evaluations of violence prevention initiatives to date is that quality early childhood education programs hold considerable promise as a primary prevention strategy. Yet despite the evidence of the effectiveness of quality programs, the United States still dramatically underinvests in such programs. It is hard to imagine how elementary and secondary schools can succeed in their violence prevention efforts if they are not assisted by efforts targeted at the early childhood years that will reduce the need for school-based efforts beginning in the elementary school years. In short, advocates of school-based violence prevention efforts should become advocates for early childhood strategies of documented effectiveness. Federal, state, and local policies that permit the dramatic expansion of early childhood education programs are the most likely paths from programs to policies.

Teacher Training in Cognitive and Behavioral Skills Development

In light of the preliminary positive findings from programs like RCCP and BrainPower, it appears that cognitive skills (e.g., accurately interpreting the social cues of other children) and social skills (e.g., mature interpersonal negotiation strategies) can be taught to children by teachers and can reduce children's risks for engaging in violence in the future. Yet even if these programs continue to demonstrate their effectiveness, they cannot possibly meet the overwhelming need unless teacher education begins to include training teachers in the theory and practice of effective conflict resolution and violence prevention. Nothing short of a profound transformation in the role of teachers in promoting social development and "emotional intelligence," and the role of teacher education programs in preparing teachers for these new roles, can possibly lead to a true violence prevention educational policy. The costs of such efforts should be borne at the teacher education end, not the curriculum delivery end, of the educational process.

Redefining Schools to Include Families and Communities

The National Institute of Justice (NIJ) released a report in early 1997 (Sherman et al., 1997) that indicated the largest proportion of antisocial and delinquent acts (presumably including acts of violence) committed by school-age children were committed between the hours of 3:00 P.M. and 6:00 P.M., when many children were "free" of adult supervision at school or home. The implications of this finding for the conceptualization and design of school-based violence prevention efforts are profound. "School" cannot be narrowly defined, and after-school hours and activities, which in some sense are the temporal and spatial links between school, community, and home, must be more explicitly brought into school-based planning.

In light of the basic research on the family and community factors that lead to the development of aggression and violence-related behaviors (see Chapters 3 and 4 of this volume), schools must not only redefine programs as policies but also redefine "school-based" to include families and communities.

Program Costs, Benefits, and Targeting

Finally, it is very important to consider two other issues as society attempts to evolve from school-based violence prevention programs to policies:

1. *Documenting the Costs and Benefits of Prevention.* David Greenwood of the RAND Corporation published a recent cost-effectiveness analysis of various crime prevention strategies (Greenwood et al., 1996). In our opinion, his controversial finding that high school graduation incentives are significantly more cost-effective in reducing crime than are three-strike programs and expansion of prison cells and early intervention programs like Head Start, will set both the policy and research contexts for discussions of crime prevention strategies for the next several years. What is clearly needed in the violence prevention arena in general, and school-based violence prevention in particular, is the same type of careful, comparative cost-benefit and cost-effectiveness analyses.
2. *Targeting Prevention Efforts.* As is well documented in other chapters in this volume (see Chapters 3 and 4), it is increasingly clear that children from different families and different neighborhoods are at different levels of risk for youth violence. How to think about differential risk (especially by family and community characteristics) and its implications for targeted versus universal prevention strategies is an old dilemma that deserves to be revisited while designing and testing various violence prevention strategies.

Conclusion

Our developmental-contextual framework, our description and analysis of extant school-based violence prevention programs, and our plea to begin to think systematically about how to move from violence prevention programs to violence prevention policies, each have implications for the type of prevention science needed in the future to reform practice and policy. Following are a few major comments on a future research agenda:

1. *Implications of the Developmental-Contextual Framework.* Using our framework to evaluate the current research, we conclude that the designers of extant programs and evaluations are better at thinking developmentally than contextually. And thinking developmentally has begun to pay off. Identifying the development of hostile attributional bias as a key process to change is a good example of program designers using current research and practice to target key processes for intervention.

The converging results from both experimental (e.g., Hudley 1994, 1995) and quasi-experimental (e.g., RCCP Research Group, 1997) studies suggest that somewhat different interventions evaluated in different ways can lead to positive change in this important developmental process that predisposes children and youth to aggression and violence. Other examples of thinking developmentally in the design and evaluation of violence prevention efforts will no doubt continue to emerge.

Surprisingly, there has been much less attention to thinking contextually in program design and in evaluation design. Do the violence prevention interventions work better in big schools or small schools? with strong student safety programs or no such programs? in African American or Latino or white communities? in very poor and dangerous neighborhoods or moderately poor and dangerous neighborhoods? In short, for what subgroups and under what conditions do the various efforts work and why? The impact of communities and neighborhoods on families and children is just beginning to become the object of systematic study (e.g., Brooks-Gunn, Duncan, & Aber, in press). The conceptual and methodological tools to evaluate program effects by context are emerging just behind (e.g., Aber, 1994; Connell, Aber, & Walker, 1995). Perhaps the greatest challenge facing a prevention science of school-based interventions is the need to think contextually.

2. *Implications of Extant School-Based Violence Prevention Programs.* Most of the extant evaluations of school-based interventions aimed at preventing violence are still in their infancy. Indeed, except for the early education/family support interventions and evaluations targeted at early childhood, all of the evaluations described in this chapter have been released in the 1990s, the majority in the last three years. Researchers will continue to analyze subsequent waves of data already collected from many of these studies; some will continue to collect longitudinal data over longer periods of time. For these reasons, it is likely to require another five to ten years for even the current cohort of studies to mature, yield results, be critiqued, and lead to more powerful program and evaluation designs.

It is difficult to be patient while such studies mature during what feels like the outbreak of an epidemic of youth violence. Yet from a scientific point of view, that is exactly what must be done. If practitioners stay the course by investing in longer-term evaluations of the most promising violence prevention initiatives (as the Centers for Disease Control and Prevention has recently committed to do), perhaps in the next decade results in this area can be definitively reviewed as Yoshikawa has done for early interventions based on programs begun one to two decades ago (Yoshikawa, 1995). In the meantime, practitioners must use the best available interim findings to make midcourse corrections in their programs.

3. *Implications of Evolving from Prevention Programs to Prevention Policies.* A third issue in the creation of a future research agenda involves how to draw on studies of prevention programs to inform the development of prevention policies. Traditionally, prevention science has established the efficacy of an intervention before it attempts to bring it to scale and evaluate its effectiveness at scale. As we have already indicated, we believe this strategy is nearly doomed to failure since schools probably cannot take the programs as designed to scale.

A few programs grew to scale before they were evaluated using traditional, rigorous true experiments, such as RCCP. But at scale, they are enormously difficult to rigorously evaluate using traditional experimental methods. To overstate the case, we can rigorously evaluate relatively small, unreplicable programs or less rigorously evaluate relatively large, varied, and demonstrably replicable programs.

The only way out of this dilemma that we can identify is through the use of both theory and meta-analysis. Some studies must establish that intervention X causally impacts on process Y or outcome Z (or both). Other studies must establish that when intervention X is implemented in the real world under normal constraints A, B, and C, that it is still associated with Y and Z (but perhaps only under some real-world conditions). The future research agenda on school-based violence prevention interventions must use theory and meta-analysis to synthesize a range of studies designed to optimize what is known about causal processes and about moderating conditions.

Note

1. Behind all these attempts at theory building is the enormous contribution of Bronfenbrenner's (1975, 1979) theory of the ecology of human development.

References

Aber, J. L. (1994). Poverty, violence, and child development: Untangling family and community level effects. In C. A. Nelson (Ed.), *Threats to optimal development: Integrating biological, psychological, and social risk factors. Minnesota Symposium on Child Psychology (Vol. 27)*. Hillsdale, NJ: Lawrence Erlbaum.

Aber, J. L., Brown, J. L., Chaudry, N., Jones, S. M., & Samples, F. (1996). The evaluation of the Resolving Conflict Creatively Program: An overview. *American Journal of Preventive Medicine, 5*(Suppl. to Vol. 12), 82–90.

Allen, J. P., Leadbeater, B. J., & Aber, J. L. (1994). The development of problem behavior syndromes in at-risk adolescents. *Development and Psychopathology, 6*(2), 323–342.

Allen, J. P., Weissberg, R. P., & Hawkins, J. A. (1989). The relation between values and social competence in early adolescence. *Developmental Psychology, 25*(3), 458–464.

Blumstein, A. (1995). Youth violence, guns, and the illicit-drug industry. *The Journal of Criminal Law and Criminology, 86*(1), 10–36.

Bronfenbrenner, U. (1975). Is early intervention effective? In M. Guttentag & E. L. Struening (Eds.), *Handbook of evaluation research* (pp. 519–604). Beverly Hills, CA: Sage.

Bronfenbrenner, U. (1979). *The ecology of human development: Experiments by nature and design*. Cambridge, CA: Harvard University Press.

Brooks-Gunn, J., Duncan, G., & Aber, J. L. (Eds.). (in press). *Neighborhood poverty: Context and consequences for child and adolescent development*. New York: Russell Sage.

Berrueta-Clement, J. R., Schweinhart, L. J., Barnett, W. S., Epstein, A. S., & Weikart, D. P. (1984). Changed lives: The effects of the Perry Preschool Program on youths through age 19. *Monographs of the High/Scope Educational Research Foundation* (Vol. 8). Ypsilanti, MI: High/Scope Press.

Collins, W. A. (Ed.). (1984). *Development during middle childhood: Years six through twelve*. Washington, DC: National Academy of Science Press.

Collins, W. A., Harris, M. L., & Susman, A. (1955). Parenting during mid-childhood. In M. H. Bornstein (Ed.), *Handbook of parenting* (pp. 65–89). Hillsdale, NJ: Lawrence Erlbaum.

Comer, J. P. (1989). Child development and education. *Journal of Negro Education, 58*(2), 125–139.

Connell, J. P., Aber, J. L., & Walker, G. (1995). How do urban communities affect youth? Using social science research to inform the design and evaluation of comprehensive community initiatives. In J. P. Connell, A. Kubisch, L. Schorr, & C. Weiss (Eds.), *New approaches evaluating community interventions: Concepts, methods, and contexts* (pp. 93–125). Queenstown, MD: Aspen Institute.

Dishion, T. J., & Andrews, D. W. (1995). Preventing escalation of problem-behavior with high-risk young adolescents: Immediate and 1-year outcomes. *Journal of Consulting and Clinical Psychology, 64*(4), 538–548.

Farrell, A. D., & Meyer, A. L. (1997a). The effectiveness of a school-based curriculum for reducing violence among urban sixth-grade students. *American Journal of Public Health, 87*(6), 979–988.

Farrell, A. D., & Meyer, A. L. (1997b). *Longitudinal evaluation and extension of the RIPP program for urban youth* (Tech. Report No. U81/CCU309966–05). Richmond, VA: Virginia Commonwealth University, Department of Psychology.

Felner, R. D., Brand, S., Adan, A. M., & Mulhall, P. F. (1993). Restructuring the ecology of the school as an approach to prevention during school transitions: Longitudinal follow-ups and extensions of the School Transitional Environment Project (STEP). *Prevention in Human Services, 10*(2), 103–136.

Fick, A. C., Lewis, M., Osofsky, J. D., & Flowers, A. (1995). *Children's safety issues and concerns: Perceptions of children, parents, and police.* Poster presented at the Society for Research in Child Development, Indianapolis, IN.

Flannery, D., Vazsonyi, A., Embry, D., Powell, K., & Atha, H. (1997). "Increasing social competence and reducing aggressive behavior among youth: Longitudinal evidence from Peace Builders." Unpublished manuscript.

Flannery, D., Vazsonyi, A., & Vesterdal, W. (1997, April). Evaluation of Peace Builders' youth violence prevention program. In J. L. Aber (Chair), *The ontogeny of conduct problems: Contexts as sources of influence and targets of intervention.* Symposium conducted at the biennial meeting of the Society for Research in Child Development, Washington, DC.

Gainer, P. S., Webster, D. W., & Champion, H. R. (1993). A youth violence prevention program description and preliminary evaluation. *Archives of Surgery, 128,* 303–308.

Galinsky, E., Howes, C., Kontos, S., & Shinn, M. (1994). *The study of children in family child care and relative care: Highlights of findings.* New York: Families and Work Institute.

Garbarino, J., Kostelny, K., & Dubrow, N. (1991). What children can tell us about living in danger. *American Psychologist, 46*(4), 376–383.

Gottfredson, D. C. (1996, May). *Violence prevention for eleven to eighteen-year-olds.* Paper presented at the Youth Violence in the United States Conference, Cantigny Estate, IL.

Greenwood, P. W., Model, K. E., Rydell, C. P., & Chiesa, J. (1996). *Diverting children from a life of crime: Measuring costs and benefits.* Santa Monica, CA: RAND Corporation.

Grossman, D. C., Neckerman, H. J., Koepsell, T., & Rivara, F. P. (1997). Effectiveness of a violence prevention curriculum among children in elementary school: A randomized controlled trial. *Journal of the American Medical Association, 277*(20), 1605–1642.

Guerra, N. G., & Slaby, R. G. (1990). Cognitive mediators of aggression in adolescent offenders: Intervention. *Developmental Psychology, 26*(2), 269–277.

Hammond, W. R. (1990). *Positive Adolescent Choices Training (PACT): Preliminary findings of the effects of a school-based violence prevention program for African-American adolescents.* Paper presented at the annual conference of the American Psychological Association, Boston, MA.

Hammond, W. R., & Yung, B. R. (1991). Preventing violence in at-risk African-American Youth. *Journal of Health Care for the Poor and Underserved, 2*(3), 359–373.

Harootunian, B. (1986). School violence and vandalism. In S. J. Apter & A. D. Goldstein (Eds.), *Youth Violence: Programs and prospects* (pp. 120–140). New York: Pergamon.

Heartsprings, Inc. (1992). *Creating a peaceful community with Peace Builders.* Tucson, AZ: Author.

Helburn, S., Culkin, M. L., Morris, J., Mocan, N., Howes, C., Phillipsen, L., et al. (1995). *Cost, quality, and child outcomes in child care centers.* Denver, CO: University of Colorado at Denver, Department of Economics.

Hudley, C. A. (1994). The reduction of childhood aggression using the BrainPower program. In M. Furlong & D. Smith (Eds.), *Anger, hostility, and aggression: Assessment, prevention, and intervention strategies for youth* (pp. 313–344). Brandon, VT: Clinical Psychology Publishing.

Hudley, C. A. (1995, March). *Reducing peer directed aggression in the elementary grades: The effects of an attribution retraining program.* Paper presented at the 61st biennial meeting of the Society for Research on Child Development, Indianapolis, IN.

Huesmann, L. R., Guerra, N. G., Miller, L., & Zelli, A. (1992). The role of social norms in the development of aggression. In H. Zumkley & A. Fraczek (Eds.), *Socialization and aggression* (pp. 139–152). New York: Springer.

Johnson, D. L., & Breckenridge, J. N. (1982). The Houston Parent-Child Development Center and the primary prevention of behavior problems in young children. *American Journal of Community Psychology, 10*(3), 305–316.

Johnson, D. L., & Walker, T. (1987). Primary prevention of behavior problems in Mexican-American children. *American Journal of Community Psychology, 15*(4), 375–385.

Keenan, K., & Shaw, D. (1997). Developmental and social influences on young girls' early problem behavior. *Psychological Bulletin, 121*(1), 95–113.

Lally, J. R., Mangione, P. L., & Honig, A. S. (1987). *Long-range impact of an early intervention with low-income children and their families.* Syracuse, NY: Syracuse University Family Development Research Program, Center for Child and Family Studies.

Lally, J. R., Mangione, P. L., Honig, A. S., & Wittner, D. S. (1988). More pride, less delinquency: Findings from the ten-year follow-up study of the Syracuse University Family Development Research Program. *Zero to Three, 8*(4), 13–18.

Meyer, A. L., & Farrell, A. D. (in press). Social skills training to promote resilience in urban sixth-grade students: One product of an action research strategy to prevent youth violence in high-risk environments. *Education and Treatment of Children.*

Miller, L. S. (1994). Primary prevention of conduct disorder. *Psychiatric Quarterly, 65*(4), 273–285.

Moore, B., & Beland, K. (1992). *Evaluation of Second Step, preschool-kindergarten: Summary report.* Seattle, WA: Committee for Children.

Muir, E. (1994). *Security in the schools: Tips for guarding the safety of faculty members and students* (5th ed.). New York: United Federation of Teachers.

New York City Department of School Safety. (1993). *Report of the school safety department for the 1992–1993 school year.* New York: United Federation of Teachers.

Olweus, D. (1994). Bullying at school: Basic facts and effects of a school-based intervention program (Annotation). *Journal of Child Psychology and Psychiatry and Allied Disciplines, 35*(7), 1171–1190.

Olweus, D. (1995). Bullying or peer abuse at school: Facts and intervention. *Current Directions in Psychological Science, 4*(6), 196–200.

Posner, M. (1994). Youth at risk: Research raises troubling questions about violence prevention programs. *The Harvard Education Letter, 10*(3), 1–4.

RCCP Research Group. (1997). *Preliminary findings from the Resolving Conflict Creatively Program.* New York: Columbia University, National Center for Children in Poverty.

Schweinhart, L. J., Barnes, H. V., & Weikart, D. P. (Eds.). (1993). *Significant benefits: The High/Scope Perry Preschool study through age 27.* Ypsilanti, MI: High/Scope Press.

Schweinhart, L. J., & Weikart, D. P. (1980). *Young children grow up: The effects of the Perry Preschool Program on youths through age 15.* Ypsilanti, MI: High/Scope Press.

Schweinhart, L. J., & Weikart, D. P. (1989). The High/Scope Perry Preschool study: Implications for early childhood care and education. *Prevention in Human Services, 7*(1), 109–132.

Seitz, V., Rosenbaum, L. K., & Apfel, N. H. (1985). Effects of family support intervention: A ten-year follow-up. *Child Development, 56,* 376–391.

Selman, R. L., Beardslee, W., Schultz, L. H., Krupa, M., & Podoresky, D. (1986). Assessing adolescent interpersonal negotiation strategies: Toward the integration of structural and functional models. *Developmental Psychology, 22,* 450–459.

Sherman, L. W., Gottfredson, D., McKensie, D., et al. (1997). *Preventing crime: What works, what doesn't, and what's promising.* Washington, DC: National Institute of Justice.

Sroufe, L. A. (1988). A developmental perspective on day care. *Early Childhood Research Quarterly, 3*(3), 283–292.

Sroufe, L. A., Carlson, E., & Shulman, S. (1993). "Individuals in relationships: Development from infancy through adolescence." In D. C. Funder, R. D. Parke, C. Tomlinson-Keasey, & K. Widaman (Eds.), *Studying lives through time: Personality and development* (pp. 315–342). Washington, DC: American Psychological Association.

Sroufe, L. A., Cooper, R. G., DeHart, G. B., Marshall, M. E., & Bronfenbrenner, U. (1992). *Child development: Its nature and course.* New York: McGraw-Hill.

Sylvester, L., & Frey, K. (1994). *Summary of Second Step pilot studies.* Seattle, WA: Committee for Children.

U.S. Department of Health, Education, and Welfare. (1977). *Violent schools–Safe Schools: The Safe School Study report to the Congress.* Washington, DC: Author and National Institute of Education.

Webster, D. W. (1993). The unconvincing case for school-based conflict resolution programs for adolescents. *Health Affairs, 12*(4), 128–141.

Williams, K. R., Guerra, N. G., & Elliott, D. S. (1996). *Human development and violence prevention: A focus on youth.* Boulder, CO: University of Colorado at Boulder, Center for the Study and Prevention of Violence.

Yoshikawa, H. (1995). Long-term effects of early childhood programs on social outcomes and delinquency. *The Future of Children, 5*(3), 51–75.

Zigler, E., & Styfco, S. J. (1993). Using policy research and theory to justify and inform Head Start expansion. *Social Policy Report, 8,* 2.

Zigler, E., Styfco, S. J., & Gilman, E. (1993). The national Head Start program for disadvantaged preschoolers. In E. Zigler & S. J. Styfco (Eds.), *Head Start and beyond: A national plan for extended childhood intervention.* New Haven, CT: Yale University Press.

Zigler, E., Taussig, C., & Black, K. (1992). Early childhood intervention: A promising preventative for juvenile delinquency. *American Psychologist, 47*(8), 997–1006.

9. Safe School Planning

RONALD D. STEPHENS

Introduction

Perhaps there is no greater challenge today than creating safe schools. Restoring America's schools to tranquil and safe places of learning requires a major new commitment: School safety must be placed at the top of the educational agenda. Without safe schools, teachers cannot teach and students cannot learn. Developing and implementing a safe school plan for each school is an essential part of this process. Safe school planning is now being recognized by school administrators as the first step in creating an appropriate learning environment for children.

A "safe school" is a place where students can learn and teachers can teach in a warm and welcoming environment, free of intimidation and fear of violence. A safe school provides an educational climate that fosters a spirit of acceptance and care for every child. It is a place where behavior expectations are clearly communicated, consistently enforced, and fairly applied. Although safe school planning can involve planning for responding to various emergencies, including natural disasters such as earthquakes and tornadoes, in this chapter the discussion focuses on the prevention of youth violence.

Safe school planning is also about the "art of the possible." Although all safe school plans share certain general features, each community should devise a plan that will best suit the needs of its schools. More than anything else, a safe school plan is a function of community will, priorities, and interests. The components are limited only by the imagination, creativity, energy, and commitment of the community. The key questions to ask are: (1) What is it we want to accomplish with regard to our schools? and (2) How do we want to make it happen?

Establishing a safe school plan is a long-term, systematic, and comprehensive process. A safe school plan addresses both the behavioral and property protection aspects of crime prevention. The best safe school plans

involve the entire community: Teachers, students, parents, law enforcement professionals, mental health professionals, business and community
leaders, and a wide array of youth-serving professionals should all be
brought to the table. Safe school planning is an inclusive and cooperative
activity (Stephens, 1994b).

Although state and federal policy makers are beginning to recognize the
need for and require schools to design safe school plans, many educators
and community leaders are at a loss as to where to begin. The strategies
described in this chapter are designed to help schools and communities
work together to reduce the opportunities for crime and violence by promoting positive learning climates.

Violence in Schools

A safe community is a prerequisite for a safe school. However, schools can
no longer be seen as "islands of safety." Violence has invaded far too many
of the nation's schools. Fistfights are being replaced by gunfights; fire drills
are being augmented by crisis drills. Nationally, of every twelve children
who are absent from school on any given day, one child stays away because
of fear (National Institute of Education, 1978). School safety has also become a leading concern for inner city teachers; they, too, are demanding a
safer environment.

Nearly three million index crimes occur on or around American school
campuses each year, according to the National Crime Survey (1987). That
figure translates to 16,000 crimes per school day, or about one every six sec-
onds that schools are in session. An index crime is an offense that, if committed by an adult, could result in arrest and incarceration. Juvenile offenders, however, are often treated differently. Many juveniles have learned
they can commit significant acts of aggression with few, if any, consequences. The juvenile court system usually withholds information related
to prior disruptive acts, treating juveniles as first-time offenders each time
they commit a crime. Throughout history, the juvenile justice system has
functioned as a nonpunitive, rehabilitative, noncriminal system. This policy is beginning to change in some jurisdictions, but for the most part, current legal practices create additional burdens, including a lack of information for teachers about the violent students they are charged to teach.

Changing Climate for Public Education

The climate for public education in many city neighborhoods has changed
dramatically in recent years. School classrooms include more children of

teenage parents, of parents who often are over-stressed, and of those who lack good parenting skills. A few years ago, approximately 10% of students enrolled were identified as "developmentally delayed," requiring special education classes. Today that number is closer to 15%. Some parents now want their children classified as special education students because they perceive that such children have increased rights and benefits. Latchkey children also represent an ever-increasing portion of the student population. Their lack of supervision at home during daytime hours suggests the need for developing programs with before- and after-school activities.

The varied cultural and ethnic makeup of inner city student populations has created social stress within the schools. This change has occurred within the context of an increasingly violent society and cities with fewer economic resources available to fund new prevention programs. The issue of personal safety looms large among students, parents, and teachers alike. Alcohol and other drugs, as well as gangs, also contribute to school violence. Moreover, society has redefined deviancy in such a way that types of misconduct that were once considered disruptive no longer even appear on school crime reports. Yet students and staff must feel safe and secure in school, and while coming to and going from school. Fear of violence affects attendance of students and causes attrition of staff, as well as interfering with the continuity of the programs that serve young people. If a safe school plan is to assist in creating an environment that allows students to achieve at optimum levels, then it must be complemented by plans for reducing violence in the neighborhood. The school is a special environment within the community, and a good school plan can help create a safe environment for learning.

Community violence, underfunding, and politics pose a special challenge for school administrators. For the most part, administrators do not design the facilities in which they work; they do not choose the students whom they serve; nor do they control the communities that often completely encircle their campuses with a community violence. The cumulative effect is a heightened challenge for today's school administrators and communities.

What is a Safe School Plan?

Why Plan?

There are two types of school administrators: those who have already faced a crisis and those who will at some point in their careers. The courts have placed school boards on notice either to create safe school campuses or to be prepared to compensate victims for their losses. By developing an effective safe school plan, administrators can prevent many crises and preclude a series of successive crises. A school administrator without a safe school plan is like a pilot without a flight plan. Inasmuch as young people are compelled to attend school, school and community leaders should be compelled to provide students with an educational climate that is safe, secure, peaceful, and welcoming. An effective safe school plan will help to reduce school violence and promote a positive educational climate to support the educational success and well-being of every student.

Safe School Planning Defined

Effective safe school planning involves three key components: (1) it identifies where you are as a district and community, specifying top concerns and/or issues; (2) it asks where you want to be; and (3) it calls for the development of a plan to deal with the difference(s) between where you are and where you want to be.

The Foundation for Safe School Planning

Before an effective safe school plan can be created, the architects of the plan must understand the forces that create safe schools. They must realize that laws and rules alone cannot address all of the issues. Adults have a special duty and obligation to care for and protect young people. In our society, there are only three categories of people who are required by law to be somewhere against their will. The first group is prisoners. They are protected against cruel and unusual punishment. The second is the mentally ill. They have similar protection. The third category is school children. Oftentimes we do not afford them the same protection. Yet if we are going to require young people to attend school, then we must provide them an environment that is safe, secure, and peaceful. This compelling duty of care defines the special relationship that exists between students and schools.

Goal of Safe School Planning

The goal of safe school planning is to create and maintain a positive and welcoming school climate, free of drugs, violence, intimidation, and fear – an environment in which teachers can teach and students can learn in a climate that promotes the success and development of all children and those professionals who serve them. Essential components of a safe school plan (Stephens, 1994b) include, but are not necessarily limited to:

- School crime reporting and tracking
- Public awareness of the community's perception of violence
- Curricula focusing on prosocial skills and conflict resolution
- Behavior/conduct/discipline codes
- Adult supervision
- Crisis management and emergency evacuation procedures
- Attendance and truancy prevention strategies
- Drug prevention tactics
- Interagency partnerships
- Staff training (e.g., in classroom management, campus supervision, conflict resolution, and social skills)
- Cultural and social awareness/respect for diversity
- Student leadership and involvement
- Parent participation
- Involvement of senior citizens
- Adequate special event management
- Crime prevention through environmental design
- Extracurricular activities and recreation opportunities
- Restitution plans for violent offenders
- Nuisance abatement
- School/law enforcement partnerships
- Screening and selection of staff (i.e., background checks)
- Violence prevention programs
- School security procedures and/or equipment
- Community service/outreach networks
- Corporate/business partnerships
- Protection of assets (e.g., risk management, access control, protection of property, and minimizing exposure to losses)
- Media and public relations representatives and management plans
- Health services
- Safe transportation
- Legislative outreach and contact
- Evaluation and monitoring

Customizing the Plan

As individual school safety plans and issues are considered, components in addition to those listed may also emerge. Safe school planning affords each community a unique opportunity to customize its own strategies for each program component chosen for examination. Limitless opportunities and strategies exist in the prevention of youth violence.

Although all safe school plans will share some of the same features, no two will be exactly the same. Each school should develop a plan that meets its unique needs and circumstances. In some schools, the school building itself and poor maintenance of the building are glaring problems. In others, gang violence is the outstanding danger. In yet another school the greatest problem may be weapons or drugs. A safe school plan is a function of the specific and unique issues the local school is facing. Consequently, every safe school plan is likely to have some variation that reflects the local community and its concerns.

Legal Aspects of Safe School Planning

An important preliminary step in safe school planning is for the school district's lawyer to conduct a review of federal, state, and local statutes pertaining to student management and school order. This review should include relevant court cases, school district policies and operations manuals, as well as labor contracts for teachers and other school staff. The legal review has two major purposes: it identifies what the law requires, and it identifies what the law allows. Every important school safety issue is embedded in existing law. Consequently, examination of the law is a necessary beginning point in safe school planning.

First, it is important to look at federal laws such as the Federal Gun-Free School Zone Act of 1994, which requires school officials who wish to receive federal funds to expel, for a minimum of one year, any student who brings, possesses, or uses a firearm on a public school campus. The district lawyer should also review the U.S. Constitution and the Civil Rights Act, as well as the Drug-Free Schools and Communities Act of 1986, which requires schools to provide prevention programs for alcohol, tobacco, and other drugs to all students. A variety of other laws pertaining to Americans with disabilities and special education (such as the Individuals with Disabilities Education Act, or IDEA) and relevant U.S. Supreme Court cases should also be reviewed.

School district policy and procedure manuals will also provide further insight as to what each local school board requires. Next, it is necessary to consider state and local laws pertaining to student management and school order. There will probably be several of them. At a minimum, the following codes should be reviewed:

- State Constitution
- Education codes
- Health and safety codes
- Penal codes, particularly juvenile justice
- Vehicle codes
- Child welfare and institution codes
- Fire codes
- Municipal codes
- School district codes
- Relevant recent state and local court decisions

It is helpful if the district lawyer can summarize in writing for the safe school planning team the least familiar provisions of the relevant laws and codes, but the lawyer should also be present at the planning meetings to guide the planners throughout their work and to ensure that the finished plan meets all the provisions of pertinent laws and policies. At the very least, if the district attorney is unable to attend all the planning meetings for whatever reason, he or she must carefully scrutinize the written draft of the plan upon its completion.

Planners need to recognize that some ideas that sound sensible may in fact violate a law or code. For instance, while it may be tempting to control campus access by chaining certain doors closed, such an action likely creates a fire code violation, endangering both students and staff and setting the stage for a serious liability problem. It is essential that legal problems not be created through establishing policies that conflict with the law, and once the final plan is developed, the district lawyer should then perform a formal review to ensure that no laws have been violated.

Practical Considerations in Policy Development

The Virginia Association of School Superintendents (1992), in a report entitled *Violence in the Schools*, recommends that members of the school board ask themselves the following questions about the safe school plan developed. Asking these questions will save school administrators and their boards a lot of grief as well as liability:

1. Is the content of the plan within the scope of the school board's authority?
2. Is it consistent with local, state, and federal laws?
3. Have legal references been included?
4. Does it reflect good educational practice?
5. Is it reasonable?
6. Does it adequately cover the issues?
7. Is it limited to one policy topic? (To combine several policies in one statement often convolutes the purpose.)
8. Is it cross-referenced to other relevant policy topics?
9. Is it consistent with the board's existing policies?
10. Can it be administered and enforced?
11. Is it practical in terms of administrative enforcement and budget?

The Planning Team

Team Membership

The safe school planning team is the driving force behind the planning process. This should include teachers, counselors, the principal, the vice principal, school security, maintenance, and the school secretary. Students should be at the heart of the process and, if age appropriate, contributors to the team. They will provide tremendous insight and direction to the safe school planning process. This group should also include a wide variety of community leaders who touch the lives of children. Examples of other essential team players include: chief of police, presiding juvenile judge, chief probation officer, local or state prosecutor, health and welfare providers, parents, business leaders, the mayor, city manager, church and community leaders, representatives from neighborhood service organizations, and representatives from mental health, corrections, parks and recreation, and emergency response teams, among others. Safe school planning initiatives are best established by community coalitions of school, law enforcement, and community leaders.

For any plan to succeed, the safe school planning team must draw upon the cultural diversity of the community it represents. When the opportunity for including diversity is overlooked, the opportunity for developing wide-ranging solutions can be severely limited. Effective safe school plans are strengthened by the participation of individuals who reflect the cultural diversity of the community. Broad participation encourages "buy-in" and support. People tend to support what they help create. Successful administrators will involve those who must do the work in the planning and evaluating. Oftentimes, planners simply ask people to "do" without gaining their insights into the process. An effective safe school plan includes a full partnership of the planning, the doing, and the evaluating.

Team Leadership

The safe school planning team may be led by anyone in the community. In some communities, the presiding juvenile judge may be the key leader. In other areas, it may be the chief of police or a school board member. Most generally, it will be the superintendent of schools. The safe school planning team provides an excellent opportunity for the chief school officer to take an active leadership role in the community. At the site level, the school principal should assume this leadership role.

Identifying who should lead the team is usually easy; however, making the team work effectively is a bit more difficult. Each community should capitalize on the unique people, resources, and levels of commitment that are present at the planning table. As a first tier priority, it is desirable to have agency heads (e.g., the police chief, the superintendent of schools, or the presiding juvenile judge) to lead, empower, and support the safe school planning team on an as needed basis. A second tier component would include agency and organization representatives who will meet on a regular basis to discuss issues and develop solutions. A third tier might be a broader advisory committee composed of community and school representatives who will meet on a regular basis, perhaps monthly or quarterly. This group can provide input and direction to the various agencies and organizations that serve young people. By establishing such a multilevel/multifaceted network, the safe school planning process can be enhanced. Such options increase participation and can improve the quality and quantity of ideas. Most importantly, such diverse efforts send a message to the community that school safety is not merely a school problem, but rather a community problem – a message that not only affirms that the school expects and needs the community's full support, but also that the problem requires a broad-based community response.

Selecting and Training the Team

The following steps can facilitate the establishment of a safe schools planning task force:

1. Identify key players in the community and school district who are willing and committed to serving on the team. There should be a district team and individual site planning teams. The district team should focus on the overall mission statement and a series of policies that will promote safe schools. The individual site plans should be compatible with the district's mission.
2. Plan a community-wide meeting about school safety. All interested parties, including students and parents, should be invited and encouraged to attend.
3. When planning the meeting, choose a date four weeks in advance to allow plenty of notice for all those wishing to attend. The letter of invitation to persons within the community should state the purpose, date, time, and place of the meeting.

Before the meeting, the executive planning team must do their homework:

1. Identify the need for safe school planning. The need for safe school planning will be determined by the key issues/top concerns that the specific school is facing (e.g., bullying, fighting, weapons, truancy). The point is to obtain some good solid data beforehand (e.g., from school crime reports). Secondly, know who to invite. There are individuals who have official authority and those who have "personal" authority because of their "influence" or expertise. Invite both kinds of individuals to the planning table.
2. Approach school and community leaders to solicit their support for the planning process.
3. Review news clips, local crime reports, and current literature in the area of school safety to present or as background for the meeting.
4. Enlist community support to create a climate of action.

Once the team is formed, its members need to educate themselves and the community about violence prevention. The team should include 25–30 people. It is a good idea to choose two or three talented people from the team to undergo specialized training in violence prevention (e.g., available through the National School Safety Center). They can then train other team members as well as members of the school and community.

Creating a Timetable

Making the planning process work requires creating a timetable for completing planning tasks. The following task sequence can help the safe school planning team get started. The planning process will require several meetings. A reasonable schedule[1] would include the following expectations:

- *First Meeting*
  Bring together key participants.
  Establish the mission and purpose.
  Set the framework for developing the safe school plan.
- *Second Meeting*
  Develop group processes for problem solving and program development.
  Identify specific issues and problems.
  Ascertain the services and talents each member brings to the team.
  Identify any local, state, and federal resources available. For example, review opportunities for state and federal demonstration programs, grants, and community action projects.
- *Third Meeting*
  Determine how the site assessment (see the "Assessing the School Safety Problem" section of this chapter) will be conducted.
  Develop a list of preliminary information to be considered before the assessment. This depends on what issues you wish to address. It is determined by identifying your key problem areas (e.g., fighting, weapons, gangs, intruders, etc.).
  Analyze the particular needs and issues of each campus.
  Identify the needs and issues of the surrounding community.
- *Fourth Meeting*
  Develop the action plan.
  Identify any constraints and special opportunities.
  Make task assignments and obtain commitments from team members.
- *Fifth Meeting*
  Draft the plan.
  Submit the draft to the district attorney for review.
- *Sixth Meeting*
  Develop an evaluation and monitoring mechanism.
  Determine who else will evaluate the plan, and how.
  Establish an evaluation schedule.
- *Seventh Meeting*
  Announce the plan to the public.
  Seek public feedback and support.

Provide training and support to each site.
Implement the plan.
* *Subsequent Meetings*
Monitor and evaluate the plan.
Make changes and refinements as necessary.
Provide team members with updated information.
Develop new and relevant strategies as appropriate.
Educate and train new members of the planning team when they join. The team should reflect changes in the community. Add replacement/new members as roles change and the community grows. On average, school boards turn over 25% every year. Safe school teams may approach a 15–20% annual turnover.
Continue to innovate and evaluate. The team should review the plan on a regular basis, at least annually.

Challenges and Obstacles to Plan Implementation

Although the meeting process is described here in "recipe" form, it is unrealistic to think that creating a safe school plan is like baking a cake. Certainly there are specific ingredients that are needed in the successful development of such a plan. However, politics often create some unusual, unexpected, and challenging situations that cannot be consistently predicted in all circumstances. One of the biggest challenges is to allay the fears and resentments that may arise when formerly independent agencies are suddenly asked to share the same "turf." Some team members may feel threatened by the new relationships. They may be uneasy about having to share ownership or information; they may feel threatened when they are required to relinquish control; or they may simply feel threatened when they are asked to do anything differently. Those age-old questions might linger: The politician may wonder, "What's in it for me?" The agency head may ask, "How will the change affect me?" The police chief may wonder, "How seriously should I take this prevention idea?" Some people simply do not like change.

It is essential for the team to develop a positive working relationship. Team building involves more than simply meeting on a regular basis. Enthusiastic leaders must work with those team members who can help create a cooperative momentum. When "foot-draggers" and recalcitrants see signs of energy and success in the process, they are much more likely to get on board. Although rotating the chairpersonship among enthusiastic team members is one option, another good idea is the periodic scheduling of management "retreats" where team building opportunities are provided. It is difficult to create a "recipe" that will ensure positive human behavior, but each team should develop its own plan for building cooperation and support. In the last analysis, a member who fails to join and support the team effort should be replaced. Safe school planning is about options, and it may be necessary to exercise some here.

Assessing the School Safety Problem

Every school should conduct an annual school safety assessment. A school safety assessment document is an evaluation and planning tool used to determine the extent of a school safety problem. It may also focus on a much broader or comprehensive area of school safety or on other school climate issues. For example, such an assessment could address gangs; weapons in school; alcohol and other drug abuse; bullying; a site evaluation of facilities including buildings, sidewalks, and landscape; policies and procedures; compliance with local and state laws; community support; parent attitudes; student attitudes and motivation; or a variety of other emerging school climate trends and concerns.

A school safety assessment, in its broadest terms, is a comprehensive review and evaluation of the educational program of a school or school district. Various issues are examined to ascertain how they affect school climate, school attendance, personal safety, and overall school security. The safety assessment includes:

- A review of student discipline problems, policies, procedures, and practices at both the school site and district level
- An evaluation of the current school safety plan and the planning process
- An assessment of the school/law enforcement partnership and the relationship with local community leaders and resources
- A review of crime prevention efforts with regard to environmental design
- A review of employee recruiting, selection, supervision, and training criteria as they pertain to school safety
- An assessment of student activities and extracurricular programs
- A review of the crisis response plan
- An assessment of the educational plan and its support for a positive school climate
- A review of the health and medical services provided on campus, by the school nurse and/or health center, as well as the local emergency medical facility serving the geographic area of the school
- A review of other such areas that may be deemed necessary in the evaluation of the campus or district

Information Gathering

In preparation for the assessment process, several resources should be gathered for the assessment team to review. These materials include:

- All security and safety-related policies of the district
- A floor plan of the school building(s)

- A site plan showing the campus boundaries and access points
- School crime reports for the previous year
- A list of known safety and security concerns of the staff, students, and parents
- The school's media file of previous news coverage
- The log of police "calls for service" generated from the school or dispatched to the school
- Risk management reports identifying insurance claims
- Maintenance/work orders related to vandalism or graffiti
- The student handbook
- The teacher/staff handbook
- Disciplinary files
- A list of students who have been sent to school as a condition of probation
- The terms of probation for any students sent to school by the courts
- PTA newsletters that address safety and security
- Labor contracts for classified and certified staff

Data Collection

Four types of data collection are needed. The first is a review of school crime reports. Every school should have a comprehensive and systematic school crime reporting process by which written records about school crime incidents are maintained and analyzed. The report should provide for some means of crime analysis to determine what incidents may be linked to other incidents, and situations that may be occurring repeatedly on the campus. Maintaining such records can serve as a valuable student management tool. These reports should be ideally complemented by community crime data obtained from local law enforcement officials.

The second type of data collection is an administrative assessment of school safety. School administrators who wish to assess the safety of their school might find the "School Crime Assessment Tool," provided at the end of this section, helpful. The "School Crime Assessment Tool" (Stephens, 1996) is a self-administered questionnaire that, when scored, helps to indicate how safe or unsafe a given school is. Each question has a specific point value as well as strategic response implications pertaining to the issue identified. These questions are merely designed to begin the evaluation process, and they are by no means comprehensive. The questions were empirically developed over time. They reflect key issues or concerns that should be considered in evaluating school safety. They serve as indicators of critical campus management issues. They are designed to heighten awareness about how the campus is managed and to help identify community factors that influence the daily management of the school. Some school administrators may wish to develop their own evaluation tools customized to their specific needs. Until that is done, however, the responses to the "School Crime Assessment Tool" provided will give the safe school planning team a lot to think about.

The third type of data collection involves surveying teachers, other school staff, students, parents, and community members regarding their perceptions of behavioral and safety issues at the school. The survey document should not only ask specific questions, but should also provide for some open-ended input. Several different questionnaire models are available from the state departments of education in Texas, California, South Carolina, and Florida.

The fourth and perhaps most important type of data collection is to talk with students, both individually and in focus groups. In an unsafe school, students usually will not spontaneously report their victimization or feelings about school safety to teachers, school administrators, law enforcers, or parents. If adults want to find out what is really going on, they must ask. Talking with students is much like a "Pocahontas adventure": you learn things you never knew you never knew. Such good information and insights improve the quality of decisions about student management. The following questions are excellent ice-breakers: "Are there areas of the campus you avoid?"; "What type of initiation rites exist for incoming students?"; "Are drugs easily available on campus?"; and "Have you ever seen a weapon at school?" The important point is to get some dialogue flowing and to establish a climate of trust. Students should be given the option of reporting such incidents anonymously. Any confidential information received should be handled appropriately by the school administrator. Students will offer some incredible insights – not only about the problems but also about solutions.

Subject Areas of Safe School Plans

The substantive scope of the safe school plan can be as broad as the creativity and commitment of the safe school planning team. Generally though, there are six overall subject areas that should be covered in the safe school plan: (1) the physical environment; (2) the social environment; (3) the cultural environment; (4) the economic environment; (5) the personal characteristics of individual students and staff members; and (6) the local political atmosphere. A seventh factor – "community will" – may sometimes transcend all of these issues.

The personal characteristics of students and staff, the school's physical environment, and the community's economic conditions are the "givens" that influence the school. (The physical environment is more difficult to

School Crime Assessment Tool

	Yes	No
1. Has your community crime rate increased over the past 12 months?	☐	☐
2. Are more than 15 % of your work orders vandalism-related?	☐	☐
3. Do you have an open campus?	☐	☐
4. Has there been an emergence of an "underground" student newspaper?	☐	☐
5. Is your community transiency rate increasing?	☐	☐
6. Do you have an increasing presence of graffiti in your community?	☐	☐
7. Do you have an increasing presence of gangs in your community?	☐	☐
8. Is your truancy rate increasing?	☐	☐
9. Are your suspension and expulsion rates increasing?	☐	☐
10. Have you had increased conflicts relative to dress styles, food service, or the types of music played at special events?	☐	☐
11. Do you have an increasing number of students on probation at your school?	☐	☐
12. Have you had isolated racial fights at your school?	☐	☐
13. Have you reduced the number of extracurricular programs and sports at your school?	☐	☐
14. Are parents withdrawing students from your school because of fear for their safety?	☐	☐
15. Has your professional development budget for staff been reduced or eliminated?	☐	☐
16. Are you discovering more weapons on your campus?	☐	☐
17. Do you lack written screening and selection guidelines for new staff at your school?	☐	☐
18. Are drugs easily available in or around your school?	☐	☐
19. Does your annual staff turnover exceed 25%?	☐	☐
20. Have you had a student demonstration or other signs of unrest within the past 12 months at your school?	☐	☐

Scoring and Interpretation: Total your affirmative answers. Multiply that total by 5. A score of 0–20 indicates there is no significant safety problem at your school. If your score is in the range of 25–45, you have an emerging school safety problem and should develop a safe school plan. A score of 50–70 indicates there is a significant potential for school violence. A safe school plan should be a top priority. If your score is greater than 70, you are "sitting on a ticking time bomb." Begin working on your safe school plan immediately. Obtain outside assistance.

change; however, there are several ways to better manage the facility, e.g., minimizing the number of entrance and exit points; removing architectural barriers that obstruct natural supervision; relocating offices and personnel to areas of the campus that do not have any or minimal natural supervision, etc.) In contrast, a school's social environment, cultural characteristics, and political components are more malleable, meaning they can be changed and improved through safe school planning and action.

The social environment of a school begins with the attitude of the principal, and should permeate the staff. Have adequate social programs, activities, clubs, sports, and community events at the school. Encourage teachers and staff to participate in extracurricular events involving their students. Students don't necessarily care how much a teacher knows, but students know how much a teacher cares. Being there and having a vibrant system of activities is the first step.

The school culture is the collection of assumptions, expectations, and knowledge that students, parents, and staff have about how a school should function and how individuals in the school should behave. A perception of belonging and commitment to the school by students and staff is an essential factor for school safety. A safe school plan could have a variety of program components or elements to support these "belongingness" factors. Safe school plans should be designed to empower communities and schools with strategies and techniques that recognize the value of every person.

Involve your local legislators in the process. Invite them to be a part of the team and let them share their vision as to how they will/can promote a safe school climate. Educate them, though, before you ask them to speak. Give them a briefing of the school's top concerns and look for common areas of interest and support.

Evaluating Safe School Plans

The burden of evaluation analyzes what has been done and suggests what remains to be accomplished. Measuring and evaluating have never been easy. Clearly there are some specific needs for developing effective evaluation techniques and measures. Program effectiveness can be evaluated on the basis of inputs, outputs, or impacts. Inputs and outputs may be the easiest to evaluate. For example, reductions in school crime reports, improvements in attendance, gains in school-level achievement test scores, and increased numbers of students completing advanced placement work can all be quantified. Impacts are the most difficult. For instance, how does one measure the effectiveness of the safe school plan in terms of crime prevention? Can one attribute crime reduction to the implementation of specific program components implemented? Is it good enough to simply know that the campus is safer? Whenever one has to measure something that doesn't exist (e.g., crimes not committed), the task becomes more difficult.

Such circumstances suggest there is a need to develop a set of objective measures and a complementary set of subjective measures. Together, such measures are more likely to constitute a fuller evaluation of safe school plan effectiveness. An initial step might be to determine what criteria will be used to evaluate effectiveness. Will the criteria include favorable crime statistics, the positive feelings of students and staff, the percentage of the annual budget devoted to safe school activities, the number of sponsored after-school programs, and/or some other measures?

To be effective, there is a compelling need to identify what works and what does not work so that limited resources can be applied with a maximum return. Following are some examples of questions that may be helpful in measuring a plan's effectiveness:

- Is school crime decreasing or increasing in terms of fewer assaults, thefts, and burglaries?
- Are student attendance rates improving?
- Are staff turnover rates increasing or decreasing?
- Is the number/percentage of administrative work orders related to vandalism and graffiti increasing or decreasing?
- Are academic test scores improving?
- Have police calls for service to the school been increasing or decreasing?
- How do students, staff, and parents currently perceive school safety?
- Are student transiency rates increasing or decreasing?
- Is community crime increasing or decreasing?
- Are the number of weapon incidents at school increasing or decreasing?

Unfortunately, there are no nationally mandated crime reporting standards nor mechanisms for evaluating the effectiveness of safe school plans. Furthermore, not all school crime is reported, because some school administrators believe that reporting crime will reflect poorly on them. To effectively evaluate school safety and school safety plans, there first must be an adequate database so progress can be measured. The greatest impediment to a good evaluation program is often the lack of adequate school crime data, followed closely by general resistance to evaluation. Generally, each community or school has been left to its own devices regarding reporting crime and/or developing effective evaluative measures of safe school plans.

Another challenge involves learning from schools that have already implemented a comprehensive plan addressing all components of safe schools. This is difficult, because each setting is unique. School safety is about identifying specific security issues and then creating a response/prevention plan. With this scenario in mind and these descriptors in place, data has begun to emerge from school systems that have implemented specific safe school components.

For instance, in Long Beach, California, the school district implemented a mandatory school uniform policy in 1995. Since its implementation, student assaults have decreased by 34%, assaults with a deadly weapon are down by 50%, sex offenses are down by 74%, and extortion decreased by 60% over the previous year. In Houston, Texas, where local law enforcement officials worked with the schools to address truancy concerns, school attendance is up and daytime burglaries are down by 70%. When young people are not in school, they are often committing acts of crime and violence in the community. In Washington, Connecticut, where a character education curriculum was implemented at Devereaux Glenholme School, student behavior problems were reduced by 50%. In Fresno, California, local probation officials and law enforcement officers joined in partnership with the schools to provide on-campus services to young people in need of supervision. As a result of their efforts, student assaults were reduced by nearly 50%. These changes have taken place with respect to specific plan components. A comprehensive program of prevention activities that focus on educational strategies, supervision strategies, mentoring, and motivating programs could have even greater results.[2]

Evaluation and monitoring should not be left to chance. It should be determined up front what will be measured, how it will be measured, who will perform the evaluation, and where and how the results will be disseminated. After data has been collected and reviewed, it is essential to keep parents, students, and school staff informed about how things are going with regard to school safety. Keeping in mind that safe school planning is an ongoing process, school administrators should ultimately incorporate results of the monitoring and evaluation process in the ongoing safe school plan.

General Recommendations for Safe School Plans

While every campus is different, there are some general elements[3] of safe school plans that would likely be beneficial for any school in the country. Following are brief descriptions of some such recommendations for safe schools.

Campus Access and Control

Control campus access. Efforts should be made to minimize the number of campus entrance and exit points used daily. Access points to school grounds should be limited and supervised on a regular basis by individuals who are familiar with the student body. Campus traffic, both pedestrian and vehicular, should flow through areas that can be easily and naturally supervised. Delivery entrances used by vendors also should be checked regularly. Parking lots often have multiple entrances and exits, which contribute to the vandalism and defacement of vehicles and school property. Vehicular and pedestrian access should be carefully controlled in these areas.

Define campus perimeters with appropriate landscaping and fencing. School campuses should lend themselves to natural supervision. Access points and campus buildings should be easily supervisable. Avoid solid block walls or other architectural barriers that obscure the playgrounds, gathering areas, or structures. Landscaped areas should be maintained in ways that promote observation and supervision. Consider decorative wrought iron rather than chain link fencing, which does little more than provide a ladder anywhere the fence is located on the campus.

Remove posters and student decorations from all window glass. Posters and construction paper covering windows block supervision. Unless glaring sun or the need for privacy mandates the covering of windows, they should be left clear or uncovered to enhance natural supervision.

Establish uniform visitor screening procedures. Specific procedures should be established to screen and monitor visitors and potential campus intruders. Signs directing persons to the office should be placed in strategic, easily visible locations and should be large enough to attract visitors' notice. Visitors should be required to sign in at the school office, state their specific business, and wear or visibly display a visitor's badge. All school employees should be advised to greet visitors or any unidentified persons not wearing a badge and direct them to the main office to ensure that these people have legitimate business at the school. Teachers and staff should be trained to courteously challenge all visitors. "May I help you?" is a kind, nonthreatening way to begin the dialogue.

Post appropriate directional signs on the campus. These signs should advise students, visitors, or other nonstudents of the conditions they agree to accept upon entering the campus, including any applicable trespassing statutes, drug-free school zone codes, weapon prevention notices, or other applicable statutes requiring public notice. A comprehensive signage program should also be created that clearly designates building names, purposes, and directional flow. Good signage minimizes confusion and provides fewer excuses for unauthorized users to trespass on the campus.

Require picture identification cards for each student and staff member (including substitutes). A school administrator is responsible not only for keeping students away from trouble, but also for keeping trouble away from students. Being able to identify enrolled students from nonstudents and visitors is critical. An effective picture identification system will enhance the control and management of the campus. Authorized parent volunteers and school visitors should also display clearly identifiable badges or name tags.

Carefully manage and appropriately monitor hall passes. Consider developing a single hall pass form to be utilized by each teacher, which provides the student's name, date, time out, time in, destination, and purpose. At the end of the day the passes would be signed by the teachers and turned in to the office. The information contained on the forms could be extremely helpful in solving campus crimes during the day because the report summarizes who was where and when. When hall pass data is combined with school crime data, the opportunity exists to leverage data in ways which enhance problem solving.

Clearly separate and segregate mixed vehicular and pedestrian functions. For instance, bus loading and unloading should be separated from parent drop-off and pick-up points. Deliveries, loading docks, and vendor access points should be clearly delineated. Visitor, staff, and student (if applicable) parking should be visibly defined. Pedestrian traffic should be clearly separated from all vehicular access. It is important to ensure that none of these functions conflicts with one another. For example, delivery trucks should not use the same route as pedestrian traffic on the campus. In addition, you would not want parents darting their cars around the bus pick-up and drop-off points. This would create a very dangerous situation.

Administrative Leadership

Mandate crime reporting and tracking. A uniform school crime reporting and record keeping system is critical to maintaining a safe and secure campus. When school administrators know what crimes are being committed on their campus, when they are committed to documenting who is involved with and where crimes are occurring, the results of this diligence speak volumes about the types of prevention strategies and supervision that should be implemented. In addition, it is important to conduct some level of crime analysis to determine what, if any, linkages exist among various aspects of criminal activity on the campus.

Place school safety on the educational agenda. School administrators tend to receive not only what they expect and deserve, but also what they measure. When the district makes a conscious decision that safe and welcoming schools are a high priority, that commitment provides the basis for the development of plans and strategies to achieve this goal. Placing school safety on the educational agenda is a mandatory first step toward safer and better schools.

Include school safety in the mission statement. The school's mission statement should include a phrase which reflects the context in which the school and district wish academic learning to take place. For instance, the phrase "to learn in a safe and secure environment free of violence, drugs, and fear" enhances the school's legal position to create and enforce policies that promote a safe, caring, and disciplined school climate. A statement of this nature can also have a powerful effect upon the validity and credibility of the school district's efforts to create and preserve a safe environment.

The Virginia Association of School Superintendents has articulated an excellent statement to assist school administrators in developing their safe school plans. Their position statement suggests: "It is the responsibility of schools and their governing authorities to provide safe schools for the children and communities that they serve. The establishment of safe schools is inseparable from the issues of violence and crime in the larger community. Safe school solutions must ultimately be pursued in the context of a commitment to create safe communities, not just safe schools. The broadest possible coordinated response of parents, educators, students, community leaders, and public and private agencies will be sought."

Develop a comprehensive, system-wide safe school plan. School safety must be placed at the top of the educational agenda on each campus and within the community. A district-wide plan should be established, complemented by a safe school plan for each school site. Programs should be developed collaboratively with parents, students, educators, law enforcers, the courts, probation and social service personnel, and religious, corporate, and other community leaders who represent the racial and ethnic balance of the community. Safe school planning is an ongoing process that must be interactively supported by pursuing vigorous interagency courses of action. Strategies should be established that focus not merely on security and supervision options, but also on educational options, including community and corporate partnerships. Plans should be reviewed, updated, and broadly disseminated annually to students, parents, and school staff. As the planning process continues, a series of other positive suggestions and strategies will emerge. Begin the process now so that positive change can occur over time.

Disseminate a summary of laws pertaining to school disorder. The summary should be drafted and developed by the district's legal counsel and disseminated through the director of security (or comparable position) to all school site administrators and security personnel in order to ensure uniformity and consistency of student supervision and management.

Establish a state-of-the-art "Emergency Operation Communications Center." This center would utilize the latest technology and allow school site administrators to make immediate contact with district-level school safety personnel. A school communications network should be established that links classrooms and schoolyard supervisors with the front office or security staff, as well as with local law enforcement and fire departments. An 800 megahertz, fully computerized public safety emergency frequency is recommended to complement this system.

Develop a clear job description of duties and responsibilities for school peace officers. A set of general orders and standard operating procedures should also be developed. The director of security (or comparable position) should develop and distribute an "Operations Manual" among all district security personnel.

Establish a crisis response plan. Through responsible planning, many potential problems can be avoided. However, there are times when a crisis is unavoidable. A good crisis response plan focuses on crisis prevention, preparation, management, and resolution. It will also identify community resources and agencies that serve students. The crisis response plan should include step-by-step procedures for the following types of crisis situations:

• Campus unrest	• Utility failure	• Assault and battery
• Chemical spills	• Weapon possession	• Suicide
• Drive-by shootings	• Hostage/terrorist	• Rape
• Kidnapping/	situations	• Molestation
abduction	• Bomb threats	• Child neglect
• Natural disasters	• Child abuse	• Unauthorized vendors
Earthquakes	• Homicide	• Search and seizure
Floods	• Intruders	• Fire
Tornados	• Student sit-ins	• Falling aircraft
Hurricanes	• Extortion	• Illness/severe injury
Tsunamis	• Motor vehicle	
	accident	

Identify specifically assigned roles and responsibilities concerning security. Specific policies and procedures that detail staff members' responsibilities for security should be developed. These responsibilities may include monitoring hallways and restrooms, patrolling parking lots, and providing supervision at before-school and after-school activities.

Work with the central administration to expand the network of alternative placement options for troubled youth. Weapon using or weapon carrying students should be removed from the mainstream educational setting and relocated at alternative sites where increased supervision and structure are provided.

Establish a restitution and community service program at district schools. Work with the presiding juvenile judge and the chief probation officer to establish a series of community service and restitution programs at school sites. Individuals who are involved in vandalism and acts of malicious mischief should have some positive means of making amends to the school and community for their infractions and offenses. Opportunities for service should be developed with the help of appropriate governmental and community agencies.

Recognize the politics of safe schools. The politics of school safety can be very delicate and turbulent. As widely diverse team members come together for safe school planning, each person and the groups they represent must be made to feel they are equally important. The safe school planning team will be no better than the example set by its chair (generally a school administrator). The following ideas can help the school administrator "rise above the politics":

- Emphasize a safe and welcoming environment for all children.
- Set goals in positive terms rather than simply focusing on combating violence; focus on developing safe schools.
- Be aware of special interest groups or political situations that should be considered. They need to be fairly represented and their views heard, yet their influence must be balanced within the larger group structure. A reasonable forum for fair representation should be made.
- Recognize that safe school planning is like a marriage or business partnership – it requires a lot of cooperation.
- Do not underestimate the value or influence of any member of the school safety planning team. Make a special effort to accept, appreciate, and work with each participant.
- Determine in advance the amount of decision-making authority to be held by the safe school planning team. Do the members have the authority to make recommendations or decisions? Communicate these responsibilities clearly to team members before they decide to serve.
- Do not attempt to force particular decisions upon the group.
- Do not have hidden agendas which require the team's "rubber stamp" of approval.
- Realize that most issues being considered do not require immediate decision. Invest the necessary time to carefully consider each issue and develop a positive decision the majority of team members agree to be the best course of action.

Establish good management practices. It is extremely important to build and continue to develop coalitions throughout the safe school planning process. Students may be the most important group to include in this process. The second most underutilized resource, next to students, are parents. Every campus should establish a "Parent Center" where parents are encouraged to participate in the educational activities of their children. Some states, such as California, have even passed laws requiring employers to release parents from their jobs for up to 40 hours per year per child, so parents can participate in school activities or meetings. The California law allows the employees to utilize vacation time, sick time, or compensable time for the school visits. Such a law is a remarkable legislative tool; it acknowledges the importance of parent involvement in the education process.

Conduct an annual review. Every school should conduct an annual school safety assessment and review of its safe school plan because safe school planning must be an ongoing process. The evaluation component is a continuing "reality check" and refinement of the safe school actions and attitudes the team wishes to create. The assessment may reveal that additional steps should be taken to improve adult supervision, revise curricula, lobby to pass legislation, redesign facilities, establish new prevention programs or student activities, etc.

The safe school planning team and the community should be involved in the evaluation process on a regular basis. (The community is involved through its representatives on the planning team and/or through open community forums.) It is important to refer to the original safe school plan, review each component, and ask the following questions:

- Is this priority on task?
- What could we do better?
- Do other options or strategies exist that we should try?
- How can we be more effective?
- How can we combine other efforts or strategies to produce better results?

At least once per year, administrators should review the school's mission statement in order to remain focused on the schools' top priority of serving and preparing young people for productive and responsible citizenship. The bottom line is, an evaluation is never finished; the evaluation process should continue on a regular basis.

Promote crime prevention through environmental design. Good facility designs cannot overcome bad management. However, outstanding management can overcome bad designs. Several things can be done to improve campus management:

- Trim or remove shrubbery that interferes with surveillance.
- Provide maximum supervision in heavy traffic areas.
- Provide strategically located public telephones with cost-free connections to emergency services.
- Relocate safe activities near typical trouble spots. For instance, consider relocating a counselor's office next to a corridor or locker bay where problems have typically occurred. Or conduct ticket sales or concession activities in or near problem areas.
- Eliminate obstacles such as trash cans and architectural barriers that block or impede traffic flow as well as supervision and surveillance.
- Use parabolic/convex mirrors in stairwells and other locations that require improved supervision.
- Replace double-entry restroom doors with an open, zigzag wall design to better monitor student behavior in restrooms.
- Utilize automatic flush valves and automatic water faucets to reduce restroom vandalism and control water consumption.
- Ensure that hallways and stairwells are large enough to adequately handle the flow of foot traffic.
- Colors and lighting also affect attitudes and behavior; use these environmental factors to help create a peaceful and pleasant school environment. For example, the color red tends to incite and encourage aggressive behavior. Earth tones – blues and browns – tend to calm.

Establish two-way communication between the front office and each classroom. Campus communications systems should include a two-way communication capability between each classroom and the office. Teachers should be able to contact the front office from any classroom; however, many schools do not have this capability. Campus supervisors, assistant principals, and principals should also have two-way radios. Each campus should have at least one cellular phone for use in emergency situations. Detention classrooms or facilities for behaviorally disruptive students (e.g., time-out rooms) should also have emergency buzzers or call buttons.

Identify and track repeat offenders. The majority of school crimes are caused by a small percentage of students. It is essential to track, monitor, and closely supervise disruptive students to discourage their continued involvement in misbehavior and crime. The following actions should be considered when planning such close supervision: place such students with experienced teachers; develop individual behavior and education plans in accordance with needs identified in the assessment process; assign a specific counselor to each student; and assign these students lockers located in areas that are clearly visible and easily supervised.

Provide close supervision, remedial training, and restitution for serious habitual offenders. Where feasible, require restitution and community service from all juvenile offenders. Create a special supervision program for the repeat offender. Such a program could include in-school suspension or alternative education offered within the district. Troublemakers should not be rewarded with time off from school or reduced class schedules. Instead, such student's training and supervision should be intensified.

Carefully screen and select new employees. One of the most important decisions that parents and communities make involves deciding who will teach, train, coach, counsel, and lead their children. (While these decisions are made by school administrators, the school board, parents, and the community should ensure that adequate record screening and selection guidelines are articulated and followed.) Keeping child molesters and pedophiles out of classrooms, schools, and youth-serving organizations is a major task. Responsible parenting and thoughtful leadership on the part of schools and other youth-serving agencies will assist in establishing appropriate safeguards for keeping child molesters away from children. Currently, "Megan's law" requiring law enforcement officials to notify neighbors when a registered pedophile moves into a neighborhood, is providing new opportunities to keep the public better informed and properly warned.

Increasing litigation against school systems and child care providers has created a compelling financial reason for conducting appropriate employee background checks to protect the safety of children. Many school systems and youth service organizations have already faced multimillion-dollar lawsuits for their failure to appropriately screen, properly supervise, and/ or remove employees who represent risks to children.

Every school system and youth-serving organization should have clear policy guidelines and procedures to "weed out" individuals who have a criminal background of misbehavior involving children. Any record-screening program must consider individual rights of privacy and due process as well as the right to a hearing when employee disqualification is involved. However, the screening program must also balance these rights with the rights of the children who will be served by the individual.

Conduct periodic joint meetings of all school staff and faculty. Discuss strategies and procedures to make the campus safer and more welcoming for students, staff, and parents. This effort can serve as the beginning for a broader and more comprehensive safe school planning effort.

Utilize existing technologies that promote crime prevention. A host of options exist relative to control of campus access, property identification, and ongoing supervision. For example, consider installing electromagnetic door-locking systems and using property control strategies such as microdot systems,[4] use surveillance cameras for difficult to supervise public areas, and other such high-tech strategies that may also be appropriate for the educational setting.

School Climate

Make the campus safe and welcoming, beginning early in the morning. School safety leadership begins at the top. There is no question that the best principals spend the majority of their time outside their offices. Staying in touch cannot be accomplished behind office walls. Begin the day by greeting students at the front door when they arrive. The way the day begins affects the climate of the entire day and has a significant impact on how it is concluded. Be present in the hall during class changes. Visit classrooms and attend special events.

Develop a nuisance abatement plan. School officials must work closely with police and community leaders to shut down "drug houses" and stop illegal group activities in the neighborhoods of schools. The local U.S. attorney, along with city and county officials, represent some excellent resources to cultivate. Their support is critical as local and regional gang, drug, and graffiti abatement strategies are developed. School officials should work with the local community in seeking cooperative solutions to nuisance abatement problems, including protecting the school site and ensuring that the walk to school is crime-free and nonthreatening.

Develop a graffiti abatement and community clean-up program. Local communities should have a policy in place that requires property owners to promptly remove graffiti. In addition there should be sanctions against offenders to appropriately prosecute them and to be able to require personal restitution.

Create a climate of ownership and school pride. Every student and staff member should feel like a key part of the school community. Such empowerment can be accomplished by involving every person in the safe school planning process (e.g., through student and staff surveys and focus group discussions), including students, parents, teachers and other school staff, and community leaders. Establish homeroom areas for faculty and students. Encourage school-sponsored groups and clubs to assume stewardship of specific hallways, display areas, or other school locations.

Establish a "Parent Center" on each campus. This center should serve to recruit, coordinate, and encourage parents to participate in the educational process. Possible activities include helping supervise hallways, playgrounds, restrooms, or other trouble spots. Classroom visitation and participation in special events should also be encouraged. Parents can tutor students in a variety of subject areas, read to children in the school library, assist with field trips and hands-on learning activities (e.g., science lab experiments), make special presentations to classes (e.g., on vocational awareness), and help to raise funds for the school. A special training program that outlines expectations and responsibilities for parents in volunteer roles can be particularly helpful. School crime decreases when responsible adult supervision is present.

Enhance multicultural understanding. Focus on stressing the unique worth of every person. Gang activity and the polarization of student groups indicate a need to develop educational programs and activities that bring students together. Such a desirable result might be brought about by using a multicultural curriculum or by instituting a process of cooperative learning. Bringing students together to work collaboratively on specific projects can also pay great dividends.

Establish a vibrant system of extracurricular programs. Schoolchildren need positive things to do. Without interesting, positive, and challenging activities, students tend to fill the void with negative activities. A safe school provides students with several options before, during, and after school.

Student Behavior, Supervision, and Management

Review the student handbook. Ensure that behavioral expectations are clearly communicated, consistently enforced, and fairly applied. School policies should also reflect behavioral expectations outlined in federal, state, county, and local statutes or ordinances.

Articulate a clearly defined locker policy. The locker policy at each school should appropriately reflect the district's custodial interest. Students and parents should be notified that the lockers are school property. Students should be advised, in the student handbook, that lockers and their contents may be searched at any time for reasons of health and safety. Distributing district-owned locks to students or requiring that students use only locks for which the school has combinations will further enhance the school's custodial position in conducting routine locker checks.

Develop and enforce a school dress code. Students and staff tend to behave the way they are allowed to dress. The courts have determined that the First Amendment rights of students to freely express themselves by their dress may be limited when student appearance conflicts with the educational mission of the school or compromises student safety. Establish a district-wide uniform dress code policy that establishes clear appearance standards for both students and staff. Gang attire should be prohibited and dress code expectations should be consistently enforced. Contradictory policies and procedures and inconsistent enforcement by staff send mixed messages to students. Involve the students and parents in developing these appearance standards. Students and parents tend to support and preserve what they have helped to create.

Review discipline and weapon possession policies. Ensure that these policies attack the problem and not simply the symptoms. Clearly distinguish between disciplinary matters and criminal offenses. Identify the school's top discipline problems and then establish a task force consisting of students, teachers/school staff, administrators, and parents to review and/or develop effective strategies and programs to address these problems. The weapon policy should reflect the Federal Gun-Free School Zone Act of 1994, which mandates a 12-month minimum suspension for the possession of a firearm on campus by a student. The student handbook should also reflect compliance with this 1994 law. Failure to comply may result in the loss of federal funds for the district.

Place students and parents on notice. At the beginning of each school year, all students and their parents or guardians should be provided with written codes of conduct outlining behavioral expectations and their sanctions. In addition to providing students and their parents with the comprehensive guidelines that establish discipline procedures and due process considerations, consider developing a one-page summary of the school rules that can be posted in strategic locations throughout the campus.

Provide adequate adult supervision. Young people need continuous responsible supervision. This may include teachers, administrators, parents, playground aides, bus drivers, counselors, cafeteria monitors, campus supervisors, and/or law enforcement or school peace officers. By all means, do not forget the option of utilizing assistance from senior citizens. Just as there are many young people who are looking for something constructive to do, there are also many senior citizens whose talents and resources are no longer being tapped. For the most part, recent studies have shown that the majority of young people feel there is a major role for adults to play in counseling and encouraging youth toward nonviolence.

Limit opportunities for the transport and storing of contraband. School systems around the country have implemented a variety of school crime prevention policies that:

- Allow only clear plastic or mesh book bags, or no book bags at all.
- Eliminate lockers completely.
- Establish a coat/jacket checking area, requiring that large articles of clothing capable of shielding weapons be left there rather than being worn or carried into other areas.
- Provide students with two sets of textbooks, one for home and one for school, in order to eliminate the need for book bags at school. Eliminating the costs of a full-scale, five-day per week/every student search (which might potentially be

necessary in a school with severe rates of violence) would save enough money to justify using this costly approach.

- Reduce the amount of time between class changes as well as extend the length of class instructional periods so students do not have to make so many class changes.

Automobile and parking policies should state that campus parking is a privilege, not a right. The parking policy should also place students on notice that when they drive their vehicles onto school property, they agree to abide by campus rules and agree to have their vehicles searched by school staff, school security, and administrators. Such searches are constitutional if the students have been placed on notice and if it is part of the school policy. Diminishing the privacy expectation can serve as a deterrent to the presence of contraband and weapons. Such a policy will also enhance the district's position for any legal action relative to search and seizure issues.

"Hard looks"/"stare downs" (or "mean mugging," "stink eye," and "mad dogging" in gang lingo) should be added as actionable offenses to the student code of conduct. Such behaviors are used to assert dominance and to intimidate staff and students. This behavior should not be tolerated at school.

Train students to take responsibility for their own safety. Encourage students to report suspicious individuals present on school grounds. Provide students and staff with a toll-free, anonymous hot line for reporting weapon and drug offenses and other criminal activity.

Conduct emergency drills. Every school should have a crisis plan, including a crisis drill for emergency situations. Whether they are drop drills, bullet drills, crisis drills, or earthquake drills, the routine is generally similar. Regardless of what they're called, do them!

Staff Training

Conduct annual school safety training programs. Prior to the start of each school year, hold training sessions for all school site administrators and security personnel to review school safety procedures and strategies. School staff and faculty should also be informed and regularly updated on school safety plans through in-service training. The training should include not only the certified staff, but also classified staff, as well as part-time and substitute employees.

Establish an active school peace officer training program. School peace officers should be academy trained and/or POST (Police Officer Standards Training) certified. Their training and their compensation should be commensurate with their responsibilities and consistent with local law enforcement agencies. This will increase the preparation and capability of peace officer personnel to meet the specific needs demanded by their position. The professional training required of school security officers today is dramatically different from that of 25 years ago. We've gone from fistfights to gun fights, from fire drills to crisis drills. School security officers must continually take part in special service and in-service training programs to stay abreast of innovative security methods and techniques. School peace officers can also enhance their professional status by participating in such professional organizations as the National Association of School Resource Officers or the International Association of School Safety Professionals.

Provide teacher training in behavior management. In-house training programs in the areas of classroom management and student behavior management should be offered for teachers and administrators. Strategies that worked 20 years ago may no longer be effective, as students no longer blindly comply. They want to know "why" and "what's in it for me." Today teacher training is more about leadership and role modeling than about managing and order giving. Teachers and others who supervise students must develop coping skills and techniques for controlling classroom behaviors and for dealing with disruptive youth and angry parents. Many printed resources from educational publishers, audio/video training programs, educational workshops/seminars, and college courses offered through universities are available in the area of behavior management today. Such skill building and training is necessary to ensure educational effectiveness as well as personal safety.

Establish an ongoing professional development and in-service training program for campus supervisors and student personnel workers. Such programs should include training techniques in conflict mediation, breaking up student fights, and handling disruptive parents and campus intruders. School site administrators must also acquire "crime-resistance savvy" and take greater responsibility in working with the school board and district staff to implement school site security programs, which will include the roles of campus supervisory staff.

Establish a physical restraint policy. The school district should establish a physical restraint policy that states that school employees may use "reasonable physical force" to maintain discipline when employees reasonably believe there is a danger to themselves or others (e.g., students).

Student Involvement

Create an active student component. Students should be actively involved in their own safety and in school safety planning, including learning conflict resolution techniques. Involve students in planning and managing student events and programs. Student participation promotes responsible student development and maturity, enabling students to be a part of the solution rather than being a part of the problem.

Implement a peer counseling and peer mediation program at every school site. Students represent some of the best agents for promoting and maintaining a safe and secure campus. An effective peer counseling program can head off many problems before they reach explosive and violent levels. In addition, students who are trained as peer counselors become wonderfully influential resources for nonviolent problem solving.

Incorporate life skills curricula. These curricula should focus on good decision making, responsible citizenship, and conflict resolution. Young people need to learn how to deal with conflict in nonviolent ways. School violence is the tangible expression of unresolved conflict. If educators can help youth identify and implement constructive conflict resolution techniques, school campuses can be made much safer. A social skills curriculum that emphasizes courtesy, thoughtfulness, and anger management will go a long way toward creating a more positive and effective campus climate. In recent years, many schools have forgotten about the "other side" of the report card, the behavior side. Clearly, success in our society requires more than just academic talent, it requires the ability to get along well with others. There are a number of promising conflict resolution programs commercially available in the marketplace. Many schools that have implemented such programs have seen fewer behavior problems among students as well as reduced tensions among staff members who have served as program instructors.

Create a student advisory council. A school administrator in south Florida, who had been experiencing significant behavior problems on his campus, brought together his 12 worst behaved students, commissioning them the "Council of Twelve." Their role was to advise and assist the principal in developing reasonable behavior standards for the most disruptive students. He pointed out to them that they had two things in common: "First, you don't want to be here and second, I don't want you here either. But the law says you must attend school and that I must provide a free public education for you. So let's figure out a way to work together." By the end of the year his campus's climate had improved dramatically. These difficult students were now part of the solution and not simply viewed as part of the problem.[5] Students (both those with behavior problems and those without) can be a powerful resource.

Develop a student crime prevention program. Components of such a program could include:

- Establishing a school crime watch program, including such groups as Crimestoppers International, the National Crime Prevention Council's Youth Crime Watch, Neighborhood Crime Watch, Block Watch, and/or other related programs.
- Establishing financial incentives for students who report school crimes.
- Involving students in campus maintenance and beautification projects.

Consider teen court as an option. Several secondary schools around the United States (e.g., Town View High School in Dallas, Texas) are establishing "teen courts" to assist administrators in the daily management and governance of school campuses. The role of teen courts is generally not to determine innocence or guilt, but rather to determine the appropriate level of sanctions or restitution to employ in cases involving student misbehavior. Former offenders must also agree to serve as participants in developing fair and meaningful consequences for misbehavior.

Building Community Partnerships

Identify community resources. School officials cannot make their schools and communities safe through their exclusive efforts. Every school district should prepare an inventory of youth-serving organizations within its jurisdiction and make this list available at each school site.

Enhance interagency cooperation by creating a partnership among youth-serving professionals. Creating safe schools is a community function. Schools alone cannot accomplish such a feat. Safe schools actively cooperate with community agencies. Campus security operations should be coordinated with local law enforcement agencies. Community support agencies such as county mental health, child protective services, departments of parks and recreation, juvenile probation, and the courts must actively work together to identify students who are potentially dangerous and to provide services that preclude them from causing further problems and assist them in their educational and personal development. By working together, community agencies and schools can develop effective educational and behavior plans to better protect the rights of students and staff while rehabilitating juvenile offenders.

Seek intensive community support and involvement in making the journey to and from school a safe one. Model programs include Safe Corridors, Neighborhood Crime Watch, and Parent Patrol. The Crimestoppers International program is another excellent way to involve the community.

Establish a close law enforcement partnership. Include law enforcers in your educational program as guest lecturers, mentors, and role models, as well as in supervision and crisis planning. Some of the most effective school peace officer programs bring officers in contact with children in the early grades and allow the officers to follow the students throughout elementary school, middle/junior high school, and high school. School peace officers can do some of their best work once they get to know students well.

Closely supervise troublemakers across agencies. A small percentage of young people create most of the school problems. There is a growing trend among schools and youth-serving agencies/professionals to begin sharing information about the serious misbehavior of juveniles. Such information sharing allows educators, law enforcers, and the courts to work together more effectively in creating appropriate educational and behavioral plans for this small but disruptive group of serious habitual offenders. Youth who commit campus and off-campus crimes should be carefully monitored. These students should be provided with special counseling, support, and referrals to appropriate community resources, including alternative schools when justified. Organizations that serve these youth, including the courts and probation, law enforcement, and social service agencies, should coordinate their activities through appropriate information sharing on a need-to-know basis.

Capitalize on the school's ability as an organizational vehicle to provide comprehensive student services. Many schools are leveraging their strategic position to serve as a comprehensive "one-stop service center" for young people. Children and youth today bring with them so many problems to school that often learning cannot take place until their other needs are met, including physical, social, and personal needs. Clearly, schools should not have to provide all of these services in addition to their educational mission. But sometimes for the educational mission to be effective these other services are required. Consequently a trend of this decade has been the evolution of public schools to full-service agencies. This includes making a school a health center and recreation center, and providing social services, counseling, probation, law enforcement, banking, and a variety of other services limited only by the imagination and creativity of the local school site administrator.

Consistently enforce the information sharing agreements. Nearly a dozen states have now passed laws requiring information sharing on juvenile offenders. In Texas, for instance, law enforcement must verbally inform school officials within 24 hours and in writing within seven days whenever a juvenile is arrested in the community. At least once annually school administrators should review their information sharing agreements to ensure they are in compliance with federal and state laws and to ensure that school administrators and education staff are doing everything possible to share such information with those who have a legitimate need to know. Special follow-up should be given by the courts to ensure that court orders (e.g., conditions of probation) and other information-sharing agreements among agencies are in compliance with court guidelines so that children can be better served. The student records policy should state that student records may be shared with any relevant teacher or school staff member or other youth-serving professional who has a legitimate need to review such information. Additionally, parents always have the right to review their children's records.

Consider placing a probation officer on campus to provide increased intensive supervision for students on probation who attend school. Exercising such an option can complement the efforts of supervisory staff, who can then invest more time reinforcing the positive behaviors of other students rather than simply disciplining troublemakers. Some schools have gone so far as to bring both law enforcement and probation officers together. They are each "cross-sworn," which means the law enforcement officers can perform the functions of probation officers and probation officers can perform the duties of law enforcement officers in prevention efforts. In Fresno, California, where this program has been piloted, campus disruptions and assaults have been significantly reduced.

Conclusion

Creating safe and orderly schools is about commitment and community will. It requires school and community leaders to articulate the quality of educational climate and learning environment they want to provide for children, and then to collaboratively and cooperatively develop the strategies that will produce the desired results. Safe school planning is about a school evaluating where it is currently, planning where it wants to be, and then implementing a series of comprehensive strategies to remediate the difference.

Essential ingredients for creating a safe school plan include the following:

- *Placing School Safety on the Educational Agenda.* This involves making a personal and collective commitment toward creating a safe and welcoming school climate.
- *Compiling and Developing the Safe School Planning Team.* Making schools safe is a joint responsibility, requiring a broad-based team with working attitudes that complement a collaborative and cooperative spirit.

- *Conducting a Site Assessment.* Determining the specific issues and concerns the local community believes are most important begins the process of customizing a relevant and meaningful safe school plan, which as a result of its pertinence will foster an increased level of community commitment.
- *Developing a Plan of Where a School Wants to Be (i.e., Setting Goals).* Such a determination includes not only the substance of what the school wants to accomplish, but also indicates additional processes by which those goals will be achieved. Articulating the goals and processes for achieving them is an important part of team building, and an essential component in creating a cooperative spirit. It is most important for team members to believe that they can individually and collectively make a positive difference in the quality of life for themselves, their community, and all the children and youth they serve.
- *Involving Students and Parents.* No plan can succeed without the integral participation of students and parents. Planners must make certain to bring these participants to the table often to collaboratively shape strategies and programs. For the most part, people do not like to have things done to them. However, they do enjoy being a part of planning, carrying out, and evaluating programs in which they have invested concern and time. All those affected by safe school plans should be involved throughout the planning process.
- *Reviewing the Law.* The law, at the federal, state, and local levels, defines what is required and what is allowed in safe school planning. Such laws, as well as district-level procedures and court orders, must be observed during the planning process.
- *Formulating a Crisis Response Plan.* Having a plan simply makes good sense. Such foresight can save time and energy and can maintain commitment when unforeseen problems arise (e.g., what to do in a hostage situation, or a campus evacuation plan). When there is no plan, the result is typically a series of successive crises.
- *Continuing Development.* No one can be an expert in all areas of safe school planning. Many of the chapters on creating safe schools have yet to be written. Consequently, strategies must be developed even while work is in progress. Who better to develop these strategies than those individuals who will be most affected by them: students, parents, school staff, and community leaders?
- *Doing the Work.* It does not take a rocket scientist to create a safe school. It does, however, require a firm commitment to school safety and believing that a positive difference can be made. Everyone must work together to ensure the success of the planning efforts.
- *Conducting a Continuing Evaluation.* Like raising children, safe school planning requires continuing attention to and reevaluation of strategies as children experience new stages of development. Evaluation is about making continuing improvements and enhancements to the school environment that are designed to serve and support the success of all children. The quality of our future will be dependent on how well educators teach and how much care is inculcated into those young people who will one day care for us and society as a whole. Safe school planning produces both immediate and long-term benefits, and should be monitored closely.

These guidelines represent the beginning of a continuing collaborative and cooperative process to create safe schools for all of America's children. Making schools safe requires a total community effort within the context of a broad spectrum of opportunities.[6]

Notes

1. The suggested timetable was modified from the Cities and Schools Plan, and modified by the author (Stephens, 1994a).
2. These results were published in newspaper articles and school district newsletters. For more information, readers should contact the superintendent's office in each of these school districts.
3. These general recommendations have been revised, expanded, and reorganized from an article previously published in *School Psychology Review* (Stephens, 1994a). They have been developed over the years as a result of the author personally conducting several hundred school site safety assessments. The recommendations provide a basis for creating and managing a comprehensive and systematic safe school plan.
4. Microdot is a system whereby property is identified and tracked in a miniaturized way. The labeling is not readable to the human eye, but the property can be tracked and traced by the miniaturized encryption.
5. This story was related to the author by Jeff Miller, principal of Holmes Beach High School in Miami, Florida.
6. Additional strategies, model assessment questionnaires, and student and staff surveys, along with sample safe school plans, are available in Safe schools: A handbook for violence prevention (Stephens, 1995).

References

National Crime Survey. (1987). *School crime: Annual statistical snapshot.* Washington, DC: U.S. Department of the Census, Center for Demographic Studies.

National Institute of Education. (1978). *Violent schools–safe schools: The Safe School Study report to the Congress.* Washington, DC: U.S. Department of Education.

Stephens, R. D. (1994a). Planning for safer and better schools: School violence prevention and intervention strategies. *School Psychology Review, 23*(2).

Stephens, R. D. (1994b, September). Planning for safer, more effective schools. *The High School Magazine,* pp. 4–8.

Stephens, R. D. (1995). *Safe schools: A handbook for violence prevention.* Bloomington, IN: National Educational Service.

Stephens, R. D. (1996, February). The art of safe school planning. *The School Administrator,* pp. 14–21.

Virginia Association of School Superintendents. (1992). *Violence in the schools,* p. 9. Charlottesville, VA: Author.

IV. Community-Based Interventions

10. Exposure to Urban Violence: Contamination of the School Environment

RAYMOND P. LORION

Introduction

This chapter examines how exposure to urban violence threatens the physical health, mental health, and educational effectiveness of those who learn, teach, and work in schools. Students, teachers, and other school staff may be exposed to urban violence in their neighborhoods, on their journey to and from school, in the school's neighborhood, or within the school itself. Whether occurring in a single setting or multiple settings, exposure to violence generates a sense of fear and leads to acts intended to reduce or control the fear. Exposure may also produce generalized emotional distress; disruptions in interpersonal relationships; problems with aggression; and, potentially, an array of cognitive, physical, and psychological dysfunctions. The effects of exposure experienced by some portion of a school's students, teachers, and staff may spread to others within that setting. As this "contagion" occurs, the school setting changes in ways that negatively alter the interactions among those within the school and that interfere with the school's capacity to achieve its educational and social goals.

In the past, community violence has been analyzed in terms of crime, using statistics (e.g., the Uniform Crime Report rates) to reveal the frequency and nature of criminal acts. These crime statistics clarify the forms of antisocial and violent behavior occurring within a setting; many of the socioeconomic, racial/ethnic, and family characteristics of both victims and perpetrators; the rates of physical injury and death associated with the violence; and the resources the community has invested in an attempt to control the violence (Lorion, Tolan, & Wahler, 1987). By contrast, this chapter focuses on the *setting* itself. To appreciate the public health implications of urban violence, one needs to understand the influence of the setting where violence occurs on the health and behavior of those exposed to these settings. (For information about a public health approach to preventing violence, see Chapter 2 of this volume.)

Definition of Terms

Before we begin, several key terms require definition. "Violence" refers to the intentional use, or threat to use force, to cause intentional injury, harm, or death to another. The qualifier "intentional" excludes from consideration injury and death resulting from unintended or accidental acts of violence. The "consequences of exposure to violent acts" refer to the effects experienced by: (1) individuals directly victimized; (2) individuals indirectly victimized because of their status as a bystander, witness, acquaintance, or loved one of a victim; and (3) individuals indirectly victimized by their awareness of, and anxiety about, the occurrence of violence within settings they occupy.

The term "community violence" locates violent acts and their consequences in a geographic setting (e.g., a neighborhood or school), an identifiable social grouping (e.g., a school class, a gang, or a nuclear or extended family), or in both. Information is now being gathered about the rates of violence within different communities and about the rates of encounters with violence by their residents. Thus far, this work has primarily focused on the urban environment; considerably less is known about the nature, frequency, and consequences of violence in suburban and rural communities. For urban settings, however, social scientists are beginning to document the health, mental health, and behavioral effects of exposure to violence.

Conceiving of exposure to violence as "toxic" implies that violence can negatively alter the sociocultural character of a setting. "Contamination" refers to the spread of these negative effects from those who have been exposed to violence to others in the setting. This ripple effect may, for example, result in increased fear and vigilance among the acquaintances of those directly exposed. Consequently, exposure to violence may cause an increase within the setting of feelings of vulnerability, or may cause people to assume that aggressive responses are both acceptable and necessary. Assumptions about the threatening quality of others, about the need to limit one's contact with others, and about the urgency of responding aggressively to actual or anticipated attacks may also color one's sense of the setting. This chapter examines the effect on the school environment as increasing proportions of its students, teachers, and staff are victimized by violence, feel vulnerable to such victimization, and engage in actions intended to reduce their actual or assumed vulnerability.

The Importance of Understanding Exposure

Schools are communities in their own right, but they are also located within a larger community, the neighborhood. Students and teachers also bring to the school their experiences with violence in the neighborhoods in which they live (Sarason, 1996). Contacts with any and all of these communities shape how students and teachers think about violence and the assumptions they make about each other. In this sense, therefore, a school setting is "contaminated" by the attitudes, expectations, and behaviors that students and teachers carry from other settings into the school, as well as by their immediate experiences within the school. Whatever its source, widespread concern about violence within a school may reduce the quality of teaching, disrupt classroom discipline, and limit teachers' availability to students before or after the school day. This same quality may reduce students' motivation to attend school, willingness to participate in extracurricular activities, and capacity to attend to and care about academic matters.

Concern with violence may similarly influence parent/child, parent/teacher, and teacher/teacher interactions. Responding to the nationwide Metropolitan Life Survey of the American Teacher, for example, teachers associated students' involvement in violent acts with parents' failure to provide supervision at home (Leitman & Binns, 1993). Other findings from this survey reveal that teachers in schools with many low-income students and poorly achieving students have very little confidence in parents' concern with or involvement in their children's schoolwork. Such attitudes make contact between homes and the school unlikely, and may prevent even the consideration of programs to involve parents in school-based activities.

In this survey (Leitman & Binns, 1993), teachers in schools marked by violence also reported their colleagues as hesitant to discipline students. If widely held in a school, such views may lead teachers to assume that ignoring violent behavior by students in class is both wise and expected. These findings support the impression that corrosive effects on settings are reflected in teachers, students, and staff behaving in ways that confirm their feelings of vulnerability and encourage them to respond to each other in a detached and self-protective manner. Understanding which factors determine the social climate of schools could help to organize and manage classrooms in ways that optimize students' learning and development of social skills. It may also increase interest in appreciating the positive and negative health consequences of a psychological sense of community, that is, of students' and teachers' sense that they value their association with the school (Brodsky, 1996; Iscoe, 1974; Macmillan, 1996).

Violence and Schools

The focus on school contexts in this chapter is not simply a convenient or arbitrary choice of social settings. Schools, especially those with large numbers of adolescents, are settings with special potential for violence as well as special potential to help children overcome the effects of exposure to violence. Levine and Rosich (1996) explain:

> Because of the salience of youth violence, the school is an important context for study. It is the single social institution where large groups of youth are located and where predatory violence, aggressive behaviors or conflicts with the potential to escalate into violence can occur. Even though research on school violence is limited, we know enough to recognize that what happens in schools can either increase the risk of violence or buffer children from it. (p. 27)

The media have repeatedly observed that exposure to urban violence is a serious concern for educators. As noted by Gardner and Resnik (1996), the media's attention to violence and its consequences both informs the public and "unfortunately . . . help[s] to perpetuate some common myths and stereotypes [about who commits violent acts and why] that will make it even more difficult to break the cycle" (p. 170). The "cycle" to which they refer is the assumed causal connection between media reports and portrayals of violence and individuals' involvement in violent acts, which, in turn, are reported by the print or broadcast media. The elimination of violent themes from television, movies, popular music, and video games is increasingly recognized as both unlikely and insufficient to eliminate the problem (American Psychological Association Commission on Violence and Youth, 1993; Gardner & Resnik, 1996; Gerbner, 1994). Rather, the emergence of a "culture of violence" in some schools must be acknowledged, understood, and countered. The quality of that culture is becoming known. Within the school setting, acts of violence range from verbal hassling to abuse; from poking and pushing others (mostly, but not exclusively, students) as they move down a hallway, to knocking them over; from verbal threats to acts of assault and even homicide; from vandalism to robbery to rape. As described by Beland (1996):

> In schools, teachers find themselves spending increasing amounts of time attending to students' disruptive and angry outbursts, interpersonal conflicts, and off-task behavior, or worse. Every day, ap-

proximately 100,000 children are assaulted at school, 5,000 teachers are threatened with physical assault, and 200 are actually attacked (Geiger, 1993). Although teachers are expected to concentrate on teaching academics, they are finding that student behavior prevents them from doing so; eventually it drives many of them from the teaching profession. (p. 209)

Such data support Phillips's (1993) conclusion that "the social and economic costs of school violence have reached alarming proportions over the last two decades" (p. 157). They also support the findings of the Metropolitan Life Survey that exposure to violence most affects students and teachers in urban schools marked by high levels of poverty and low academic achievement (Leitman & Binns, 1993).

Whatever the specific experiences of students and teachers, their behavior in such settings becomes understandable when considered in terms of the context. Before implementing interventions to prevent violence that impose expectations on others (e.g., teachers, parents, and peers) who are assumed to be available to support students at risk for violence, one must measure the demands the setting makes on those others. As noted previously, many teachers suffer injuries at the hands of aggressive students (Beland, 1996). Others feel tense throughout the day. Presently, little is known about the emotional toll taken on teachers who fear their students and dread their work settings. Even less is known about how the atmosphere within such settings influences personal interactions generally, and the expression of anger and aggression between faculty and students and within each of these groups.

Documenting Exposure

Before one can design interventions to control the effects of exposure to urban violence, one must document its occurrence and impact. Are many children frequently exposed to violence in our country? Most of the research studying this subject relies on the questionnaire used in Richters and Saltzman's (1990) Survey of Children's Exposure to Community Violence. After surveying children in different populations and settings, Richters and associates, as well as other researchers, found that many children in the United States are indeed exposed to violence (see Lorion & Saltzman, 1993; Martinez & Richters, 1993; Osofsky, Wewers, Hann, & Fick, 1993; Richters & Martinez, 1993; see also Hill & Madhere, 1996; Singer et al., 1995).

Adding to this information, Jenkins and her associates studied African American children's encounters with violence (Bell, Hildreth, Jenkins,

Levi, & Carter, 1988; Bell & Jenkins, 1993; Jenkins & Thompson, 1986). They interviewed students enrolled in grades 2–12 about: (1) knowing someone who was a victim of violence; (2) having witnessed violent events in *real life;* (3) having been a victim of a violent incident; and (4) having perpetrated a violent act.

Table 10.1, utilizing data from five studies, lists the percentages of children in several age groups and grade levels who were victims of, or had witnessed, specific types of violence themselves.[1]

Table 10.1 reveals that the percentage of children surveyed who had been exposed to various types of violence varied greatly across settings (ranging from none to percentages in the mid forties), but confirms that exposure is primarily an urban experience. Apfel and Simon (1996), speaking of communities characterized by "communal violence," described them as settings in which *"every child* has witnessed or expects to witness violence and has been or expects to be violated" (pp. 4–5; my emphasis). Although that statement is not literally true of any of the settings studied thus far, it is evident that some children in some urban settings do have frequent encounters with violence, a pattern confirmed in Leitman and Binns' (1993) report on the Metropolitan Life Survey.

Although exposure to violence cannot be described as being at "epidemic" proportions in all of the nation's schools, findings from the Metropolitan Life Survey and the data in Table 10.1 indicate students and teachers in some urban schools regularly confront violence. Such schools are characterized by high proportions of students from impoverished families and by inadequate academic performance. Most of the violence to which students are exposed occurs in their home neighborhoods and in the neighborhood surrounding the school rather than in the school itself. Nevertheless, significant violence occurs in schools. Approximately one in eight students reports carrying some form of weapon to school, and significant numbers of students report having seen or discussed violent events in school. The most frequently reported forms of violence in school are pushing and shoving. At the same time, a sizable minority (approximately 20%) of students report that threats involving a weapon and forms of assault in school represent a major problem for them (Leitman & Binns, 1993).

Schools with High Levels of Exposure

My own interest in focusing on exposure to violence as a setting characteristic of schools derives from personal observations in urban schools and from research I conducted there. Awareness of students' sense of vulnerability became, for me, an inescapable aspect of conducting school-based research. Each year, this awareness intensified as I returned to the same schools. In discussing with me the design for a substance involvement survey and an associated drug prevention program in 1988, the principal of a Maryland elementary school argued that students' lives were at far greater risk from bullets and bullies than from cigarettes and drugs. He described how, at the end of each day, he had to "sweep the school" and send home children who were afraid to return to violent neighborhoods and homes. His comments led me to include questions concerning exposure to violence in my survey.

Two years later, another elementary school principal described how, almost daily, she received teacher reports of children unable to sit calmly or attend to lessons, seemingly because of fear and constant vigilance. Such students were known by teachers to have been exposed to events such as exchanges of gunfire or encounters with a lifeless or bleeding victim of violence. The principal explained that order was difficult to maintain in the hallways and on the playground as children excitedly competed to relate the most violent encounter. In these verbal exchanges, the students often denied their fear and appeared to identify and empathize more with the perpetrators than the victims.

This principal expressed the most concern about the reactions of many perpetrators of violence against other students when brought to her office. She sensed their lack of guilt, regret, or empathy for the pain they inflicted.[2,3] Within six months she announced her retirement, because of the haunting sense that increasing numbers of her students had become numb to issues of life and death, pain and suffering, and hope for the future. Tearfully, she explained she could no longer attend funerals of students or their loved ones.

In a third school, middle school students described to me the sexual and aggressive tension pervading the hallways with each change of class. In their words, "anything" (e.g., an unwanted look, touch, or rumor) might trigger a fight. To avoid a serious, and potentially dangerous, confrontation, touches often elicited no overt response. At other times, the failure to respond was considered especially risky. Students described the need to be vigilant throughout the day and to decide which response was appropriate under which conditions. Depending on those involved, it was essential they be prepared to respond with equal or greater intensity to a provocation (real or imagined). As the students explained, a violent event was likely to occur as retaliation for some "offense" past, present, or future. For this reason, they rarely relaxed in that middle school.

Table 10.1. *Percentage of youths reporting direct and indirect exposure to violence across five studies*

	Percentage who had been victims of an event						
	Richters & Martinez, 1993 Parents' report		Martinez & Richters, 1993 Childrens' report		Osofsky et al., 1993	Bell & Jenkins, 1993	Saltzman, 1992
N	77	51	—	37	53	997	170
Grade level	1-2	5-6	1-2	5-6	—	—	5-6
Age	—	—	—	—	9-12	16-19	9-13
Setting	Urban	Urban	Urban	Urban	Urban	Urban	Urban
Gender (M/F)	51/49	52/48	—	—	—	—	51/49
Shooting	3	6	—	11	—	—	—
Stabbing	1	4	—	6	0	3.2	14
Sexual assaults	0	2	—	22	1.9	4.3	15
Mugging	9	8	—	6	3.8	2.5	—
Physical threat	5	14	—	47	—	—	23
Drug trade	4	6	—	9	—	—	31
Drug use	1	4	—	0	—	—	—
Arrest	—	—	—	11	—	—	—
Punch/hit/slap	—	—	—	—	—	—	—
Illegal weapon	—	—	—	—	—	—	71
Forced entry/other	3	6	—	37	—	—	—
Forced entry	—	—	—	3	—	—	—
Dead body outside	—	—	—	—	—	—	19
Murder	—	—	—	—	—	—	—
Suicide	—	—	—	—	—	—	—
Woundings	—	—	—	—	—	—	—
Serious accidents	—	—	—	—	—	15.9	33
Weapons used	—	—	—	—	—	10.9	—
Robbery	—	—	—	—	—	—	—

Percentage who had witnessed an event

	Richters & Martinez, 1993 Parents' report		Martinez & Richters, 1993 Childrens' report		Osofsky et al., 1993	Bell & Jenkins, 1993	Saltzman, 1992
N	77	51	—	37	53	997	170
Grade level	1–2	5–6	1–2	5–6	—	—	5–6
Age	—	—	—	—	9–12	16–19	9–13
Setting	Urban	Urban	Urban	Urban	Urban	Urban	Urban
Gender (M/F)	51/49	52/48	—	—	—	—	51/49
Shooting	9	14	47	31	—	—	—
Stabbing	13	4	31	17	26.4	39.4	26
Sexual assaults	1	4	—	43	18.9	34.6	30
Mugging	25	43	45	3	3.8	—	—
Physical threat	17	18	—	22	—	—	41
Drug trade	5	12	—	67	—	—	43
Drug use	53	61	69	22	—	—	—
Arrest	37	20	88	74	—	—	—
Punch/hit/slap	39	38	—	44	—	—	—
Illegal weapon	18	20	—	58	—	—	73
Forced entry/other	5	10	—	39	—	—	—
Forced entry	5	0	—	14	—	—	—
Dead body outside	16	16	37	23	39.6	—	24
Murder	3	4	—	9	5.7	23.5	43
Suicide	0	3	—	3	1.9	—	15
Woundings	—	—	—	29	49.1	—	—
Serious accidents	11	—	—	74	71.7	—	50
Weapons used	—	—	—	—	—	55.1	48
Robbery	—	—	—	—	—	—	—

Data Sources: Bell & Jenkins, 1993; Martinez & Richters, 1993; Osofsky et al., 1993; Richters & Martinez, 1993; Saltzman, 1992.

Participating in focus group discussions on school violence, some high school students proudly boasted to me of the ease with which they could intimidate other students, teachers, and school staff. They echoed the view that tension was always present in their school buildings, playgrounds, and buses. Academic work, for students there, was viewed as secondary to the need to recognize warning signs of impending trouble. Among the participants in the focus groups, fatigue and tension seemed widespread. Drugs, sex, and violence seemed to have merged into a mosaic of options to reduce their pervasive sense of vulnerability and tension. One student, in fact, noted he used alcohol to help him handle the day's tensions.

I observed both urban and suburban schools. Many, but not all, of the students in these schools received reduced cost or free lunches. Many students were "latchkey kids," while others went home to a waiting parent or responsible caretaker. Many students described their trip to and from school as very tense because of actual or threatened conflicts encountered along the way. Because of parental concerns about safety, many students in these schools (regardless of grade level) were confined to their homes during non-school hours. One parent described this practice to me as a necessary form of "protective custody"; their children likened it to "house arrest."

Exposure and Emotional Distress

Scientific evidence of these observations continues to be found. Research to date supports the conclusion that exposure to violence is psychologically toxic. Saltzman (1992), for example, observed significantly higher levels of generalized emotional distress in fifth and sixth graders who reported the highest levels of exposure to violence. Support for this link is provided by several studies (Bell & Jenkins, 1993; Hill & Madhere, 1996; Martinez & Richters, 1993; Osofsky et al., 1993; Richters & Martinez, 1993). In addition to finding a similar association between exposure and reported feelings of depression, anxiety, anger, and general stress, Singer and colleagues (1995) noted low scores for self-esteem and social competence among those adolescents reporting high levels of exposure to violence.

In numerous studies, exposed children reported both emotional and physical symptoms of depression and many indications of stress-related disorders. They were more likely to describe themselves as feeling sad, anxious, and afraid. They reported difficulty attending to schoolwork, had trouble concentrating, and found it difficult not to be distracted by memories of traumatic events and sights. Exposed children have, understandably, been described as suffering from post-traumatic stress disorder (PTSD)

(Eth & Pynoos, 1985), the severe anxiety experienced by many Vietnam War veterans. Except for the fact that for many children exposure is an ongoing rather than a past experience, the diagnosis of PTSD seems quite appropriate.

Exposure and Aggressive Behavior

It is reasonable to ask whether exposure to violence is related to a person's subsequent antisocial and violent behavior. In their study of nearly 4,000 high school students, Singer and his associates (1994, 1995) found a significant link between exposure to violence and increased aggression, conduct disorder, and truancy. Exposed youths (especially males) were more likely to engage in "preventive" violence (i.e., to hit someone before being hit); to use a weapon; and to otherwise engage in aggressive, predatory behavior. In a study of 225 urban African American adolescents, researchers also found a significant relationship between exposure to and involvement in aggressive and violent acts (Durant et al., 1994).

In his study of nearly 2,000 high school students, Saltzman (1995) found exposure significantly predicted involvement in antisocial and violent acts, independent of peer, family, and other factors known to contribute to such behavior. Rubinetti's (1996) preliminary study of the specific factors linking exposure with aggressive and violent behavior suggests involvement in violent activities is most likely to be found in youths with decreased levels of empathy, hopefulness, and self-esteem, the very symptoms generally found in exposed youths.

Effect of Exposure on Learning and Teaching Abilities

Exposure has measurable effects on cognitive, psychological, and physical functions related to learning and teaching (see Hill & Madhere, 1996; Osofsky et al., 1993; Richters & Martinez, 1993; Saltzman, 1992, 1995; Singer et al., 1995). For example, exposure appears to influence cognitive functions known to affect learning, such as arousal, memory, concentration, abstract reasoning, vigilance, and emotional reactivity (Singer et al., 1995). The cognitive effects have significant implications for what and how teachers teach, and for what and how students can learn. Exposure also appears related to rapid fluctuation of emotions, and, as previously noted, to a lack of empathy, to depression, anxiety, hopelessness, and an inability to control impulses (see, e.g., Lorion & Saltzman, 1993; Martinez & Richters, 1993; Rubinetti, 1996; Saltzman, 1995; Singer et al., 1995). These emotional states affect learning and have implications for instructional methods, classroom management techniques, and school discipline, and also for evaluating the emotional status of students, teachers, and other school staff.

The extent to which exposure negatively affects basic physical functions such as digestion, metabolism, the immune system, the growth rate in children, sleep-wake cycles, and dream patterns has yet to be studied systematically. Some links have already been reported. If such links continue to be confirmed,[4] it is likely exposure has an impact on the physical comfort, stamina, and well-being of students, teachers, and staff as they carry out their respective responsibilities in schools. Inconsistent attendance due to tardiness or absenteeism due to physical illness, fatigue, or stress in either a teacher or student can further disrupt not only their respective teaching and learning experiences but those of other students as well. Very preliminary findings have been gathered relating exposure to violence in late adolescence to self-reported sleeping disorders, chronic fatigue (not to be confused with "chronic fatigue syndrome," or the Epstein-Barr virus), and a low startle threshold (Cooley-Quill, personal communication, February 11, 1997).

Confirmation that exposure can cause chronic fatigue and constant vigilance may provide new explanations for such students' academic difficulties, reliance on preventive violence, and for their aggressive or defensive responses to ambiguous personal interactions. Stress-related physiological changes might negatively alter the behavior of children or teachers observed in a classroom or on a playground. Fatigue combined with constant vigilance, for example, might reduce a student's or teacher's acceptance of ambiguity or tolerance for stress. In either case, a quality of the setting becomes the link between any provocation and retaliatory or even preventive aggression on the part of a student or a disciplinary response on the part of a teacher.

The Effect of Exposure on the Setting

Evidence is mounting that exposure to violence has toxic consequences for emotional, behavioral, cognitive, and overall physical functioning. It is likely the effects of exposure documented thus far combine, in ways yet to be understood, to increasingly erode an individual's resistance to further exposure. As a result of behavior by those exposed, it is likely school settings become qualitatively different and acquire characteristics that not only result in further exposure but also exacerbate the effects. Theories linking environmental characteristics to emotional and behavioral development in children can help to clarify how exposure changes settings.

More than six decades ago, Lewin (1935) asserted the importance of environmental factors in interpreting human behavior. In his theory of "psychological ecology" (1944), he argued there is a process of mutual influence, or a "transaction," between the individual and the environment, and if one studies the characteristics of the environment and the individual, one can to a fair degree predict behavior.

If one applies Lewin's theory to violent acts occurring in a school, one can analyze them by determining when, how, and where they occur; who is present at the time; and how each person present interprets the events and the options available for responding to those events. The way in which those elements combine gives meaning to the violent act and determines how it will influence subsequent events. Among those events are the responses of others to the violence; the likelihood of its continuation by its perpetrator(s); and the likelihood of its adoption by others. As noted later in this chapter, one potential outcome is that those exposed come to see others' acts as threatening and aggressive, whether they are so or not. As a result of this process, violence becomes a defining and expected part of the school environment.

Schoggen (1989) argued that studies of settings ought to focus especially on "the ecological environment," or "the objectively observable *standing patterns of behavior* of people – that is specific sequences of people's behavior that regularly occur within particular settings" (p. 2). Barker and his colleagues determined that knowledge of situational characteristics of particular school settings resulted in better prediction of children's behavior than knowledge of the characteristics of individual children (Barker, 1968; Barker & Gump, 1964; Barker & Schoggen, 1973; Barker & Wright, 1951; Schoggen, 1989). Across a number of settings, children acted more like each other within a given setting than like themselves across settings.

Barker and his colleagues used the concept of "behavior settings" to describe such person-setting linkages. Wicker (1979) explains this process as follows:

> Behavior settings are self-regulating, active systems. They impose their program of activities on the persons and objects within them. Essential persons and materials are drawn into settings, and disruptive components are modified or ejected. It's as if behavior settings were living systems intent on remaining alive and healthy, even at the expense of their individual components. . . .
>
> . . . to summarize some of the essential features of behavior settings. Most of them can be presented in a single sentence: A behavior setting is a bounded, self-regulated, and ordered system composed of

replaceable human and nonhuman components that interact in a synchronized fashion to carry out an ordered sequence of events called the setting program. (p. 12)

Although the potential of Barker's theory has yet to be fully mined, his concept of behavior setting offers one avenue for understanding the influence of exposure to violence on school climates. (See also Levine & Perkins, 1987; Moos & Insel, 1974; Wandersman & Hess, 1985, for illustrations of the potential richness of this perspective.) The work of Barker and his colleagues suggests that schools with high levels of exposure will "pull" for aggressive and defensive behaviors generally and violent reactions specifically (see, e.g., Barker, 1968; Barker & Gump, 1964; Barker & Schoggen, 1973; Barker & Wright, 1951; Schoggen, 1989). According to Barker's theory, students tend to respond aggressively and defensively to ambiguity; teachers are likely to interpret ambiguous behaviors and situations as threatening and to anticipate violent rather than nonviolent responses. Increasingly, in such settings, the behavior of individuals becomes motivated by fear and anxiety and organized around the avoidance or control of violence, aggression, and a sense of vulnerability.

How setting characteristics translate into behavioral patterns is explained, in somewhat clearer detail, in transactional models that have evolved from Lewin's original work (1935, 1944). Bronfenbrenner's (1977, 1979) focus on how individual development (e.g., intelligence quotient, or IQ; temperament) and setting (e.g., parental responsiveness) influence one another led Sameroff (Sameroff & Chandler, 1975; Sameroff & Fiese, 1989) to propose a model for understanding the causes of developmental problems. In Sameroff's view, a child's emotional and behavioral development emerge through an ongoing sequence of transactions among: (1) responses by an individual to situational circumstances and demands; (2) alterations of those situational circumstances and demands as a function of the individual's responses; and (3) responses by an individual to that altered situation. Within Sameroff's model, individuals and settings evolve continually over time. This element of the theory suggests behavior can be positively shaped through controlled changes in the individual, the context, or both.

Sameroff's model offers a basis for linking variations in behavior to settings. In effect, unyielding settings would constrain behaviors within certain well-defined parameters. In the most recent version of the model, Sameroff and Fiese (1989) explicitly say that societal (and, presumably, setting and subgroup) expectations influence people's definitions of the behavioral roles available to them and, in that way, set contextual limitations on developmental outcomes. If the behavioral expectations and definitions in a school are for violent encounters and intentions, the elements are present for the school (or certain parts of the building) to become behavior settings for violence. Leitman and Binns's (1993) findings that school locker rooms, restrooms, and hallways are perceived by students as the primary sites for violence may confirm this view.

Integrating Transactional and Environmental Perspectives

Barker's (1968) work, especially in schools (e.g., Barker & Gump, 1964), stresses the fact that educational settings generally, and their components (e.g., classrooms, gyms, hallways) in particular, are *existing* behavior settings. The question, therefore, is not solely whether exposure to violence is sufficient to influence behavioral demands but also whether it is sufficient to alter behavioral demands already operative within a setting. In essence, does exposure change either the physical characteristics or the shared assumptions about how people are expected to behave within school settings? If so, how?

The answers to both of these questions depend on resolving a series of issues. First, can exposure to violence be reliably and validly measured? (This issue appears to have been resolved previously in this chapter.) Second, can its presence and level be consistently associated with distinct behavioral patterns? Work to date has begun to provide a body of evidence confirming links between exposure to and the perpetration of violent acts. What must be studied, however, are the behavioral responses of those whose exposure leads to avoidance and withdrawal rather than retaliation. Third, can the mechanisms by which exposure negatively changes existing behavioral expectations in a school be controlled in order to reverse the pattern? Can schools marked by high levels of exposure to violence be "reshaped" to reduce both the occurrence and the negative effects of exposure? An answer to this question depends on the success with which interventions, based in schools, neighborhoods, or both, can be designed, implemented, and evaluated.

Conclusion

Exposure to urban violence has a potentially powerful toxic effect on many different settings. If inescapable and uncontrolled, exposure may corrode the positive effects of any of the human resources within any of the settings. Within schools, general resources include the students, teachers, and staff, as well as the opportunities for learning in classrooms, the library, on athletic fields, and in other settings. For those resources to be used, however, those who come to school to learn, teach, or work must feel secure in the setting and trust each other's intentions. Interventions to reduce violent incidents in schools have been reviewed by Tolan and Guerra (1994), and are also discussed in other chapters of this volume.

As noted, however, much of the violence to which students are exposed does not occur in schools but in the neighborhoods surrounding schools and in the neighborhoods in which the students live (Leitman & Binns, 1993). Thus, interventions must be designed that allow students, teachers, and staff to experience the school setting as a "no-fire zone," free both of violence and exaggerated attention to its occurrence. To achieve that positive status, schools will have to join with their surrounding communities in violence prevention efforts, and open their doors during nonschool hours to serve as safe havens where children can play and engage in positive, developmentally valuable academic, interpersonal, and recreational activities. Schools must design programs that detect traumatized students, teachers, and staff, and offer access to crisis intervention or stress management resources. Most important of all, responding to the toxic consequences of exposure to violence requires educators and the community to understand the reality of exposure and its negative effects.

Notes

1. Test-retest reliability (at a one-week interval) for the "Things I Have Seen and Heard" scale with a small sample (N=21) was 81. Only limited reliability information is available for other survey scales.
2. This same observation is noted in a striking description by Gardner and Resnik (1996) of a group of high school students' reactions to the film about the Holocaust entitled *Schindler's List* (1994, MCA Universal Films). The striking thing about these students was "their inability to empathize with the human suffering being portrayed." The authors commented, "This incident reinforces the notion that young people today are hardened to violence because of their constant exposure to it through the media" (p. 167).
3. Rubinetti (1996) reports additional evidence of the link between lack of empathy and the perpetration of violent acts in her study of adolescent participants in a juvenile court diversion program. Rubinetti found the connection between exposure and involvement in antisocial and violent acts appeared to be the participants' resulting sense of hopelessness, lack of empathy, and low self-esteem. Similarly, Beauford (1994) observed success of a conflict mediation program for middle school students' academic and psychosocial functioning depended on their acquisition of social-interpersonal skills and a sense of self-efficacy.
4. The author and colleagues are designing a series of studies to examine these as-

pects of exposure in cross-sectional samples ranging from preschoolers to young adults.

References

American Psychological Association Commission on Violence and Youth. (1993). *Violence and youth: Psychology's Response. Vol. I: Summary report of the American Psychological Association Commission on Violence and Youth.* Washington, DC: American Psychological Association.

Apfel, R. J., & Simon, B. (Eds.). (1996). *Minefields in their hearts.* New Haven, CN: Yale University Press.

Barker, R. G. (1968). *Ecological psychology.* Stanford, CA: Stanford University Press.

Barker, R. G., & Gump, P. V. (1964). *Big school, small school: High school size and student behavior.* Stanford, CA: Stanford University Press.

Barker, R. G., & Schoggen, P. (1973). *Qualities of community life: Methods of measuring environment and behavior applied to an American and an English town.* San Francisco: Jossey-Bass.

Barker, R. G., & Wright, H. F. (1951). *One boy's day.* New York: Harper & Row.

Beauford, J. (1994). "Social problem solving, empathy and self-worth as factors which "insulate" children against maladaptive school outcome." Unpublished doctoral dissertation, University of Maryland, College Park.

Beland, K. R. (1996). A schoolwide approach to violence prevention. In R. L. Hampton, P. Jenkins, & T. P. Gullota (Eds.), *Preventing violence in America* (pp. 209–232). Thousand Oaks, CA: Sage.

Bell, C. C., Hildreth, C. J., Jenkins, E. J., Levi, D., & Carter, C. (1988). The need for victimization screening in a poor, outpatient medical population. *Journal of the American Medical Association, 80,* 853–860.

Bell, C. C., & Jenkins, E. J. (1993). Community violence and children on Chicago's southside. *Psychiatry: Interpersonal and Biological Processes, 56,* 46–54.

Brodsky, A. E. (1996). Resilient single mothers in risky neighborhoods: Negative psychological sense of community. *Journal of Community Psychology, 24,* 347–364.

Bronfenbrenner, U. (1977). Toward an experimental ecology of human development. *American Psychologist, 32,* 513–531.

Bronfenbrenner, U. (1979). *The ecology of human development.* Cambridge, MA: Harvard University Press.

Durant, D. H., Cadenhead, C., Pendergast, R. A., Slavens, G., & Linder, C. W. (1994). Factors associated with use of violence among urban black adolescents. *American Journal of Public Health, 84,* 612–617.

Eth, S., & Pynoos, R. (Eds.). (1985). *Post-traumatic stress disorder in children.* Washington, DC: American Psychiatric Press.

Gardner, S. E., & Resnik, H. (1996). Violence among youth: Origins and a framework for prevention. In R. L. Hampton, P. Jenkins, & T. P. Gullota (Eds.), *Preventing violence in America* (pp. 157–178). Thousand Oaks, CA: Sage.

Geiger, K. (1993, January 14). *Violence in the schools.* Statement presented at a news conference given by the president of the National Education Association, Washington, DC.

Gerbner, G. (1994). *Violence and drugs on television: The cultural environment approach to prevention.* Philadelphia, PA: Annenberg School for Communication.

Hill, H. M., & Madhere, S. (1996). Exposure to community violence and African American children: A multidimensional model of risks and resources. *Journal of Community Psychology, 24,* 26–43.

Iscoe, I. (1974). Community psychology and the competent community. *American Psychologist, 29,* 607–613.

Jenkins, E. J., & Thompson, B. (1986, April). *Children talk about violence: Preliminary findings from a survey of black elementary school children.* Paper presented at the Nineteenth Annual Convention of the Association of Black Psychologists, Oakland, CA.

Leitman, R., & Binns, K. (1993). *The Metropolitan Life survey of the American teacher – 1993: Violence in America's public schools.* New York: Louis Harris and Associates.

Levine, M., & Perkins, D. V. (1987). *Principles of community psychology: Perspectives and applications.* New York: Oxford University Press.

Levine, F. J., & Rosich, K. J. (1996). *Social causes of violence: Crafting a science agenda.* Washington, DC: American Sociological Association.

Lewin, K. (1935). *A dynamic theory of personality: Selected papers* (D. K. Adams, trans.). New York: McGraw-Hill.

Lewin, K. (1944). Constraints in psychology and psychological ecology. *University of Iowa Studies in Child Welfare, 20,* 17–20.

Lorion, R. P., & Saltzman, W. (1993). Children's exposure to community violence: Following a path from concern to research to action. *Psychiatry: Interpersonal and Biological Processes, 56,* 55–65.

Lorion, R. P., Tolan, P. H., & Wahler, R. G. (1987). Prevention. In H. C. Quay (Ed.), *Handbook of juvenile delinquency* (pp. 383–416). New York: John Wiley & Sons.

Macmillan, D. W. (1996). Sense of community. *Journal of Community Psychology, 24,* 315–326.

Martinez, P., & Richters, J. E. (1993). The NIMH Community Violence Project, II: Children's distress symptoms associated with violence exposure. *Psychiatry: Interpersonal and Biological Processes, 56,* 22–35.

Moos, R. H., & Insel, P. M. (Eds.). (1974). *Issues in social ecology.* Palo Alto, CA: National Press.

Osofsky, J. D., Wewers, S., Hann, D. M., & Fick, A. C. (1993). Chronic community violence: What is happening to our children? *Psychiatry: Interpersonal and Biological Processes, 56,* 36–45.

Phillips, B. N. (1993). *Educational and psychological perspectives on stress in students, teachers and parents.* Brandon, VT: Clinical Psychology Publishing.

Richters, J. E., & Martinez, P. (1993). The NIMH Community Violence Project, I: Children as victims of and witnesses to violence. *Psychiatry: Interpersonal and Biological Processes, 56,* 7–21.

Richters, J. E., & Saltzman, W. (1990). "Survey of exposure to community violence: Parent report version." Unpublished measure, National Institute of Mental Health, Child and Adolescent Disorders Research.

Rubinetti, F. (1996). "Empathy, self-esteem, hopelessness. and belief in the legitimacy of aggression in adolescents exposed to pervasive community violence." Unpublished doctoral dissertation. University of Maryland, College Park.

Saltzman, W. R. (1992). "The effect of children's exposure to community violence." Unpublished master's thesis, University of Maryland, College Park.

Saltzman, W. R. (1995). *Exposure to community violence and the prediction of violent antisocial behavior in a multi-ethnic sample of adolescents.* Unpublished doctoral dissertation, University of Maryland, College Park.

Sameroff, A. J., & Chandler, M. J. (1975). Reproductive risk and the continuum of caretaking casualty. In F. D. Horowitz, M. Hetherington, S. Scarr-Salapatek, & G. Siegel (Eds.), *Review of child development research* (Vol. 4) (pp. 187–244). Chicago: University of Chicago Press.

Sameroff, A. J., & Fiese, B. H. (1989). Conceptual issues in prevention. In D. Shaffer, I. Phillips, & N. B. Enzer (Eds.), *Prevention of mental disorders, alcohol and other drug use in children and adolescents* (DHHS Publication No. [ADM] 89–1646) (pp. 23–54). Rockville, MD: Department of Health and Human Services, Office for Substance Abuse Prevention.

Sarason, S. B. (1996). *Revisiting "the culture of the school and the problem of change."* New York: Teachers College Press.

Schoggen, P. (1989). *Behavior settings: A revision and extension of Roger G. Barker's* Ecological Psychology. Stanford, CA: Stanford University Press.

Singer, M. I., Anglin, T. M., Song, L., & Lunghofer, L. (1994). *The mental health consequences of adolescents' exposure to violence.* Cleveland, OH: Case Western Reserve University.

Singer, M. I., Anglin, T. M., Song, L., & Lunghofer, L. (1995). Adolescents' exposure to violence and associated symptoms of psychological trauma. *Journal of the American Medical Association, 273,* 477–482.

Tolan, P., & Guerra, N. (1994). *What works in reducing adolescent violence: An empirical review of the field.* Boulder, CO: University of Colorado, Center for the Study and Prevention of Violence.

Wandersman, A., & Hess, R. (1985). *Beyond the individual: Environmental approaches and prevention.* New York: Haworth Press.

Wicker, A. W. (1979). *An introduction to ecological psychology.* Monterey, CA: Brooks/Cole.

11. Community Policing, Schools, and Mental Health: The Challenge of Collaboration

STEVEN MARANS & MARK SCHAEFER

Introduction

The epidemic of youth violence in our nation is both the result of and a major contributor to serious developmental damage to many American children. The crisis is a clarion call, requiring one to rethink the ways in which educational, mental health, and law enforcement services are delivered, in order to achieve a primary focus on the mental health of the family and child.

A public health model for understanding and enhancing the relationship between children, families, and basic community services is presented in Chapter 2 of this volume. The public health perspective adds needed new dimensions to the understanding of the nature and scope of the youth violence epidemic, as well as bringing new concepts, tools, and measures for intervention.

This chapter considers the impact of violence and related risk factors on child and youth development and reviews some of the efforts that have been made to improve neighborhood safety and promote prosocial behavior. It examines three major systems that serve the developing child: school, mental health services, and neighborhood police. Our case studies illustrate how a coordination of these three systems can better serve children and families. An integrated approach can best foster early intervention and prevention, applying what is known about children's developmental needs.

Poverty, marital disruption, domestic violence, family breakdown, parental unemployment, substance abuse, unsafe housing, poor physical health, and an overburdened educational system are just a few of the circumstances that take a huge toll on the development of children in urban centers. For these children, the world is a dangerous and threatening place in which to grow up. Their world is crime-ridden streets, where schools and playgrounds belong to gangs and drug dealers. It is dilapidated homes with broken windows, poor heating, peeling lead paint, rats, and garbage. It is a world in which children grow up afraid and ashamed of the way they live, where they learn basic survival skills before they learn to read. Some of these disadvantaged children succeed and prosper despite adversity, but too many face limited futures outside the economic, social, and political mainstream.

Most poor children in America are in double jeopardy. Whether in the inner city or in desolate rural areas, they experience the most health problems but have the least access to medical care. They are at the highest risk of academic failure but often attend the worst schools. They may be most vulnerable to the short- and long-term effects of exposure to violence and live in homes and neighborhoods with the highest concentration of violent events. Their families experience the most stress but have the fewest social supports (Commission on Children, 1992).

Mental Health Effects of Exposure to Violence

The number of potential psychological casualties of violence far outnumber the physically wounded seen in emergency rooms. At Boston City Hospital it was reported that one out of every ten children seen in the primary care clinic had witnessed a shooting or stabbing before the age of six: half in the home, half on the streets. The average age of these children was 2.7 years (Taylor, Zuckerman, Harik, & Groves, 1992). And, in New Haven, Connecticut, 41% of 6th, 8th, and 10th grade students had seen someone shot or stabbed in the preceding year (New Haven Public Schools, 1992; Schwab-Stone et al., 1995). Parents of six- to ten-year-olds living in a low-income, *moderately* violent neighborhood in Washington, D.C., reported that 84–90% had witnessed violence to others, broadly defined (Richters & Martinez, 1993). Twenty-five percent of the 1st and 2nd graders had witnessed a mugging, 13% had seen a stabbing, and 16% had happened upon a dead body outdoors. More than 30% of the children in the 5th and 6th grades reported they had personally seen someone shot. Finally, in a survey of 3,735 students in grades 9–12, Singer and colleagues (1995) found that among males in some schools, as many as 21% reported seeing someone sexually assaulted, 82% had witnessed a beating or mugging at school, 46% had seen someone attacked or stabbed with a knife, and 62% had witnessed a shooting. In both of the latter studies, having witnessed violence was significantly associated with reports of depression, post-traumatic stress disorder, anger, and/or anxiety.

Mental Health Effects in Children and Families

When children witness or are the direct victims of violence, psychological trauma may follow, as the normal capacity to anticipate, adjust to, and assimilate events and emotional experiences is severely undermined. When the capacity to anticipate and contain exceptional dangerous events is lost, behavioral and mental systems are immobilized. When the individual is rendered passive in the face of events that are threatening to his or her body and mind, a cascade of psychological and physiological processes ensue. The violent events are remembered differently from other events, and the experience is handled in a special fashion. In response to exposure to violence, children and adults alike may develop specific symptoms, such as disruptions in patterns of sleeping, eating, toileting, sustaining attention, and relating to others, and may experience generalized fearfulness and flashbacks of the violent event (American Psychiatric Association, 1994; Marans, 1994; Pynoos, 1993; Pynoos, Steinberg, & Wraith, 1994; Terr, 1991). Chronic exposure to violence is associated with increased depression and anxiety, lower school attainment, and greater alcohol use among adolescents and adults (Garbarino, Dubrow, Kostelny, & Pardo, 1992; Martinez & Richters, 1993).

All too often the children who shoot and stab others have themselves been beaten and neglected for many years and progress from the role of frightened victim to the role of frightening assailant (see Chapter 4 of this volume). Tragically for the child and society, perpetration of violence represents another adaptation to chronic exposure to violence. Actively engaging in violent behavior may be one of the significant long-term adaptive responses to chronic passive experiences of witnessing or being victimized by violence (Widom, 1989).

Impact of Violence on Neighborhood Cohesion and Social Support

An entire community's experience of fear, loss, and despair often serves as the broader context in which a child's capacity to achieve increasing mastery of his or her immediate environment is severely undermined. When added to other aspects of social adversity – for example, multigenerational poverty; parental unemployment; substandard housing, education, and medical care; and racial discrimination – acute and chronic exposure to violence becomes a powerful element that erodes a community's sense of order and capacity for problem solving.

Adults confronted by unrelenting community violence may adopt a range of denial and avoidance responses. They may be unable to listen and attend to children's needs in the aftermath of traumatic events, as a natural consequence of their own attempts to protect themselves from feelings of vulnerability, fear, and traumatic disorganization. The same factors may keep extended family, friends, and neighbors from listening to traumatic narratives and providing distressed individuals with appropriate support. Many residents of violent urban neighborhoods may have a strong psychological investment in avoiding open discussions of their chronic experience of fear and helplessness, in part because few people in the community are emotionally available to share the burdens of community members who are exposed to violence. In many poor urban and rural settings, the instability of families and the extended community places a special burden on the social institutions called upon to respond to both victims and perpetrators of violence.

For many American children development has occurred in environments that provide neither consistent structure nor a basic sense of safety, both of which are crucial to the sense of mastery and achievement children need to develop as they mature. As a result, from early in life, these children lack the internal psychological structure necessary for achieving a sense of autonomy, competence, and pride in academic, social, and personal endeavors. When children are reared in environments lacking the family and community structures that support healthy development, institutions outside the family may be the only source for the needed structure and supports for children whose limitations, insecurity, and lack of inhibition manifest themselves in problem behaviors in the classroom and on neighborhood streets.

The Challenge of Multidisciplinary Intervention

Whether as victims, witnesses, or perpetrators of violence, children's psychological reactions are all too often ignored or misunderstood by the professionals (i.e., police, teachers, physicians, lawyers, probation officers) with whom they come in contact. This negligence is compounded by frequent failures of communication and coordination among those adults who potentially play the most significant roles in some children's lives. As a result, the strategies for intervening on children's behalf in the wake of violent events typically tend to be fragmented, inadequate, and ineffective.

Youth-serving professionals must develop an understanding of the child behaviors that may reflect exposure to violence, such as inattention in class; underachievement or academic failure; isolation from the peer group; and provocative acts, clowning, aggression, and oppositional behavior. There is also a need to understand the link between learning difficulties, low self-competence, dropping out of school, and criminal behavior. Without this knowledge, the opportunity to consider specialized and integrated interventions across domains is missed.

For example, in addition to having contact with police who arrive on the scene, the children who witness violence are also students in a school system, may have contact with health care providers, and, in some instances, have been involved with child welfare authorities or other social service agencies. However, it is rare that these professionals know each other, let alone consult with each other in order to recognize and then respond to children's needs. Similarly, many of the children and adolescents who enter the juvenile justice system are already known to the schools, child welfare agencies, mental health clinics, and other social services because of family disruption, truancy, disruptive behavior in the home or community, or substance abuse. Nevertheless, judicial decisions about how to intervene in the lives of these children and their families are frequently made with little if any consultation among the institutions that regularly come in contact with them, and often without any professional evaluation of the children's psychological or developmental status by any of the agencies.

The systematic absence of informed, coordinated interagency responses may be in part the result of professionals' efforts to respect the privacy of the children and families they serve. This is seen most clearly in the strict rules of confidentiality that shield children's records in the juvenile justice system. The absence of agency collaboration also reflects, however, the sense of insularity, distrust, and futility that often pervades the various professionals and agencies involved with the children most affected by community violence and at high risk of suffering its psychological consequences.

Yet today, educators, police, and mental health practitioners have begun to seek new, more effective institutional responses to the crisis confronting American children. The time is ripe for exploring collaboration *among* institutions that have, in the main, traditionally operated in isolation. In order to examine the conceptual and practical implications of collaboration among education, mental health professionals, and police, we shall first review the changes occurring in each system.

Three Key Youth-Serving Community Institutions

Public Schools

American public schools hold a unique position in the community. They are expected to provide the knowledge and skills necessary for their students to succeed in a highly competitive and rapidly evolving marketplace. In addition, the schools are asked to set an example, to lead rather than follow on the heels of community change. By default, in the past three decades, public schools have increasingly been pressed to assume a role in public health, public safety, and the inculcation of morals, as well as to address the various ways in which social and psychological development in children has gone awry.

Quite apart from federal legislation, many of the pressures for such school changes have arisen from within local communities. The problems faced by inner city schools threaten the safety and integrity of all members of a school community, both school staff and students. The problem behaviors resulting from escalating divorce, child abuse and neglect, violence, gangs, drugs, vandalism, unprotected sex, and teenage pregnancy have threatened to undermine the central mission of public schools. In populations at high risk, whether or not school leaders see it as their mission, they have been left with little choice but to address the problems associated with a deteriorating community, if only because those problems interfere with a school's capacity to educate students.

School initiatives to cope with community problems embody a public health approach. They represent a full range of anti-violence programs. Strategies for controlling school violence include the installation of metal detectors, random locker searches, and juvenile offense tracking to increase detection and conviction of serious and/or repeat offenders (Centers for Disease Control and Prevention, 1991). Some school districts have developed alternative schools, nonviolence contracts, mentoring programs, parent educational involvement, clothing regulations, and contingency and incentive programs (see, e.g., Butterfield & Turner, 1989; Sabatino, Heald, Rothman, & Miller, 1978; Sarmiento, 1989; Toby, 1980).

Prevention programs are similar in structure to traditional school health programs, but they have adopted numerous psychoeducational approaches from the fields of education, social work, and psychology. They often involve a special curriculum, workshops, or series of group sessions that address children's knowledge, assumptions and beliefs, behavior change, and life skills building. Areas commonly addressed include alcohol and drug abuse, anger management, bullying, conflict resolution, dropping out, empowerment, gang affiliation, peer pressure, problem solving, vandalism, social competence, self-esteem, sexual abuse, racism, and interpersonal negotiation/mediation (see, e.g., Burt, Resnick, & Matheson, 1992; Carter, n.d.; Committee for Children, 1989; Feindler, Marriott, & Iwata, 1984; Gainer, Webster, & Champion, 1993; Hammond et al., 1990; Harris &

Associates, 1993; Kaufman, 1993; Kohl, 1993; Moore & Beland, 1992; National School Safety Center, 1988; Pastorino, 1991; Roden, 1991; Swan & Poertner, 1990).

Still other school programs have emphasized a rapid response by the school to crises and violence, in order to minimize their impact (Harper, 1990; Nelson & Slaikeu, 1984; Peterson & Straub, 1992; Schonfeld & Kline, 1994). Similarly, since the early 1960s, a growing number of cities have begun to assign police officers to specific school districts and to develop their own security operations, using both police and civilian patrol staff on school campuses (Burgan & Rubel, 1980; Rubel, 1990). Although initially the police were used by schools primarily to respond to crises – such as fights, vandalism, and traffic problems – increasingly, new approaches, including school/police liaison programs, school resource officers, anti-truancy programs, and drug education programs, have focused on "crime and order problems while improving police/student contacts and relations" (Kenney & Watson, 1992).

The Safe Passage program and the SMART (School Management and Resource Teams) program are two of the more promising problem-oriented approaches to school violence that have emerged in recent years. Following the tragic stabbing of a student returning home from school by subway, the Abraham Lincoln High School in Brooklyn, New York, initiated the Safe Passage program. The program coordinated school dismissal times with train schedules and assigned uniformed police officers to ride in the last three subway cars, which were designated as Safe Passage Cars. In the first three years following the program's inception, there was not a single incident in any of the Safe Passage Cars (Chancellor's Advisory Panel on School Safety, 1993).

The SMART program is an effort to improve school safety and discipline by combining computer-based incident tracking with school team building and interagency coordination. A computerized system allows the participating school districts to record each misbehaving student's disciplinary infractions and criminal acts. SMART teams, including students, parents, teachers, school support staff, law enforcement/security officers, and administrators, use these data to devise action plans and monitor results. The program relies on interagency collaboration and the efficient use of existing resources to minimize the need for additional funds (Moora, 1995).

Many school-based programs appear to have had significant success in accomplishing their specific goals. However, for both scientific and practical reasons, it is important to evaluate programs rigorously and learn whether or not they work at all, what works for whom, whether there are unintended positive or negative consequences, what are the effective in-gredients, and what is the cost-effectiveness of such school-based pro-grams.

Most important, but generally neglected in evaluation, is the need for an overarching frame of reference that reflects the principles of child psychia-try and child development. Within such a frame, program evaluation would emphasize the program's influence on children's overall develop-ment, in addition to the reduction of specific behaviors and symptoms. In keeping with this notion, many schools have come to recognize the positive effects of a fundamental change in a school's philosophy, mission, or cli-mate, even when these restructurings are not specifically for the purpose of addressing school violence. Such "whole school" changes are measura-ble (see Chapter 7 of this volume). One such program, the nationally rec-ognized Comer School Development Program (Comer, 1986; Comer & Haynes, 1990) provides a model for collaboration in which social and psy-chological principles are applied to all aspects of school programming. The model involves the introduction of school-based planning and manage-ment teams that guide an elementary school's attention to issues that affect overall climate and quality of the educational experience. This model has been replicated nationwide and recently extended to middle and high schools. Evaluations of the Comer model have shown promise for facilitat-ing both academic and social development among children in at-risk urban communities.

Mental Health Services

Recent data suggest children with mental health problems continue to be underserved, and only a minority of those who receive services are seen in mental health settings (Costello, 1994). The preponderance of services of-fered to children at risk of mental health problems is provided by schools (Leaf, 1993; Zahner, Pawelkiewicz, Defrancesco, & Adnopoz, 1992). A mi-nority of children in the child protective system receive services from the mental health system (Landsverk, 1993), despite estimates that more than 50% have serious levels of mental disorders (Hoagwood & Rupp, 1994). Data are not readily available regarding how many children affected by vi-olence receive services, even though studies suggest children's victimiza-tion by and/or exposure to violence is alarmingly high (e.g., New Haven Public Schools, 1992; Osofsky, Wewers, Hann, & Fick, 1992; Taylor et al., 1992). It is likely that few referrals are made, perhaps in part because the first symptoms of exposure (e.g., social withdrawal, inattention, muted affect, loss of interest in activities, sadness, fearfulness, avoidance) often are not disruptive to others, or do not seem serious enough to arouse great concern among adults in a child's home, neighborhood, or classroom.

Nonetheless, during the past 25 years, mental health services for children have evolved rapidly. Since 1970, new community-based services have proliferated, and the creation of the Child and Adolescent Service System Program (CASSP) by the National Institute of Mental Health in 1984 reflected a concerted effort to rethink and restructure the system of children's mental health services (Meyers, 1985).

CASSP emphasizes the importance of collaboration among key service stakeholders, typically education, mental health, and social services. Many sites established local interagency teams to deal with problems in coordinating service delivery and resolving funding disputes in the course of providing increasingly intensive care. In several states and urban centers, CASSP has been reasonably successful in supporting the development of a coordinated system of services for children and adolescents with a severe emotional disturbance (SED) (Day & Roberts, 1991; Schlenger et al., 1992). Unfortunately, federal guidelines for SED eligibility exclude children with a "social maladjustment," those children who engage in delinquent or criminal behavior that would probably warrant a diagnosis of "conduct disorder." Consequently, law enforcement, probation, and juvenile justice agencies usually have not been included in interagency discussions, in part because they offer such limited therapeutic services. Furthermore, CASSP has not emphasized the needs of the less severely disturbed or at-risk children routinely encountered in schools and in the justice system. Care for children who are not classified as "emotionally disabled" has usually not been the focus of these systems, although there are indications that this may change (England & Cole, 1992).

With the advent of managed health care, the focus has been on economic reform of the public and private mental health system. The earliest managed care organizations, and most of the current private sector ones, have emphasized cost cutting and, therefore, time-limited care in "less restrictive" (i.e., less costly) environments. For Medicaid-funded medical and behavioral health services, managed care initiatives have focused on improving access to services by offering care within the community. Along with these new services, the application of developmental principles to the work of fundamental community institutions – for example, schools (Comer, 1980), social welfare services (Solnit, Nordhaus, & Lord, 1992), and law enforcement agencies (Marans, 1994; Marans & Cohen, 1993) – will increasingly serve to support and supplement the mental health care that has traditionally been provided in the psychiatric consulting room for individuals, families, and small groups.

Police Departments

In the 1970s, the police in urban areas began to ask fundamental questions about the way they operate. The delivery of police services in urban areas had become high-speed, high-tech, anonymous, and tough. The neighborhood police officer on the beat had long been abandoned in search of the more efficient, professional law enforcement officer. This new breed of police officer had left the street corner to work in a patrol car with a partner, plugged into a central dispatch center by a sophisticated communications system. Police calls came to be viewed as an unending demand that needed to be handled quickly and efficiently, so patrol units were not "out of service" too long handling any one incident.

Centralized dispatch of officers, rotating assignments and shifts, random patrolling, and other traditional policing measures increased the separation between police and community members. This "social distancing" (Bureau of Justice Assistance, 1994) was reinforced by increasingly sophisticated communications systems (e.g., 911 calls must be answered immediately, regardless of the urgency of the calls). In addition, rather than placing an emphasis on understanding the types of services requested and the quality of contacts with the public, reliance on computer-generated statistics placed greater emphasis on the number of calls for police service and the efficiency of response times (Bureau of Justice Assistance, 1994). In fact, these reactive attempts at crime fighting proved unsuccessful in lowering the crime rate (Wycoff, 1982). Controlled studies of intensified motor patrols in targeted high-crime areas indicated no significant changes in rates of victimization, arrests, or in the public's perceptions of the quality of interactions with the police (Kelling, Pate, Dieckman, & Brown, 1974; Schnelle, Kirchner, McNees, & Lawler, 1975; Sherman, 1990). Every attempt by the police to staunch the demand for their services seemed to fail (Kelling & Moore, 1988; Bureau of Justice Assistance, 1994).

The police began to discover that, in an effort to gain efficiency and respond to the ever-growing demand on their services, they had lost their once valued connections to the neighborhoods and the communities they were sworn to serve and protect. They had lost much of their ability to prevent or deter crime and to intervene early in problems developing. As the late Lee Brown, former national secretary of drug policy and former chief of police in New York City, Atlanta, Georgia, and Houston, Texas, observed,

"The police were not part of the community" but rather had grown "apart from it" (Brown, 1990). Because of this critique, police began to rethink their fundamental relationship to the communities they served and increasingly recognized the value of much that had been lost in the modern era. The police began to embrace the concept, once found too threatening, of working with communities in a new partnership to identify problems and work together toward their solution.

Goldstein (1977) developed and advanced the concept of "problem-oriented policing," which emphasized identifying, addressing, and solving the root causes that lead to repeated calls for service. Problem solving in this way is among the most substantial functions of policing. It requires moving away from "a reactive, incident-oriented stance to one that actively addresses the problems that continually drain police resources" (Bureau of Justice Assistance, 1994). A study of early efforts to shift to a more proactive, community-oriented approach to policing in San Diego, California, reported increases in officers' job satisfaction, problem-solving activities, and regular involvement with members of the communities in which they worked (Boydstun & Sherry, 1975).

The increased use of foot patrols was studied in Newark, New Jersey, in the late 1970s (Pate, Wycoff, Skogan, & Sherman, 1986). There were no significant differences in reported crimes, arrests, or victimization in areas in which foot patrols were tried and discontinued over a year. Nonetheless, "residents in areas with foot patrols perceived a significant decrease in crime and favorable attitude toward police and police services" (U.S. Department of Justice, 1995, p. 121).

The study conducted by Pate, Wycoff, Skogan, and Sherman (1986) evaluated a controlled intervention in Newark that focused policing efforts on addressing physical and social disorder thought to be directly linked to crime. This program, based on the "broken windows" theory (Kelling & Moore, 1988), increased police involvement and availability in neighborhoods by adding "storefront" police substations to foot patrols and also increased crime prevention measures, such as more rigorous enforcement of penalties for nuisance crimes and traffic violations, ongoing block watches, use of the neighborhood substations for accepting crime reports, and canvassing neighborhoods to identify fear and problems. In the experimental areas, citizens' satisfaction with the police and their neighborhoods increased, while concerns about disorder and property crimes decreased significantly relative to comparison areas.

Other innovations involving varying levels of increased problem-solving partnerships with the police and the community have been evaluated

(Lindsay & McGillis, 1986; Pate et al., 1986; Schnelle et al., 1975). Typical of the findings in neighborhoods where these changes in police practice have been implemented is the striking contrast between the minimal effects these efforts have had in preventing crime and the neighborhood residents' perceptions of a decrease in crime, physical danger, and social disorder, and increased satisfaction with the police and the neighborhood (U.S. Department of Justice, 1995). Kelling and Moore (1988) point out that a highly visible police presence helps to reduce fear, which is more closely correlated with social disorder than with crime. Fear of crime limits community activity and empties streets, which in turn leads to increased crime. Mobilizing the community can broaden the range of preventive measures through a partnership of citizens and police (Kelling & Moore, 1988). Although the array of programs nationwide had much in common, little uniformity in details of implementation was found (Goldstein, 1990). In a definitive report on community policing, the Bureau of Justice Assistance (BJA) (1994) outlines several key ingredients for effective community policing practices:

- Developing mutual trust and community partnerships that define mutually agreed on priorities
- Exceeding standard law enforcement in recognizing the value of activities that contribute to the orderliness and well-being of the community and its members (e.g., helping crime victims, resolving family and community disputes, making referrals for those at risk, and providing models of positive/good citizenship)
- According respect and sensitivity to all citizens in an evenhanded, just fashion
- Using in-depth knowledge of neighborhoods as the basis for understanding root causes of difficulties and engaging in problem solving
- Using law enforcement agencies as catalysts for mobilizing resources at the national, state, and local levels to address contemporary problems more successfully

The U.S. Department of Justice's Office of Community Oriented Policing Services identifies community partnerships and problem solving as the essential "complementary core components" to a community policing strategy (Office of Juvenile Justice and Delinquency Prevention, 1995). In reviewing the available controlled studies of problem-oriented policing strategies, the Office of Juvenile Justice and Delinquency Prevention (OJJDP) report points out none of the sites included both of the core components. In addition, crime reduction has been taken as the measure of success for such strategies. The BJA report (1994) suggested a shift from crime reduction statistics to the following qualitative measures:

- Numbers and types of community partnerships formed
- Qualitative policing differences defined by effectiveness, efficiency, and equity
- Creativity in response to community problems
- Use of community resources as part of police response

- Community involvement with police (both informal and formal means of regular engagement in the process of identifying problems and developing intervention strategies)
- Change in nature of calls from crime reports to requests for social assistance
- Change in roles and responsibilities of police personnel (e.g., decentralized decision making), reflecting the shift to greater engagement and problem-solving functions within the community
- Control of calls for service (e.g., prioritizing calls, developing alternatives for nonemergency calls)
- Increased job satisfaction for officers

When considering the effect of the role of policing both on the quality of life of families and on children's development, it may be especially important to examine those models of community policing that have an impact on reducing fear, mobilizing community involvement in problem-solving partnerships, and enhancing the community's sense of security. These goals may not only be more realistic than the current emphasis on crime reduction, but may also prove more meaningful measures of outcome.

In many communities across the nation, different versions of community policing are being implemented. In a sample of 2,314 municipal and county police and sheriffs' departments, 50% had either implemented or were in the process of implementing community policing (Wycoff, 1982). They have shared a number of features, including permanent assignments, neighborhood-based substations, specific training and interagency involvement, and regularly scheduled meetings with community members.

The police have moved back into the neighborhoods by returning to the beat and manning neighborhood substations. They have participated in community councils, and citizen/police management teams focusing on beat maintenance, collaborative strategies, and problem solving have supplemented traditional strategies such as police sweeps, tactical planning teams, and SWAT (Strategic Weapons Attack Team) operations. In many departments, police officers have returned to street corners, housing projects, and neighborhoods and are encouraged to become part of the communities in which they serve, working with the citizens on their beat to improve the quality of life in the neighborhood (Goldstein, 1990; Kelling, 1988). Schools have also been targeted. Throughout the country, police officers have moved into the classrooms to educate children at risk through various programs.

Among the best known of this last type of program is Project DARE (Drug Abuse Resistance Education), sponsored jointly by the Los Angeles, California, Police Department and the Los Angeles School District, which targets young adolescents at risk of substance abuse (Ennett et al., 1994; Kochis, 1995; Rosenbaum, 1994). The DARE program has gained wide acceptance and is the most widely disseminated police-related program across the nation. However, evaluations of DARE have found little evidence that the program has met its goal of preventing substance abuse and delinquent/criminal activities, but considerable evidence that it improves children's attitudes toward the police (Ennett et al., 1994). In a related study in Scotland, Hopkins (1994) investigated a police/schools liaison program designed to improve relations between police and youth. Although adolescents developed favorable attitudes toward school-based officers, these attitudes did not generalize to officers in the community. Indirect effects of this program on client, family, or community were not examined. Available assessments of DARE have evaluated only the original DARE model, which covered only the fifth and sixth grades. Currently, there is a model that is continuous from K-12. The revised program is too new for definitive evaluation, but continuity of presentation has been shown to be highly important in other programs through which changes in *behavior* of children and adolescents have been achieved. However, the continuity of presentation across developmental phases seems more likely to result in sustained changes in the behavior of children and adolescents.

A search of the literature on police/mental health partnerships uncovered only one program that addressed the needs of citizens who were victims of violence, the Crisis Intervention Support Unit (CISU), for adults. In their examination of this adult program, Fein and Knaut (1986) focused on counseling and casework and offered a descriptive account of client characteristics, use of staff time, services provided, and so forth, but no data regarding the program's impact on clients, the police, or the broader community.

In the community-based, problem-oriented approach to policing, a new role and job description for officers has begun to emerge. An emphasis on prevention, deterrence, and intervention has evolved. Community organizing, networking, and social service referrals are becoming necessary everyday skills for community police officers. The community-based model of policing emphasizes that in a given neighborhood, order can best be maintained when officers are able to sustain relationships with community members and local support services, working together to identify problems, hazards, and fears, and to develop solutions for them (Goldstein, 1977; Kelling, 1988).

In order to be effective in their new roles within communities, and to guard against being overwhelmed by the volume of problems they address in their efforts to prevent crime, officers need a framework for understanding the children and families with whom they work, and they need new partners who can assist in dealing with the challenges and tragedies they encounter every day. The shift from a solely reactive to a proactive role for community-based police officers is based on developing and sustaining relationships with members of a community, as well as increasing the array of available interventions. In both arenas, officers need an expanded conceptual frame of reference, as well as additional resources and partners, in order to share the burden of increased demands (Marans et al., 1995).

Child Development and Community Policing (CD-CP): The New Haven Model

Description of the Model

The New Haven, Connecticut, model of community-based policing has adopted a city-wide strategy for developing partnerships between officers and the neighborhoods in which they work. Central to this strategy are the shared concerns about the safety and welfare of children and families and the role that officers can play in fostering favorable development. In New Haven, police are increasingly being recruited from the types of communities they patrol. In addition, all the officers are placed in neighborhoods on long-term assignments; each is provided with a personal beeper; small neighborhood, often storefront, substations have been built in each district of the city; policing activities in each district are supervised by a high-ranking officer who develops and coordinates problem-solving strategies in conjunction with substation management teams composed of officers and community members; and substations are used as around-the-clock centers for after-school activities, community mediation, and neighborhood meetings. Each of these innovations aims to build and strengthen partnerships between the police and the citizens for whom, and increasingly with whom, they work.

It is in the context of this shift in policing philosophy and practice that the Child Development-Community Policing (CD-CP) program has been developed in New Haven (Marans, 1994). The program, a collaboration between the Yale Child Study Center and the New Haven Department of Police Service, attempts to reorient police officers in their interactions with children in order to optimize the psychological roles they can play as providers of a sense of security and positive authority and as models for identification in ways that would not have occurred in an impersonal, incident-driven approach to policing. In addition, through a reorientation of their traditional relationships with police professionals, the program aims to extend the roles mental health clinic professionals may play in the lives of children and families exposed to community violence.

Though police officers come in daily contact with children who are victims, witnesses, and perpetrators of violence, they generally have neither the professional expertise, the time, nor the other resources necessary to meet these children's psychological needs. Conversely, mental health professionals in local clinics may be professionally equipped to respond to children's psychological distress following episodes of violence, but the acutely traumatized children who are most in need of clinical service are rarely brought to outpatient clinics until months or years later, when chronic symptoms or maladaptive behavior brings them to the attention of parents, teachers, or the juvenile courts. Valuable opportunities are therefore lost to intervene at the moment when professional contact could provide both immediate stabilization and bridges to a variety of ongoing services.

Core elements of the Child Development-Community Policing (CD-CP) program capitalize on new trends in policing and the necessity of changing the ways in which mental health services are delivered to some of the most vulnerable members of the nation. The program has five central components (Marans, 1994; Marans & Cohen, 1993):

1. A core seminar for rank-and-file officers on the principles of lifespan development and human functioning
2. A training fellowship that exposes district police supervisors to clinical services and liaison with social services
3. A training fellowship for mental health professionals that orients them to police practices
4. A 24-hour per day consultation service for officers, children, and families who are directly involved in violent incidents
5. An ongoing case conference for officers and mental health professionals during which both clinical and policing interventions for victims and perpetrators of violence are discussed

The CD-CP collaboration is based on the premise that although a violent event may cause responses that can damage a child's development, it may also be viewed as a window of opportunity for applying what has been learned in the consulting room and for delivering services to such children through a coordinated effort by diverse agencies.

Over the past four years, hundreds of rank-and-file officers and dozens of senior police supervisors have been trained in the principles of child development and acute traumatic response. Working collaboratively with mental health professionals, police in New Haven have referred more than 500 children who have witnessed and experienced violence, as well as dozens of children who have committed serious violent offenses. These children have often been seen by a mental health professional within minutes of the police response to murders, stabbings, beatings, maiming by fire, death by drowning, and gunfire. The children and their families have been seen individually and as part of larger groups in their homes, at police substations, at school, in their neighborhoods, at the police station, and within the Yale Child Study Center.

The possibilities created by a police/mental health partnership continue to be actively explored at the CD-CP program's original site. Thus far, the program has emphasized through several mechanisms early intervention within the community, as well as alternatives to sentencing for arrested persons:

- A coordinated police/mental health response to children and families who are victims of or witnesses to violence. The program seeks to optimize the acute and post-acute response of the police and mental health clinicians who begin their work at the scene of a violent event.
- A police/mental health response to children indirectly affected by neighborhood violence and the aftermath of a violent event. Police and clinicians engage other systems and contexts, e.g., they work together with parents and/or teachers to arrange a discussion with peers in a child's school or classroom.
- Police identification and referral of children involved in pre-delinquent activities who demonstrate psychiatric problems (e.g., depression, poor impulse control, psychotic behaviors) that place them at risk of victimization, violence, or serious delinquent behaviors.
- Consultation by clinicians with police and juvenile probation officers, and, when indicated, therapeutic intervention with children charged with various delinquent and violent offenses. The focus is on juveniles who are at risk of repeat offending, but for whom extended detention or incarceration is not available or appropriate.

Each of these points of collaboration offers the potential for prevention of violence, although as yet data to support the effectiveness of this partnership in reducing rates of violence are not available. Research opportunities will expand as more such programs are established. Similar programs have been piloted in Framingham, Massachusetts, and Newark, New Jersey. Under the auspices of the U.S. Department of Justice's Office of Juvenile Justice and Delinquency Prevention, the CD-CP program will be implemented and evaluated in Buffalo, New York; Charlotte, North Carolina; Nashville, Tennessee; and Portland, Oregon.

Case Studies

When officers work from small substations rather than from central headquarters, they observe and experience the lives of children and families in their districts much more accurately. They generally know who the "players" are and where trouble is brewing and why; and they see and often know the many victims of violence – not only those who are shot, stabbed, or beaten and their assailants, but the many child witnesses who observed the events in horror or ran for safety. As the police become more engaged with the communities in which they work, they create an opportunity to provide broader-based strategies for problem solving.

The scene of a crime may be a situation where the officer recognizes that without intervention the damaging effect of a child's exposure to a grisly event will be expressed in symptoms at home, at school, and later, on the streets. Consultation with a mental health collaborator begins the process of examining the emotional/developmental needs of the child, which may include follow-up contact with the neighborhood officer, counseling for the parents, individual treatment for the child, and coordination with the school to optimize support for the child and family and to mediate the larger school community's response to danger and tragedy.

Case Study 1. The CD-CP model is illustrated by the following case (Marans et al., 1995). At midday on a late spring day, shots rang out. A school bus filled with eight five- to six-year-old children was caught in the crossfire of rival drug dealers. The bus was hit by gunfire; a six-year-old boy was shot in the head. The bus went to a nearby middle school where the children were met by police officers and emergency medical personnel. Officers trained in the CD-CP program were the first to greet the children and also contacted members of the Consultation Service to join them at the middle school. The boy who was shot was taken to the hospital. He survived surgery and suffered some neurological impairment for which he continues to receive rehabilitative services. The remaining children were taken inside the middle school building by police officers, who immediately began coordinating efforts to summon the parents of each of the children to the middle school. The officers described their central aim as protecting the children from the excitement surrounding the shooting – camera crews, multiple police personnel, onlookers – and securing the most immediate source of comfort possible – reuniting them with their parents. The children were *not* interviewed by the officers about the shooting. The officers explained that, while in the past this would have been part of the standard approach in an investigation, the reality was that any information about the shooting from the children was not immediately necessary and would only "retraumatize the children, especially when what they needed the most was to be with their parents."

The CD-CP clinicians arrived on the scene within ten minutes of the shooting. They were briefed by the police already on the scene and taken to the gym where the seven young children were sitting on the floor. Middle school personnel attempted to engage the children in a discussion about what they had seen, but the children remained quiet, clutching their knees and staring into the distance. The CD-CP clinicians were introduced to the school personnel who moved to the background as the clinicians began to work with the children. The clinicians had brought paper and markers. They sat down with two children each, asking one, then the other child if he or she would like to draw a picture. Each child quietly declined but when asked if they would like the clinician to draw something the response was unanimously positive, as was the requested content of the pictures: "Draw my mommy." Each child was asked what the speech bubble that went along with the drawing of the face should say. The children's instructions for faces fell in two categories: happy and sad. The speech bubble words alternated between "I'm so happy to see you" and "I was so sad and worried about you." After engaging in the drawings, the children grew more verbal and began to make inquiries about where their mothers were and when they would arrive. All of the children also expressed concern that perhaps their mothers had been hurt and might not be coming for them. The senior police officer on the scene, a CD-CP Fellow, came over and told the children and clinicians that each of their parents had been located and was on the way to the school.

One of the children asked a clinician to draw a picture of a head. "Whose head?" the clinician asked. "Um, a boy's head . . . that just got shot with a bullet." The rest of the children overheard this request and immediately turned their attention to the picture. The clinician requested details in order to complete the picture and asked if any of the children wished to add something themselves. Three children scribbled the same ingredient with a red marker – blood from the head wound that soon covered much of the page. While there were some questions about what was happening to the classmate who had been shot, the majority of the children's questions and comments had to do with curiosity about bodily functions (e.g., "How much blood does the body have?" and "Can parts of the body fall off?"), and quickly turned to a more spirited group discussion about various physical feats each could perform. The discussion continued to be punctuated by the sidelong glances to the door as parents began to arrive to pick up their children. Each parent was seen briefly by a clinician, given a telephone number to call any time with questions regarding their children's experience, and asked if they could be contacted for follow-up assessments.

While the crime scene was secured and the criminal investigation was begun, similar attention was paid to the emotional needs of all of the neighborhood children who were indirectly affected by the violence. All aspects of the response to the shooting – including the ways of informing both the middle school and elementary school communities about the shooting; briefing parents and school personnel; consulting with teachers, school administrators, and parents about how to respond to children in the classroom and at home; and making additional clinical services available – were coordinated and carried out by the Child Development-Community Policing program in conjunction with the school system. Officers trained in the CD-CP program were able to communicate information about the shooting in formal briefing sessions with parents and school personnel and informally in their encounters with the children who approached them on the street. They delivered information about the circumstances and background of the shooting, as well as communicating their understanding about the meanings of adult expression of rage and feelings of helplessness in an effective and sensitive manner that indicated their sophistication about the complexity of responses of individuals exposed to violence.

The CD-CP officers and clinicians were able to influence broader community responses to the shooting as well. They successfully argued that, while making some adults feel less helpless, using squad cars to escort school buses the day after the shooting would only exacerbate the children's concerns about safety. In a similar vein, with greater appreciation for children's anxiety and vulnerability, officers were able to discuss their concerns about the children as they negotiated with the media who gathered around the children's school soon after the shooting and in the days that followed. As a result, the intrusiveness and associated excitement of cameras and a barrage of questions directed to the children and their families were minimized. As a consequence of the CD-CP responses to the shooting incident, in this situation, the police were seen not merely as the harbingers of tragic news and violence but as sources of effective authority, concerned about the safety and emotional well-being of the affected children and families.

Five of the seven children received brief follow-up psychotherapy because of enduring post-traumatic stress disorder symptoms – disruptions in sleeping, eating; increased separation anxiety; and hypervigilance, generalized anxiety, and avoidant behaviors that were not part of the premorbid history. Two vignettes offer illustrations of the ways in which developmental phase and individual circumstances determine the context and specific meaning given to the disturbing external event. Each case example represents a condensation of material that emerged over the course of two to four months of treatment once and twice a week.

Beverly, five and one-half years old, had sat across the aisle from her classmate when he was shot. Her previous school functioning was good, as was her adaptation in an intact family that included a mother, father, and ten-month-old brother. Her developmental history was unremarkable. After the shooting, however, Beverly's difficulties with sleeping and eating, multiple new fears, and need to remain close to her mother continued unabated for two weeks before her parents agreed with a clinician's recommendation for individual work with the child in conjunction with parental guidance.

In her individual sessions, Beverly repeatedly returned to the scene of the shooting, reviewing an increasing array of details in both play with toy figures and in her drawings. Each narrative ended with Beverly looking and stating that she felt scared or "bad." Over time, the therapist probed these feelings further – either within the action of the play or the narrative that accompanied the pictures. Beverly would elaborate that she felt scared that the bullet might have hit her and very bad because her friend had been hurt. In one session, she drew a picture of herself and her friend on the bus. She drew the bullet tracking around her head on an eventual path to the head of her classmate. She grew quiet and looked forlorn. With the clinician's suggestion that there was a connection between her feelings and the story that lay behind the picture, Beverly revealed a secret whose telling spanned many sessions and was accompanied by a dramatic reduction and final resolution of her presenting symptoms.

The first part of the secret was that for several days before the shooting, Beverly had been reprimanded by the driver for bad behavior on the bus. Beverly thought that perhaps the bullet had really been meant for her as punishment. Later, she told the therapist that her "bad" behavior had really been about her teasing and poking at the very classmate who was shot. The third part of the secret was about her baby brother. With great anxiety, Beverly reported that she had teased the baby on numerous occasions and that, in fact, she often wished her brother was no longer around. With this, the source of her worry and guilt became more clear. She was able to articulate her fear that somehow her bad wishes about pesty brothers had come true in the shooting of her schoolmate and that her wishes would be discovered and severely punished. The therapist pointed out that Beverly was punishing herself as if the reality of the scary event had somehow been under her magical control.

Beverly's hostile wishes toward a rival baby brother and their displacement onto a schoolmate was not unusual. However, for Beverly, the *realization* of these wishes – if only in the displacement – constituted the central source of her overwhelming anxiety and traumatization. In addition, her sense of "magical control" reflected both age-expectable phenomena augmented by reliance on magic for the purposes of restitution and recovery. That is, a belief in magical control would revise the original experience of traumatization, or absence of control, in the shooting – even if the belief in magic might also lead to a tremendous sense of responsibility for and guilt about the real and imagined events.

Miguel, another classmate age five, presented multiple symptoms. He was the youngest in a family of six. Both parents and a 19-year-old brother worked, one sister was in high school, and the other in middle school. Prior to the shooting, Miguel had had no difficulty sleeping, leaving home for school, or engaging in activities away from home. This changed dramatically after the shooting of his classmate. He insisted on sleeping with the light on throughout the night, departures from home were very upsetting for him, and in the remaining days of school he complained of sickness in order to avoid attending.

It was not until several weeks into the treatment that Miguel could reveal in his play that he was terrified that the persons responsible for the shooting of his classmate would come to shoot him and all the members of his family. The fact that the shooters had been arrested and remained in jail did nothing to alleviate Miguel's fears or symptoms. However, his ability to express this central worry opened the door to further exploration, clarification of his thoughts, and greater mastery over a very frightening experience.

What lay behind Miguel's fear of being shot was his attempt to explain to himself why the shooting had happened and perhaps, with this explanation, to feel more able to predict similarly dangerous events. However, the explanation Miguel developed was limited by condensation and concrete thinking typical of his phase of development. Miguel eventually was able to explain the following ideas to his therapist and then to his parents. He had learned in school about how bad drugs are and that in addition to the terrible things they do to the body they also make people violent and are the cause of fights between drug dealers. When the shooting started and the bus was hit by gunfire, Miguel assumed the shooting was about drugs and if the school bus was being shot at, it must somehow be involved with drugs. If the school bus was involved in drugs and he was on the school bus, then he must somehow be connected with drugs, and if he was involved in drugs then so must his family be. If he and his family were involved with drugs, they too would fall victim to gunfire just like his classmate.

While there was no indication at all that the family was involved with drug use or dealings, the dangers were brought home to Miguel as a powerful response to being shot at and seeing blood flow from the bullet wound in his friend's head. While generating considerable fear, Miguel's explanation relied on the cognitive resources available to him and provided the basis for altering the traumatic episode. In the version of *his* making, Miguel was able to anticipate the danger – he expected assailants to come after him – and he defended against the danger: he remained hypervigilant, staying up at night, staying close to home, and keeping his family nearby. Understanding Miguel's solution in the context of phase-specific concerns and capacities helped Miguel to unravel and clarify the distinction between his fantasy configurations and the factual information, and led to a resolution of his developmental crisis and the attendant symptoms.

Where phase-appropriate concerns associated with the body, sibling rivalry, and magical and concrete thinking played a crucial role in understanding and addressing the nature of trauma for Beverly and Miguel, another incident illustrated an adolescent version of overwhelming, disorganizing anxiety.

Case Study 2. In this case (Marans et al., 1995), collaboration between police and mental health professionals helped avert retaliation and possibly bloodshed following the robbery of a high school student. Mark, age 15, was robbed at gunpoint on a Friday evening. He'd been walking with friends when two men put a reportedly large caliber semiautomatic weapon in his face and demanded all of his money and jewelry. Mark had been walking behind several of his friends and they were unaware of what occurred in an alley off the sidewalk. Mark later reported the men repeatedly shoved the weapon in his face and told him they would shoot him. After taking his valuables the assailants fled and Mark ran home. He ran into his room crying uncontrollably, hid on the floor of his closet, and in spite of his mother's urging, Mark refused to come out. After a while, a sobbing Mark told his mother what had occurred and she phoned the police.

Each of the three officers who arrived had been trained in the CD-CP's child development seminars, and the supervisory officer had completed the fellowship. As one of the officers approached the bedroom, Mark began to scream. The officer told him he had heard what had happened to him and realized the holdup was a terrifying experience. Mark would not look at the officer and yelled at him to leave the room. The officer was about to leave when the supervisor pointed to his gun and utility belt. With this, the officer removed his holster and weapon, explaining to Mark that he would leave them outside the room, as he understood how frightening guns might be to Mark. Mark continued to sob and shake uncontrollably, but allowed the officer to help him out of the room and accepted the suggestion that he go to the emergency room for treatment. A Consultation Service clinician was called and Mark was met at the E.R.

During the course of the interview, Mark was only able to look at the clinician after a comment was made about how feeling very frightened could make a guy feel small and helpless – a very undesirable feeling for a 15-year-old. Mark began to talk about the events, repeating the same scene and his assailants' commands to him over and over. The repetition then began to include some slight alterations in the facts, and Mark protested that he should have "grabbed the gun and kicked each of the [attackers] in the balls." He described the size of the gun muzzle as huge and insisted he thought they would kill him with this huge weapon.

As his shaking, hyperventilating, and sobbing subsided, Mark began to talk about the earlier part of the evening. He explained that before being robbed he had been "hanging back from [his] 'homeboys' because they were with their ladies" and he wanted to "give them space." He shyly told the clinician that he didn't have a girlfriend and then quickly exploded with rage and then tears. He said he wanted to get a gun and kill the guys who had "messed with him." He said he didn't deserve what had happened to him – he was a good student in school and had just completed an important history paper. He explained that all of the thin gold chains he wore, he'd bought for himself – clarifying that he was not to be lumped together with "low-life drug dealers." Mark began to cry again, as he swore revenge. The clinician commented that it felt humiliating to have to feel so terrified and that Mark was wishing that he could undo his experience. Mark replied that if he had a gun or had disarmed his attackers, he wouldn't have to feel as though he'd "wimped out." The clinician agreed that feeling powerful would certainly be the opposite of what he had experienced with a gun in his face.

Mark then brightened and looked up, suddenly exclaiming that now he remembered the gun more clearly – it wasn't a nine-millimeter semiautomatic; it was a BB gun. As the acute terror diminished, he was also able to remember the make of the car his assailants drove off in, as well as clear descriptions of the two men. His fantasies of revenge began to take another form as Mark talked about helping the police make an arrest. At his request,

Mark spoke with the detective involved in the case to offer the information he had recovered in the course of the interview. Two hours after the admission to the emergency room, Mark was discharged.

Mark was seen in two follow-up sessions in which he continued to review the events of that Friday evening. The fantasies of what he should have done were intermingled with talk of the mortification of feeling helpless and the increasing recognition that, in fact, there was nothing he could have done to alter what had occurred. When his difficulties with sleeping and hypervigilant feelings abated, Mark declined further clinical contact. However, over the following several weeks one of the three responding officers stopped in on Mark regularly for brief chats during the course of usual patrol. In the last clinical follow-up, eight weeks after the incident, Mark had still not bought a gun and instead of continuing to recite numerous violent revenge fantasies, spoke of the latest academic demands at school and of his newfound friendships with the cops on his beat. While he had not forgotten the terror or rage associated with his experience, Mark added that his good memory had been instrumental in helping the police to arrest the two men who had attacked him. And, as he said, "That felt really good."

Evaluation of CD-CP

Efforts to evaluate the CD-CP program are currently under way. In addition to the descriptive statistics, this evaluation aims to explore the effect of the collaboration on the professional development of participating officers and mental health professionals. It is hypothesized the program will have a range of favorable effects contributing to officer effectiveness, job satisfaction, and flexibility in problem solving. A survey documented for officers has been developed that provides a way of measuring attitudes related to sensitive response to children's needs: (1) officer knowledge of child development, (2) dogmatism versus circumspection, (3) awareness of the experience of children, (4) contact with youths, (5) comfort in expressing emotions, (6) comfort in responding to child witnesses of violence, and (7) general receptivity to a mental health perspective. A comparable survey for mental health workers assesses their knowledge and attitudes related to policing and law enforcement.

Although these surveys reveal the wider range of direct benefits from the program, they do not address other fundamental questions regarding additional benefits to the community. More specifically, what is the impact, if any, that a police/school/mental health partnership has on community well-being, as evidenced in rates of crime, fear of crime, and trust in the police? Furthermore, how do the nature and scope of such a partnership translate into specific benefits in terms of policy change and spin-off partnerships or community initiatives?

It appears there are significant law enforcement benefits arising from the development of relationships between officers and members of the community. When there is community perception of a more personally engaged and personally responsive police force, officers have noted greater cooperation in intelligence gathering following a crime, as well as in problem solving related to the prevention of criminal activity. For example, in 1991, SWAT operations in New Haven occurred, on average, once per week. From 1992 to 1995, the need for SWAT operations has decreased to no more than two times per year. In New Haven, the closure rate of homicide investigations is approximately 95%, as compared to a national average of 40–50% (New Haven Police Department Lieutenant Mike Sweeney, personal communication, August 1995). The efforts of a local, state, and federal task force have dismantled three major violent drug operations, netting major federal convictions with federal time.

The most important question these surveys should answer, however, is whether there are measurable improvements in the lives of children whose experience is dominated by multiple, chronic risks such as parental unemployment, ill health, substance abuse, poverty, and neglect. These are the children who have a high risk of experiencing or perpetrating violence.

CD-CP officers demonstrate empathy to the children involved in a violent incident, respond in a manner that is understanding and supportive, and make referrals for immediate on-site clinical support. Important possible outcomes would include reduced rates of post-traumatic stress disorder symptoms over the short term, and reduced risk of social withdrawal, depression, or aggressive behaviors over the long term. While this would be a tall order for a single episode of relatively brief contact with an officer and what is typically a brief involvement with a clinician, nonetheless expectations of this sort may be within reach when these brief contacts are embedded in a context of friendly neighborhood familiarity, as well as a long-term pattern of contacts throughout childhood covering a broad range of issues. Such interventions might include an officer's caring and sensitive response in the wake of domestic violence, occasional supportive contact with a school- or community-based police officer, or firm but respectful contact with an officer in the context of probationary and therapeutic interventions. Prosocial behavior and reduced violence may be among the gains.

The Juvenile Justice System: The Challenge of Collaboration

For far too many inner city children whose exposure to violence, poverty, and other adverse conditions has gone unnoticed, the juvenile justice system may be the first and most significant point of intervention in lives that have already deviated from optimal developmental pathways. Juvenile justice is still largely a self-contained system. Once in the system, youths are unlikely to be put into contact with other agencies. Before the coordination of police and mental health interventions, it was equally unlikely the children seen through the police's CD-CP Consultation Service would have come to the attention of education, mental health, or social service systems until they experienced serious emotional and behavioral disturbances months or years later.

Opportunities for Collaboration

Collaboration between the police and juvenile authorities can identify those accused juveniles who are most troublesome and dangerous to the community, so that prosecutors may vigorously seek their secure detention or else alternatively devise conditions for their release that will be sufficiently supervised to provide reasonable safety for the community. Community-based police officers may also be able to provide information about juvenile offenders whose behavior is related to family difficulties or to identify sources of support for a child in the community. This may help to provide necessary support structures for a child as a condition of probation. In this regard, neighborhood officers, who often know delinquent youths prior to their involvement in criminal activity, and who will likely come in contact with them again on probation or after their release from institutions, are in an ideal position to collaborate with probation and other social service professionals to create and tailor community-based alternatives to secure detention.

Such efforts can further an officer's efforts to maintain community safety and prevent additional crime. Community residents who know that an officer remained involved in a case after completing the arrest and juvenile court referral are more likely to feel protected by the police. An officer who initiates psychological treatment, job training, or a well-supervised community placement for a child as part of a juvenile prosecution is also less likely to be seen as the enemy by the child and his or her family.

Similarly, school personnel can provide juvenile authorities with valuable information about an accused child's history of attendance, academic performance, and social behavior, and, in collaboration with probation officers and neighborhood police, can provide structure and guidance for youths who are in trouble.

Mental health professionals can inform the judicial process about a child or adolescent's internal experience of his or her violent behavior and its meaning in the context of the child's previous life history and previous responses to mental health interventions, and can make recommendations for future treatment, including external conditions necessary to support psychological treatment. In many situations, psychotherapy would be useless when attempted as an isolated response to delinquent behavior but might form an important part of a coordinated team response that includes the necessary external structure.

This successful approach to collaboration can be seen in New Haven, Connecticut, where police and probation officers are beginning to work together in a systematic way for the first time. These two groups of professionals have begun a CD-CP affiliated pilot project in which supervision and monitoring of juvenile offenders are shared and integrated. Probation officers are relocating from a central office to community substations. Neighborhood police officers are supervising community service projects for neighborhood youths on probation, and are able to provide more detailed information to probation officers about violations through regular contact during the course of daily beat shifts. Overall the collaboration has yielded decreasing numbers of juvenile offenders for whom incarceration is the only option. Even though New Haven currently refers twice the number of juvenile offenders to the criminal justice system as two other Connecticut cities, it sends only half as many juveniles to correctional facilities as Hartford, and three times fewer than Bridgeport. This suggests that, in the community in which the collaboration was developed, the alternatives to incarceration have increased significantly.

This form of collaboration also improves the effectiveness of external controls for juveniles who require consistent supervision. This is reflected in the fact that there have been no outstanding arrest warrants for juvenile offenders in the New Haven city district where neighborhood probation officers, police officers, and mental health professionals have been working together as part of the CD-CP program (Richard Aldridge, personal communication, June 1995). In addition, as an offshoot of the CD-CP program, local probation, school personnel, child welfare, police, and mental health professionals are coordinating services regarding the assessment, disposition, and case supervision of juvenile offenders.

Barriers to Collaboration

Collaborative activities tend to breach traditional professional boundaries. Schools and social service agencies have often chosen to remain distant from the juvenile justice process, precisely in order to maintain good working relationships with the children and families with whom they are involved, as well as to focus exclusively on their own work. A collaborative approach to juvenile delinquency requires all of the professionals involved with children to reexamine the traditional concepts of their work.

Interagency collaborations, especially in the days preceding a defendant's court appearance, also raise serious questions about breaches of accused children's rights to privacy and to the presumption of innocence. A school, for example, may have no business knowing of a child's arrest prior to conviction, and similarly, information about a child's psychological status, family troubles, or prior reputation with the police should have no bearing on the determination of whether a crime was committed by the child.

In the juvenile justice system, a defendant's legitimate assertion of due process rights often impedes intervention. However, due process rights should not stand as an insurmountable barrier to intervention that will serve a troubled child's longer-term interests in developing social skills and in containing impulses of dangerous behaviors likely to place the child at risk for future injury and/or involvement with the adult prison system. Parents may sometimes waive the right to strict confidentiality or to pretrial postponements in the interest of obtaining much needed and wanted services.

Police, probation officers, mental health clinicians, educators, and other service professionals involved with a child convicted of a crime need to engage collaboratively with the child and family in coordinated efforts to provide appropriate structure, support, and ongoing positive relationships with adults. When the juvenile justice system is equipped with a wider range of coordinated interventions – for example, increased probation and police supervision in the community; intensive clinical services for the child and family; highly structured school-based programs; and supervised group living arrangements that combine vocational, educational, and clinical services – accused delinquents and their families may be engaged in thinking about the children's long-term interests. In this context, the crisis of a child's arrest can be used to seek, rather than to avoid, prompt intervention. Similarly, when there are appropriate alternatives to incarceration, prosecuting and defense attorneys will be in a better position to understand an adolescent's needs and advise about options that address the need for external controls when internal controls have failed.

This is a very recently emerging area of collaboration. Published accounts of such collaborations are still rare. There is an urgent need for well-designed, rigorous research in this area.

New Directions for Research

Both practical and ethical objections may be raised to the use of a classic experimental design, consisting of random assignment of children to a treatment program and a control group of untreated children, to test the effectiveness of programs like CD-CP. However, a quasi-experimental long-term design in a large city could allow for a better investigation than is ordinarily undertaken. Cook and Campbell (1979) offer a comprehensive look at some appropriate research designs. The methodological issues are too complex to cover in detail here, but this is a crucial area for research. Such research is felt by many to be both justified and feasible in social experiments where the stakes are high.

The quasi-experimental design does include experimental and control comparisons. Selecting a control school within a single community helps protect against a variety of factors that might invalidate the results, such as changes in employment, school reform, and the like. Nontraditional models such as CD-CP are likely to be implemented in communities where new programs are encouraged. It is important that both the experimental and control districts be involved in the same study. Even when potentially distorting factors have been avoided and known threats to the validity of the study have been minimized, sample sizes need to be large and expectations modest.

Attempts to evaluate a model of this type should involve more than a simple comparison of experimental and control groups on some outcome measure (Bickman, 1989). It should also assess how the program was implemented, its content, and its effect on known risk factors in the multiple social contexts involved (Bronfenbrenner, 1979; Connell, Kubisch, Schorr, & Weiss, 1995; Garbarino, 1985). State and local policy changes, interagency linkages, and home/agency linkages may also emerge from the original, limited partnership.

Finally, the individual children at the center of these networks and the children's experiences with family, school, and helping adults should be carefully considered from a psychological, and particularly a developmental, perspective. This means evolving beyond the exclusive use of behavior checklists, self-reports, and structured interviews as indicators of outcome and change over time, and into the realm of clinical case studies. The case study approach can provide an important supplement to theoretical models and the deceptively simple explanations they sometimes offer about risk factors and protective or therapeutic factors. If funding were available for a randomized, controlled study across comparable *cities*, this would be very useful. Although such research is very expensive, it might be possible with public/private partnerships.

Conclusion

Over the course of development, the majority of children succeed in negotiating both internal and external demands and achieve healthy growth and development using the order, stimulation, and opportunities provided by families, schools, and communities. Too many children fail, however. In many cases, the reasons for the failure are neither simple nor obvious. These negative outcomes are not simply the result of family or school, but rather reflect a complex interaction among social, cognitive, emotional, constitutional, biological, and family factors. There may be internal problems, such as anger, depression, self-criticism, hostility, apathy, and indifference, and behavioral problems, such as defiance, or flagrant rebellion and other forms of oppositional behavior. In other cases, a child in school may consistently fail to meet deadlines or complete assignments, do work hastily or haphazardly, or come to class late or not at all, revealing other internal problems: limited motivation, ambition, self-discipline, or pleasure in mastery. There may not be enough encouragement, structure, or guidance from the family and broader social environment. Self-defeating motivations may come from social intimidation, a need for immediate gratification, involvement in the drug trade, exploitation, violence, vandalism, or other antisocial behavior. In these instances of retarded or failed development, the role of the mental health professional may become key in assessing the whole child in order to engage in coordinated planning that involves parents, the schools, psychological services, and in many cases the criminal justice system.

Although families and schools serve as the primary training grounds for children's socialization, the "laws of the land," at least ideally, reflect the external boundaries for expected behavior and participation in school and the broader community. At their best, agents of the law can serve as benign figures of authority who represent social aspirations and requirements for order, safety, and justice, and who constructively intervene when the individual, family, and/or community crosses the line of the law and contravenes these requirements.

Police also can provide children and families with a sense of security and safety through rapid, authoritative, and effective responses at times of difficulty. All too often, however, children's contacts with police officers typically arouse threatening rather than comforting and positive feelings.

In the psychological lives of inner city children, the appearance of police officers in the context of aggression makes them objects of children's and families' rage; their arrival "after the fact" strengthens children's view of society as unprotective; and the role of police as symbols of the dominant culture may shape children's view of them as representatives of an alien, uncaring outside world (Marans & Cohen, 1993).

Without special awareness and training of police, contacts between police and children are sometimes harsh, and police officers, especially in the midst of a crisis, may be thoughtless about children's emotional needs. Such negative encounters may further reinforce a child's view of society as uncaring and aggressive. Thus, these experiences may strengthen a child's idea that hostile behavior – being rough and tough, bullying, acting strong – is not only appropriate and reasonable in certain situations but is the normal mode of adult functioning.

Our call for collaboration among community organizations is not new – similar calls have been issued for many years, and from many sources. The successful model of CD-CP, however, in its sixth year as of 1997, demonstrates that traditional "turf boundaries" of social institutions can be overcome when a shared frame of reference is applied; that this type of collaboration has great potential for improving the lives of American children; and that we are beginning to accumulate evidence that it can work.

References

American Psychiatric Association. (1994). *Diagnostic and statistical manual of mental disorders* (4th ed.). Washington, DC: American Psychiatric Press.

Bickman, L. (1989). Barriers to the use of program theory [Special issue]. *Evaluation and Program Planning, 12*(4), 387–390.

Boydstun, J., & Sherry, M. (1975). *San Diego community profile: Final report.* Washington, DC: Police Foundation.

Bronfenbrenner, U. (1979). *The ecology of human development: Experiments by nature and design.* Cambridge, MA: Harvard University Press.

Brown, L. P. (1990). Neighborhood-oriented policing [Special issue]. *American Journal of Police, 9*(3).

Bureau of Justice Assistance. (1994, August). *Understanding community policing: A framework for action* [Monograph]. Washington, DC: U.S. Government Printing Office.

Burgan, L., & Rubel, R. (1980). Public school security: Yesterday, today and tomorrow. *Journal of the American Medical Association, 266,* 23–42.

Burt, M. R., Resnick, G., & Matheson, N. (1992). *Comprehensive service integration programs for at-risk youth: Executive summary.* Washington DC: Urban Institute.

Butterfield, G. E., & Turner, B. (Eds.). (1989). *Weapons in schools: NSSC resource paper.* Malibu, CA: National School Safety Center.

Carter, S. (n.d.). *Evaluation report on New Mexico mediation in the schools, 1989–90* (Unpublished report). Albuquerque, NM: New Mexico Center for Dispute Resolution.

Centers for Disease Control and Prevention. (1991). Weapon-carrying among high school students: United States, 1990. *Morbidity and Mortality Weekly Report, 40*(40), 681–684.

Chancellor's Advisory Panel on School Safety. (1993). "Rethinking school safety: The report of the New York City school."

Comer, J. P. (1980). *School power: Implications of an intervention project.* New York: Free Press.

Comer, J. P. (1986). School experiences and preventive intervention. *Resource papers to the report of the National Mental Health Association commission on the prevention of mental-emotional disabilities,* 67–69.

Comer, J. P., & Haynes, N. M. (1990). Helping black children succeed: The significance of some social factors. In K. Lomotey (Ed.), *Going to school: The African-American experience* (pp. 103–112). New York: State University of New York Press.

Commission on Children. (1992). *Beyond rhetoric: A new agenda for children and families.* Washington, DC: Library of Congress.

Committee for Children. (1989). *Second Step, grades 6–8, pilot project 1989–90: Summary report.* Seattle, WA: Author.

Connell, J. P., Kubisch, A. C., Schorr, L. B., & Weiss, C. H. (Eds.). (1995). *New approaches to evaluating community initiatives: Concepts, methods, and contexts.* Washington, DC: Aspen Institute.

Cook, T. D., & Campbell, D. T. (1979). *Quasi-experimentation: Design and analysis issues in field settings.* Chicago: Rand McNally College Publishing.

Costello, E. J. (1994). *Preliminary findings from the Great Smoky Mountain study.* Presentation at the National Institute of Mental Health, Rockville, MD.

Day, C., & Roberts, M. (1991). Activities of the Child and Adolescent Service System program for improving mental health service for children and families [Special section]. *Journal of Clinical Child Psychology, 20*(4), 340–350.

England, M. J., & Cole, R. F. (1992). Prevention as targeted early intervention. *Administration & Policy in Mental Health, 19*(3), 179–189.

Ennett, S., Tobler, N., Ringwalt, C., & Flewelling, R. (1994). How effective is drug abuse resistance education? A meta-analysis of Project DARE outcome evaluations. *American Journal of Public Health, 84*(9), 1394–1401.

Fein, E., & Knaut, S. A. (1986). Crisis intervention and support: Working with the police. *Social Casework: The Journal of Contemporary Social Work, 67*(5), 276–282.

Feindler, E., Marriott, S. A., & Iwata, M. (1984). Group Nager control training for junior high school delinquents. *Cognitive Therapy and Research, 8,* 229.

Gainer, P. S., Webster, D. W., & Champion, H. R. (1993). A youth violence prevention program description and preliminary evaluation. *Archives of Surgery, 128,* 303–308.

Garbarino, J. (1985). *Adolescent development: An ecological perspective.* Columbus, OH: Charles E. Merrill.

Garbarino, J., Dubrow, N., Kostelny, K., & Pardo, C. (1992). *Children in danger: Coping with the consequences of community violence.* San Francisco: Jossey-Bass.

Goldstein, H. (1977). *Policing a free society.* Cambridge, MA: Ballinger.

Goldstein, H. (1990). *Problem oriented policing.* Philadelphia: Temple University Press.

Hammond, W. R. (1990). *Positive Adolescents Choices Training (PACT): Preliminary findings of the effects of a school-based violence prevention program for African-American adolescents.* Columbus, OH: Ohio State Commission on Minority Health.

Harper, S. (Ed.). (1990). *School crisis prevention and response: NSSC resource paper* [Grant No. 85-MU-CX-0003 from the U.S. Department of Justice, Office of Justice Programs, Office of Juvenile Justice and Delinquency Prevention]. Malibu, CA: National School Safety Center.

Harris, L., & Associates. (1993). *Racism and violence in American high schools: Project TEAMWORK responds.* Boston: Northeastern University, Center for the Study of Sport in Society.

Hoagwood, K., & Rupp, A. (1994). Mental health service needs, use, and costs for children and adolescents with mental disorders and their families: Preliminary evidence. *Mental Health, United States* [Publication 94–3000]. Rockville, MD: U.S. Department of Health and Human Services.

Hopkins, N. (1994). School pupils' perceptions of the police that visit schools: Not all police are "pigs." *Journal of Community and Applied Social Psychology, 4*(3), 189–207.

Kaufman, S. (1993). *Assessment of implementing conflict management programs in 17 schools: First year report of the school demonstration project.* Amherst, MA: National Association for Mediation in Education.

Kelling, G. L. (1988). The evolving strategy of policing. *Perspectives on policing series.* Cambridge, MA: Harvard University, Kennedy School of Government, and U.S. Department of Justice, Program on Criminal Justice Policy and Management.

Kelling, G. L., & Moore, M. H. (1988). From political to reform to community: The evolving strategy of police. In J. R. Greene & S. D. Mastrofski (Eds.), *Community policing: Rhetoric or reality.* New York: Praeger.

Kelling, G. L., Pate, T., Dieckman, D., & Brown, C. E. (1974). *The Kansas City preventive patrol experiment: A summary report* (p. 118). Washington, DC: The Police Foundation.

Kenney, D., & Watson, S. (1992). Improving school safety by empowering students. *The Educational Forum, 57,* 50–62.

Kochis, D. S. (1995). The effectiveness of Project DARE: Does it work? *Journal of Alcohol and Drug Education, 40*(2), 40–47.

Kohl, J. (1993). School-based child sexual abuse prevention programs. *Journal of Family Violence, 8*(2), 137–150.

Landsverk, J. (1993). Methodological challenges in mental health services research with children and families in the child welfare system. Unpublished manuscript.

Leaf, P. (1993, October). *Service use from the MECA study.* Presentation at the Annual Conference of the American Association of Public Health.

Lindsay, B., & McGillis, D. (1986). Citywide community crime prevention: An assessment of the Seattle program. In D. P. Rosenbaum (Ed.), *Community crime prevention: Does it work?* (p. 124). Beverly Hills, CA: Sage.

Marans, S. (1994). Community violence and children's development: Collaborative interventions. In C. Chiland & G. Young (Eds.), *Children and violence* (pp. 109–124). Northvale, NJ: Jason Aaronson.

Marans, S., Adnopoz, J., Berkman, M., Esserman, D., MacDonald, D., Nagler, S., Randall, R., Schaefer, M., & Wearing, M. (1995). *The police mental health partnership: A community based response to urban violence.* New Haven, CT: Yale University Press.

Marans, S., & Cohen, D. J. (1993). Children and inner-city violence: Strategies for intervention. In L. Leavitt & N. Fox (Eds.), *Psychological effects of war and violence on children* (pp. 218–301). Hillsdale, NJ: Lawrence Erlbaum.

Martinez, P., & Richters, J. E. (1993). The NIMH community violence project: II Children's distress symptoms associated with violence. *Psychiatry, 56,* 22–35.

Meyers, J. C. (1985). Federal efforts to improve mental health services for children: Breaking a cycle of failure [Special issue]. *Journal of Clinical Child Psychology, 14*(3), 182–187.

Moora, L. G. (1995). "School safety: Promising initiatives for addressing school violence." Report to the Ranking Minority Member, Subcommittee on Children and Families, Committee on Labor and Human Resources, U.S. Senate, United States General Accounting Office [GAO/HEHS-95-106].

Moore, B., & Beland, K. (1992). Alternative education for behaviorally disordered youths: A promise yet unfulfilled. *Behavioral Disorders, 11*(2), 98–108.

National School Safety Center. (1988). *Gangs in schools: Breaking up is hard to do.* Malibu, CA: Author.

Nelson, E., & Slaikeu, K. (1984). Crisis intervention in the schools. In K. Slaikeu (Ed.), *Crisis intervention: A handbook for practice and research.* Newton, MA: Allyn & Bacon.

New Haven Public Schools. (1992). *Social Development project evaluation 1991–92: Final report* (pp. 179–196). New Haven, CT: Author.

Office of Juvenile Justice and Delinquency Prevention. (1995). *Bridging the child welfare and juvenile justice systems.* Washington, DC: National Institute of Justice.

Osofsky, J., Wewers, S., Hann, D., & Fick, A. (1992). Can they feel safe again? The impact of community violence on infants, toddlers, their parents and practitioners. In J. Osofsky & E. Fenichel (Eds.), *Zero to three.* Arlington, VA: National Center for Clinical Infant Programs.

Pastorino, R. (1991). *The mediation process – Why it works: A model developed by students.* Grinnell, IA: Iowa Peace Institute.

Pate, A., Wycoff, M., Skogan, W., & Sherman, L. (1986). *Reducing fear of crime in Houston and Newark: A summary report.* Washington, DC: Police Foundation.

Peterson, S., & Straub, R. (1992). *School crisis survival guide: Management techniques and materials for counselors and administrators.* West Nyack, NY: Center for Applied Research in Education.

Pynoos, R. (1993). Traumatic stress and developmental psychopathology in children and adolescents. In J. Oldham, M. Riba, & A. Tasman (Eds.), *American Psychiatric Press review of psychiatry, Vol. 12* (pp. 205–238). Washington, DC: American Psychiatric Press.

Pynoos, R., Steinberg, A. M., & Wraith, R. (1994). "A developmental model of childhood traumatic stress." Unpublished manuscript.

Richters, J. E., & Martinez, P. (1993). The NIMH community violence project: I Children as victims of and witnesses to violence. *Psychiatry, 56,* 7–21.

Roden, M. (1991). A model secondary school date rape prevention program. In B. Levy (Ed.), *Dating violence: Young women in danger* (pp. 267–278). Seattle, WA: Seal Press.

Rosenbaum, D. P. (1994). *The challenge of community policing.* Thousand Oaks, CA: Sage.

Rubel, R. (1990). Cooperative school system and police responses to high risk and disruptive youth. *Violence, Aggression and Terrorism: An International Journal.*

Sabatino, D. A., Heald, J. E., Rothman, S. G., & Miller, T. L. (1978). Destructive norm-violation school behavior among adolescents: A review of protective and preventive efforts. *Adolescence, 13*(52), 675–686.

Sarmiento, L. (1989). Schools ban hats over gang activity. *Social Policy, 20*(2), 13–14.

Schlenger, W., Etheridge, R., Hansen, D., Fairbank, D., & Onken, J. (1992). Evaluation of state efforts to improve systems of care for children and adolescents with severe emotional disturbances: The CASSP Initial Cohort study. *Journal of Mental Health Administration, 19*(2), 131–142.

Schnelle, J. F., Kirchner, R. E., McNees, M. P., & Lawler, J. M. (1975). Social evaluation research: The evaluation of two police patrolling strategies. *Journal of Applied Behavior Analysis, 8,* 119, 121.

Schonfeld, D. J., & Kline, M. (1994). School-based crisis intervention: An organizational model. *Journal of Crisis Intervention and Time-limited Treatment, 1*(2), 155–166.

Schwab-Stone, M., Ayers, T., Kasprow, W., Voyce, C., Barone, C., Shriver, T., & Weissberg, R. (1995). No safe haven: A study of violence exposure in an urban community. *Journal of the American Academy of Child and Adolescent Psychiatry, 34*(10), 1343–1352.

Sherman, L. W. (1990). Police crackdowns: Initial and residual deterrence. In M. Tonry & N. Morris (Eds.), *Crime and justice, Volume 13* (pp. 123–126). Chicago: University of Chicago Press.

Singer, M. I., Anglin, T. M., Song, L. Y., & Lunghofer, L. (1995). Adolescents exposure to violence and associated symptoms of psychological trauma. *Journal of the American Medical Association, 273*(6), 477–482.

Solnit, A. J., Nordhaus, B. F., & Lord, R. (1992). *When home is no haven: Child placement issues.* New Haven, CT: Yale University Press.

Swan, H. L., & Poertner, J. (1990, April). *Preventing violent behavior of children through classroom instruction in nonviolent problem-solving.* Paper presented at the National Symposium on Child Victimization, Atlanta, GA.

Taylor, L., Zuckerman, B., Harik, V., & Groves, B. (1992). Exposure to violence among inner-city parents and young children. *ADJC, 146,* 487–494.

Terr, L. (1991). Childhood traumas: An outline and overview. *American Journal of Psychiatry, 148*(1), 10–20.

Toby, J. (1980). Crime in American public schools. *Public Interest, 58,* 18–42.

U.S. Department of Justice. (1995). *Guide for implementing the comprehensive strategy for serious, violent, and chronic juvenile offenders.*

Widom, C. (1989). Child abuse, neglect and adult behavior: Research design and findings on criminality, violence, and child abuse. *American Journal of Orthopsychiatry, 59,* 355–367.

Wycoff, M. W. (1982). Evaluating the crime effectiveness of municipal police. In J. R. Greene (Ed.), *Managing police work: Issues and analysis* (p. 118). Beverly Hills, CA: Sage.

Zahner, G., Pawelkiewicz, W., Defrancesco, J., & Adnopoz, J. (1992). Children's mental health service needs and utilization patterns in an urban community: An epidemiological assessment. *Journal of American Academy of Child and Adolescent Psychiatry, 31*(5), 951–960.

12. Tailoring Established After-School Programs to Meet Urban Realities

MARCIA R. CHAIKEN

Introduction

The pressing need for after-school programs for children in the inner city has been well described in other chapters of this volume (see Chapters 1, 2, and 6). To help prevent violence, children and youth need safe places to go and positive activities to do.

Schools are places where effective programs can help stem the harm of youth violence. But children and teens are in school for a relatively limited amount of time. Children age nine to 14 typically spend about 60% of the time they are awake outside the school setting (Timmer, Eccles, & O'Brian, 1985). And violent crimes by juveniles are typically committed during after-school hours – between 2:30 in the afternoon and 8:30 at night (Snyder & Sickmund, 1995).

Around the nation, currently there are more than 500 organizations receiving federal funds to prevent youth problems[1] and about the same number of privately funded organizations providing activities during nonschool hours (Pittman & Wright, 1991). Many of these organizations focus on a single problem, such as drug use, or developing a single proficiency, such as an athletic skill; but research has shown such approaches are not likely to prevent violence or delinquency (Lipsey, 1992; Tolan & Guerra, 1994). While others stress comprehensive approaches that in theory should work, most of these short-term programs will at best have only short-term effects. And, as many researchers (see, e.g., Sherman et al., 1997) have found, many organizations lack the stability and experience needed to implement well-designed approaches to preventing youth violence.

This chapter describes new urban initiatives by national organizations with proven ability to work with children and teens: Boys and Girls Clubs of America, Boy Scouts of America, Girls Incorporated, Girl Scouts of the

U.S.A., National Association of Police Athletic Leagues (PAL), National 4-H Council (sponsored by the U.S. Department of Agriculture 4-H and Youth Development Service), and the YMCA of the U.S.A. Many of these organizations offer a variety of age-graded programs based on an understanding of the developmental skills that all children need to master. All are highly regarded throughout the United States for their success in helping children to develop into "complete" young adults (Larson & Kleiber, 1993).

In a recent survey of these organizations[2] (LINC, 1994), data were provided by 579 sampled affiliates collectively serving 21,000 children in after-school programs on a typical weekday. Exemplary approaches described in this chapter were initially nominated by survey respondents and then selected for case studies by a panel of experts in the fields of youth development, community development, delinquency, and policing for crime prevention. By design, about half the affiliates in the survey were located in big cities with high crime rates. Case studies concentrated on organizations successfully recruiting adolescents – both boys and girls – from neighborhoods experiencing significant youth problems.

Not all of these organizations have traditionally focused on city children. The 4-H Clubs, for example, originally served farm children and emphasized agriculture. Boys and Girls Clubs and Girls Incorporated, on the other hand, have long been serving children in economically impoverished urban neighborhoods. The YMCA, though it has numerous suburban branches, also traditionally focused on cities, owned its own buildings (though not necessarily in the most troubled areas), and offered special recreation opportunities to city children, such as aquatics. PALs were especially intended to combat juvenile delinquency by including in its sports activities children at risk for delinquency. Boy Scouts and Girl Scouts have long served cities as well as small towns and suburbs.

The most destitute urban neighborhoods, however, have in the past been underserved by most youth organizations (Carnegie Council on Adolescent Development, 1992). If asked, many children in these areas wistfully wish for places and activities that others take for granted: "safe parks and recreation centers . . . libraries with the latest books, videos, and records . . . chances to go camping and participate in sports . . . long talks with trusting and trustworthy adults who know a lot about the world . . . and opportunities to learn new skills" (p. 43).

Today, communities as well as youth organizations themselves are realizing that no other groups are better equipped than traditional youth organizations to help troubled inner city children and teens by providing enjoyable and educational recreation and other necessary resources they fail to find elsewhere (Wynn, 1987). With their carefully designed, long-term, age-graded programs, their extensive experience, their highly trained staffs, and their fiscal and administrative skills, they are well prepared for this task.

Many of these organizations have in recent years been turning their attention especially to the needs and harsh realities of inner city children. The 4-H Clubs, in addition to serving rural children, now offer programs specially designed for at-risk youth (Bogenschnieder, Small, & Riley, n.d.) – including, for example (until funding cuts in the mid 1990s), outreach to teen prostitutes in Washington, D.C. The YMCAs now offer programs in school gyms and other locales besides their own buildings. Boys and Girls Clubs, and Girls Incorporated, in addition to their already strong offerings for lower income city children, are also experimenting with new locations for their programs, such as public housing projects. Girl Scouts and Boy Scouts, in addition to their proven age-graded programs appropriate for all children, are putting special emphasis on developing new programs intended to help inner city adolescents deal with violence and other contemporary issues. Several national organizations still specialize in designing gender-appropriate programs; but, to meet community needs, many of their affiliates are introducing adaptations to serve both girls and boys.

In some cities youth organizations are also active participants in diverse, comprehensive, community-wide anti-violence efforts undertaken by a broad coalition of groups, agencies, and citizens. Typically, in these cities the police role is changing dramatically with respect to children and youth at risk for violence. Police are becoming a crucial part of these efforts to provide mentorship and a variety of skill-enhancing after-school activities for children and teens already experiencing problems, as well as helping keep after-school program areas safe. Four examples of highly innovative, community-sponsored programs in three cities (Arlington, Texas; Bristol, Connecticut; and Spokane, Washington) are described in case studies later in this chapter.

Resource Needs

Finding the resources needed to establish after-school programs in economically depressed areas is a major challenge. At a minimum, a viable program requires an adequate meeting place that is safely accessible, funding, well-trained leaders who understand children's needs, challenging, age-graded activities, and community support.

Meeting Places

Although some organizations own their own buildings, many must find meeting places elsewhere. Among organizations responding to the LINC survey (1994), more than 70% meet in places provided rent-free. About 25% meet in youth clubs or youth centers, about 25% in schools, and 25% in churches or other buildings owned by religious organizations. Programs are also provided in community centers, buildings administered by city parks departments, buildings owned by nonprofit institutions such as hospitals, and, more recently, in police department substations.

An ideal meeting place has enough room to provide separate spaces for different types of activities: a check-in counter; a relatively large game area, with table games such as "fooz ball" and billiards; a gym or large space for team sports; an area for messy arts and crafts activities in which spills and splatters are no problem; quiet places to do homework or have a one-to-one conversation; and a room or corner for computer activities. Some centers serving children of all ages have a section that is set aside just for teenagers.

In many urban areas, it is not safe for children and youth to travel alone to the meeting place. Many organizations that can afford them buy vans and use them to transport children, but the costs, which include insurance, are high. A newer idea is to bring the meeting place to the children. Schools are an obvious choice. Although few children find a classroom attractive after a long day of sitting at desks, even a gymnasium, cafeteria, auditorium stage, or a separate bungalow on school grounds can provide enough change of scene and enough room for activities. In Arlington, Texas, local affiliates of three national organizations divide responsibility for providing separate school-based programs; from the time school lets out until early evening children can attend activities led every day there by Boys and Girls Clubs, the YMCA, or Girls Incorporated. In Spokane, Washington, rather than serving separate schools, organizations coordinate the rotation of their programs between the same schools; students can participate in a 4-H Club one day and in Scouts the next.

Bringing the meetings close to children's homes is another solution. Boys and Girls Clubs and other organizations have started to meet in community rooms or vacant apartments in public housing developments. Participants, adult residents, and on-site housing managers interviewed (LINC, 1994) all highly approved of this arrangement. The managers experienced a drop in vandalism and other property destruction. The children not only enjoyed the activities and the safety, they liked being able to get home fast and they enjoyed the frequent, positive comments they received from adult residents about their efforts to improve the buildings and public areas. Parents liked knowing their children were happy and safe and that they were receiving help with their homework.

Funding

Funding for community-based affiliates of national youth organizations primarily comes from private nonprofit sources such as the United Way and other community fund-raising efforts. For organizations with their own buildings, local capital campaigns are a major source of funds for building and maintaining facilities.

Neither the federal government nor state governments provide sustained funding for most traditional youth organizations. The notable exception are 4-H Clubs, which are sponsored by the U.S. Department of Agriculture's Youth Development Service program and run as part of county extension offices. But because of severe cuts in funding for the extension services, many offices are being eliminated and 4-H Clubs along with them – so even the youth organization most closely tied to the government is rapidly losing federal support.

Some federal funds for delinquency reduction efforts are available. For example, Boys and Girls Clubs receive a relatively large proportion of all federal crime prevention funds and use them for efforts such as gang intervention. Girls Incorporated received a small grant for reviewing the needs of girls in the juvenile justice system in the mid 1990s. However, most federal and state funds for violence and delinquency prevention have gone not to established youth organizations but to relatively short-term "innovative" programs that generally receive little support from either the nonprofit or the private sectors (Wilson-Brewer, Cohen, O'Donnell, & Goodman, 1991).

Fund-raising for youth development programs therefore falls to the organizations' leaders. Because the major source of funding is local, neighborhood youth organization leaders must have the grit, determination, and entrepreneurial skills to win over local nonprofit organizations, corporate executives, philanthropic organizations, and influential community leaders. In communities where many needs of residents of all ages are unmet, after-school programs can be a very hard sell. Youth organizations are much better positioned for obtaining funding when they are part of a city-wide collaboration between public and private organizations to prevent crime and violence. More funding is usually provided when youth organizations work together and form partnerships with other community-based agencies. As the case studies presented later in this chapter show, businesses can make superb contributions, not only in terms of funding but in terms of leadership and volunteering.

Organization Traditions

Certain traditions of national youth organizations present difficulties in inner city neighborhoods, but organizations are finding ways to maintain their customs and still meet the needs of these children and youth. Uniforms, for example, are powerful symbols of belonging, but the traditional uniforms of some organizations, paid for by participants, are too expensive for many children and their families. Some organizations have replaced their expensive uniforms with relatively inexpensive pants and tee-shirts. Others use a hand-me-down system, and still others have persuaded local businesses to pay for the uniforms of children who cannot afford to buy them. Businesses may also help to provide equipment for camping and other activities.

Since paying dues is a form of commitment, most youth organizations are reluctant to drop their dues entirely, but to help children living in poverty some solutions are to provide "scholarships" or to charge lower dues in economically depressed neighborhoods. Others use a sliding scale related to family income.

Volunteer leadership by adult volunteers is a highly valued tradition in most youth organizations, and many have depended heavily on parents. In inner city neighborhoods, however, parents may lack parenting skills, and fathers are often absent. In addition, parents and other potential adult leaders often have no childhood experience with the organizations and therefore lack both the experience and the motivation to become leaders. To address this problem, some organizations have recruited retirees and other residents who have successfully raised their own children and enjoy working with children and youth. In several cities, some local corporations allow their employees time off during business hours to volunteer. Girl Scouts, in several cities, are temporarily providing leaders from their professional staff while preparing mothers and other community adults to become troop leaders.

Keeping Order

Vandalism and other property crime can drain resources needed by after-school programs. Violent crime can make staff and participant recruitment difficult.

Table 12.1. *Problems with participants dealt with by 579 organizations, 1993–1994 Program Year*

Problems	N	%
Abuse/neglect at home	114	19.7%
Attacked someone at program site	99	17.1%
Committed other type of illegal act	60	10.4%
Brought weapon other than gun to program site	43	7.4%
Brought drugs to program site	21	3.6%
Brought gun to program site	13	2.2%

Note: Estimated number of children served daily=21,000.
Source: LINC, 1994.

Crime in the Meeting Place

It is very likely in high-crime neighborhoods that crime and violence will have to be dealt with in and around the youth organization meeting place. Among the organizations that responded to the LINC survey (1994), vandalism was the most common offense, followed by theft, and then by violence (see Table 12.1) such as grabbing, punching, or choking, and less often, assaults and threats with weapons. Most offenders were children or teens, more often outsiders than participants, but adults from the neighborhood were responsible for some crimes against the youth organizations.

Various anticrime measures have been tried. Putting locks on doors, gates, cabinets, and closets to limit access and protect possessions and equipment is one strategy. Requiring a responsible adult to accompany participants when they leave the meeting place is another. And anticrime programs are frequently offered as activities.

The LINC survey (1994) showed that in areas with high crime rates, a close working relationship between the organization providing the after-school activities and the police was the one factor significantly associated with less crime in the meeting place. Swift responses by the police to emergency calls from the meeting place is of course essential; however, the informal presence of police as everyday visitors and program leaders, actively supporting the children's activities, appears to be even more important. Their friendly presence in the meeting place not only provides much greater safety for children but is changing the whole relationship between children, neighbors, and the police in some communities.

Discipline

Not just "good kids" are recruited by affiliates of national organizations; the LINC survey (1994) shows they are successfully attracting many young participants who are either victims of violence and/or delinquent themselves. Youth organization staff know from long experience that most children from violent homes and crime-ridden neighborhoods cannot be expected to be mannerly when they first participate in after-school programs. The key components needed to maintain order are clear-cut rules; staff who know how to use age-appropriate and positive forms of discipline; and, for adolescents, participation in making the rules.

The rules in the main branch of the Arlington, Texas, Boys and Girls Clubs, for example, are stated in positive, "do" terms. They include important general principles (e.g., "Treat others as you would want to be treated," and "Respect one another") as well as specific rules about behavior (e.g., "Walk in the building"; "Keep your hands and feet to yourself"; and "Speak in courteous language only"). Consequences are spelled out clearly: they range from a time-out (when a child is required to sit quietly, with legs crossed and hands folded in the lap), to suspension from the program, to calling the police (for serious crimes). The object of the discipline is to gradually teach the participants the value of self-control, rather than simply to impose control upon them, and staff members there know how to make children and youth feel valued and respected as people even when their disruptive behavior must be disciplined. This style of discipline may, over time, teach important lessons about nonviolence to the participants.

Following are the rules formally endorsed by the teenagers at the Teen Center in Arlington, Texas:

- It is assumed that all who come to the Teen Center will:
  Take care of the center
  Obey all laws
  Respect the neighborhood
  Treat all with mutual respect
- The following are examples of behaviors that will result in being asked to leave the building:
  Smoking in the building
  Leaving trash for others to pick up
  Refusing to cooperate with staff
- The following are examples of behaviors that will result in the police being called and legal action being pursued:
  Stealing
  Destruction of property
  Threatening harm

Violence
Possession of illegal substances

An additional rule the Arlington teenagers decided was critical, and voluntarily observe, is a ban on any gang symbols in the center. The teenagers realize that allowing gang symbols increases the chances of gang activity in the center, and although many of the participants claim to be gang members, the center is considered neutral territory. Additionally, weapons of any type, including sticks or metal objects, by agreement are not brought into the center.

Because of the large number of teenage boys in the center and the past involvement of many in violence, all staff members are consciously vigilant and constantly monitor all the meeting place areas. Except for restrooms and the photography darkroom (used only under the supervision of an instructor), an unwritten rule is that doors to all rooms occupied by participants must stay open at all times. Teenagers are allowed to bring their own audio equipment, as long as they use earphones, but another unwritten rule is no loud music. One staff member explained, to prevent trouble, "We need to use all our senses: seeing, hearing, smelling [for smoke], feeling [gut reactions], touching . . . but not physical touching. But the sense we use most is common sense."

Situations in which staff members need to step in and remind the teen participants about the rules commonly involve questions of "respect." The adolescents are very sensitive to challenges from other teenagers made, for example, during a basketball game. Given the frequent violent outcomes on the surrounding streets in similar situations, the adolescents nearby become tense, and telltale "noise" begins. Staff alert to the needs and values of the teenagers immediately break the tension with a simple take-charge action (e.g., blowing a whistle, giving a time-out sign, or simply walking over to the locus of the challenge), focus the teens on the clear-cut rules, talk quietly to the participants involved in the challenge, and then ask for an instant replay (in the basketball example). No one is blamed, everyone "saves face," and respect is maintained.

Of course, the activities themselves are also an alternative to activities that commonly result in violence. Adolescents in these programs are often thoroughly engaged in positive activities that demand their full attention and distract them from youth violence.

Program Activities

There is no doubt that among the thousands of members enrolled in the organizations studied, the children and teenagers who consistently participate in their activities find them enjoyable (LINC, 1994). The high numbers of participants (an average of 21,000 on a typical day in 1993 in 579 organizations) alone testifies to the attractiveness of the opportunities provided.

Additional evidence is provided by the extent to which the participants are visibly engaged in activities. Except for an occasional youth assigned to a disciplinary time-out for breaking one of the rules, it is uncommon to see a participant who is not actively focused on a particular game or program activity. The keys to this active engagement are realistic challenges and meaningful rewards. An undercurrent of good-natured moaning and groaning often accompanies intense efforts of participants carrying out a variety of activities from homework lessons to physical endeavors; and a constant murmur of encouragement from the staff and other participants acknowledges the difficulties being faced. But shouts of success and acknowledgments of success frequently ring out when math assignments are completed, for example, or a group project reaches the desired goal.

There is no randomness to these events. Careful preparation on the part of the organizations' national program staff and equally careful implementation on the part of the local staff ensure regular challenges and rewards for children and teens at different stages of development and of different abilities. Most programs developed by national organizations are firmly grounded in current research findings about developmental needs, and they address the real concerns of children growing up in any culture (e.g., universal concerns among young adolescents about sexuality) and the real concerns of children growing up in the inner city. Programs are designed for children and adolescents of specific ages and specific developmental stages. And local staff are trained to implement the program materials using interactive training techniques.

The results of years of development of and training for delivering particular programs is manifested in the behavior of the participants. Places where youth organizations are providing programs for large groups of school-age children have a familiar ring, whether they are Boys and Girls Clubs, the YMCA, Girls Incorporated, or other organizations. Enthusiastic staff or adult volunteers provide direct supervision and encouragement to small groups of the youngest children, who sprawl on the floor coloring pictures, using building materials, or playing simple board games. Children in the middle elementary grade range, in larger groups, rambunctiously play games involving running, jumping, tossing balls, and other enlivening physical skills; others create colorful objects with a wide variety of arts and crafts materials, while discussing day-to-day experiences about school or home, praising each other's creations, and occasionally bickering over the only sheet of purple paper or container of glue.

Children approaching adolescence may assist younger children in arts and crafts projects; play one-to-one competitive table games such as fooz ball or pool; practice team sport skills; prepare for community performances, such as a play; or "hang out" with a staff member of the same gender and curiously quiz him or her about personal issues such as: "What movie did you see with your girlfriend?"; "How come you were at school so late last night?"; or "Is the guy who drove you here your brother or your boyfriend?"

Typically the noise level is high, with chattering children, and compared to school settings the multitude of activities may seem chaotic. But in separate corners or side rooms designated as "quiet areas," children work with adults on homework assignments, sit transfixed at a computer terminal, or are engrossed in a story being read to them. Occasionally a child sits disconsolately in a time-out area waiting out a penalty for breaking a rule, or a child may be off in an out-of-ear-shot corner discussing a problem or concern with a staff member.

Toward early evening, parents or other family members often arrive, waiting impatiently for the children being picked up to prepare to leave. Most of the children are not eager to end their activities and leave their friends. Before they leave, the participants can be seen more than willingly washing paint brushes, sweeping floors, neatly stacking sports equipment, or completing other cleanup activities. The youngest children won't leave before they receive a good-bye hug from a staff member. Each departing child receives a compliment about his or her achievement that day, a mention of upcoming events, and a warm smile: "Thanks for the really good cleanup job you did today, Billy. Don't forget, next time you get to pick the activity."

Adolescent Participants

Although most younger children enjoy traditional program activities such as crafts and relay races, by the end of junior high/middle school or high school many adolescents in all social groups begin to drop out of youth organizations, because they no longer find the activities challenging or the adult leaders attuned to their interests. This is a critical problem, since all adolescents need support from and opportunities in the community for building competencies in six essential areas: health/physical, personal/ social, creative/cognitive, vocational, communal ethics, and citizen participation (Pittman & Wright, 1991). More specifically, especially in neighborhoods with high rates of violence, adolescents need opportunities to build and practice basic life skills known to be integral to healthy adolescent development: "problem-solving skills, planning and decision-making skills, cognitive strategies for resisting peer and media influences, skills for increasing self-monitoring and self-regulation, and coping strategies to deal with everyday stresses" (Hamburg, 1990, p. 3).

A major study of youth-serving organizations in urban areas (McLaughlin, Irby, & Langman, 1994) found that although adolescents first come to places with teen programs because they are looking for fun, they are more likely to participate regularly if:

- An environment has been created by program administrators and staff in which individuals are valued and youth are considered to be resources rather than problems for their community; there are clear rules for behavior and membership, but there is flexibility in responding to the real crises faced by many teens in urban settings; and the adults are attuned to the interests, aspirations, and values of adolescents and treat them with the same amount of respect as adults while at the same time recognizing that like all children, they still need to be protected.
- Activities for teens present real challenges and experiences in planning, preparing for, and publicly presenting projects they and their communities truly value; sufficient activities are presented to allow for choice, but teens are encouraged to try activities that will develop competencies through hands-on experience and practice; and teens are urged to meet the challenges presented by the activities by prodding, nagging, teasing, and loving.
- Outreach to the teens and adults in the community is an ongoing process that involves messages that are understandable to teens and other community members, and activities encompass other neighborhood institutions and people who are integral to the day-to-day lives of the teens.

Among the youth organizations responding to the LINC survey (1994), almost three-fourths (72%) have adolescent participants. To increase teen participation in urban areas, many youth organizations are developing and testing new programs designed specifically for urban teenagers and are training their professional staff and volunteer leaders to lead them. Some of these programs are popular with inner city teenagers. Boys and Girls Clubs' "Smart Moves," for example, is a primary prevention program that facilitates small group discussions about real temptations many young teenagers face every day, such as alcohol use and premature sexual activity. This program helps adolescents learn how they can refuse to take serious risks without seeming "not cool" or becoming social outcasts. In one children's center visited for the study, the participants clearly liked this activity. When the time for Smart Moves was announced in the game room, the younger children looked on with envy and the older teenagers nodded knowingly as the young teenagers dropped their games and raced to the next room to take part.

Another example is the Girls Incorporated "Teens for Teens" program, designed to help adolescents from troubled communities realize their ability to bring about positive change in their neighborhoods. Under the direction of older adolescent interns, groups of young teenagers (in some cities, boys as well as girls) learn about factors that affect their own health and that of others in the community. After deciding which local problems are most important they carry out prevention projects in their communities.

For many inner city Teens for Teens participants, violence is one of the most serious health threats. Participants found that the program helped them to advocate successfully for changes in their neighborhoods that made their lives safer. For example, participants in one high-crime neighborhood presented a convincing argument to members of the local school board asking for a bus to take them home at the end of their after-school program. The board, realizing from the presentation that the teens were learning much from but were beginning to drop out of the program because they wanted to get home before dark, rerouted a late afternoon bus from a neighboring school for their use. In another community, teenage girls identified sexual assault as a serious problem and asked the police department to train them and their schoolmates in self-defense. The assignment was given to a female police officer who, having been a victim herself as a teen, was eager to teach the course. A large group of students participated with high interest, and, as one outcome, continued to call on this officer as a trusted adviser after the training was complete.

Girls Incorporated's "Connections Advocacy" program was designed for adolescent girls ages 12–15 who are often absent from school, have started to experiment with health-threatening behaviors, show signs of depression, experience sudden declines in academic performance, and lack family support. After a year of grappling with and overcoming initial implementation problems, two cities had highly visible accomplishments. In one case, the juvenile facility director in Rapid City, South Dakota, reported that the program broke the pattern of girls cycling in and out of the juvenile justice system. As a result, local funding was then made available for the program for Rapid City boys.

Adult mentors (the advocates) were selected on the basis of empathy, friendliness, ability to listen, and a mature understanding of teenagers' needs. They interacted with the adolescents informally in activities that the teens enjoy but they also listened carefully to their "idle chatter" in order to discern clues about individual needs. When activities were planned, time for talking with participants in small groups or individually was always taken into account.

Through participation in the Connections Advocacy program, the teens learned that they could make responsible decisions and take actions to improve their lives. The advocates encouraged the teens to act in situations they used to think were beyond their control and helped them to find realistic ways to effect change. The advocates provided trust, encouragement, and tangible support as the teenagers worked to achieve their goals. When they failed (as inexperienced adolescents often do), the advocates did not blame them but instead encouraged them to see what could be done differently and to try again (Chaiken, 1995).

Activities for teenage boys in the inner city must provide opportunities for status; peer group approval; independence; and tests of physical, personal, and social endurance that boys of that age crave but tend to otherwise find in street violence. Sports are often the "hook" that lures these boys into youth organizations, but they will stay if the organizations provide suitable activities for them. A vivid example observed on a particular site visit was an Explorer Scout in his uniform deftly handling a horse from the mounted police unit while other teenagers wearing gang colors or symbols looked on with obvious awe and envy.

The need for thrills and independence many teenage boys experience can be satisfied by presenting unusual, yet positive, challenges. For example, although wilderness adventures certainly provide thrills, for many inner city youth trips out of their own neighborhoods in the city can be frightening ventures into uncharted territory. For example, most of the urban teens observed as part of one research project displayed great bravado when planning forays to distant corporations in financial districts or to major universities or medical complexes as part of a project they were carrying out. But in retrospect, as they regaled the other participants with their success in negotiating the new places and social environments, they admitted how uncertain they had been about where they were going and whether they could ever find their way back. "Man, I thought I was gonna haveta live in Brooklyn!" one teen from the Bronx reported, after venturing into lower Manhattan for the first time and boarding the wrong subway train. Their pride in having accomplished this adventure successfully (which did require courage) was evident.

Case Studies of Innovative Youth Programs

Youth organizations working alone in a city to help children and youth are on an uphill road. Youth organizations working in cities where a community-wide, collaborative effort to improve the lives of children and youth is under way have a much better chance of success. Four outstanding youth programs[3] in three cities are described in the case studies that follow. These cities have made a comprehensive, community-wide effort to promote changes that will help prevent violence and crime in threatened neighborhoods. Rather than trying to bring about change using child-by-child approaches, they have taken a long, hard look at themselves as communities, determined what changes are needed, and have acted to make those changes happen. Each of these cities has, as a result, used an intensely collaborative approach that brings together all available resources – city government and agencies, national youth affiliates, local youth-serving agencies, local residents, business leaders, churches, schools, police officers, and juvenile justice agencies. These are cities in which certain deteriorating neighborhoods had recently experienced rapid social change accompanied by increasing crime and violence rates. In response, the cities adopted the kind of community-wide public health prevention efforts advocated in this volume, and their efforts clearly appear to have made a difference.

In some cases, the initial impetus came from residents who did not want to watch their neighborhoods deteriorate further. In other cases, alarmed city government officials and business leaders led the way. In all three cities, the crucial role of providing positive recreation activities for children and youth in preventing delinquency and youth violence was recognized and energetically addressed. These three cities also drew widely on the varied expertise of national youth organizations, both for their traditional programs and for help in designing innovative ones especially suited to their communities. A crucial factor helping to ensure the success of several of these community efforts was the extensive support offered by the police, who, in the new spirit of community policing, not only supported but actively participated in these innovative after-school programs for children. Juvenile justice authorities also cooperated by helping to ensure that juvenile offenders whose offenses were minor were supervised within the communities' youth programs rather than being sent to reformatories, which often simply reinforce violent behavior.

Strong partnerships were also forged between professionals in youth development, such as mental health professionals and social workers, and professionals in other youth-serving agencies such as schools, police, and the juvenile justice system. A major purpose of these partnerships was to ensure that decisions for individual children were made on the basis of a comprehensive review of the child's situation: family, school, mental health, and developmental status. Housing local youth-serving professionals together can make such collaboration much easier. In Spokane, Washington, for example, representatives from key city agencies have their offices together in "Community Oriented Police Services (COPS) Shops," neighborhood buildings that serve as both community centers and police substations.

Several of these cities' neighborhoods have community centers that provide a place for numerous essential activities, including extensive before- and after-school and weekend programs for children. Outstanding features of these community center programs for children are the impressive number of hours and days when activities are offered, the variety of activities offered, and the extensive involvement of community residents, local organizations, and city agencies in making the programs succeed.

Case Study 1: Bristol, Connecticut, Family Center for Girls and Boys

Bristol, Connecticut, is a primarily blue-collar town of 60,000 that has accommodated successive waves of various ethnic and racial groups. The previously homogeneous city has been altered by pockets of poverty in the central area and the development of upscale homes in the outlying areas. Bristol began experiencing "big city problems" such as child neglect and teen pregnancy.

Unlike larger cities that have undergone population change, many of Bristol's families have been living there for generations. Many business owners were raised in Bristol and now contribute time to the school mentoring program. Along with churches, clubs, and fraternal organizations, the Bristol Family Center for Girls and Boys is an organization that has been an anchor in the community for generations.

In Bristol, needs assessment for children was spearheaded by the city's Youth Services Bureau, a state-mandated agency funded jointly by the state and the municipality that coordinates all community youth services and also provides direct services. The agency was instrumental in the formation of the Greater Bristol Community Leadership Team, with the mission of aiding families and individuals. Comprised of local officials, representatives of community groups and business groups, and directors of public and private agencies and service organizations, the team designated public safety as a top priority and stressed organizing neighborhoods and improving access to services. On the basis of surveys of the needs of the city's children, they concluded that after-school programs were essential.

Bristol used several approaches to gain and maintain widespread support for these programs: community workshops, in which community leaders learned to collaborate on behalf of children; experiential programs to engage city officials and directors of influential organizations; and neighborhood outreach to broaden the base of neighborhood support.

The membership of the board of the Bristol Family Center for Girls and Boys shows the breadth of the community's involvement in the center. It consists of an assistant superintendent of schools, the president of one of the leading local industries, a CPA, an insurance company administrator, an employee of a city department, a local bank's investment manager, and several retired residents.

The Bristol Family Center, a two-story brick building on a downtown street, built more than 60 years ago, boasts a modern gymnasium and a swimming pool. The center attracts children from all over the city. It is open from early morning, when preschoolers are dropped off for child care, to 9:00 P.M., when teens finish swimming, gymnastics, dance classes, and other activities. Among the numerous children served are day care children, schoolchildren, teen parents and their babies, young offenders assigned by the Bristol Juvenile Review Board to carry out community service, and children with physical disabilities.

The Bristol Family Center is affiliated with Girls Incorporated, and many of the activities are typical of the organization's offerings. Participants can choose from an extensive menu of activities designed to foster their physical, social, psychological, and intellectual development, including sports, discovery, and creative play activities designed for various age groups from early childhood through high school. Adolescents have their own programs, including science projects and activities that involve off-site participation in wider community events; they also are employed formally or informally as staff assistants and take responsibility for helping younger children who need assistance. Many younger children arrive at the Center immediately after school and stay until their parents finish work; toward early evening it is common to see the youngest participants looking tired but content as they cuddle up to or lean on the older participants and "help" them prepare decorations for the center.

Offerings also include a "Young Parent Program" for adolescent parents. In collaboration with schools, classes are held at the Bristol Family center so that pregnant teens and young mothers can finish their education. Day care for infants and toddlers with young parents is provided at the Center and in Bristol schools. Parenting classes are offered for both young mothers and fathers, and counseling is also provided to help these teenagers deal with normal adolescent stresses compounded by parenthood. Home visits by Family Center staff provide needed attention to young mothers and fathers. Adult mentors for the mothers are also trained and provided by the center. Although cases of teen pregnancy have not declined in Bristol, the number of teen mothers who complete high school has risen from approximately 11% to about 85%; the number of teen mothers having second babies has greatly decreased; and very few cases of child neglect or abuse are now found among the teen parents.

The Bristol Family Center for Girls and Boys participates with the Bristol Police Department and the Youth Services Bureau in a program that provides an alternative to detention for juvenile offenders. The coalition also involves the Bristol schools, other youth development organizations, the Department of Probation, and both public and private agencies providing clinical services for school-age children and their families. Representatives from these agencies review cases of juveniles who have been detained by the police. Alternative options for a plan of action for each child are discussed. For first-time adolescent offenders involved in minor crimes, one alternative is restitution through community service; in these cases a Family Center representative can volunteer to place the teen as an aide in one of the center programs, where participation may aid the teen's positive development while fulfilling the community service requirements. Adolescents who receive a "sentence" of community restitution in the center must sign a contract with the Bristol Juvenile Review Board that specifies the number of hours they are to work in a set calendar period. The hope is, of course, that participation in Family Center activities will become an attractive alternative to delinquency. Center staff say adolescents assigned such community service often participate voluntarily after their sentences have been served.

Case Study 2: Arlington, Texas, Teen Center

Located between Dallas and Fort Worth, Texas, Arlington (population 270,000) is the home base for several major corporations and boasts one of the best-educated populations in the nation. Arlington is undergoing rapid growth, however, with an influx of well-to-do commuters as well as large numbers of low-income families fleeing the economically depressed larger cities. The city now has enclaves of primarily African American or Latino families living in large complexes of apartments for low-income residents. Both long-term residents and more recent arrivals are concerned by the rapid growth, strain on services, and the changing nature of the city.

Two primary strategies were used to deal with rising crime and violence rates in Arlington's impoverished neighborhoods. One was the City of

Arlington Crime Prevention Action Plan, designed by more than a hundred residents and community professionals. Establishing after-school programs was one of the key recommendations made by several task forces that helped create the plan.

At the same time, in order to build a collaboration to address youth issues, the Arlington Human Service Planners convened a group of citizens and youth service professionals to explore issues concerning the city's children. The group included a United Way official and representatives from seven youth organizations, including Boys and Girls Clubs, the YMCA, and Arlington Youth Services; representatives from city agencies that serve children, including the police department, the public library, and the Department of Parks and Recreation; liaisons from the mayor's office, the University of Texas at Arlington, and coalitions of religious organizations; representatives from civic and business groups; representatives of the school district and PTA; and community volunteers. Together the group assembled a wealth of information about the status of children in Arlington, about neighborhoods where problems were most intense, and about groups and agencies that could help. A planning commission nominated by the group designated for first emphasis programs for low-income minority children. The policy set by this group of concerned residents was clear and directive: not only was the continued viability of the city a major concern, but the healthy development of children was considered to be a cornerstone of the community's social structure.

In 1992, the Arlington Youth Services opened the Teen Center as part of their ongoing adaptation of services to help address these concerns. The Teen Center occupies a medium-size, one-story concrete building, formerly used by the Department of Parks and Recreation, in one of the older city areas in southeast Arlington. An especially valuable feature of this and other innovative centers is the many hours of service it offers. The Teen Center is open seven days per week: on schooldays until 9:00 or 10:00 P.M., and on weekends from 10:00 A.M. to 6:00 P.M.

The Teen Center is an affiliate of Girls Incorporated and also works with the YMCA, city youth agencies, and churches. Members of the women's auxiliary for Arlington Youth Services provide hours of on-site administrative support services as well as helping hands for creative projects and an annual gala fund-raiser. The Teen Center attracts up to one hundred participants per day, both boys and girls ages 11–18.

At the Teen Center the vast proportion of participants are minority members, some with gang affiliations. The primary neighborhood from which participants are drawn had been experiencing a surge of youth violence, and a relatively large number of participants were previously involved in some of the most serious incidents, including homicides.

The Arlington Teen Center also cooperates in a juvenile diversion program, offering alternatives to detention, and a small number of participants have been assigned to the Teen Center by the courts. The majority of participants, however, have been recruited through initial outreach to teens who have already been experiencing difficulties, including contacts with police, in neighborhoods where most teenagers never previously had the opportunity to participate in constructive activities during nonschool hours.

One critical barrier to participation – the need to get safely to and from the Teen Center – has been overcome by Arlington Youth Service vans that make frequent runs between participants' neighborhoods and the center.

The teen participants have created strict rules regarding their own behavior and, when tempers flare, are prompted to follow these rules by the staff. Arlington Police Department patrol officers regularly drop by the center, beginning in late afternoon, and remain to watch and cheer basketball games. Their presence helps staff keep adolescent conflicts in check and is key to local residents' willingness to have the Teen Center in their neighborhood.

Teenagers interviewed made clear that part of the reason they like to spend many hours playing basketball in the Teen Center was because they knew that a staff member was available as a referee when issues of respect arise: "Archie, he knows when to say 'chill'; on the streets . . . no Archie to say chill, so we fight."

Case Study 3: Spokane, Washington, Nevawood Youth Volunteers and Family Focus Program

Spokane, Washington, like other cities in the Northwest, has a long history of forming coalitions to address shared problems. In recent years Spokane has experienced an influx of new residents spanning the economic and ethnic spectrum, including impoverished people of European ancestry, Native Americans, and recent immigrants from Southeast Asia and East India. Rising crime and violence rates prompted a community-wide prevention effort.

Both of the programs detailed in this case study are examples of successful collaboration involving (among others) private citizens, government, a local university, city police, business leaders, youth agencies, and youth organizations. In both of the neighborhoods described, beyond the critical actions of neighborhood residents who asserted the need for change, the contributions of a responsive city government, a police department ready to go far beyond the traditional definition of policing, a federally sponsored program designed to help not just children but families and entire neighborhoods, and both traditional and innovative programs of national youth organizations (e.g., Girl Scouts, Boy Scouts, 4-H/Spokane County Extension Programs) are interesting features.

The Nevawood COPS Youth Volunteers. The Nevada and contiguous Lidgerwood neighborhoods (known collectively as "Nevawood") were never the highest crime-rate areas in Spokane, but the community had begun to experience a rising crime rate with more burglaries, vandalism, and youth violence. In reaction, neighborhood Girl Scouts and their troop leader were instrumental in the forming of the Spokane Police Department's Nevawood COPS (Community Oriented Police Services) program and its youth group, the Nevawood Youth COPS Volunteers. Public safety was the original focus, but the Youth COPS Volunteers' activities now include a range of some distinctively attractive recreation opportunities for adolescents, both boys and girls, as well as a variety of community service programs.

The Nevawood Youth COPS Volunteers were founded as part of a community service project by a local Girl Scout, whose troop leader had encouraged in the troop a high level of enthusiasm and a strong belief in the capacity of youth to accomplish social change. This teenager organized her sister scouts to recruit other neighborhood adolescents who could be trained by the police as youth volunteers to help prevent crime. She persuaded a local business owner to provide a facility on Mt. Spokane for the training and to provide "a hiking excursion, swimming, horseback riding, and a meal" for each trainee. In addition to the many teenage girls who wanted to join, neighborhood boys who had never before thought of scouting as "cool" also asked to participate.

One of the volunteers' first projects was to reclaim the deteriorating Nevawood neighborhood park. By documenting its run-down condition, they secured repairs from the city's parks department. They then held overnight campouts there (protected by the police).

Over the following years the Youth COPS Volunteers undertook several anticrime programs such as "Knock and Nag," a project to remind residents to lock their doors, and "Alley Watch," occasional 6:00 P.M. to 2:00 A.M. vigils (supervised by the police) in areas with high burglary rates. In addition, they held a blanket drive for homeless and other needy people.

The Youth COPS Volunteers were also publicly recognized for their other creative efforts. One activity drew on local culture as a way to create a sense of competence and self-esteem among the girls. For an area-wide Girl Scout campout, the girls decided to entertain the other troops with a jump rope demonstration. Performing to music, their ability to tumble, turn, and do splits amazed the audience. The jumping was such a hit that this subgroup of the Girl Scouts/Youth COPS Volunteers, known as the "Side Steps," is now often called on to perform at community fund-raisers and city events. Side Steps currently includes original members now in high school and college, and younger girls who emulate their older counterparts both on and off the stage.

The Nevawood Youth COPS Volunteers currently have more than 60 participants, both girls and boys, most in their mid-teens. (The girls are still organized into a Girl Scout troop.) The Youth COPS Volunteers run their meetings entirely on their own. They decide as a group which of the many projects requested by the community to tackle. They form ad hoc committees to take responsibility for each project they agree to do, with meetings held in places that provide recreation opportunities, such as a commercial indoor playground.

The Youth COPS Volunteers have received extensive support, from the beginning, from COPS, the Spokane Police Department's Community Oriented Police Services, one of the most innovative community policing programs in the country. The police assisted the Girl Scouts in founding the Nevawood Youth COPS Volunteers, supervised the crime watch program, and performed the training at Mt. Spokane, in effect providing several unique activity programs. COPS has been instrumental, both in Nevawood and in a West Central Spokane neighborhood (described following) in assisting youth groups.

The police not only support and actively participate in neighborhood-sponsored programs, they have also originated youth programs themselves throughout the city, such as a program to prevent drunken driving by teens on prom night, which has had spectacular success, and a popular Boy Scout Explorer post, which has offered unique activities for many teens. This program, founded by the Spokane police in 1987, goes well beyond conventional scouting. To prepare younger adolescents to meet the rigorous Explorer Scout criteria, the police offer leadership training for students in the eighth and ninth grades, which includes not only physical exercise but communications skills, teamwork, and leadership skills; this training is available to girls as well as boys.

Family Focus in West Central Spokane. The West Central Spokane community is a multiethnic neighborhood that has experienced some of Spokane's worst social problems, including violent crime. Fear of crime and the destruction of social support networks were among the serious problems that threatened the welfare of children in this neighborhood. The Family Focus program, along with the neighborhood's COPS organization, has helped to achieve a remarkable turnaround in this area of the city.

Family Focus seeks to break down social isolation, bolster parenting and other life skills, and bring neighbors together for mutual day-to-day support and assistance. Administered by Washington State University's Spokane County Cooperative Extension, the program has engaged intensively in community outreach. Door-to-door visits by its Family Resource Assistants (now called Extension Educators) were carried out to recruit neighborhood residents for the program. Family Focus activities now take place throughout the West Central Spokane neighborhood: in parents' homes; in a small local COPS West police substation-cum-community center; and in the West Central Community Center, constructed in the early 1980s as a federal Housing and Urban Development-funded project.

In the early 1990s, before Family Focus and COPS West began their outreach initiatives, the West Central Community Center had difficulty attracting participants despite their modern building. Today the center is a beehive of activity. During the day, developmentally delayed adults are cared for by trained providers until their caregivers return from work. COPS West and Family Focus representatives often meet there with school administrators and the center's director to plan neighborhood activities, such as "Neighbors Day," on which many local youth groups participate annually in a parade and general celebration. An extensive program of before- and after-school activities for children is also offered.

K.A.R.E. (Kids Achieve through Recreation and Enrichment) Club activities supervised by West Central Community Center professional staff are available school days from 7:00 A.M. to 6:00 P.M. Activities provided by outside organizations, such as martial arts and dance classes, can take place until 9:00 P.M. On a typical day, children are dropped off at the Community Center in the early morning by parents on their way to work. Instead of waiting in empty homes and walking to school alone, elementary schoolchildren stay at the center, which offers a choice of activities, until a van takes them to school. The very youngest often choose a small-group quiet activity, in which they can talk with a staff member about experiences that worry or interest them. Many of the older children choose to join the 4-H's "Early Morning Club" activities. They enjoy the hands-on activities accompanied by useful information. For example, one project in which various flower patterns were used to make refrigerator magnets led to a simple botany lesson and a discussion of good food in the refrigerator – and of "why your head feels funny" if one eats lunch early and misses one's meal at lunchtime.

After school, and until early evening, the West Central Community Center is filled with children doing a variety of things. Snacks and homework (with help) come first, followed by a choice of age-graded K.A.R.E. programs. On some days a Girl Scout meeting will be in progress as well. The center has supplemented its own 4-H programs by working with the local Girl Scout Council to found Girl Scouts in the neighborhood. Since most of the local mothers are not familiar with scouting, the council provides a trained adult Girl Scout leader for the present but is working to prepare mothers to lead the troop by involving them in Girl Scout events.

COPS West, a police-sponsored citizens' group, was organized in 1991 through the joint efforts of citizens, business owners, and the Spokane Police Department. (The original motivation was a resident's horror at several crimes against children in the area.) The COPS West administration, staffed by community volunteers (many of whom are Family Focus participants or graduates); the Neighborhood Resource Officer (NRO) assigned as a liaison by the Spokane Police Department; and, more recently, representatives from the district attorney's office and the juvenile justice system, all have offices in the COPS West building, which serves as the local police station.

Both traditional and innovative neighborhood policing techniques are used by COPS West members. Teams of neighbors are trained in dispute resolution and respond to calls involving conflicts between community children and teens or other residents, if the Neighborhood Resource Officer believes police intervention is not required. Adult members patrol the streets both before and after school, to make sure children are safe and that older teens are not harassing each other or younger children. COPS West and Family Focus also cooperate in many community projects, and both offer children's activities at the West Central Community Center.

In West Central Spokane, a close bond between uniformed police officers and residents has been forged through joint participation in upbeat community events, and the police have functioned as positive mentors for children and youth. Integral to the community events are the neighborhood children and teens – both through their participation in COPS Junior Volunteer Groups and through the youth groups formed at the West Central Community Center. The Neighborhood Resource Officer is highly visible at many community events and coalition meetings and, in an independent study of the department's NRO program, was judged to be carrying out activities very responsive to the community's needs.

Together COPS West and Family Focus have achieved documented success in creating a safer community. According to the Spokane Police Department, the effort resulted in a 40% decrease in crime in the West Central Spokane neighborhood between 1991 and 1994. The neighborhood, formerly known as "Felony Flats," now takes pride in having one of the lowest crime rates in the city.

Conclusion

Approaches by national youth organizations typically embody the characteristics known to prevent youth violence and delinquency and promote wholesome development: (1) they are comprehensive, attempting to ameliorate more than a single factor associated with delinquency and simultaneously focusing on multiple problem behaviors; (2) they are appropriate for children of specific ages and developmental stages; and (3) they continue over the long term, certainly more than a few months, and often lasting several years (Chaiken & Huizinga, 1995).

National organizations and their affiliates recognize the lack of proven after-school programs urgently needed by children and teens in urban neighborhoods. Many are working hard to overcome this deficit. In the process, they are learning some important lessons about tailoring their traditional approaches to meet inner city realities. Following are the key ingredients common to the promising approaches that have taken place in Bristol, Connecticut, Arlington, Texas, and Spokane, Washington:

- *High Standards Are Maintained and Assistance in Meeting Them Is Provided.* Children and teens in economically depressed neighborhoods want and need the same high standards, challenges, and traditions as participants in more affluent areas. Realistically, they often need more support and resources for meeting these challenges than children and teens whose families are better prepared to help them. Mentors, advocates, tutors, donors, and other community volunteers provide extra resources and support.
- *Rules Are Clearly Stated and Consequences Are Explicitly Defined.* Organizations are successfully recruiting children and teens who perceive violence and delinquency as normal behavior. These children and youth need and want violence- and crime-free places to go during after-school hours. They are willing to follow rules and accept discipline as long as the rules and the consequences for infractions are fair. Time-outs for rule violations are commonly used, are usually sufficient to calm the most agitated child or teen, and typically are considered fair by all.
- *Activities Are Varied, Active and Interactive, Challenging, Goal-Directed, and Humorous.* Without stimulating, fun activities, the youngest participants typically whine and sulk, older children create destructive games, and adolescents leave – and don't voluntarily come back. Affiliates of national organizations draw on decades of experience in providing stimulating activities; participants are encouraged to select those they find most rewarding and enjoyable. Bored participants are rare.
- *Activities for Engaging Teens Are Based on Current Knowledge of Adolescent Develop-*

ment. Recently, knowledge about adolescent needs has begun to provide a solid basis for national organizations' after-school programs. Programs take into account hormonal changes in early adolescence and the implications for gender-appropriate activities. Findings about the timing of complex social, psychological, and cognitive changes help determine which activities to provide for teens at different stages of development. For boys and girls in early adolescence, after-school programs productively channel their energy and enthusiasm for communal projects to better their communities. Older teens are given opportunities for developing their individual leadership and employment skills.

- *The Same Strategies for Teens with "Normal" Adolescent Development Are Recognized as Essential for Adolescents Already in Trouble.* Young parents, gang members, and juvenile offenders are recognized to have many of the same interests and concerns as teen participants whose behavior has been less troublesome. Experienced and trained program staff realize these youth respond best to approaches that are appropriate for their ages and stages rather than their presenting problems. Staff are realistic about what teens can and cannot comprehend and do. They are also realistic about the long-term social and psychological support all adolescents need to avoid day-to-day problems and to assume adult responsibilities. Rather than finding essential resources at home or school, many of these teens are dealing with serious difficulties – abuse, AIDS (acquired immune deficiency syndrome), drug use, alcoholic parents, and other urban ills. Staff know that one organization alone cannot meet all these teens' multiple needs.
- *Partnerships Are Created to Meet the Multiple Needs of Youth.* While the case studies detailed in this chapter were selected because of specific programs, it is clear that program success is contingent on cooperation among a spectrum of agencies. Three levels of coordination are involved: coordination among neighborhood-based organizations, including schools and before- and after-school programs; teamwork among city and county government agencies; and cooperation of the "movers and shakers" in a city, including CEOs of local corporations and nonprofit organizations.
- *The Organizations Collaborate with the Local Police.* Police departments are key players in many cooperative efforts to prevent youth violence. Chiefs and other top-ranking police actively participate on youth organizations' advisory boards. Officers of all ranks lead traditional youth services, serve on juvenile review boards, and help select and monitor youth assigned to community service. Community police officers help identify needs of neighborhood children, help keep program sites safe, and reassure neighborhoods that teen center participants will not become unruly.

Bristol, Arlington, and Spokane are not alone. Around the country, many affiliates of national youth-serving organizations are working hand in hand with police and others in their communities to provide programs children and teens need and want during after-school hours. Hopefully, a growing number of cities will recognize these programs' promise and support similar efforts.

Notes

1. As of 1996, according to John Gladstone, U.S. Department of Agriculture (personal communication, October 1996), more than 540 federally funded organizations

were listed on PAVNET, the World Wide Web site where a consortium of federal agencies provides information about prevention programs receiving federal funds.
2. The survey and case studies were carried out by LINC with sponsorship by the Carnegie Corporation of New York (B6025) and the National Institute of Justice (94IJCX0015).
3. These case studies incorporate information gathered by the author from on-site observations; interviews with a wide spectrum of policy makers and practitioners in each city; discussions with groups of program participants; and from documentation of community problems, program participation, practices, and results.

References

Bogenschnieder, K., Small, S., & Riley, D. (n.d.). *An ecological risk-focused approach for addressing youth-at-risk issues.* Chevy Chase, MD: National 4-H Center.

Carnegie Council on Adolescent Development. (1992). *A matter of time: Risk and opportunity in the nonschool hours.* New York: Carnegie Corporation of New York.

Chaiken, M. (1995). *An evaluation of the Girls Incorporated Connections Advocacy activities: Advances for sound adolescent development executive summary.* New York: Girls Incorporated.

Chaiken, M., & Huizinga, D. (1995). Early prevention of and intervention for delinquency and related problem behavior. *The Criminologist, 20*(6).

Hamburg, B. (1990). *Life skills training: Preventive interventions for young adolescents, report of the Life Skills Training Working Group.* Washington, DC: Carnegie Council on Adolescent Development.

Larson, R., & Kleiber, D. (1993). Daily experiences of adolescents. In P. Tolan & B. Choler (Eds.), *Handbook of clinical research and practice with adolescents* (pp. 125–145). New York: John Wiley and Sons.

LINC. (1994). *National survey of youth-serving organizations.* Cosponsored by the Carnegie Corporation of New York [B6025] and the National Institute of Justice [94IJCX0015]. Alexandria, VA: Author.

Lipsey, M. W. (1992). Juvenile delinquency treatment: A meta-analytic inquiry into the variability of effects. In T. Cook (Ed.), *Meta-analysis for explanation* (pp. 83–126). New York: Russell Sage Foundation.

McLaughlin, M. W., Irby, M., & Langman, J. (1994). *Urban sanctuaries: Neighborhood organizations in the lives and futures of inner-city youth.* San Francisco: Jossey-Bass.

Pittman, K. J., & Wright, M. (1991). *A rationale for enhancing the role of the non-school voluntary sector in youth development.* Washington, DC: Carnegie Council on Adolescent Development.

Sherman, L. W., Gottfredson, D., McKensie, D., et al. (1997). *Preventing crime: What works, what doesn't, and what's promising.* Washington, DC: National Institute of Justice.

Snyder, H. N., & Sickmund, M. (1995). *Juvenile offenders and victims: A national report (March 19, 1995 Preview).* Washington, DC: U.S. Department of Justice, Office of Juvenile Justice and Delinquency Prevention.

Timmer, S. G., Eccles, J., & O'Brian, I. (1985). How children use time. In F. T. Juster & F. B. Stafford (Eds.), *Time, goods, and wellbeing.* Ann Arbor, MI: University of Michigan, Institute for Social Research.

Tolan, P., & Guerra, N. (1994). *What works in reducing adolescent violence: An empirical review of the field.* Boulder, CO: University of Colorado at Boulder, Center for the Study and Prevention of Violence.

Wilson-Brewer, R., Cohen, S., O'Donnell, L., & Goodman, I. (1991). *Violence prevention for young adolescents: A survey of the art.* Washington, DC: Carnegie Council on Adolescent Development.

Wynn, J. (1987). *Communities and adolescents: An exploration of reciprocal supports.* Chicago: University of Chicago, Chapin Hall Center for Children.

V. Conclusions

13. An Integrated Approach to Violence Prevention

DELBERT S. ELLIOTT, KIRK R. WILLIAMS,
& BEATRIX HAMBURG

Introduction

The objective of this concluding chapter is to summarize key findings and recommendations of the previous chapters in this volume. The summary is organized around identified themes that cut across chapters and flow from the general approach described in Chapter 1 – the ecological, life course, developmental perspective. The specifics of these chapters will not be reiterated; the reader should refer to individual chapters for detailed information. Rather, our summary is selective, noting findings and recommendations that illustrate the identified themes. This chapter closes with a summary of recommendations for youth violence prevention policy and practice, drawn from the chapters.

The previous chapters have presented different perspectives representing multiple academic disciplines and research traditions. The task now is to begin integrating these perspectives, often complementary, into a more comprehensive approach to understanding and preventing violence. We offer the ecological, life course, developmental approach as a framework for organizing the perspectives, research findings, and prevention recommendations of the previous chapters. For simplicity, this framework will be referred to subsequently as the ecological-developmental approach. We identify five themes related to the developmental approach and illustrated by the results reported in some, if not all, of the chapters of this volume.

Theme 1: The Interconnectedness of Family, Peer Group, School, and Neighborhood

The first theme bears on the ecological nature of the ecological-developmental approach. Recall that human development does not occur in isolation from other human beings. Instead, people live in social contexts that influence their developmental processes. For example, most Americans are connected to families of some sort living in neighborhoods situated within larger communities. Moreover, as children grow older, they become involved in increasingly larger social spheres of influence, ranging from family and friendship groups to schools, workplaces, and other social institutions within communities. The ecological nature of the developmental approach denotes more than just the interrelationships among individuals in social contexts. It also signifies the overlapping connections among these increasingly larger social spheres of influence. Hence, what goes on in the workplace can influence family relations, for example. These, in turn, can influence neighborhood dynamics and the conditions of school settings serving those neighborhoods.

Many of the chapters speak to the theme of interconnections among multiple social contexts and their impact on schools. A major emphasis is that many social institutions traditionally responsible for youth development are "losing ground." This deterioration is a major cause of the youth violence problem and increasingly puts pressure on schools to compensate for other institutional failures. Consider some illustrations drawn from the chapters:

- There is a changing climate for public education. More students are becoming parents themselves, are developmentally delayed, "latchkey" children, etc. These changes affect the environment, including safety issues, of schools (Chapter 8).
- Many pressures have been put on schools in recent years. In addition to their traditional educational role they are now often expected to assume a role in public health, public safety, teaching morals, and addressing social and psychological problems in youth development (Chapter 10).
- For many of the nation's children, development has occurred in environments that provide neither consistent structure nor a basic sense of safety and, therefore, these children lack the internal psychological structure necessary for achieving a sense of autonomy, competence, and pride in academic, social, and personal endeavors (Chapter 10).
- School leaders have been forced to address the problems of deteriorating communities because those problems interfere with schools' capacity to educate children (Chapter 10).

A second dimension of this theme is the idea that "no school is an island," particularly pertaining to the waves of violence that sweep from families and neighborhoods into the schools. Understanding and preventing youth violence, therefore, requires attending to the interconnectedness between families, schools, and their neighborhoods. Many of the chapters address this theme, as illustrated by the selected comments following:

- Aggression in the home does relate to aggression in the school, and certain risk factors in the home predict aggression in the school (Chapter 4).
- Violence trends in communities have had a direct impact on schools as violence and the implements of violence have spilled into classrooms, corridors, and playgrounds (Chapter 6).
- Many of the risk factors for being the victim of firearm violence derive from behavioral and environmental factors external to the school environment (Chapter 6).
- The availability of and attitudes toward firearms by children's families and communities are likely to be an important influence on the firearm violence problem in and around schools (Chapter 2).
- The strongest predictors of school violence rates are local neighborhood crime rates, or direct measures of community disorganization. Students attending school bring with them the problems of their families and residential communities. In this sense, school violence is a reflection of neighborhood context and student body composition (Chapter 5).

The interconnections among social contexts and their impact on schools also have major implications for prevention efforts. These interrelationships must be taken into account when developing and implementing such efforts. A comprehensive strategy that attends to the multiple social contexts in which youth live and function, including schools, has much greater promise for successfully stopping or reducing youth violence. This is clearly one of the important messages of the developmental approach and the authors of the chapters offer a number of points bearing on this issue. Consider some illustrative comments about schools, their connections to other social settings, and the prevention of youth violence:

- Better violence prevention results will be achieved if school-based interventions are nested within a coordinated, well-designed prevention system involving the whole community (Chapter 7).
- A multipronged approach that includes the community, families, and the school itself is the most promising strategy for both understanding and controlling school violence (Chapter 5).
- "School-based" must be redefined to include the family and community (Chapter 8).
- The best safe school plans involve the entire community (Chapter 9).
- After-school programs must be part of a comprehensive, communitywide effort to prevent violence (Chapter 12).

Theme 2: The Dynamic Interaction between Individuals and Social Contexts in the Process of Development

The second theme pertains to the consequences of violence for schools and the functions of violence for individuals within their social settings. This theme is consistent with two different aspects of the developmental approach. First, a major assumption is that social contexts can shape the process of human development. Specifically, participation in multiple social contexts, having varying significance at different stages in the life course, influences the way people think, feel, and behave. However, the behavior of individuals, in turn, can shape social settings. In short, youth development takes place through a dynamic interaction between children and adolescents and their social environments. For example, youth violence can have major consequences for the general climate of schools. This point is illustrated by the following comments from the chapters:

- Children who witness firearm violence can suffer from psychological trauma, and the impact of firearm injuries on children can adversely affect individual development and the educational climate of a school (Chapter 6).
- Whatever its source, widespread concern about violence within a school may reduce the quality of teaching, disrupt classroom discipline, and limit teachers' availability to students before or after school. It also may reduce the students' motivation to attend school, willingness to participate in school activities, and capacity to care about academic matters (Chapter 10).
- School violence is toxic: it can negatively alter the sociocultural characteristics of a setting (Chapter 10).

A second aspect of the person in context developmental approach is that violence may express frustration or hopelessness for some youths striving but failing to master the tasks relevant to their developmental stage. Such mastery helps youths make healthful adjustments to various life circumstances and prepares them for passages into new settings and developmental stages. Nonetheless, violence may acquire functional value for other youths. It may become a method in and of itself for accomplishing developmental tasks when conventional opportunities are unavailable or unworkable in their social contexts (e.g., establishing respect in the eyes of others, an important task in adolescence, through the intentional use of violence). This aspect is relevant to the second identified theme, particularly the functions of violence for youth. Again, consider some illustrative points drawn from the chapters:

- Violence is a way of resolving disputes, but it is also a way of achieving other developmental goals and personal needs (Chapter 3).
- Violence is an important way to develop and maintain dominance hierarchies (Chapter 3).
- Five goals important to adolescence that may be achieved through violent acts are: (1) achieving and maintaining high status or respect, (2) materialism, (3) power and control, (4) "rough justice" and self-help, and (5) risk taking and impulsivity (Chapter 3).

Theme 3: Effective Prevention Efforts Require Collaboration

The third theme is captured in a single word – collaboration. Consistent with the ecological-developmental approach, the prevention of violence involves building relationships among representatives of all public and private sectors that touch on the lives of youth. Comprehensive prevention strategies are needed that address multiple risk and protective factors in the different but overlapping social contexts relevant to the developmental stages of youth. Building such strategies requires the collaborative input of adults responsible for delivering needed services to youths, but the building process should also listen to the voices of the youths themselves. Listed following are comments illustrating this theme:

- There is a need for collaborative efforts by every social institution affected by youth violence at local, state, and national levels (Chapter 6).
- Collaboration is critical in order to ensure comprehensiveness of surveillance, intervention design, evaluation, and dissemination tasks (Chapter 2).
- Schools must join with surrounding communities in violence prevention efforts (Chapter 9).
- In order to collaborate, professionals in the various institutions need to reexamine the traditional concepts of their work that frequently set up barriers to collaboration (Chapter 11).
- Youth organizations working in cities where there is a community-wide collaborative effort to improve the lives of children have a much better chance of success (Chapter 12).

Theme 4: The Need for a Public Health Approach to Violence Prevention

The fourth theme constitutes a major emphasis of this book. The public health strategy should be used to assess the nature and extent of the youth violence problem and to plan and carry out violence prevention programming. These activities involve the step-by-step procedures delineated in Chapter 2: public health surveillance; risk and protective factor identification; intervention design, implementation, and program monitoring as well as short- and long-term outcome assessment; and dissemination of the results to inform public policy and promote effective prevention efforts. As stated in Chapter 1, these steps provide operational guidelines necessary to apply the developmental approach to the study and prevention of youth violence. The terminology used throughout all the chapters is influenced by the public health strategy, but this theme is particularly pronounced in Chapters 2 and 6. Consider the following illustrative comments:

- The techniques of public health have been effective in reducing the burden of many other preventable or controllable conditions, and framing violence as a public health problem can be an important strategy in violence prevention (Chapter 2).
- The public health model shifts the intervention focus from the individual to the population, which is crucial for changing behavior on a community-wide level (Chapter 2).
- Violence intervention must be based on risk factors identified through careful epidemiological surveillance and analysis (Chapter 2).
- The public health approach provides a multidisciplinary, scientific approach explicitly directed toward identifying effective approaches to prevention (Chapter 6).

Theme 5: Effective Programs and Strategies for Preventing Violence

Apart from the specific results reported throughout this volume, the authors also made numerous recommendations for addressing the problem of youth violence in American schools. We close this chapter by listing examples of these recommendations, which constitute the fifth theme. They are organized around three intervention strategies: systemic changes for schools, programs for individual youths, and public policy positions.

Targeting entry points for intervention is an important part of planning and implementing youth violence prevention efforts. Such efforts may be crafted specifically for individuals, such as skill enhancement programs (e.g., anger management and conflict resolution training, social problem solving, reading readiness, tutoring, etc.). However, they also may be designed for system reform, such as improving family relations, the quality of the school climate, the prosocial orientation of peer groups, or improving the service capacity of community agencies. System reform efforts alter the social contexts of youths' lives, from the immediate to the more distant, with the primary objective to support healthful youth development and the prevention or reduction of youth violence. Here are some illustrative recommendations for policy and/or practice concerning system (i.e., school) reform:

- Schools can play an important role in strategies to rebuild families and neighborhoods by serving as multi-service centers, providing young people at risk and their families with services not available elsewhere in the community (Chapter 5).
- Schools must provide the explicit development and promotion of norms of nonviolence (Chapter 7).
- "School" cannot be narrowly defined, and after-school activities, which in some sense are the temporal and spatial link between school, community, and home, must be more explicitly brought into school-based planning (Chapter 8).
- Schools must open their doors during nonschool hours to serve as safe havens where children can play and engage in positive, developmentally valuable academic, interpersonal, and recreational activities (Chapters 9 and 12).
- Schools must develop programs that detect traumatized children, teachers, and school staff and offer crisis intervention or stress management resources (Chapter 10).
- A school administrator without a safe school plan is like a pilot without a flight plan (Chapter 9).
- A type of intervention that holds promise for having an immediate impact on firearm injuries and violence among school-age children is requiring and promoting the safe and secure storage of firearms (Chapter 6).

Besides recommendations for policy and practice concerning system reform efforts, the authors also offered recommendations for programs targeting individual youth. Listed following are some examples of these recommendations:

- The most effective school responses to violence and delinquency will be those that develop the social resources (capital) of their students (Chapter 5).
- Interventions should be specifically designed to address gun-related events rather than simply interpersonal disputes (Chapter 3).
- Theater and role playing, in which facilitators "unpack" (i.e., decompose and analyze) the stages and sequence of violent events, taking into

account the provocative and steering behaviors of bystanders in the context, are a promising violence prevention strategy (Chapter 3).
- Interventions combining early childhood education and family support have demonstrated the ability to prevent aggressive behavior and later violence-related outcomes (Chapter 7).
- The Safe Passage, SMART, and New Haven Child Development-Community Policing (CD-CP) programs are promising violence prevention efforts (Chapter 11).
- A highly visible police presence helps reduce fear within communities (Chapter 11).
- The Comer School Development Program organizational model holds promise for facilitating academic and social development among children at risk in urban areas (Chapter 11).
- After-school activities for teenage males in the inner city must provide opportunities for status, peer approval, independence, and tests of physical, personal, and social endurance (Chapter 12).

The reader is encouraged to refer to the individual chapters for more specific research findings and recommendations for violence prevention policy and practice, whether targeted for system reform or programming for individual children and youth. We have simply tried to provide an overview of the themes in this volume, particularly those relevant to the developmental approach, and illustrations from specific chapters that are consistent with these themes.

Conclusion

We hope the perspectives, findings, and recommendations of this book will be infused into a variety of services and programs designed to promote healthful youth development and to prevent youth violence in American schools. Surely prevention efforts will differ from one place to the next, since the cultural and community environments of schools vary across the United States. Prevention efforts must be sensitive to these issues in meeting the needs of the diverse population of youth in this country. Moreover, a clear message throughout this book is that implementing prevention strategies requires "buy-in" and relationship building among the social contexts most relevant to the lives of the nation's youth. The overall goal is to improve the quality of their lives, and this volume is offered with the hope of stimulating collaborative and informed efforts to achieve that goal.

Author Index

Subject Index

399